Mental Illness
Popular Media

Mental Illness in Popular Media

Essays on the Representation of Disorders

EDITED BY
LAWRENCE C. RUBIN

Foreword by Jonathan Metzl

McFarland & Company, Inc., Publishers
Jefferson, North Carolina, and London

LIBRARY OF CONGRESS CATALOGUING-IN-PUBLICATION DATA

Mental illness in popular media : essays on the representation
of disorders / edited by Lawrence C. Rubin ; foreword by
Jonathan Metzl.
p.   cm.
Includes bibliographical references and index.

ISBN 978-0-7864-6065-6
softcover : acid free paper ∞

1. Mental illness in mass media.   I. Rubin, Lawrence C.,
1955–
P96.M45M46 2012
362.2—dc23   2012004953

BRITISH LIBRARY CATALOGUING DATA ARE AVAILABLE

Front cover design by David K. Landis (Shake It Loose Graphics)

Manufactured in the United States of America

*McFarland & Company, Inc., Publishers
Box 611, Jefferson, North Carolina 28640
www.mcfarlandpub.com*

Acknowledgments

I remember the day I found out that the Popular Culture Association had given my first volume, *Psychotropic Drugs and Popular Culture: Medicine, Mental Health and the Media* (McFarland 2006), the Ray and Pat Browne Award for best anthology. I had a Sally Field moment — "They like me, they really like me!" What they liked, really, was the way in which I brought together a chorus of talented voices that understood the myriad ways in which our culture has become, as Simon Gottschalk called it, "a chemically gated community." I was fascinated by the messages in the many forms of popular media that the road to better living is through chemistry. While the ensuing reviews of that volume have been mixed, I believe that for a brief moment in time, I helped to enrich the conversation. I am grateful to the Popular Culture Association, to those who contributed to that volume, and to people who bought the book.

Each of the essays in the present volume seeks understanding of the ways in which social construction of mental illness is represented in popular culture. Whether in the bold graffiti of sidewalk artists, the subtle subtext of a blockbuster film, or the alluring prose of a Broadway play, they seek to highlight messages about what it means to be psychologically fit and psychologically disordered.

As always, I want to express my deep and abiding love for my wife, Randi; my son, Zachary; and my daughter, Rebecca. Each of them, in their own way, has helped me to appreciate the power of popular culture, whether it is in the form of a mindnumbingly violent video game, the seemingly random perturbations in the life of Hannah Montana, or in the complexity of the plots and personalities in literary fiction. I am truly blessed to have my parents, Esther and Herb, in my life. They beam every time I put pen to paper and then send copies of my writings to distant relatives. Finally, I am indebted to Grace Bernard, my competent and ever-so-patient assistant.

Table of Contents

Foreword

Jonathan M. Metzl

Psychology and popular culture have long been inexorably linked, and understandably so. In differing ways, both domains aggregate projected imaginations. Both are concerned with understanding cathexes, longings, perspectives, attitudes, and memes. And both use language and representation to anatomize inchoate communal anxieties and desires.

For much of the latter half of the twentieth century, the relationships between psychology and popular culture flowed in rather predictable narrative trajectories. Films from Cavalcanti's *Dead of Night* to Olivier's *Hamlet* to Hitchcock's *Spellbound* drew freely on psychological or psychoanalytic concepts of subjectivity in order to portray the troubled inner lives of filmic characters. Starting in the 1960s and 1970s, film theorists appropriated Lacanian theories of the "gaze" in their analyses of films, while psychoanalytic literary theorists applied analytic principles to the study of literary texts. Meanwhile, popular representations of mental illness served as metaphoric critiques of American political culture. Anitole Litvak's 1948 film *The Snake Pit* exposed American viewers to gendered conditions in state mental hospitals. Samuel Fuller's 1963 *Shock Corridor* depicted the asylum as a "street" in which the problems of American modernity drove its inhabitants to insanity. And Milos Forman's 1975 *One Flew Over the Cuckoo's Nest*, based on the 1962 Ken Kesey novel, warned of the dangers of state authoritarianism.

These and other examples demonstrate the rich historical resonances between psychological, psychiatric, and popular cultural sensibilities. But they also suggest how the study of these resonances was, for a long time, rooted in a set of heuristic models, such as classical psychoanalysis or literary studies, that emphasized somewhat linear relationships between psychology and popular culture. Psychology remained a totalizing analytic system, represented as psychology *per se*, while the culture it examined was culture with a capital "C," as manifest in classic works of literature or mainstream films.

Recent scholarship has created new ways to explore how psychology and culture are not only distinct entities, but also forms of knowledge and expression that mirror, critique, reinforce, and even disprove one another over time. Awareness of the fluidity of this relationship has allowed new generations of scholars to expand how psychological study understands many diverse popular cultures, and at the same time to explore the cultural aspects of psychology. This new focus has upended the once top-down relationship between psychology and popular culture. Scholars now understand the overlap between the two domains, not just as a set of psychological "facts" that disseminate downward, but also as a set of mutually affecting rhetorics and representational schemas that themselves reflect larger economies and demands.

As the essays in this book demonstrate, this new focus allows scholars to expand the analytic focus of the field beyond questions of identity into newly political terrain. To be sure, many authors collected here are concerned with the ways that various popular cultures represent matters of mental illness and mental health. But their analyses of sources as disparate as Batman films, Broadway musicals, print media, internet sites, Canadian graffiti, and Nigerian home videos reveal how the rhetorics of mental health and its discontents are made to stand in for a much wider set of assumptions and ideologies. The essays thus reveal how definitions of mental illness, mental health, and even of psychology itself intersect with discourses of race, gender, law, capitalism, and globalization. Such embeddedness can lead to enhanced stigmatizations of particular groups. Essays by Laura Tropp, Shawn Phillips, Julian Vigo, and Elizabeth EnglandKennedy show how cultural representations propagate negative views of postpartum mothers, persons with disabilities, lesbians, and persons with attention deficit disorder, respectively. But cultural representations also allow the means of forming new opinions or communities, or for fighting back, as essays by Jeff Johnson, Wanda Little Fenimore, and Lawrence Rubin suggest.

Playing devil's advocate, one might argue that psychological and popular cultural studies simply represent a new form of psychomedicaliazation, in which ever-expanding psychological frameworks place endlessly expanding cultural sites under their purview.

To be sure, skepticism about over-psychologizing everyday life remains vital in our present, over-psychologized era. Yet the essays collected here demonstrate how medicalization can have potentially liberating functions in addition to potentially colonizing ones. In differing ways, the authors also show how attention to representations of psychological issues allows for a means of exposing the oft-troubling agendas that lie behind constructions of mental illness. And, they demonstrate the importance of ongoing awareness of psychological and cultural issues during an age when so many vital topics — stigma, advertising, identity, betterment, desire, torture — combine the two discourses in exceedingly complex ways.

Ultimately, recognition of the psychological aspects of popular cultures enables deeper understanding of our collective and projective selves and of the forces involved in constructing them.

Jonathan M. Metzl is the Frederick B. Rentschler II Chair of Sociology and Medicine, Health, and Society and the director of the Program in Medicine, Health, and Society at Vanderbilt University. His books include The Protest Psychosis *(2010);* Against Health *(ed., 2010);* Difference and Identity in Medicine *(ed., 2005); and* Prozac on the Couch *(2003).*

Introduction

LAWRENCE C. RUBIN

Last night I saw upon the stair
A little man who wasn't there
He wasn't there again today
Oh, how I wish he'd go away[1]

A few semesters back, I was given the opportunity to construct an under-graduate course of my choosing. Eager to break free of the constraints of the traditional undergraduate psychology curriculum, I decided to bring together two of my professional passions — popular culture and psychopathology. The course, "Mental Illness and the Movies,"[2] gave students (and me) the chance to explore the ways in which American film captures the heights and depths of the human experience. Who can possibly forget Jack Nicholson's portrayal of sociopath R.P. McMurphy in *One Flew over the Cuckoo's Nest,* Olivia de Havilland's depiction of the fragile Virginia Cunningham in *The Snake Pit,* Dustin Hoffman's powerful rendering of the autistic Raymond Babbitt in *Rainman* or Patty McCormack's frightening Rhoda Penmark in *The Bad Seed*? Students, particularly the younger ones who had never seen these movies, instantly appreciated the powerful and compassionate depictions of mental illness these films offered.

Due to popular demand, or perhaps the desire to escape experimental psychology or research statistics, I was once again asked to construct a course that would somehow catch the attention of students already sated on Freud, Pavlov and Kitty Genovese.[3] How to capture the imagination and stimulate both the intellect and curiosity of students raised on social media, video games, and fast food? The resulting course, "Psychology and Popular Culture," explored the ways in which foundational research in the field of Psychology was reflected in every facet of popular culture — from cartoons to commercials

5

to fast food. Students immersed themselves in the course and came away more savvy and psychologically sophisticated consumers of all things popular.

Soon after these courses debuted, I was given the opportunity to create a new division of the Popular Culture Association (PCA), Mental Health & Mental Illness and Popular Culture. My call for papers was greeted with interest from scholars all over the globe. The proposed topics ranged from stigmatization of the mentally ill in Nigerian film to the psychologically traumatizing effect of piloting simulated warrior drones and to the gendering of hysteria in 19th-century France. Each topic was more fascinating than the last, and choosing between them for representation at the 2010 annual conference of the National Popular Culture and American Culture Association in St. Louis was a challenge.

On the heels of that conference and the energy of the presenters, I turned my efforts to this volume and once again reached out to scholars and clinicians interested in exploring the unique crossroads of mental illness and popular culture. It was my hope that this call would generate interest both here and abroad in the ways in which the full range of popular culture has been used as a conduit to deepen our discourse around and understanding of mental illness. My hopes have been exceeded.

The essays in **Section One**, "Mental Illness Depicted in Popular Culture," address how various specific forms of psychiatric disorder have been addressed in film, on stage, and in literature. Jeffrey K. Johnson's "The Hero with a Thousand Dysfluencies: The Changing Portrayals of People Who Stutter" compares the way that popular culture venues have traditionally presented people who stutter with new narratives that display stutterers as heroes. Elizabeth S. EnglandKennedy's "Representations of Attention Deficit Disorder: Portrayals of Public Skepticism in Popular Media" focuses on media representations of attention deficit disorder (with and without hyperactivity) and the ways in which these portrayals intensify cultural stereotypes. Debra Merskin's "Smooth Operator: The Compensated Psychopath in Cinema" describes the subclinical expression of psychopathy and how it is romanticized in Hollywood cinema. Shawn M. Phillips's "The Most Dangerous Deviants in America: Why the Disabled Are Depicted as Deranged Killers" asks how people with disabilities have been negatively typecasted in popular culture, particularly in slasher/horror films and stories. Laura Tropp's "Off Their Rockers: Representation of Postpartum Depression" explores such questions as how "madness" and "craziness" are associated with postpartum depression, who is represented as shouldering the burden of the illness, and how depictions of this illness position the role of motherhood in society. Julian Vigo's "Lesbianism and the Fourth Dimension: The Psychotic Lesbian" analyses the popular cultural media representations of the lesbian as insane — from the popular lesbian, knife-wielding doppelgänger in *Basic Instinct* to the very "real life" interpretation of "Celestia." Finally, Alena Papayanis's "'The Veteran Problem': Examining Contemporary Constructions of Returning Veterans" revolves around the image of the "damaged" war veteran by drawing both from case studies and media analysis in order to deconstruct the popular mis-characterization of the veteran as dangerous.

The essays in **Section Two**, which is entitled "Popular Culture Genres and Mental Illness," pull back the lens, so to speak, in order to understand how various genres of popular culture are utilized to communicate our often confusing and conflictual relationship with the mentally ill. Esther Terry's "Musical Storm and Mental Stress: Trauma and Instability in Contemporary American Musical Theater" offers a study of the depiction of mental illness and treatment in Broadway musicals. Wanda Little Fenimore's "Bad Girls: From Eve to Britney" examines media portrayals of three contemporary "bad" girls — Lindsay Lohan, Britney Spears, and the late Amy Winehouse — all of whom have a history of sexual promiscuity, substance abuse, mental illness, and run-ins with the law, and asks, Are they really "bad girls?" Sarah J. Rudolph's "Evolving Stages: Representations of Mental Illness in Contemporary American Theater" considers the various iterations of the relationship between gender and mental illness on the American stage and situates them on the larger landscape of popular culture. Katie Ellis's "New Media as a Powerful Ally in the Representation of Mental Illness: YouTube, Resistance and Change" seeks to understand the way in which homemade videos convey messages of mental health and mental illness. Finally, my own "On the Wings of Icarus: Exploring the Flawed Superhero" asks why it is so compelling to construct our superheroes as wounded warriors.

The essays in **Section Three**, entitled "Mental Illness and Popular Culture Abroad," investigate the fascinating ways in which popular culture reflects mental illness outside the United States. Kimberley White's "The Aesthetics of Mad Spaces: Policing the Public Image of Graffiti and Mental Illness in Canada" explores the way that the narratives of madness, disease and disorder have been taken up in the representation and regulation of graffiti as a social problem and as sign of social danger in Toronto. Philippa Martyr's "Beyond Beyond Reason: Images of People with Mental Disabilities in Australian Film Since the 1970s" examines Australian film's portrayal of mental illness in the last thirty years, from the production of Australia's first self-consciously "psychiatric"-themed film, *Between Wars*, to the present. Saheed Aderinto's "Representing 'Tradition,' Confusing 'Modernity': Love and Mental Illness in Yoruba (Nigerian) Video Films" illuminates the intersection of love, sexuality, masculinity, and mental illness in Nigerian home video, drawing evidence from a particular Yoruba movie entitled *Ayo ni Mofe*. And finally, Lee Knifton's

"Reframing Mental Health and Illness: Perspectives from the Scottish Mental Health Arts and Film Festival" takes us to the Scotland to investigate a grass-roots movement that has impacted the perception and treatment of people with chronic psychiatric disorders.

NOTES

1. From the poem "Antigonish" by Williams Hughes Mearns (1875-1965), this was the chilling mantra of the serial murderer/dissociative identity disordered protagonist in the film Identity (2003).

2. For an excellent discussion of the many ways in which psychopatholgy has been depicted in cinema, see Danny Wedding, Movies & Mental Illness (Cambridge, MA: Hogrefe, 2005).

3. Kitty Genovese was a New Yorker who was brutally murdered in the early 1960s while neighbors reportedly failed to assist. Her story became the subject of a subsequent body of social psychology literature on the topic of "bystander apathy" and "diffusion of responsibility."

BIBLIOGRAPHY

The Bad Seed. Directed by Mervyn LeRoy. 1956. Burbank, CA: Warner Bros. Pictures, 2004. DVD.

One Flew Over the Cuckoo's Nest. Directed by Milos Forman. 1975. Hollywood, CA: United Artists, 2002. DVD.

Rainman. Directed by Barry Levinson. 1988. Hollywood, CA: United Artists, 2000. DVD.

The Snake Pit. Directed by Anatole Litvak. 1948. Los Angeles, CA: Twentieth Century Fox Film Corporation, 2004. DVD.

SECTION ONE

Mental Illness Depicted in Popular Culture

1

The Hero with a Thousand Dysfluencies

The Changing Portrayals of People Who Stutter

Jeffrey K. Johnson

Mentally and physically challenged characters have appeared for decades in popular culture mediums like film, television, and genre fiction. Traditionally, creators have often constructed these characters to be the embodiments of a disorder or impediment, and thus these creations have commonly borne little to no resemblance to actual human beings. Frequently, a mentally or physically challenged character acted as either comic relief or a story point, but he/she rarely was allowed to be lifelike. Although popular culture portrayals have begun to change over the last few years, one of the slowest types to evolve is the character in film, television, and popular fiction who stutters.

Generally, before the late twentieth century, a person who stuttered was almost never shown to be a three-dimensional character and often was merely seen as the embodiment of a speech impediment. Interestingly, within the last decade or so writers and artists have together created a new crop of films, television shows and children's stories that showcase a person who stutters as a hero.

This chapter will compare the way that popular culture venues have traditionally presented people who stutter with new narratives that display stutterers as heroes. The differences between the traditional and new narratives reveal a fascinating change in not only how society views people who stutter but also how cultural normality is being refined.[1]

The Commonplace Stutterer

Chances are that most people have met someone who stutters. It is estimated there are about 50 million people worldwide who stutter or about one out of every 120 people have the dysfluency issue.[2] A good technical definition of stuttering is "the interruption of the flow of speech by hesitations, prolongation of sounds and blockages sufficient to cause anxiety and impair verbal communication."[3] Although this definition is a little unwieldy, it does highlight the important facts that stuttering creates choppy, hard-to-understand speech and the impediment is often linked to fear and/or anxiety. While most would not be able to create a coherent definition, many people believe that they understand stuttering and believe themselves to be experts regarding the dysfluency. Possibly because stuttering is so commonplace, or maybe because it involves a seemingly easy part of everyday life (speaking), a large number of people believe that stuttering can be easily cured if the stutterer would try harder or calm down.

These popular (mis)conceptions have led to cultural and social understandings of stuttering that often have little basis in reality and which, nevertheless, many citizens have accepted as factual. For decades, American popular culture generally portrayed people who stuttered as two-dimensional embodiments of a speech impediment. Motion pictures, television, comic books, and even popular fiction portrayed stutters in crude, stereotypical, and derogatory ways that were meant to amuse or entertain. Stutterers could be funny, weak, or evil, but could almost never be a well-rounded person or a hero. Above all, in almost every case, in popular culture the most important part of a stutterer's existence was his/her speech impediment. People who stuttered were defined by their speech impediment and how the impediment, not the character, could service the story. [4]

Making a Change

For decades, popular culture genres including film, television, and popular literature had fashioned stuttering characters to create easy humor, showcase a weak or nervous character, or to mark a character as evil. Stuttering was often seen as a deformity that writers could use to create feelings of amusement, pity, or anger, and the stuttering character was generally only a vehicle to produce a reaction or to drive a plot forward. Stutterers could be silly, sad, nervous, or mean, but they could almost never be a hero. To be a hero, a character had to be upstanding and appealing, two qualities that many viewers, readers, and writers did not associate with those who stuttered. Stuttering was too great a physical, social, and maybe moral deformity to allow a stuttering character to become a hero. Interestingly, this bias appears to have begun to change during the late part of the twentieth and early part of the twenty-first centuries. While numerous popular culture narratives still portray stutterers as funny, weak, and altogether unappealing, several new stories include characters who stutter — not just stuttering characters. These films, television programs, and popular books create more well-rounded characters than before and often the person who stutters becomes the story's hero. This change presents a new popular culture understanding of both people who stutter and the role of the American hero in general. These novel narratives highlight a hero who stutters and ask readers and viewers to rethink their understanding of physical challenges and to recast their notion of the hero.

The Stuttering Hero

Popular culture outlets have long had an affinity for characters with disabilities. Writers often joke that a Hollywood actor can quickly gain an Oscar nomination by portraying a character with a physical and mental challenge. From Daniel Day Lewis's portrayal of Christy Brown and his battle with cerebral palsy in *My Left Foot* to Marlee Matlin's cinematic turn as a deaf cleaning lady in *Children of a Lesser God*, the Academy of Motion Picture Arts and Sciences often rewards these difficult acting roles. Critics and audiences cheer when the characters overcome numerous difficult challenges and the films provide viewers of all ages with heartwarming moments and celluloid life lessons. Although advocates argue whether these characters provide positive attention or are merely profiting on sentimentality and voyeurism, the writers and actors generally attempt to create characters that are not just a physical embodiment of their disabilities. Sometimes these portrayals fail miserably, but occasionally they create physically and mentally challenged characters that resemble real people.

Likewise, often television versions of these narratives turn into overly-hyped "disease of the month" showcases that produce characters that become just as one-dimensional as Mister Magoo or Porky Pig cartoons. Sometimes, though, characters become more than just a jumble of clichés and well-worn narrative devices. As mentioned previously, until recently characters who stutter have had little chance of receiving balanced portrayals in major popular culture narratives. Recently, some creators' attitudes have seemingly changed and stutterers have become the heroes of several notable stories. This change marks an interesting turn of events and highlights a sharp contrast from earlier, more clichéd popular culture narratives. It also highlights an example of popular culture taking the lead and addressing real-life issues that are still widely misreported in news and entertainment stories.

Real Life Stuttering Disinformation

It bears mentioning that the new popular culture stuttering narratives are not only a change from fictionalized accounts of stuttering across various genres but also from numerous contemporary "real life" stories. Each year many news and entertainment sources produce stories that explain to readers how a famous person "overcame" stuttering through force of will or a special technique and is now cured of the annoying/ debilitating condition. These stories reinforce the notion that stuttering is a malady that must be cured before a person can become successful and whole. This idea closely follows the characterization of many stutterers in popular culture that are seen as too weak or uninspiring to become the narrative's hero. The true-life reports describe and reinforce the idea that before a person can become the narrative's hero, he/she must cure his/ her stuttering. Two examples of this are the stuttering actors Emily Blunt and James Earl Jones. Emily Blunt, the actor best known for her role in the motion picture *The Devil Wears Prada*, is a stutterer who had a severe dysfluency as a child. Numerous newspaper and website articles report that Blunt cured her speech impediment by faking an accent and training to become an actor. Most of these texts proclaim that Blunt only became famous and successful because she was smart and brave enough to overcome her stuttering. Many of the articles' titles reveal this bias, such as Popeater.com's "'The Devil Wears Prada' Star Emily Blunt: How I Beat My Stutter."[5] "Emily Blunt's childhood stutter 'anguish'" at *MSNBC Celebrity*,[6] and PerezHilton.com's "Emily Blunt Opens Up About Se-S-Secret Stutter Past."[7] These articles and others like them reveal that a stuttering Emily Blunt could never have been the hero of the story and could not have been taken as seriously as her fluent counterpart.

Darth Vader Stutters?

James Earl Jones is an actor renowned for his deep voice and iconic vocal tones. Besides providing the sound bite that informs viewers that "This is CNN," Jones is best known as voicing the villain Darth Vader in the *Star Wars* films. Because of this, many members of the public find it surprising that Jones is a stutterer, and a number of news and entertainment articles focus on how the world renowned actor "cured" his stuttering. Jones could only become a successful Hollywood hero after he "beat" his stuttering and took control of his life. Although Jones has publicly stated many times that he still stutters, just in a more controlled and less frequent manner, the articles' authors create narratives in which Jones is completely fluent through his own hard work and force of will. An October 8, 2002, *People Magazine* article proclaims, "James Earl Jones Conquers Stuttering" and portrays the actor as a hero who defeated his internal foe.[8] The *Daily Record* claims that Jones "overcame [a] childhood stutter" and gives the impression that Jones could not have been successful had he not overcome his dysfluency issues.[9] Like the numerous accounts regarding Emily Blunt's stuttering, multiple article present Jones's stuttering as an enemy which he battled and defeated. In these accounts Jones is the conquering hero whose quest is to destroy his flaw. Article authors relate Blunt, Jones, and other stutters to Joseph Campbell–like heroes whose mission is to struggle and overcome their enemy. These articles imply that if these popular figures had continued to stutter, then their lives could have been less productive and far less heroic. Although Blunt and Jones are the heroes of the narratives, they are heroes because they defeated their stuttering. They would not have been depicted as such had they not vanquished this enemy. In this way, they are not heroes who stutter, but rather heroes who once stuttered and overcame the malady in order to be successful. These real-life accounts make it even more surprising and exceptional that several authors have created popular culture narratives in which stutterers are now lead characters and heroes. In these cases, fictional popular culture texts are creating characters who are more well-rounded than non-fictional accounts.

Children's Heroes

While non-fiction writers often create narratives that fall back on clichéd and negative understandings of people who stutter, heroic and original characters who stutter have begun to appear in several popular culture venues. Not surprisingly, one of the first popular culture outlets to include well-rounded heroic characters who stutter was children's literature. Books written for children have long attempted to teach lessons and to introduce young readers to the different types of people in the world. It would seem a natural fit that numerous children's stories teach about stuttering and how the hero learns to deal with his/her dysfluency. A number of these stories do take the main character on a hero's quest in an attempt to resolve his/her fluency issues. What is surprising is that almost none of these tales end with the person who stutters being "cured" or finding a way not to stutter anymore. Generally, the end of the story focuses on a way for the protagonist to live with his/her stuttering and to better understand who he/she is. Although the stutterer finishes the hero's quest, the stuttering is not defeated but rather accepted and modified, which is the most expected and true-to-life outcome. This is quite different from many other popular culture accounts and the real life narratives that were discussed previously.

In these children's stories stuttering does not define a character as weak or funny, or showcase a problem that must be solved. Instead, they attempt to present characters who stutter as people who can sometimes control their stuttering but never "cure" it. These children's stories are unique because they do not present a clichéd stutterer or a malady that needs be overcome. Rather, these narratives showcase a person who stutters and explore the challenges and accomplishments of that character. These stutterers who are often only seen for a few pages, are three-dimensional characters in ways that other characters who stutter are not. In other words, children's books often provide a believable outlet for creating narratives that define and project characters who stutter as heroes.

Mary Marony

There are several children's books that portray people who stutter as main characters and heroes. One of the most noteworthy narratives is a series of children's books by author Suzy Kline that revolves around the life of a young girl named Mary Marony who stutters. In the multiple-book series, Mary is a seven-year-old girl who must deal with a number of trials and situations that are exacerbated by her speech impediment. Mary must confront a series of real-life issues that would challenge any young girl, but are made more difficult because she stutters. In 1992's *Mary Marony and the Snake*, Mary starts attending a new school and has to deal with not only socially acceptable fears such as snakes, but also with stuttering-centric anxieties such as saying her name in front of her new teacher and classmates. Saying one's name is often extremely challenging for a person who stutters because he/she cannot substitute another word or phrase if difficulties arise. This often causes a large amount of fear and anxiety and results in the dysfluent person avoiding situations in which he/she must say his/her name. Although this situation can be painful, it also is a part of a stutterer's life and should be treated as such. By including both socially acknowledged fears and stuttering-specific challenges in the book, Suzy Kline creates a realistic narrative that allows for a character who is more than a series of clichés, who reacts to her world realistically and displays both fear and courage as a real person would. In this book Mary visits a speech therapist and begins to work on controlling and reducing her dysfluency. There is no magical cure and her problems and challenges do not quickly vanish, but rather she is shown as a heroine who tackles every problem that is placed in her way.[10]

Mary's Later Adventures

In the 1993 book *Mary Marony Hides Out*, Mary confronts her fears of speaking with strangers when she hides from an author whom she desperately wants to speak to. Mary is so embarrassed by her stuttering that she tries to avoid contact with this authority figure and is even willing to hide in order to circumvent the uncomfortable situation. Nervousness and avoidance are not usually traits associated with heroes and are instead most often connected to weak characters and villains. In this book Mary is the hero because she acts in a realistic manner and eventually confronts and challenges her fears. Although Mary is still afraid, she does not let her fear become debilitating, but rather learns how to control it and to do the things that she desires. This is a good lesson for both children and adults alike as the story showcases Mary as the hero who grows socially and emotionally.[11]

In *Mary Marony, Mummy Girl*, Mary confronts a classmate who makes fun of her stuttering. Notice Mary's growth in the course of these three adventures. The heroine who began the first book afraid to say her name and who hid from a role model in the second book is now standing up for herself against someone who teases and taunts her. Mary is still worried and anxious in this book and is not the supremely confident hero seen in many popular culture venues. Instead, she is a heroine who works hard to do the right thing in spite of her fears. She confronts the bully not in a stereotypical physical way, but rather creates a plan to embarrass him and show the rest of her class that he also is scared and anxious, just like her. Although Mary's bully does not have a speech impediment, he does have other challenges and obstacles in his life and Mary easily points out this fact. Mary evens the playing field and turns the table on an aggressive bully who does not understand how hurtful his actions are. In doing so, she defends herself and others around her, becoming more a hero than she was in the previous stories.[12]

Interestingly, in 1995's *Mary Marony and the Chocolate Surprise*, very little of the story revolves around Mary's stuttering. Although the speech impediment is a part of Mary's overall makeup, it has little to do with the plot. In this story, Mary succumbs to her desire to win a contest and cheats in order to win. Resorting to cheating in order to get what she wants is something that the reader would not associate with Mary and thus comes as a surprise. The prize of lunch with a teacher is something that Mary would very much like; she simply does not know how to otherwise express these feelings and desires. The book ends with Mary understanding why cheating is wrong and learning a valuable life lesson. Although most of her actions seem unheroic, Mary is repentant and eventually does the right thing.[13] Notably, though, Mary's speech impediment plays almost no role in the story. In these four books alone Mary changes from a scared girl who avoided saying her name in front of others, to a flawed heroine whose stuttering only serves as a small part of her character. Importantly, Mary's quest does not "cure" her stuttering or explain how she overcame her dysfluency as many other past tales would have. This change marks a heroic quest that resembles a Campbellian heroic arc and showcases a realistic hero who stutters rather than a clichéd stuttering hero.

Other Children's Books with People Who Stutter

There are a number of other children's books with characters who stutter, and many of them fall back on the same clichés and unimaginative characterizations as other types of stories.[14] A growing number of stories like the Mary Marony tales do feature strong and well-balanced stuttering characters. An example is a 2008 book by Laurence Yelp for young adults titled *The Dragon's Child*. In this fictionalized account of a true story, a family travels to the United States from China and faces a number of trials and tribulations. One plot point is a father who punishes his young son because the child stutters. Eventually, the son learns that his father only wants to help him to cure his stuttering and does not realize that the added pressure only makes it worse. The child's stuttering is a small element and it is presented as one of many difficulties that the family must face as they immigrate to a new country. The young man is presented as a hero who overcomes these problems and eventually becomes the head of a large and successful family.[15] In Peadar Ó Guilín's 2007 action-adventure novel *The Inferior*, Stopmouth, a character who stutters, proves himself to be quick, strong, and brave and is clearly the tale's hero. This is unusual because action-adventure stories have rarely presented characters who stutter as heroes, and in this tale, Stopmouth's speech difficult is just one impediment that he must face on his hero's journey.[16] In Laurie Lears's 2000 picture book *Ben Has Something to Say: A Story About Stuttering*, young Ben must overcome his stuttering to save a dog from the pound. Ben does not find a cure for his stuttering, but rather decides that he must be brave and speak even though he does not like that he stutters. Ben's heroic actions do not change his stuttering but rather change him and those around him.[17] These stories, and several others, showcase new children's tales in which characters who stutter are presented as heroes. This change in children's stories marks a cultural shift and displays a new, much needed perspective: one in which children are taught that anyone can be a hero, even if they stutter.

It's Rocket Science

In recent years, some film and television creators have followed children's books and created narratives in which characters who stutter are portrayed as both heroes and interesting characters. Although this was not always the case, a new breed of electronic narrative is emerging that highlights the strengths of characters who stutter and showcase their heroic actions. One of the most obvious films that features a heroic character who stutters is Jeffrey Blitz's *Rocket Science* (2007). The motion picture is based around Hal Hefner, a shy fifteen-year-old who stutters and wants to be accepted by those around him. At the beginning of the film, Hal is approached by Ginny Ryerson, who asks him to join her on the debate team so that she can win a championship. Ginny claims that she likes the fact that Hal stutters because it allows her to mold him into the debater she wishes him to be. Hal trains with Ginny and practices his debating skills, but is still very dysfluent and has a difficult time participating in the practice debates. Hal continues to practice, but Ginny secretly changes schools and debate teams and Hal performs poorly at his first debate, stuttering badly and watching Ginny win first place. Hal is heartbroken, and after being kicked off of his school's debate team, he recruits Ginny's former partner Ben to be his new partner for the championships. Ben trains Hal to sing his debating points to the tune of "The Battle Hymn of the Republic" and the two practice intensely for the competition. Hal and Ben's team is disqualified at the debate championship, but Hal confronts Ginny and tells her that eventually he will come out on top. The movie ends with Hal talking to his father and stuttering so badly that he is unable to say "rocket science," the film's title.[18] Although Hal does not beat Ginny, debate well, overcome his stuttering, or solve any of his problems, he is the film's hero. Hal works hard to become better and get what he wants. He fights against his stuttering and his other problems and becomes much more confident and self-assured. Hal does not find some instant cure for his stuttering, but instead realizes that he must accept it as a part of who he is and work to be more fluent. Hal accepts both that he stutters and that life is difficult and messy, but there are no other options. Although this is not the typical path of the conquering hero, it is heroic nonetheless.

Mad Men

Although children's authors and film creators have begun to craft narratives involving heroic stutterers, there are very few television shows that prominently feature dysfluent heroes. It is unclear why this is so, but one would assume that if motion pictures and other popular culture narratives continue to include heroic characters who stutter, then television will eventually follow suit. One recent example of a minor television character who stutters appears in the fourth season of the AMC television series *Mad Men.* The critically lauded series follows the lives of advertising agency employees during the 1960s and explores social and cultural changes and themes in both the past and the present. The show has not only been a hit with viewers and

critics but also is the rare program that has become a part of the national consciousness. Because the show has become a cultural touchstone for many, it is important that a character who stutters was included in episode nine of the fourth season, entitled, "The Beautiful Girls." In the episode the advertising executives meet with three brothers who own and operate Fillmore Auto Parts, with whom they discuss possible ideas for a new advertising campaign. The brothers are generally unhappy with the suggestions and the parties argue about what should be done. Two of the brothers do most of the talking and fight with each other and with Don Draper, the series' main character, about the advertising campaign's direction. The third brother, Sean, remains mostly silent throughout the process, and when he finally speaks, he strongly stutters. Although he stutters, Sean provides the voice of reason and the brothers' clearest argument against Don Draper's proposed campaign. Draper has been trying to force the three brothers to do things his way, although they employ him to provide them with what they want. Sean at first claims that he does not know what he thinks of the campaign and then states, "Why do we have to convince him?" The "him" in this sentence is Draper, and Sean is asking why Don acts like they work for him and not vice versa? Although Sean has a small role and does not say very much, he is the one person in the room who appears to have the courage and common sense to state the obvious.[19] While it may be a stretch to call Sean Fillmore a hero, he does speak with knowledge and clarity even though he stutters. Sean's stuttering had nothing to do with the plot and was never mentioned during the episode or later in the season. Sean's stuttering was a characteristic, much like eye or hair color, that neither pushed the story forward nor held it back. This small role on a hit television series demonstrates that a character who stutters can be important for qualities other than his/her stuttering. Although this may not be heroic, it is true to life and an important message for viewers and creators alike.

Is The King's Speech *Heroic?*

One cannot discuss recent popular culture narratives that include characters who stutter without mentioning Tom Hooper's film *The King's Speech*. The 2010 motion picture has won numerous awards including the Best Picture Oscar. Numerous critics have praised the film, and it is generally thought to be a motion picture about a brave and heroic young man who overcomes adversity and thus becomes a stronger and more self-assured person. Randy Myers, a critic for the *Contra Costa Times* stated that the film, "tells a universal story about a man confronting his fears and finding confidence in his own voice."[20] Lisa Schwarzbaum of *Entertainment Weekly* notes, "Even a king can have a common stutter, this sturdy backstairs-at-the-palace drama assures.

Even a king could do with some trusted help. Even a king must find his own voice."[21] Joe Neumaier from the New York Daily News writes the film "concerns the colossal effort by England's King George VI to defeat a debilitating stuttering problem."[22] Film audiences appear to enjoy the film as much as reviewers; users of the film site Rotten Tomatoes gave the motion picture a 96 percent positive rating.[23] Although the film has been has been well-received and many audience members and critics appear to believe that it presents a valuable lesson, does *The King's Speech* present a heroic character who stutters or does the film merely revive antiquated notions of weak characters who stutter?

The Speaking King

The King's Speech focuses on the British king George VI, a stutterer who wants to speak more fluently so that he can address his subjects via the radio. King George has battled his stuttering his entire life and has not been able to come to terms with his dysfluency. During the course of the film, the king and his speech therapist, Lionel Logue, work on various fluency techniques and the film ends with George VI successfully giving a radio speech at the beginning of World War II.[24] The motion picture presents George VI as a heroic individual who bravely battles his stuttering and eventually wins. As the king gives his speech, he triumphs over his impediment and becomes a powerful, full-voiced person. It is often difficult to determine if George VI fits the definition of a hero who stutters, as presented in this paper. Although the George VI is clearly the hero of the film, he is presented as heroic because many audience members would assume that he cures his stuttering and becomes a fluid speaker. If the king had continued to perform his job as a dysfluent stutterer, the motion picture's viewers would have seen him as a failure. In this manner, George VI is not a hero who stutters, but rather a hero because he stops stuttering. If one watches the film closely though, it is clear that the king does not stop stuttering; he merely manages to learn to speak fluently at times. In this way, the film presents a hero who stutters, and not a clichéd character who needs to become fluent before he can be heroic.

Conclusion

The inclusion of heroic characters who stutter in several popular culture venues showcases a new cultural understanding of stuttering and other people with physical and mental challenges. In the past, characters who stuttered were reduced to clichéd caricatures that were often used to draw laughs or sympathy, or to move the plot along. By crafting three-dimensional heroic stuttering characters, creators highlight a new type of popular hero. Instead of a hero who overcomes and defeats his stuttering and thus becomes a "whole" fluent person, these heroes learn to deal with their dysfluency issues and to better understand who they are. Although this may at first sound pedestrian rather than heroic, it encompasses the daily experience of real stutterers who cannot cure their speech impediments by sheer force of will. This new type of heroic character who stutters showcases an American society more willing to accept realistic heroes who have true-to- life challenges. Children's books and films have begun to include these kinds of characters, and one should expect television programs to soon follow suit. If this is in fact a growing trend, then it is one that should be welcomed for the new and distinctive voices that now can be heard. Although characters who stutter have long been a part of mainstream popular culture, it is only recently that their true heroic voices have been heard.

NOTES

1. The author would like to assert that he does not believe that stuttering is either a mental illness or a psychological condition. Although some characteristics of stuttering may be akin to types of mental illnesses, these are only surface associations. While many members of the general public may wrongly associate stuttering with mental or psychological conditions, researchers have found a possible genetic basis for some forms of the speech impediment and other scientists have found additional potential biological causes.

2. Marc Shell, *Stutter* (Cambridge, MA: Harvard University Press, 2005), 1.

3. Jock A. Carlisle, *Tangled Tongue: Living with a Stutter* (Toronto: University of Toronto Press, 1985), 4.

4. For a better understanding of how stutterers were portrayed in a number of popular culture genres in the past please see Jeffrey Johnson, "The Visualization of the Twisted Tongue: Portrayals of Stuttering in Film, Television, and Comic Books," *The Journal of Popular Culture* 41, no. 2 (2008): 245–261.

5. "'The Devil Wears Prada' Star Emily Blunt: How I Beat My Stutter," *PopEater*, June 7, 2010, accessed December 15, 2010, http://www.popeater.com/2010/06/07/emily-blunt-stutter/.

6. "Emily Blunt's Childhood Stutter 'Anguish,'" *MSN Celebrity*, September 6, 2010, accessed December 15, 2010, http://celebrity.uk.msn.com/news/gossip/articles.aspx?cp-documentid=153700525.

7. Perez Hilton, "Emily Blunt Opens up About Se-S-Secret Stutter Past," *Perez Hilton.com*, June 8, 2010, accessed December 22, 2010, http://perezhilton.com/2010-06-08-emily-blunt-opens-up-about-se-s-secret-stutter-past.

8. Stephen M. Silverman and Jennifer Blaise, "James Earl Jones Conquers Stuttering," *People Magazine* online edition, October 8, 2002, accessed December 17, 2010, http://www.people.com/people/article/0,,624807,00.html.

9. Brian McIver, "How James Earl Jones Overcame Childhood Stutter to Produce Galaxy's Most Evil Voice," *Daily Record* online edition, June 16, 2010, accessed December 15, 2010, http://www.dailyrecord.co.uk/showbiz/celebrity-interviews/2010/06/16/how-james-earl-jones-overcame-childhood-stutter-to-produce-galaxy-s-most-evil-voice-86908-22337035/.

10. Suzy Kline, *Mary Marony and the Snake* (New York: Putnam's, 1992), n.p.
11. Suzy Kline, *Mary Marony Hides Out* (New York: Putnam's, 1993), n.p.
12. Suzy Kline, *Mary Marony Mummy Girl* (New York: Putnam's, 1994), n.p.
13. Suzy Kline, *Mary Marony and the Chocolate Surprise* (New York: Putnam's, 1995), n.p.
14. For a list of children's books featuring characters that stutter please see Tahirih Bushe and Richard Martin, "Stuttering in Children's Literature," *Language, Speech, and Hearing Services in Schools* 19 no. 3 (1988): 235–250; and http://www.mnsu.edu/comdis/kuster/kids/kidsbooks.html.
15. Laurence Yelp, *The Dragon's Child* (New York: HarperCollins, 2008).
16. Peadar Ó Guilín, *The Inferior* (New York: David Fickling Books, 2007), n.p.
17. Laurie Lears, *Ben Has Something to Say: A Story About Stuttering* (Morton Grove, IL: Albert Whitman, 2000), n.p.
18. *Rocket Science*, directed by Jeffrey Blitz (West Hollywood, CA: Picturehouse Films, 2007).
19. *Mad Men*, "The Beautiful Girls," AMC, Season 4, episode 9, 2010.
20. Randy Myers, "Review: 'The King's Speech' Is a Royal Accomplishment," *Contra Costa Times* online edition, December 10, 2010, accessed December 20, 2010, http://www.mercurynews.com/movies-dvd/ci_16808951?nclick_check=1.
21. Lisa Schwarzbaum, "The King's Speech (2010)," *Entertainment Weekly* online edition, December 30, 2010, accessed December 31, 2010, http://www.ew.com/ew/article/0,,20444629,00.html.
22. Joe Neumaier, "'King's Speech' Review: Colin Firth Is perfection in Tom Hooper's Classy Drama about King George VI," *New York Daily News* online edition, November 26, 2010, accessed December 26, 2010, http://www.nydailynews.com/entertainment/movies/2010/11/26/2010-11-26_kings_speech_review_colin_firth_is_perfection_in_tom_hoopers_classy_drama_about_.html.
23. "The King's Speech," *Rotten Tomatoes*, December 30, 2010, accessed December 30, 2010, http://www.rottentomatoes.com/m/the_kings_speech/.
24. *The King's Speech*, directed by Tom Hooper (London, UK: See Saw Films, 2010), DVD.

BIBLIOGRAPHY

Carlisle, Jock A. *Tangled Tongue: Living with a Stutter*. Toronto: University of Toronto Press, 1985.
"'The Devil Wears Prada' Star Emily Blunt: How I Beat My Stutter." *PopEater*, June 7, 2010. Accessed December 31, 2010. http://www.popeater.com/2010/06/07/emily-blunt-stutter/.
"Emily Blunt's Childhood Stutter 'Anguish.'" *MSN Celebrity*, September 6, 2010. Accessed December 15, 2010. http://celebrity.uk.msn.com/news/gossip/articles.aspx?cp-documentid=153700525.
Hilton, Perez. "Emily Blunt Opens up About Se-S-Secret Stutter Past." *Perez Hilton.com*, June 8, 2010. Accessed December 22, 2010. http://perezhilton.com/2010-06-08-emily-blunt-opens-up-about-se-s-secret-stutter-past.
Johnson, Jeffrey. "The Visualization of the Twisted Tongue: Portrayals of Stuttering in Film, Television, and Comic Books." *The Journal of Popular Culture* 41, no.2 (2008): 245–261.
The King's Speech, directed by Tom Hooper. See Saw Films: London, UK. 2010.
"The King's Speech." *Rotten Tomatoes*, December 30, 2010. Accessed December 22, 2010. http://www.rottentomatoes.com/m/the_kings_speech/.

Kline, Suzy. *Mary Marony and the Chocolate Surprise*. New York: Putnam's, 1995.
_____. *Mary Marony and the Snake*. New York: Putnam's, 1992.
_____. *Mary Marony Hides Out*. New York: Putnam's, 1993.
_____. *Mary Marony Mummy Girl*. New York: Putnam's, 1994.
Lears, Laurie. *Ben Has Something to Say: A Story About Stuttering*. Morton Grove, IL: Albert Whitman, 2000.
Mad Men. "The Beautiful Girls." AMC, Season 4, episode 9. 2010.
McIver, Brian. "How James Earl Jones Overcame Childhood Stutter to Produce Galaxy's Most Evil Voice." *Daily Record* online edition, June 16, 2010. Accessed December 16, 2010. http://www.dailyrecord.co.uk/showbiz/celebrity-interviews/2010/06/16/how-james-earl-jones-overcame-childhood-stutter-to-produce-galaxy-s-most-evil-voice-86908–22337035/.
Myers, Randy. "Review: 'The King's Speech' Is a Royal Accomplishment." *Contra Costa Times* online edition, December 10, 2010. Accessed December 20, 2010. http://www.mercurynews.com/movies-dvd/ci_16808951?nclick_check=1.
Neumaier, Joe. "'King's Speech' Review: Colin Firth Is Perfection in Tom Hooper's Classy Drama about King George VI." *New York Daily News* online edition, November 26, 2010. Accessed December 26, 2010. http://www.nydailynews.com/entertainment/movies/2010/11/26/2010–11–26_kings_speech_review_colin_firth_is_perfection_in_tom_hoopers_classy_drama_about_.html.
Ó Guilín, Peadar. *The Inferior*. New York: David Fickling Books, 2007.
Rocket Science. Directed by Jeffrey Blitz. 2007. West Hollywood, CA: Picturehouse Films, 2007. DVD.
Schwarzbaum, Lisa. "The King's Speech (2010)." *Entertainment Weekly* online edition, December 30, 2010. Accessed December 31, 2010. http://www.ew.com/ew/article/0,,20444629,00.html.
Shell, Marc. *Stutter*. Cambridge, MA: Harvard University Press, 2005.
Silverman, Stephen M., and Jennifer Blaise. "James Earl Jones Conquers Stuttering." *People Magazine* online edition, October 8, 2002. Accessed December 31, 2010. http://www.people.com/people/article/0,,624807,00.html.
Yelp, Laurence. *The Dragon's Child*. New York: HarperCollins, 2008.

2

Representations of Attention Deficit Disorder

Portrayals of Public Skepticism in Popular Media

Elizabeth S. EnglandKennedy

Although Attention Deficit Hyperactivity Disorder is not generally considered a mental illness per se, it sometimes is.[1] Additionally, ADHD is a common co-diagnosis of several other mental illnesses,[2] and some medications are prescribed for both (e.g., Concerta). Further, like mental illnesses, ADHD is a "hidden" disability: not immediately visible to others and situationally concealable. The National Survey of Children's Health found that the incidence of childhood ADHD was 9.5 percent in 2007, a 21.8 percent increase since 2003. The CDC describes ADHD as "...the most commonly diagnosed neurobehavioral disorder of childhood."[3] The estimated rate for adults is 2.5 percent[4]; other estimates place incidence at nearly 10 percent in the overall population.[5] Nonetheless, ADHD continues to be poorly understood by the public.

This chapter focuses on media representations of ADHD and how they reinforce stereotypes, often presenting inaccurate information and reflecting cultural suspicions and stigmatization. I introduce ADHD and then briefly explain diagnostic procedures and the importance of methylphenidate, the first and most commonly prescribed medication. After describing audience characteristics that affect perceptions and interpretations of media models, I describe historic representations of disability to contextualize this analysis. I then discuss depictions of characters with ADHD in U.S. mass media and how they reflect and shape understandings of people labeled as having ADHD. Last, I offer suggestions for advocates who want to counter current representations.

Attention Deficit Disorders

Attention Deficit Hyperactivity Disorder was first formally recognized in the Diagnostic and Statistical Manual 3rd version (DSM-III) in 1980.[6] DSM-III delineated three sub-types: "Attention Deficit Disorder with Hyperactivity (ADHD)," "Attention Deficit Disorder without Hyperactivity (ADD)," and "Residual Type" (also "ADD"). This last was used for adult diagnoses, as ADHD had previously been considered a childhood developmental disability. In 1994, DSM-IV renamed it "Attention Deficit/Hyperactivity Disorder."[7]

Attention deficit disorders of all types (hereinafter, "ADD") are medicalized conditions; individuals are "diagnosed" and typically prescribed medication to control associated behaviors. Diagnosis is primarily based on behavioral observations (ideally, in homes, classrooms, and other school or workplace settings), psychoeducational tests, computer-delivered tests, and/or trial medication regimens.[8] Genetic and other medical tests are sometimes used. Although pediatricians and other medical personnel may prescribe medication without gathering additional information,[9] a team approach to diagnosis is preferred. Teams ideally include family members, school personnel (when applicable), and professional diagnosticians.[10]

Incidence is reflected in methylphenidate prescription rates (most often Ritalin and time-release Concerta), the primary mode of medical treatment.[11] These rates are rising: In 1995, 12.5 million prescriptions were written for Ritalin and other stimulant medications for ADD; by 2000, the number had risen to 20 million.[12] Globally, prescriptions of methylphenidate increased 80 percent from 2004–2008. In 2009, 75 percent of the world's supply of Ritalin was consumed in the U.S. Its use continues to increase.[13]

Ritalin is a Schedule II substance under the Controlled Substances Act. (The category includes codeine and morphine.) The U.S. Food and Drug Administration strictly limits production levels. Following a 1993 report on ADD on the news show *20/20*, demand for Ritalin increased so dramatically that pharmacies' supplies were exhausted, resulting in a government-approved production quota increase (a 700 percent increase between 1990 and 1997).[14] Subsequently, additional medications have been approved for treatment of the condition. Many physicians prefer the newer medications because of (1) limitations on methylphenidate, (2) market releases of generic forms, (3) pharmaceutical marketing campaigns, (4) concerns about abuse of oral forms, and (5) consumer requests.

Audience Engagement and Attitude Formation

Media representations affect how people understand and perceive disability.[15] Understandings of disability are more effectively created when audiences actively construct meaning while attending to the presentation. Langer & Chanowitz describe two key modes of engagement: "mindlessness" and "mindfulness." In the former, individuals watch unreflectively without cognitively processing what they experience; they do not try to interconnect cues or information. Previously formed categories are evoked in a routinized manner, along with stereotypical attributions and beliefs. Mindful viewers reflect on what they see and attempt to integrate it with other knowledge and cues. Stereotypes can be questioned in such cases and new attitudes can be constructed. "When mindful, one actively constructs categories and draws distinctions. When mindless, one relies on already constructed [sic] categories."[16] This theoretical model refers to diametrically opposed modes of engagement. However, these are more usefully conceived as the endpoints of continua of attentiveness and thoughtfulness.

Some researchers claim that U.S. culture inherently promotes mindlessness and discourages reflection, describing it as production-oriented rather than process-oriented.[17] Television and movies are more often watched for entertainment value than for cognitive challenge, and therefore tend to be watched in a state of "mindlessness." However, when constructed in ways that promote mindfulness, such as including information and realistic depictions, media representations of characters with disabilities can provide new, more humanizing representations and counteract negative models and stereotypes. Media producers who want to change perceptions of persons with disabilities must therefore be especially conscious of the need to overcome barriers to mindfulness.

How mindfully a viewer approaches a piece of media depends on characteristics of the viewer (both enduring and specific to the moment) and of the piece being watched. Generally, certain genres of movies and television shows are watched more mindfully than others. Comedies, romances, and action shows are more often considered to be pure entertainment than are dramas, mysteries, or "art" films. Watching "entertainment" does not necessarily lead to mindlessness in viewing. However, it is more likely that viewers will not watch it mindfully. Wood points out, "Entertainment is not, as we often think, a full-scale flight from our problems, not a means of forgetting them completely, but rather a rearrangement of our problems into shapes ... which disperse them to the margin of our attention."[18] Similarly, Auden states, "What the mass media offers us is ... entertainment which is intended to be consumed like food, forgotten, and replaced by a new dish."[19] This is especially problematic for ADHD portrayals, which are most commonly presented in popular comedies and satires.

Mindfulness is more probable when stimuli are novel. Depictions supporting cultural stereotypes are more likely to cause viewers to lapse into mindlessness, reinforcing the perspective. If reinforcement is frequent enough, mindfulness decreases and the invoked cognitive set rigidifies. If a representation of a given disability (or of "the disabled") is presented in a sufficiently powerful way, rigidification can occur within a single exposure.[20] In either case, stereotypes are no longer questioned.

If negative stereotypes persist unquestioned, they "normalize" and are more easily and unreflectively enacted. This makes it harder for individuals with disabilities to counter such portrayals and their associated prejudices and discrimination. If the representation does not conform to stereotypes, mindfulness is enhanced. Beliefs and attitudes are re-evaluated and can be reshaped. In these cases, images of persons with disabilities can be powerful agents of change, able to alter audiences' perceptions, understandings, and attitudes.

Character portrayal also affects audiences. The character must be readily identifiable as a person with a disability for viewers to respond mindfully. This identification can happen early in the story or be used as a "plot twist" later, but is crucial for initiating mindfulness. The timing and means of disability disclosure must be considered carefully. Individuals made aware of a disability may make inaccurate observations about the character and/or project cultural stereotypes if the character has not been sufficiently humanized before disclosure.[21] If an audience has formed a close identification with a character that later is identified as having a disability, these stereotypes can be called into question.

Analytic Framework: Historical Media Representations of Disability

This analysis draws upon a variety of models, beginning with those from films of the 1920–1940s, which primarily drew upon theater and literature portrayals; none of these are actively positive. Characters were portrayed as Demonic (angry, vengeful, violent, and/or soulless), Charity Cases (pitiable, helpless), Realistic (pragmatic, part of society), or Survivors (long-suffering, stalwart, outsiders).[22] Later analyses of television and movie depictions provided an overlapping categorization, also used in the current inquiry. Negative stereotypes again dominated: (1) sinister, evil, and criminal (morally culpable); (2) pitiable and pathetic; (3) unable to live a successful life; (4) a burden; (5) maladjusted or unable to adjust to the disability; (6) better-off-dead; and/or (7) "supercrips," defined below.[23]

Some of these categories were not found in the representations of people with ADHD analyzed below. For example, the weak, self-pitying character who cannot adjust to life with a disability until rebuked by a non-disabled individual did not emerge.[24] Similarly, representations of people whose disabilities are so distressing or painful that the characters become suicidal were not found.[25]

The "supercrip" image was only seen once, perhaps because most of the characters with ADHD were familiar to audiences as members of "average" families who appeared in most or all episodes. A "supercrip" is an individual with disabilities who does more and performs better than is possible for most nondisabled people.[26] It is often offered as an inspirational model, a portrait of "...courageous or heroic superachievers ... presumed deserving of pity — instead of respect — until he or she proves capable of overcoming a physical or mental limitation through superhuman feats."[27] This was not how the "supercrip" portrayal was used in the *Simpsons* episode described below.[28]

Movies provided the most common media portrayals of individuals with disabilities until 1978, when television shows increasingly began to included them.[29] Television programming tends to include more realistic portrayals of individuals with disabilities than movies. Although most are watched for pleasure or escape, some are specifically designed to inform the public. Informational programming (e.g., *60 Minutes*) has been effective in decreasing stereotypes and improving attitudes toward persons with disabilities.[30] Providing direct information is intended to enhance mindfulness. However, sometimes this programming is watched unreflectively while other in-home activities are going on, and/or at the end of the day when viewers are tired. Thus it may not have the desired effect.

Television programming can be a powerful tool for activists: A 1991 study indicated that television had become a powerful mode for changing perceptions and attitudes.[31] Other studies, often grounded in social learning theory, support the premise that television is a powerful instructor of sociocultural values and attitudes.[32] Indeed, it has become cultural common sense [33] that television is especially powerful for such instruction, even when unintentional.

Recent depictions more frequently show characters with disabilities facing and confronting discrimination,[34] and as integrated into social worlds rather than serving only as a socially marked "other." This change might reflect increasing activism by persons with disabilities and the increasing emphasis on independence and public participation fundamental to this activism. However, while many representations of disability have become more humanistic and realistic, this is not true of representations of ADD.

Methods

Online compendia sites such as TV Tome (http://www.tvtome.com) and MovieTome (http://www.movietome.com/) were searched to ensure that the sample was as exhaustive as practically possible. To be included, ADHD had to be integral to the piece; e.g., included in a major plot sequence or point, as a major character's characteristic, or as a central theme. Pieces were only included if they were available to mainstream audiences and recognized as being of high quality at the time the original article was written.

One movie, *Pecker*,[35] was included. It was nominated for the Grand Prix Asturias Award at the 1998 Gijo´n International Film Festival and won a Florida Film Critics Circle award in 1999. All television series won a variety of awards, including multiple Emmys and Annies and at least one other. By far, the most decorated program was *The Simpsons*, nominated for 130 awards in the U.S. and internationally, winning 80. (For full and continually updated listings, see http://www.snpp.com/guides/awards.html and http:// www.imdb.com/title/tt0126604/awards). Additional analysis is based on over 10 years' academic and ethnographic research on ADD, including relevant medications, diagnostic procedures, and sociocultural models.[36]

Media Portrayals of Characters with ADD

Media portrayals of ADD reveal negative cultural stereotypes and skepticism about its validity as a "legitimate" disability, including views that it is overdiagnosed, overmedicated, and morally suspect. In this section, I discuss representations of ADD in the movie *Pecker* and animated television social parodies. In these, only children are portrayed, reflecting the belief that this is not a category of adult disability.[37] Social parodies typically present caricatures of culturally-held beliefs. The fact that they are almost the only representations of ADD in programming thus far may indicate that the culture at large does not see ADD as a serious or disabling condition.

DIAGNOSIS

Diagnosis is portrayed as cursory at best, easily accomplished by people with little or no training. Children are diagnosed for exhibiting age-appropriate behaviors or reacting to caffeine in coffee (presented as an age-inappropriate beverage). This reflects a cultural perception that parents are overly reliant on medical opinions rather than on "common sense."[38] Little Chrissy, the youngest sibling in *Pecker*, is diagnosed from a distance by a doctor from Child Protection Services (CPS) who enters the household with a bottle of Ritalin in her purse. She informs the family that CPS employees saw Little Chrissy's picture in the newspaper and diagnosed her with Attention Deficit Hyperactivity Disorder. She presents the bottle and tells them that "she needs Ritalin," and they should "...just think of this as Mommy and Daddy's little helper."

The parents, who had not previously seen Little Chrissy's high levels of physical activity, fidgeting, and resistance to authority as a problem, comply unquestioningly. They reframe their understanding of her behaviors to fit the diagnosis, decide that the prescription is "for her health," and immediately try to persuade her to take "the medication." Chrissy is suddenly no longer a high-energy, willful child, but a person who is unable to live a successful life: a maladjusted burden.

Bobby Hill, the son on "King of the Hill,"[39] is diagnosed after eating four bowls of "Cookie Crunch" cereal (the last with extra sugar at his father's suggestion) and exhibiting increasingly "hyperactive" behavior as a result. This reflects the popular misconception that ADD is caused by excessive sugar intake.[40] In school, his behavior is disruptive in ways commonly associated with ADD: His speech is impulsive, he interrupts his teacher suddenly and repeatedly, repeats and pre-empts her speech, rocks his desk violently, and generally behaves aggressively. When told to go to the nurse's office, he runs, breathing rapidly and heavily. It is significant that he is sent to the nurse's office, as problems of behavioral misconduct are usually referred to a principal or vice-principal. This implies that Bobby's behaviors (all personally atypical) should be treated medically rather than disciplinarily.

The nurse diagnoses Bobby on the spot with ADD, using information from a pamphlet in a rack in her office. She tells Hank, his father, that Bobby "...has probably had it for years..." despite the fact that he had not previously exhibited these behaviors. She recommends "...putting him on one of the many popular ADD medications now available." Confronted with the choice between medication and sending him to "...the special school across town," in which not all the children at his grade level can button their own shirts, Hank and Peggy Hill opt for medication: Ritalin.

His parents accept the diagnosis unquestioningly, without looking into alternative reasons for why Bobby is suddenly exhibiting behaviors so unusual for him. The exception is Hank's conjecture that, "...[I]t *is* called Attention Deficit Disorder. Maybe the boy's not getting enough attention." Hank finds support for the diagnosis based on his own experience: "...I *have* noticed the boy's mind wanders sometimes when I'm lecturing him. A mental disorder would explain that." Regular audience members who have seen Hank lecture Bobby recognize this comment as indicating that Bobby's wandering mind is an expected response of a boy his age in that circumstance, rather than a symptom of ADD. In combination, these scenes index the lack of information held by or given to parents of diagnosed children.

Two episodes of the animated social satire *South Park* feature ADD: "Gnomes"[41] and "Timmy 2000."[42] In "Gnomes," fellow student, Tweek, is assigned to work with the four main characters (Stan, Kyle, Cartman, and

Kenny) on a current events report. They resist this at first, saying they will be unable to work with him, but the teacher insists. Tweek shakes constantly, occasionally flinching or spasming: one or both of his eyes closes, and his head jerks down to one shoulder. His hair is in constant disarray, his voice is high-pitched and explosive, he screams when he feels threatened or becomes the center of attention, and he repeatedly states that he "...can't take that kind of pressure." Overall, Tweek presents himself as helpless, pitiable, maladjusted, and unable to succeed at school.

Tweek's parents give him coffee throughout the episode, both brewed and as packaged grounds to eat. They also give coffee to all five boys on a study night. After drinking it, they run in circles, jump on the bed and from it into a toy pile, yell, talk rapidly, and collapse in exhaustion with upset stomachs. Behind this "hyperactivity," the musical score is high-pitched and fast-tempo, reinforcing the frenetic atmosphere. The point is clearly made that coffee can induce "hyperactive" behavior, i.e., behavior that looks like ADD. Later, Kyle suggests to Tweek's mother,

> KYLE: Hey, do you ever think maybe you shouldn't give your son coffee?
>
> MOM: Why, how do you mean?
>
> KYLE: Like, look at him (points) He's always shaking and nervous.
>
> (Tweek's right eye closes as he spasms and emits a slight scream.)
>
> MOM: (chuckles warmly) Oh, that. He has ADD, Attention Deficit Disorder. That's why he's so jittery all the time.

The boys (and viewers) make a connection that the mother has not: Tweek does not have ADD. He needs to stop drinking coffee. This questions the legitimacy of diagnostic procedures for ADD and the potential for overdiagnosis. ADD is not re-addressed in the episode.

When Timmy (and subsequently all South Park second-graders) are "tested" for ADD in "Timmy 2000," the doctor reads them the novel *The Great Gatsby* and then asks questions about trivial details. When testing Timmy (as the school counselor and principal fall asleep while listening), the doctor asks, "OK, now, Timmy, can you tell me, in Chapter 7, what kind of car did Gatsby drive?" When group-testing the other children, the doctor asks, "In Chapter 12, what kind of bottles did Miss Van Tappan talk about?" Satirizing the memory and aural attention tests of many ADD evaluations, some the children fall asleep during group testing, while others sit with torpid expressions, their eyes half-closed. Kenny hits his head rhythmically against a cupboard.

The characters' responses and the obvious triviality of the questions index societal skepticism about the validity of diagnostic tests and the cultural belief that age-appropriate behaviors are being medicalized. This is reinforced when Sheila and Sharon (Kyle and Stan's mothers) swap confirmatory stories:

SHARON: Yes, I should have known. It all makes sense now. I never could get Stanley to pay attention when his grandfather told him stories about the '30s.[43]

SHEILA: I know what you mean. Kyle gets so hyper sometimes he runs around and screams like a little eight-year-old.

KYLE: I am eight.

Kyle confirms the audience's belief: He does not have ADD, but is being a "normal boy."

These episodes portray parents as unquestioningly accepting of "professional" diagnoses, whether or not the person is actually trained in evaluation or is using accepted diagnostic methods. They also reflect cultural perceptions that parents are comfortable medicating their children based on suspect diagnoses. As social satire, these scenes speak to the power of allopathic medicine, the medicalization of ADD, and an unquestioning acceptance of formal institutional authority by the average parent, who is largely uninformed about ADD.

MEDICATION AND SIDE EFFECTS

These depictions also reflect cultural conceptualizations of medications prescribed for ADD and their potential side effects. When the *South Park* boys' mothers first buy their Ritalin, only Cartman's mother asks about side effects. She is told he "...might experience a small lack of energy," and "...might start seeing little pink Christina Aguilera monsters" (with the singer's head, pink bug bodies, and oversized teeth). Although momentarily nonplused, she makes the purchase. Subsequently, Cartman becomes the only character to experience these side effects until he is "cured" when Chef gives him lemonade spiked with the antidote "Rittle-out."

The South Park boys react in two different ways to their prescriptions: Cartman and Kenny accept the medicalization, while Stan and Kyle (the more "mainstream" and generally practically-minded of the four) initially reject it, telling their friends they never intended to take it. Cartman and Kenny convince them to take it:

CARTMAN: Hey, guys, have you been taking your Ritalin?

STAN: HUH? No, we're not actually gonna take that stuff.

CARTMAN: No, guys, you gotta try it. It makes you feel good.

KENNY (pleasurably): Hmmm.

Stan and Kyle then take Ritalin from Cartman's bottle. From this point on, the boys are "on Ritalin," self-dosing without adult supervision. They carry bottles of it, eating pills frequently. The number of pills taken varies, with no apparent justification.[44] Society's concern about the potential for abuse of Ritalin and similar medications is illustrated through their constant self-administration of pills.

Once they begin taking Ritalin, the children change in many ways. Their voices become monotone, their emotional range diminishes, and they behave in personally inappropriate ways: Cartman suggests a group trip to a concert without mocking Kenny's poverty, Kenny enunciates clearly, and Stan and Kyle do not complain to Chef during lunch. Worst of all (from Chef's and their own non-medicated points of view), they all develop a taste for Phil Collins's music rather than the heavy metal sound of "Timmy and the Lords of the Underworld." Under the influence of Ritalin, they agree with Phil Collins (as depicted) that, "...[P]eople like Timmy should be protected and kept out of the public's eye," a statement they would otherwise reject. These behavioral deviations highlight the sociocultural belief that Ritalin changes personalities as well as "symptoms."

Nor do the Hills ask about side effects. When Hank gives Bobby his first Ritalin pill, he says, "In about half an hour, you're going to be interested in stuff that would normally bore the pants off you." Bobby experiences side effects similar to but more realistic than those of the *South Park* boys: His voice becomes monotonous, his affect flattens, and he falls asleep while waiting to be allowed to take his next dose. His attention to the sound of a fly's legs is hyperfocused; the fly fills both the screen and the soundtrack. He counts the ridges on all the checkers in a set, indicating a tendency to fixate on details.

In the *Simpsons* episode "Brother's Little Helper,"[45] Bart experiences paranoia as a side effect of taking too much "Focusyne" while self-medicating.[46] This is not considered problematic until he steals a tank and knocks a satellite from the sky, portraying him as losing sanity; becoming sinister, criminal, and arguably Demonic; and gaining superhuman ("supercrip") military abilities under Ritalin's effects.

In *Pecker*, Little Chrissy becomes lethargic, staring vacantly into space with her mouth hanging open after ingesting Ritalin. Her mother interprets her heavy breathing as indicating Chrissy needs additional medication, which she gives. Bobby Hill's parents, who pointedly frame Ritalin as a "medication" rather than a "drug," also give him his pills. Taking "drugs" (vs. "medication") may, in this context, indicate that the person is morally suspect and/or criminal and that the substance has potential for abuse.[47]

The fear that nondiagnosed family members might abuse the "drug" is also evidenced: The parents of all the *South Park* boys try Ritalin, as does Bobby's cousin. She hopes the "smart drug" will help her focus on studying. However, it gives her so much energy that she cooks and eats a family brunch, tunes the car, and fixes the mower while the family is at a recital. (Increased energy and appetite are potential side effects of Ritalin.) These examples can be read as indicating that parents are unconcerned about possible side effects and overly trust doctors, criticisms that have been levied against both parents (who are viewed as naive) and doctors (who are viewed as overprescribers, poor diagnosticians, or dismissive.[48] These representations and the Hills' insistence on framing Ritalin as a "medication" also reflect a social contradiction: There has been a "war on drugs" in the U.S. since the Reagan presidency, yet until recently schools routinely medicated large numbers of children with a Schedule II "drug." Popular newspapers and magazines depicted long lines of children in elementary schools waiting for the school nurse to dole out "medications" as indexing this contradiction. These and other mass media portrayals reflect negative stigmatization of medications, as well as of ADD itself.

PERCEPTIONS OF ADD

Negative stigmatization of ADD is clear in how Hank talks about Bobby's diagnosis. He tells Peggy that it means Bobby is "crazy," i.e., unable to live a successful life, and potentially a Charity Case or Survivor. Later, he explains to Bobby that, "...technically, they call it a disease... But not a regular disease like you get in your body. It's a much more rare disease in your brain." Bobby's cousin Luanne, who lives with them, assumes he might overnight have forgotten who she is. Hank protests, saying, "He has ADD. He didn't get hit in the head." Nonetheless, her comment indicates a belief that people with ADD have poor cognitive abilities and are therefore unable to live successful lives.[49]

In "Timmy 2000," the entire second-grade class self-refers for testing after learning that Timmy's diagnosis excuses him from all homework. This action can be interpreted as reflecting a cultural belief that children who have been labeled ADD are inappropriately claiming a sick role and are actually lazy,[50] using their diagnosis to excuse them from work they "should" be performing. When Timmy first exhibits problematic behavior, Stan tries to explain:

> STAN: Uh, Mr. Garrison, haven't you figured it out? Timmy's retarded.
>
> MR. GARRISON: Don't call people names, Stanley.
>
> STAN: But he is.
>
> MR. GARRISON: Now, Timmy, you need to work on your study skills.

The teacher believes Timmy is intelligent but is not trying hard enough, foreshadowing the other children's attempt to use the diagnosis as an excuse to avoid work. Although it is never clear whether Timmy is diagnosable as "retarded," his limited vocabulary and range of social behaviors clearly indicate that unmodified academic assignments are probably inappropriate. However, the other children seize on the "ADD" label and use it to avoid work (until "rescued" by Chef):

> CARTMAN (waiting in line to buy Ritalin): That's right. I have a bad case of ADD — no more homework for me!
>
> KYLE (defending his "diagnosis" to Chef): Yes, but now we don't have any homework, so we can go see Timmy play downtown at Mile High Stadium.

Chef's reaction both models and reflects a common reaction to the perception that children with ADD are simply "lazy," rather than students who need accommodations. He says, "Dammit, children, you don't need drugs to make you pay attention in school. In my day if we didn't pay attention we got a belt to the bottom. Now they try to do everything with drugs." He also later shows the children's parents a video depicting an "...exciting drug-free treatment..." that involves adults hitting a screaming child and yelling, "Sit down and study!" The nostalgic desire for a return to a more discipline-oriented school system and the need for parents to administer more discipline are clear in U.S. discourses on education and child-rearing.[51] This position holds that parents are letting themselves be directed by their children instead of exerting parental control. As a result, children are not taught appropriate social and work-related skills. Such discourses are referenced through Chef's actions and statements. The stereotypes in these episodes are common in U.S. society[52] and can lead to discrimination that, in turn, can create self-fulfilling prophecies of failure and negatively impact self-esteem and self-efficacy.

Conclusion

The media representations discussed throughout this chapter are not realistic. Second-graders cannot refer themselves for testing. Diagnosis is not based on a single behavioral episode, does not use pamphlet checklists, and does not rely on an answer to a single, trivial question. These caricatures ridicule ADD as a diagnostic category. Although some diagnoses are made by "trying out" medications to see if they can "prevent" the undesired behaviors, many carefully consider the person's behavioral history. These portrayals also indicate that Ritalin is the only medication for ADD. (The exception, "Focusyne," is fictional.) This is not the case, as described above. Further, Ritalin does not cause all depicted side effects and has no "antidote." No character's diagnosis is plausible to the audience (with the possible exception of Little Chrissy, for whose behavior alternate explanations are also plausible).

These episodes feature skepticisms and concerns reinforced by popular press articles: ADD is overdiagnosed and misdiagnosed, it is a childhood-only disorder, Ritalin is overprescribed, and children are being misdiagnosed based on behaviors that are culturally perceived as age-normal or are misread.[53] However, the one-sidedness of the portrayals indicates that viewers are correct to deny ADD's validity as a disability. This reinforces the belief that real people who claim the label must be victims of the medical and/or education systems, malingerers, criminals, lazy, or insane: They are maladjusted, pitiable and pathetic, unable to live a successful life, possibly criminal, and potentially a burden. There are no positive portrayals. Rather, diagnosed individuals are depicted as inappropriately claiming the sick role and needing to be taught the error of their ways. In this line of reasoning, problems ultimately lie in the individual.

These movies and television series are viewed as entertainment and/or as social satire. They are "read" unreflexively or as pieces of media that reflect known flaws in sociocultural systems and processes, and they reinforce the stereotypes and factual inaccuracies they model. Nonetheless, these portrayals are rarely targeted by parents, persons with disabilities, or activists as being problematic.

In the U.S., causes of disability are often located within the physical and/or moral person,[54] shifting attention away from sociocultural and environmental causes of difficulty, and making people with disabilities responsible both for their own integration into society and for educating the public. These presentations of disability allow people who are not currently disabled to avoid facing their own prejudices or the need to change environments.

For those invested in reducing the power of such portrayals, it is imperative to find ways to negate them or to balance them with more positive representations. Media policy changes are unlikely to diminish negative stereotyping. For example, adding a category to television and/or movie ratings would probably have little impact on adults' viewing decisions and might make the process so cumbersome that media makers would forego this voluntary process. Further, the current system has been criticized for inconsistency, insufficient use of external reviewers, and failure to properly educate audiences. Another complaint is that the system simply does not work,[55] perhaps because there is no enforcement system. Finally, labeling some depictions as inappropriate through use of a ratings system would close the door to some educational techniques. Arguably, to counter negative stereotypes, it may be necessary to depict them in order to expose them as preparation for education.

It is more likely that group and individual activists would be effective media watchdogs. For example, groups such as the National Organization on Disability could provide media makers with lists of experts who could serve as consultants (not censors) and could more actively disseminate information on how to effectively and appropriately write about disability. More specialized advocacy groups (e.g., the Attention Deficit Disorder Association or Children and Adults with Attention Deficit/Hyperactivity Disorder) could work as media consultants and as media advocates. Groups that regularly publish position papers on disability policy, such as the American Association of People with Disabilities, could take public, strong stances regarding stereotypes and misinformation in mass media. The work of similar organizations can serve as a template for initial efforts, e.g., the National Disability Authority of Ireland, the Irish Radio and Television Commission, and the United States' NAACP.

Increased emphasis on media literacy in schools and through mass media can teach viewers how to spot and counteract negative stereotyping. A wide variety of curricula and materials exist for school use, but many do not include actually analyzing popular television shows and movies. No such education is produced for adults. In addition, activist groups could create Public Service Announcements and similar spots to increase the likelihood that audiences will question media presentations. Commercials by the American Legacy Foundation's "Truth" campaign against teen smoking are potentially useful models.

Showing anti-smoking commercials before a movie with characters who smoke "inoculates" nonsmokers against the message that smoking is "OK." Advocacy organizations could create similar trailers to be shown before films and at the beginning of DVDs, as has been successful in anti-smoking campaigns. To increase the likelihood that these would be watched mindfully, a variety should be produced and selections periodically renewed.

Images of persons with disabilities have changed greatly over the years. Characters have moved from being primarily portrayed in unrealistic or stereotypic ways to being depicted as mainstreamed people. This is not true of characters with ADD. Few media representations of ADD exist, and most are inaccurate. This is unfortunate, given current estimates of the increasing rates of ADD diagnoses.

Cultural skepticisms and concerns regarding diagnosis and medication are clearly reflected in these ADD portrayals; universally, they mirror and confirm societal doubts concerning the validity of the diagnostic category. They reflect and reinforce negative and inaccurate beliefs that adults do not have potential diagnoses of ADD; diagnosis is quickly made and is not grounded in valid methods; medications are "abused" by children and family members; adults overlook side effects and do not properly supervise medications; and the label is used to excuse poor performance, cheating, or avoiding work. Unless advocates and others who are in positions to counter these portrayals do so, negative stereotypes and attitudes are likely to remain unchanged. Fortunately, media representations can be equally powerful vehicles for changing models, understandings, and attitudes of individuals diagnosed with ADD.

NOTES

1. Kate Kelly and Peggy Ramundo, *You Mean I'm Not Lazy, Stupid, or Crazy? A Self-Help Book for Adults with Attention Deficit Disorder* (New York: Scribner, 1993), 106.

2. Lucy Cumyn, Lisa French and Lily Hechtman, "Comorbidity in Adults with Attention-Deficit Disorder," *Canadian Journal of Psychiatry*, 54 (2009): 682.

3. "Increasing Prevalence of Parent-Reported Attention-Deficit/Hyperactivity Disorder Among Children — United States, 2003 and 2007," *Centers for Disease Control and Prevention MMWR: Morbidity and Mortality Weekly Report* 59 (2010): 1439.

4. Viktoria Simon et al., "Prevalence and Correlates of Adult Attention-Deficit Hyperactivity Disorder: Meta-Analysis," *The British Journal of Psychiatry* 194 (2009): 206.

5. Ilina Singh, "Doing their Jobs: Mothering with Ritalin in a Culture of Mother-Blame," *Social Science and Medicine* 59 (2004): 1193; Lawrence H. Diller, *Running on Ritalin: A Physician Reflects on Children, Society and Performance in a Pill* (New York: Bantam Books, 1998), 71.

6. It was included as "Hyperkinetic Reaction of Childhood" in DSM-II and not recognized in the original DSM.

7. Michael Cohen, *The Attention Zone: A Parents' Guide to Attention Deficit/Hyperactivity. Disorder* (Washington, DC: Taylor and Francis, 1998), 13–15; Diller, *Running on Ritalin*, 56–57.

8. Cohen, *The Attention Zone*, 62–64.

9. Diller, *Running on Ritalin*, 71–72.

10. Cohen, *The Attention Zone*, 59–64; Diller, *Running on Ritalin*, 195–213; James A. McLoughlin and Rena B. Lewis, *Assessing Special Students*, 4th edition (New York: Macmillan College Publishing, 1994), 149–150.

11. Robert Foltz, "Medicating Our Youth: Who Determines Rules of Evidence?" *Reclaiming Children & Youth*, 19 (2010): 11.

12. Kate Zernike and Melody Petersen, "Schools' Backing of Behavior Drugs Comes Under Fire," *New York Times*, August 19, 2001, accessed January 1, 2011, http://www.nytimes.com/2001/08/19/us/schools-backing-of-behavior-drugs-comes-under-fire.html?ref=katezernike.

13. Foltz, "Medicating Our Youth," 11.

14. Diller, *Running on Ritalin*, 37.

15. Jack A. Nelson, "Broken Images: Portrayals of Those with Disabilities in American Media," in *The Disabled, the Media, and the Information Age*, ed. J. A. Nelson (Westport, CT: Greenwood Press, 1994), 184; Stephen P. Safran, "The First Century of Disability Portrayal in Film," *Journal of Special Education* 31 (1998): 467; Joseph P. Shapiro, *No Pity: People with Disabilities Forging a New Civil Rights Movement* (New York: Random House, 1993), 12, 16; Otto F. Wahl and J. Yonatan Lefkowits, "Impact of a Television Film on Attitudes Toward Mental Illness," *American Journal of Community Psychology* 17 (1989): 525–6.

16. Ellen J. Langer and Benzion Chanowitz, "Mindfulness/Mindlessness: A New Perspective for the Study of Disability," in *Attitudes Toward Persons with Disabilities*, ed. Harold E. Yuker (New York: Springer Publishing, 1988), 69.

17. Langer and Chanowitz, "Mindfulness/Mindlessness," 74.

18. Paul K. Longmore, "Screening Stereotypes: Images of Disabled People in Television

and Moving Pictures," in *Images of the Disabled: Disabling Images*, eds. A. Gartner and T. Joe (New York: Praeger Press, 1987), 65.

19. Wystan H. Auden, *The Dyer's Hand and Other Essays* (Toronto: Random Books, 1968), 83.

20. Langer and Chanowitz, "Mindfulness/Mindlessness," 70.

21. Beatrice Wright, "Attitudes and the Fundamental Negative Bias: Conditions and Corrections," in *Attitudes Toward Persons with Disabilities*, ed. Harold E. Yuker (New York: Springer Publishing, 1988), 10.

22. Leonard Kriegel, "The Cripple in Literature," in *Images of the Disabled: Disabling Images,* eds. A. Gartner and T. Joe (New York: Praeger Press, 1987), 35–40.

23. Robert Bogdan et al., "The Disabled: Media's Monster," in *Perspectives on Disability: Text and Readings on Disability*, ed. M. Nagle (Palo Alto, CA: Health Markets Research, 1990), 138–41; Nelson, "Broken Images," 5–9.

24. Marilyn J. Phillips, "Damaged Goods: Oral Narratives of the Experience of Disability in American Culture," *Social Science and Medicine* 39 (1990): 851–2, 855.

25. Longmore, "Screening Stereotypes," 69–70; Nelson, "Broken Images," 7–9.

26. Joseph P. Shapiro, "Disability Rights as Civil Rights: The Struggle for Recognition," in *The Disabled, the Media, and the Information Age*, ed. Jack A. Nelson (Westport, CT: Greenwood Press, 1994), 16–19; Shapiro, *No Pity*, 16–18.

27. Shapiro, *No Pity*, 16.

28. The "supercrip" image is offensive to many persons with disabilities (Shapiro *No Pity*, 16–18) who see it as demeaning the less dramatic struggles that people with disabilities regularly face, and as implying that they are somehow "...failures if they haven't done something extraordinary" (Longmore, 75–76; Nelson, 6; Shapiro *No Pity*, 16–18). The struggles of people with hidden disabilities are especially devalued, as a necessary quality of "supercrips" is that their difficulties are clearly evidenced and seem painful, in order to underscore the point that the superheroic "supercrip" is overcoming "insurmountable" obstacles (Shapiro *No Pity*, 17–18). The extreme skills of theft and the use of military equipment that Bart Simpson exhibits in the analyzed episode can be interpreted as a parody of the "supercrip" image.

29. Keith E. Byrd and Timothy R. Elliott, "Media and Disability: A Discussion of Research," in *Attitudes Toward Persons with Disabilities*, ed. Harold E. Yuker (New York: Springer Publishing, 1988), 83.

30. Byrd and Elliott, "Media and Disability," 89.

31. Nelson, "Broken Images," 2.

32. Patricia M. Greenfield, *Mind and Media: The Effects of Television, Video Games, and Computers* (Cambridge: Harvard University Press, 1984), 37–41.

33. Clifford Geertz, *Local Knowledge: Further Essays in Interpretive Anthropology* (New York: Basic Books Publishers, 1983), 75–6.

34. Longmore, "Screening Stereotypes," 75–6.

35. *Pecker*, directed and written by John Waters, 1998.

36. Elizabeth S. EnglandKennedy, "Performing the Label 'LD': An Ethnography of U.S. Undergraduates with Learning Disabilities," (PhD diss., University of Arizona, 2002).

37. Such beliefs have increased the difficulties experienced by diagnosed adults (Kelly & Ramundo, 26). Notable exceptions are seen in advertisements selling medications for "adult ADD." These often portray adults with ADD as dizzied, confused, and inattentive to business meetings or other events before using the medication. In other words, when unmedicated, they are maladjusted and unable to live a successful life, hence potentially pitiable and pathetic.

38. Jeanne M. Stolzer, "Attention Deficit Hyperactivity Disorder: Valid Medical Condition or Culturally Constructed Myth?" *Ethical Human Psychology and Psychiatry* 11 (2009): 114.

39. *King of the Hill.* "Peggy's Turtle Song," Episode 22, Season 1, first broadcast May 10, 1998, by FOX, directed by Jeff Myers and written by Greg Daniels, Brent Forrester and Mike Judge.
40. For a discussion of this belief, see Diller, 142.
41. *South Park,* "Gnomes," Episode no. 17, Season 2, first broadcast December 16, 1998, by COM, directed by Trey Parker and Matt Stone and written by Trey Parker and Matt Stone.
42. *South Park,* "Timmy 2000," Episode no. 4, Season 4, first broadcast April 19, 2000, by COM, directed by Trey Parker and Matt Stone and written by Trey Parker and Matt Stone.
43. U.S. culture presumes that such an experience would be "boring" for eight-year-old children. Other episodes indicate that Stan does not like to hear his grandfather's stories because he finds them irrelevant and dull.
44. In actual practice, a school nurse dispenses medication during the school day, or the child takes a long-acting medication, such as Concerta. At home, parents frequently dispense medication, especially to younger children.
45. *The Simpsons,* "Brother's Little Helper," Episode no. 2, Season 11, first broadcast November 3, 1999, by FOX, directed by Mark Kirkland and written by George Meyer.
46. Compare this to "Folcalin XR," the extended release medication dexmethyl-phenidate hydrochloride.
47. Methylphenidate is used without prescription for study and recreational purposes; the U.S. Department of Justice's Office of Diversion Control reports that an estimated 4.8 percent of people aged 18–25 had used methylphenidate other than as prescribed, and an estimated 1.61 million people in the overall population had done so at some time in their lives. The youngest age group reported was eighth-graders (http://www.deadiversion.usdoj.gov/drugs_concern/methylphenidate.htm).
48. e.g., Diller, *Running on Ritalin*, 196, 198, 315; Thom Hartmann, *Beyond ADD: Hunting for Reasons in the Past and Present* (Grass Valley, CA: Underwood Books, 1996), 130.
49. Jonathan Mooney and David Cole, *Learning Outside the Lines* (New York: Fireside, 2000), 15–17.
50. Kelly and Ramundo, *You Mean I'm Not...,*" 5–6, 12–13; Talcott Parsons, *The Social System* (Glencoe, IL: Free Press, 1951), 285–287.
51. Nancy Gibbs, "Who's in Charge?" *Time* 158 (2001): 40–49; Richard DeGrandpre, *Ritalin Nation: Rapid-Fire Culture and the Transformation of Human Consciousness* (New York: W.W. Norton, 2000), 46–48.
52. e.g., Hartmann, *Beyond ADD*, 12.
53. e.g., Diller, *Running on Ritalin*, 7–8, 11; Foltz, "Who determines Rules of Evidence?" 11; Lyn Nell N. Hancock and Pat Wingert, "Mother's Little Helper," *Newsweek*, 127 (1996), 2; Stolzer, "ADHD: Valid Medical Condition or Culturally Constructed Myth," 6–10; Roberta Waite, "Women with ADHD: It Is an Explanation, Not the Excuse du Jour," *Perspectives in Psychiatric Care* 46 (2010): 182, 186–7.
54. e.g., Richard DeGrandpre, *Ritalin Nation: Rapid-Fire Culture and the Transformation of Human Consciousness* (New York: W.W. Norton, 2000), 38; Hartmann, *Beyond ADD*, 5, 7, 13, 150–58, 164; Thomas G. Finlan, *Learning Disabilities: The Imaginary Disease* (Westport, CT: Bergin & Garvey, 1994), 15, 37; Longmore, "Screening Stereotypes," 66–74.
55. George Gerbner, "The Ratings Rant, V-Chip Gyp, and TV Violence Shuffle: What are the Real Issues?" *Peacework* 290 (1998): 16–17.

BIBLIOGRAPHY

Auden, Wystan H. *The Dyer's Hand and Other Essays.* Toronto: Random Books, 1968.
Bogdan, Robert, Douglas Biklen, Arthur Shapiro, and David Spelkoman. "The Disabled:

Media's Monster." In *Perspectives on Disability: Text and Readings on Disability*, edited by M. Nagle, 138–42. Palo Alto, CA: Health Markets Research, 1990.

Byrd, E. Keith, and Timothy R. Elliott. "Media and Disability: A Discussion of Research." In *Attitudes Toward Persons with Disabilities*, edited by Harold E. Yuker, 82–95. New York: Springer Publishing, 1988.

Cohen, Michael. *The Attention Zone: A Parents' Guide to Attention Deficit/Hyperactivity Disorder*. Washington, DC: Taylor and Francis, 1998.

Cumyn, Lucy, Lisa French, and Lily Hechtman. "Comorbidity in Adults with Attention-Deficit Disorder." *Canadian Journal of Psychiatry* 54 (2009): 673–683.

DeGrandpre, Richard. *Ritalin Nation: Rapid-Fire Culture and the Transformation of Human Consciousness*. New York: W.W. Norton, 2000.

Diller, Lawrence. H. *Running on Ritalin: A Physician Reflects on Children, Society and Performance in a Pill*. New York: Bantam Books, 1998.

EnglandKennedy, Elizabeth S. "Performing the Label 'LD': An Ethnography of U.S. Undergraduates with Learning Disabilities." PhD diss., University of Arizona, 2002.

Finlan, Thomas G. *Learning Disabilities: The Imaginary Disease*. Westport, CT: Bergin & Garvey, 1994.

Foltz, Robert. "Medicating Our Youth: Who Determines Rules of Evidence?" *Reclaiming Children & Youth* 19 (2010): 10–15.

Geertz, Clifford. *Local Knowledge: Further Essays in Interpretive Anthropology*. New York: Basic Books Publishers, 1983.

Gerbner, George. "The Ratings Rant, V-Chip Gyp, and TV Violence Shuffle: What are the Real Issues?" *Peacework* 290 (1998): 16–17.

Gibbs, Nancy. "Who's in Charge?" *Time* 158 (2001): 40–49.

Greenfield, Patricia M. *Mind and Media: The Effects of Television, Video Games, and Computers*. Cambridge: Harvard University Press, 1984.

Hancock, LynNell N., and Pat Wingert. "Mother's Little Helper." *Newsweek* 127 (1996): 50–57.

Hartmann, Thom. *Beyond ADD: Hunting for Reasons in the Past and Present*. Grass Valley, CA: Underwood Books, 1996.

"Increasing Prevalence of Parent-Reported Attention-Deficit/Hyperactivity Disorder Among Children — United States, 2003 and 2007." *Centers for Disease Control and Prevention MMWR: Morbidity and Mortality Weekly Report* 59 (2010): 1439–1443.

Kelly, Kate, and Peggy Ramundo. *You Mean I'm Not Lazy, Stupid, or Crazy? A Self-Help Book for Adults with Attention Deficit Disorder*. New York: Scribner, 1993.

Kriegel, Leonard. "The Cripple in Literature." In *Images of the Disabled: Disabling Images*, edited by A. Gartner and T. Joe, 31–63. New York: Praeger Press, 1987.

Langer, Ellen J., and Benzion Chanowitz. "Mindfulness/Mindlessness: A New Perspective for the Study of Disability." In *Attitudes Toward Persons with Disabilities*, edited by. Harold E. Yuker, 68–81. New York: Springer Publishing, 1988.

Longmore, Paul K. "Screening Stereotypes: Images of Disabled People in Television and Moving Pictures." In *Images of the Disabled: Disabling Images*, edited by A. Gartner, and T. Joe, 65–78. New York: Praeger Press, 1987.

McLoughlin, James A., and Rena B. Lewis. *Assessing Special Students*. 4th edition. New York: Macmillan College Publishing, 1994.

Mooney, Jonathan, and David Cole. *Learning Outside the Lines*. New York: Fireside, 2000.

Nelson, Jack A. "Broken Images: Portrayals of Those with Disabilities in American Media." In *The Disabled, the Media, and the Information Age*, edited by J. A. Nelson, 1–24. Westport, CT: Greenwood Press, 1994.

Parsons, Talcott. *The Social System*. Glencoe, IL: Free Press, 1951.

Phillips, Marilynn J. "Damaged Goods: Oral Narratives of the Experience of Disability in American Culture." *Social Science and Medicine* 39 (1990): 849–57.

Safran, Stephen P. "The First Century of Disability Portrayal in Film." *Journal of Special Education* 31 (1998): 467–79.

Sargent, James D. "Smoking in Movies: Impact on Adolescent Smoking." *Adolescent Medicine* 16 (2005): 345–70.

Shapiro, Joseph P. "Disability Rights as Civil Rights: The Struggle for Recognition." In *The Disabled, the Media, and the Information Age*, edited by Jack A. Nelson, 59–67. Westport, CT: Greenwood Press, 1994.

_____.*No Pity: People with Disabilities Forging a New Civil Rights Movement*. New York: Random House, 1993.

Simon, Viktoria, Pál Czobor, Sára Bálint, Ágnes Mészáros, and István Bitter. "Prevalence and Correlates of Adult Attention-Deficit Hyperactivity Disorder: Meta-Analysis." *The British Journal of Psychiatry* 194 (2009): 204–211.

Singh, Ilina. "Doing their Jobs: Mothering with Ritalin in a Culture of Mother-Blame." *Social Science and Medicine* 59 (2004): 1193–1205.

Stolzer, Jeanne M. "The ADHD Epidemic in America." *Ethical Human Psychology and Psychiatry* 9 (2007): 109–116.

_____. "Attention Deficit Hyperactivity Disorder: Valid Medical Condition or Culturally Constructed Myth?" *Ethical Human Psychology and Psychiatry* 11 (2009): 5–15.

Wahl, Otto F., and J. Yonatan Lefkowits. "Impact of a Television Film on Attitudes Toward Mental Illness." *American Journal of Community Psychology* 17 (1989): 521–28.

Waite, Roberta. "Women with ADHD: It Is an Explanation, Not the Excuse du Jour." *Perspectives in Psychiatric Care* 46 (2010): 182–196.

Wright, Beatrice. "Attitudes and the Fundamental Negative Bias: Conditions and Corrections." In *Attitudes Toward Persons with Disabilities*, edited by Harold E. Yuker, 3–21. New York: Springer Publishing, 1988.

Zernike, Kate, and Melody Petersen. "Schools' Backing of Behavior Drugs Comes Under Fire." *New York Times*, August 19, 2001. Accessed January 1, 2011. http://www.nytimes.com/2001/08/19/us/schools-backing-of-behavior-drugs-comes-under-fire.html?ref=katezernike.

3

Smooth Operator
The Compensated Psychopath in Cinema

Debra Merskin

More than destroying the peace, the psychopath shatters our complacency that comes from not knowing that dangerousness cannot be detected by body type or by a psychological interview; psychopathy reveals itself by a sudden eruption of the will that exists in a hybrid mental state between sanity and madness...[1]

Paul Bernardo, Jeffrey Dahmer, Clifford Olson, and John Wayne Gacy are individuals typically and publicly associated with the symptomatology of psychopathy. News media present and sensationalize the horrors committed by these killers. However, the majority of psychopaths pass by us everyday unnoticed.[2] In particular the *compensated* psychopath (CP) is someone so cool, so charming, and so enticingly unavailable that he often proves irresistible, particularly to women. Several media portrayals glamorize and romanticize the CP such as the character Gordon Gekko in *Wall Street* and *Wall Street: Money Never Sleeps*. In the Showtime television series *Dexter*, actor Michael C. Hall plays a forensic bloodstain pattern analyst who, in his spare time, engages in serial killer vigilantism. His work with the Miami Police Department provides cover for his fascination with killing. He is handsome, accomplished, charismatic, and thereby appealing to women.

This chapter describes this subclinical expression of psychopathy and how it is romanticized in Hollywood cinema, for "movies are the main medium through which dangerous individuals are presented to the public."[3] I first briefly describe the relationship between media representations and public views of those with psychological challenges. This is followed by a discussion of psychopathy. Then Guggenbühl-Craig's concept of the "compensated

44

psychopath" is presented.[4] This individual is a functional variation of a psychopath who is able to pass in society. Importantly, the CP lacks eros, but is aware of its lack. Guggenbühl-Craig uses the term "eros" in a wide sense, not as a substitute for only the erotic or sex, but as an approach to life. Finally, the largely uncriticized romantic idealization of CP is discussed as it is expressed in several films, for "psychopaths abound in cinema."[5] The chapter concludes with a discussion of the potential consequences of this romanticiziation.

Media and Mental Health

That the media influence not only how people perceive others but also how they perceive themselves is well documented.[6] One of the most neglected areas of representation in media, and arguably one of the most inaccurate when presented at all, has to do with issues of mental health. According to Braun, "The media are the public's most significant source of information about mental illness."[7] Even if portrayals of individuals with psychological challenges are positive, they affect how so-called "normal" people view them, how people with psychological problems view themselves, and how mental health workers view clients.[8] Furthermore, whether positive or negative, stereotypical representations contribute to "false beliefs, confusion, conflict, and a delay in receiving treatment."[9] Psychopathy, a complex array of symptoms, exists along a continuum. Definitions vary considerably and representations in popular media vary from the most dramatic, full-blown variety to more subtle variations, discussed in the following sections.

The Nature of Psychopathy

Psychopathy is "a historically ill-defined concept."[10] It has been viewed as a medical problem, a philosophical quandary, and an individual failing. Portrayals range from the dangerous individual, the freakish and monstrous, to the quietly perverse. Early conceptualizations of the constellation of personality characteristics considered psychopathic were considered by psalmists as extreme violence, "immoral behavior, pride, vanity, grievousness, a sense of invulnerability, deceitfulness, and manipulation."[11] During the 19th century, many physicians argued there were "men who were of sound reason and intellect, but when it came to the moral realm were 'deranged.'"[12] They described individuals who had no sense of right and wrong, no feelings of guilt or shame for wrongdoing, and had a marked propensity to lie, cheat, and engage in other activities which normal society considered reprehensible.[13]

The early 20th century saw a narrowing of the definition of psychopathy to refer more to disordered personality with a specific set of symptoms including "aggression, impulsivity, and antisocial behavior."[14] In the second half of the 20th century, symptoms were further limited to describe a disorder with specific affective, behavioral, and interpersonal characteristics. Based on clinical observations, more nuanced definitions evolved.[15] For example, in 1964, Hervey Cleckley articulated several main features of psychopathy:

1. Superficial charm and good intelligence
2. Absence of delusions and other signs of irrational thinking
3. Absence of nervousness or other neurotic manifestations
4. Unreliability
5. Untruthfulness and insincerity
6. Lack of remorse or shame
7. Anti-social behavior without apparent compunction
8. Poor judgment and failure to learn from experience
9. Pathologic egocentricity and incapacity for love
10. General poverty in major affective reactions
11. Specific loss of insight
12. Unresponsiveness in general interpersonal relations
13. Fantastic and uninviting behavior under the influence of alcohol
14. Impersonal, trivial, and poorly integrated sex life
15. Failure to follow any conscious life plan[13]

Intending to generate a common definition of the symptomatology of a psychopath given the wide range of uses and misuses of the term in everyday and clinical life, psychologist Robert Hare and colleagues developed criteria to help clinicians diagnosis the illness.[17] What emerged from the work Hare began in the 1960s was a 40-point scale known as the Psychopathology Check-list (PCL-R). It was revised in 1991 and reduced to 22 items.[18] Drawing on Hare's work, the psychopath is "characterized primarily by a lack of conscience: Psychopaths are incapable of remorse, an incapacity that frees them to offend repeatedly—not necessarily to kill but to prey on others without experiencing guilt."[19]

Hence, "for 150 years, science has known of the psychopath's existence; for at least 140 years, scientists have quarreled over the definition of this disorder."[20] According to the *Diagnostic and Statistical Manual of Mental Disorders—Fourth Edition (DSM-IV-TR)* of the American Psychiatric Association, psychopathy (also referred to as dyssocial personality disorder and sociopathy) and its constellation of symptoms are classified under "Antisocial Personality Disorders."[21] An essential, early childhood characteristic of this disorder is "a pervasive pattern of disregard for, and violation of, the rights of others."[22] This behavior continues throughout adulthood. Three broad dimensions that are independent of antisocial behavior typically characterize it: (1) narcissism (arrogant and deceitful interpersonal style), (2) callous–unemotional traits (deficient affective experience), and (3) impulsivity (impulsive and irresponsible behavioral style).[23] Psychopathy manifests in "an interpersonal style that is dominant, forceful, deceptive, and grandiose, by an affective deficiency evidenced by a failure to experience remorse or guilt, and by behavior that can be described as impulsive and reckless."[24]

In addition to characteristics such as lack of remorse, callousness, pathological lying, charm, parasitic lifestyle and other traits, researchers discovered that "the popular image of the psychopath as a remorseless, smiling killer — Paul Bernardo, Clifford Olson, John Wayne Gacy — while not wrong, [was] incomplete."[25] Many of the traits associated with psychopathy are also present, to varying degrees, in so-called "normal" persons, such as egocentrism, impulsiveness, guiltlessness, callousness, and immaturity. Thus, the challenge is determining when, where, or how the symptoms or constellation of symptoms cross the line into pathology.

Psychopaths are difficult to identify; therefore demographics are hard to come by, for at least two reasons. First, psychopaths don't seek therapy because they don't recognize they have personality flaws.[26] Second, studies of psychopathy are often conducted among persons who are institutionalized.[27] There are, however, some commonalities. For example, "males outnumber females by at least 5:1, and that they almost always come from severely disturbed families."[28] Cleckley's *The Mask of Sanity* is the classic description of the clinical features of psychopathy. These include guiltlessness, lack of insight and judgment, lovelessness and lack of empathy, disordered interpersonal relationships, and fearlessness.[29] These characteristics are described in greater detail in the following sections.

Guiltlessness

A psychopath, particularly the compensated variety discussed later, recognizes that other people have consciences. They use this knowledge to manipulate others via feigned remorse to avoid punishment. According to Cleckly,

> He shows almost no sense of shame. His career is always full of exploits, any one of which would wither even the more callous representatives of the ordinary man. Yet, he does not, despite his able protestations, show the slightest evidence of major humiliation or regret. This is true of matters pertaining to his personal and selfish pride and to esthetic standards that he avows as well as to moral or humanitarian matters.[30]

Lack of Insight and Judgment

The psychopath is often surprised that people are upset by his actions or behavior. "Psychopaths can be thought of not as being hypocrites, but as actually not understanding or using language in the same way other people do."[31]

Lovelessness and Lack of Empathy

Completely egocentric, the psychopath values others only for the pleasure they might give him. He is superficially charming, makes friends easily, and manipulates wildly. He is admired for the ability to distance himself from his emotions. "The psychopath is unable to feel sorry for others in unfortunate situations or put himself in another's place, whether or not they have been harmed by him."[32] This characteristic makes him attractive to many women who find his emotional unavailability exciting and challenging. Thus, the psychopath uses his appeal to manipulate others by using sex. Heterosexual psychopathic men "tend to be sexually precocious, have sex with a larger number of women, have more illegitimate children, and are more likely to separate from their wives than non-psychopathic men."[33] This trait, evident in life and amplified in cinema, functions as an "opportunistic, exploitative sexual strategy"[34] and is thought to increase in highly mobile populations where reputational costs are less likely to be incurred.

Disordered Interpersonal Relationships

While psychopaths enter into sexual relationships, they are unable to form meaningful bonds. Often promiscuous, they are typically interested in relationships of dominance and power, enjoy being in positions of power over women, and will often humiliate or joke at a woman's expense. They employ a "deceptive or 'cheating' strategy in their social interactions."[35]

Fearlessness

Remarkably, fear or anxiety that would normally be associated with risky endeavors is something the psychopath lacks. He is typically reckless and risks his own life and those of others. When framed as acts of bravery, this behavior often results in the psychopath being admired, respected, and placed in further positions of power. "Even under concrete circumstances that would for the ordinary person cause embarrassment, confusion, acute insecurity, or visible agitation, his relative serenity is likely to be noteworthy."[36]

Impulsiveness

Impulsiveness is the characteristic that is usually the undoing of the psychopath who feels invulnerable. Considering his need for continual stimulation and excitement, he sometimes makes mistakes because there is no concern for consequences.

These traits appear alone or in different combinations among everyone some of the time. There are those individuals who do not exhibit the full-blown constellation of characteristics, who are psychopathic, but can almost invisibly live among us, and are in fact often rewarded in western culture — the *compensated* psychopath.

The Stranger Beside Us

While it is the criminal psychopath who makes headlines, the reality is there are few "pure psychopaths."[37] There are individuals who "approach the psychopathic extreme," but "are not totally wanting in morality."[38] Jungian psychologist Adolf Guggenbühl-Craig labeled this type a "compensated psychopath" (CP).[39] The CP is identifiable by five primary symptoms:

- An "inability to love."[20]
- "A missing or deficient sense of morality."[21]
- The "absence of any psychic development."[22]
- A background of deep, nihilistic depression.
- A "chronic background fear."[23]

These (mostly) men manage to fit in, and in fact succeed in American society, particularly in the business and political worlds, in part because they "are graced with a kind of charisma."[44] Cleckley wrote:

> In these personalities ... a very deep-seated disorder often exists. The true difference between them and the psychopaths who continually go to jails or to psychiatric hospitals is that they keep up a far better and more consistent outward appearance of being normal. The chief difference ... lies perhaps in whether the mask or façade of psychobiologic health is extended into superficial material success.[45]

Furthermore, "Everything about him is likely to suggest desirable and superior human qualities, a robust mental health."[46] Yet, to those who carefully observe him, it is clear something is not quite right. For example, CPs are logical to the point of rigidity, have extremely high personal standards to the level of narcissism, and are free from many symptoms that might bring an individual to therapy, such as low self-esteem or relationship problems. Since

CPs rarely end up in a therapist's office, their behavior goes virtually undetected until something significant, and usually tragic, happens.

Lacking a "divine spark," a Self that individuates in a moral sense, the CP must construct a persona.[47] This persona, defined as "the character that we present to others, or the symbolic masks we wear," only appears to be terribly concerned with the well-being and whereabouts of the target of interest.[48] However, lacking an internal moral compass, he sees the world as a stage upon which a performance is needed. If anything this personality type overcompensates, as do people who lack, for example, a good sense of time and thus constantly look at their watches. "You can't appeal to his conscience. He just doesn't care. He takes what he needs and moves on to the next victim.... Like vampires, they exploit people to feed off the energy the game arouses."[49] Robert Hare's definition of psychopath fits the CP to a T:

> Social predators who charm, manipulate, and ruthlessly plow their way through life, leaving a broad trail of broken hearts, shattered expectations, and empty wallets. Completely lacking in conscience and in feelings for others, they selfishly take what they want and do as they please, violating social norms and expectations without the slightest sense of guilt or regret.[50]

When caught in lies, the CP, being free from feelings of guilt, is able to quickly recover and explain and/or rationalize away the situation, providing seemingly reasonable explanations. These justifications mask an underlying lack of compassion and morality.

> If psychic health were defined as freedom from inhibitions, complications, or compulsions, and freedom from all scruples, psychopaths would be prime candidates. It is this freedom, which makes psychopathic sexuality so attractive for others, particularly those acutely aware of the complications, inhibitions, and contradictory nature of their own sexuality.[51]

CPs tend to seek occupations "where those with whom they work will help maintain a moral rigidity, occupations where a strict morality is the order of the day."[52] They are attracted to vocations that provide the opportunity to exert power such as law, law enforcement, clergy, medicine, business, and politics. They seem sincere, trustworthy, forthright, and of high moral standards, but are "always distinguished by egocentricity."[53] They are highly motivated and skilled at social climbing, "regardless of the cost to people or morals."[54]

The CP's characteristics are often rewarded in everyday life. A *New York Times* article about financier Bernard Madoff, who infamously operated a $50 million Ponzi scheme, referred to him on the one hand as an "affable, charismatic man," "reclusive, at times standoffish and aloof," but also as "quiet, controlled, and closely attuned to his image, down to the most minute detail."[55] Some journalists say he stole simply for the fun of it, "exploiting every relationship in his life for decades while studiously manipulating financial regulators."[56] In fact, an FBI agent referred to Madoff as a psychopath. Sensationalism? Perhaps, but the article nevertheless illustrates what is commonly rewarded in political and business culture — the ability to remain detached, hence unencumbered by emotions when making decisions, a powerful drive for self-preservation, and lack of remorse when making difficult choices. As such, psychopaths usually believe they are beyond the law, beyond suspicion, and "tend to strongly believe that they're special."[57]

Thus, the psychopath we should be most concerned about is "the socially well adjusted psychopath."[58] These "'sub clinical' psychopaths" are "the charming predators who, unable to form real emotional bonds, find and use vulnerable women for sex and money (and inevitably abandon them)."[59] "Seductive, manipulative, cruel, egocentric, callous, affectionless, and unfaithful" these men use sensuality to control and dominate (mostly) women.[60]

CPs are often envied for their ability to stand back and apart from emotional involvement. Many women, particularly emotionally vulnerable women, fall for the male psychopath because he appears to share their interests and passions:

> ... He will talk to a woman who is interested in poetry about poetry. He doesn't care about poetry but he will quote poets! ... and even sexually he will be better because his sexual life is absolutely healthy. Normal sexual life is so complicated, so full of strange ideas and obsessions and desires.... It's one of the most complicated things in life and in many ways shows some of the most perverse things. The only sexually normal man or woman is a psychopath, sexuality just functions, and a man psychopath and a woman psychopath — they can make love to anybody, anytime, anyplace, doesn't matter, because it's just going, there is no inhibition of any kind. That's why they are so good at making money.[61]

Popular culture portrayals tend to emphasize the CP's finesse and largess in the business and political spheres. Their access to power and resources functions as an aphrodisiac.

The CP in Popular Culture

As described in this chapter's introduction, because many people have limited personal experience with and are relatively uninformed about various mental health conditions except for what they see and hear in media, these portrayals are very important. "For better or worse, movies and television contribute significantly to shaping the public's perception of the mentally ill and those who treat them."[62] The film *Silence of the Lambs*, for example, is said to have inaccurately portrayed psychopaths as smarter than average: "The popular idea that psychopathic offenders have higher levels of intelligence is somewhat inconsistent with scholarly research that has produced mixed results on their interrelationship."[63] Furthermore, it is important to identify portrayals that on the surface do not appear to be those of full-blown psychopathy.

On the printed page and in moving images, the CP takes center stage. Literary treatments include Shakespearean tragedies, European fairy tales, and Victorian literature and lore. The combination of allure, horror, attraction, and repulsion fluidly operate as tools in the CPs bag of tricks. The power of illusion is another technique. Oscar Wilde's *The Picture of Dorian Gray*, for example, tells the story of a protagonist who never ages. He has sold his soul to remain eternally youthful. He seduces women, betrays his friends, yet, in true CP form, "he does not know fear and sadness."[64] Television is filled with both full-blown psychopathy, but also the more subtle, covert variety. Programs such as *Desperate Housewives* feature a cast of characters (Orson, Zach Young, Betty Applewhite, George Williams, Eddie Orlofsky) who are able to integrate themselves into communities and while they might be considered curious or strange, manage to live double lives. The character Don Draper on AMC's television hit *Mad Men* is so driven to succeed that he routinely cheats on his wife, is willing to leave his children in order to indulge his desires, will do anything (including lying, stealing another man's identity) in order to succeed in the advertising business. His emotional unavailability, physical attractiveness, and business aplomb make him a sexual magnet for women. The Showtime series *Dexter* leads viewers to sympathize with the main character (Michael C. Hall) who is unable to bond with others, "feigns nearly every aspect of normal human relating," is handsome, and is desirable because of his lack of emotions.[65] Yet, as do so many representations of compensated psychopaths, the program explains away what he does because he ritualistically murders those who have harmed others.

Compensated Psychopaths in Cinema

Not only does the viewer experience a dissociative state while viewing films in which the circumstances of ordinary life are suspended, but some cinematic portrayals of psychologically challenged individuals are sympathetic, such as *Three Faces of Eve*, *David and Lisa*, *Ordinary People*, and *A Beautiful Mind*. Less positive portrayals are colorful, exciting, frightening, and as "the embodiment of pure evil they serve as marvelous foils for the hero, who can feel entirely justified in rubbing them out."[66] The psychopath's ability to act without remorse and take risks without fear of reprisal makes him a fascinating subject for cinema. Full-blown psychopathy is obvious in the horror genre, in particular in slasher films such as *Friday the 13th, Halloween, Cape Fear, The Silence of the Lambs,* and *The Texas Chainsaw Massacre* and the *Elm Street* series.[67] Psychopaths, lacking all self-control and gripped by uncontrollable desires, are predatory as well. Norman Bates in *Psycho* is an example. The inability to control one's impulses was highlighted in the character Mark Lewis in *Peeping Tom* (1960) who photographs, as he impales, women. The character Buffalo Bill (Ted Levine) in *Silence of the Lambs* is helpless in the face of his obsession, whereas Hannibal Lecter (Anthony Hopkins) controls his madness.

Whereas early psychopaths in cinemas were characterized as sadistic villains, a more refined, covert, elite criminal variation exists as well. Examples include:

- The classic 1955 film *Night of the Hunter* (1955), in which Robert Mitchum plays a self-appointed preacher who preys upon a gullible widow in hopes of "relieving" her of money hidden by her deceased husband.
- Martin Scorsese's Tommy DeVito and "Nicky" Santoro (Joe Pesci) in films *GoodFellas* and *Casino* respectively.
- A mental patient (J.T. Walsh) in *Sling Blade* who brags to Karl Childers (Billy Bob Thornton) about kidnapping and murdering women.
- The character John Doe (Kevin Spacey) in *Se7en* who is a religious fanatic who murders people according to the Seven Deadly Sins.
- Michael Keaton's character in *Pacific Heights* (1990), a professional bad tenant whose "mannerisms, so fresh and antic, seem unbearably threatening when they mask an ugly agenda; his insouciant, plastic face seems terrifying when it's hiding motives."[68]
- Quentin Tarantino's 1992 film *Reservoir Dogs* features career criminal Mr. Blonde (Michael Madsen) who casually murders a roomful of people.
- Grimsrud (Peter Stormare) in *Fargo* is a reserved villain who says little and kills without remorse or forethought.
- Alonzo Harris (Denzel Washington) in Antoine Fuqua's *Training Day*, a corrupt detective who believes he is above the law.
- Vincent (Tom Cruise) in Michael Mann's *Collateral* plays a professional killer.
- Daniel Plainview (Daniel Day-Lewis) in *There Will Be Blood* is a hate-filled, paranoid oilman who is pathologically competitive.

- Anton Chigurh (Javier Bardem) in *No Country for Old Men* is a hit man who kills without hesitation almost everyone he meets.
- Hans Landa (Christoph Waltz) in *Inglourious Basterds* is a happy-go-lucky SS officer who clearly enjoys playing with, tormenting, and killing people.

I argue, however, that there is another psychopathic character in cinema who is less obvious, less flashy, and in some ways more dangerous because of his near invisibility and simultaneous support in the culture. The *compensated psychopath* similarly defies convention, breaks rules, and fearlessly flaunts convention. He is predatory and to be feared, and yet he is alluring, manipulative, powerful, and successful. In fact, his emotional unavailability and dangerousness makes him attractive to girls and woman as a romantic ideal. Some of his characteristics that make for good drama include:

- High intelligence and a preference for intellectual stimulation (music, fine art, wine).
- A somewhat vain, stylish, almost "cat-like" demeanor.
- Prestige, or a successful career or position.
- A calm, calculating, and always-in-control attitude.[69]

Gordon Gekko in *Wall Street,* Richard Gere in *Internal Affairs* (1990), or Ben Kingsley in *Sexy Beast* (2001): These compensated, sexy psychopaths are able to insert themselves into normal people's everyday lives and make them believe they are trustworthy, strong, and reliable. Actor Kevin Spacey in *Se7en* (1995) and *The Usual Suspects* (1995) passes for normal in society and yet is a deranged killer. Jack Torrance in *The Shining* occupies a seemingly normal life with a wife and child, yet snaps during winter isolation as a caretaker at a closed-for-the-season lodge.

An obvious illustration of a compensated psychopath in cinema is the character Patrick Bateman (played by actor Christian Bale) in the 2000 film *American Psycho.* Based upon Bret Easton Ellis's 1991 book of the same name, Bateman, the main character, is a Wall Street executive so taken by his own physical appearance and prowess that competition among peers for the best business card or most expensive suit elicits a murderous response. But it is his ongoing internal dialogue that reveals his psychopathy:

> There wasn't a clear, identifiable emotion within me, except for greed and possibly, total disgust. I had all the characteristics of a human being—flesh, blood, skin, hair—but my depersonalization was so intense, had gone so deep, that the normal ability to feel compassion had been eradicated, the victim of a slow, purposeful erasure. I was simply imitating reality, a rough resemblance of a human being, with only a dim corner of my mind functioning.[70]

A subtler example of CP is found in the 1987 film *Wall Street*, which presented the unemotional, amoral Gordon Gekko (Michael Douglas), who was not only physically good-looking, but also attractive in part because he was so unreachable. His good looks, compulsion to duty and order, exaggerated conscientiousness, aplomb, take-no-prisoners business savvy, and resultant financial success resulted in a sexy persona unfazed by an ethics of discovery. Gekko says to aspirant Bud Fox, "It's not a question of enough, pal. It's a zero sum game, somebody wins, somebody loses."[71]

In the 2010 sequel, *Wall Street: Money Never Sleeps*, Gekko returns after his prison stint. He *appears* to have changed, or those around him believe him to be reformed, particularly his daughter, with whom he works toward reconciliation. In the end, however, his words and actions are only intended to restore him to financial strength. The portrayal of the real Wall Street in this film is described in *The New York Times* as "a mess, a morass, a snarl of contradictions large and small — a magnet for envy and indignation, fear, and worship."[72] The market is an apt metaphor-Gekko as well.

The largely uncriticized idealization of the CP as top boyfriend material is evident in the *Twilight* book series and movies. This romantic idealization flies under the radar of contemporary concern for girls' psychic and physical well-being. In the book series and in the films, the main character, Bella, becomes completely dependent on Edward, desires him in part because he seems unattainable, and is willing to die and live a new life of predation in order to be with him. For example, early in *Twilight* she says,

> About three things I was absolutely positive. First, Edward was a vampire. Second, there was part of him — and I didn't know how potent that part might be — that thirsted for my blood. And third, I was unconditionally and irrevocably in love with him.[73]

The appeal of the forbidden, dangerous, and thus exciting is a persona real CPs cultivate and are amplified characteristics in vampires, who are consistently attractive because of "their combination of deathless good looks and decadent sexuality."[74] Thus, for many of the same reasons, real girls and women are attracted to the vampire mystique. Therapist Linda Hilburn writes:

> Vampires are the quintessential bad boys of the preternatural universe. They don't follow any human rules or laws. Imagine James Dean with fangs. Or Captain Jack Sparrow rising from his coffin. They're also examples of extraordinary men. Women in therapy often report disappointment with the "human" males they're in relationship with. Would a handsome vampire sit in front of the television, scratching his stomach and drinking beer? Are women lusting after the undead Homer Simpson? Probably not. Imagining a heart-stoppingly-gorgeous man hovering outside your window is much more fun. Most of my clients would open the window.[75]

The characterization of Edward as a desirable male poses a danger to real girls-as-eventual-women's sense of self and development and to the idea of the power dynamics in real relationships with boys-as-eventual-men. Moreover, in cultures such as the U.S. in which a premium is placed on youth, eternal life and fixed ethereal beauty is a hard-to-resist combination. The attraction is "all about the titillation of imagining the monsters we could be if we just let go," said a fashion designer, adding "we're all fascinated with corruption, the more glamorous the better," and the idea of "devouring, consuming, possessing someone we desire."[76] Male vampires presented in media as romantic partners are typically drawn to victims who are emotionally vulnerable. Teen and pre-teen girls who are wrestling with changing bodies, psyches, and sex role identities are a vulnerable audience. Thus the vampire story "resonates with girls because it perfectly encapsulates the giddiness and the rapture — and the menace — that inherently accompany romance and sex for them."[77]

Conclusion

The goal of this chapter was to explore the CP as an unnamed variation of a potentially dangerous manifestation of psychopathy that is at the least rewarded, but more often idealized in cinema. Whether it is the sex appeal and intrigue of Wall Street winners such as Gordon Gekko or the exotic seductiveness of Edward Cullen to teen girls and their middle-aged mothers, the CP has been constructed as a romantic ideal. This has at least two implications. First, the CP as a sympathetic, even tragic figure is an example of the culture ignoring the gender specificity of serial killing. Cameron and Frazer ask:

> Why ... is it usually men who are driven to kill women, and only very rarely that women kill men? Why are there no female sadistic sex-killers and why are there so many men of this type? What is the connection between murder and the erotic? What is the difference between 'normal' men and killers? To ask these questions ... is to ask something about men — or more precisely, about the construction of masculine sexuality in our culture.[78]

In the various incarnations of the *Twilight* saga, for example, while Edward Cullen feeds on animals other than humans, he is always only a bite away from a change in the menu, which is part of his appeal to Bella. She says, "Common sense told me I should be terrified. Instead, I was relieved to finally understand. And I was filled with compassion for his suffering, even now, as he confessed his craving to take my life."[79] Even more frightening is once Bella realizes this, she says of her choice to be with him, that the "decision was ridiculously easy to live with. Dangerously easy."[80]

This soul, personified in Bella, is in flux in teen girls, toggling between girlhood and womanhood. Having the boyfriend or girlfriend of one's dreams can seem like life or death to an adolescent. However, in the case of this story's heroine, the consequences are literal. A 2006 survey by Teen Research Unlimited for example, revealed that teens are experiencing more physical and psychological abuse than in previous years, and that girls in particular had been "hit, punched, slapped, or kicked while in a relationship."[81] Furthermore, parents did not know about the abuse in many cases because their teen either didn't tell them about it or minimized the seriousness of the violent behavior (68 percent).[82]

The second implication is the importance of taking popular culture portrayals seriously. It would be easy to dismiss cinema as only harmless entertainment. Yet research suggests that not only does the viewer experience a dissociative state while viewing films, during which the circumstances of ordinary life are suspended, but also, "No other art form pervades the consciousness of the individual to the same extent and with such power as cinema."[83] While the characters may be purely fictional, the power of story, of mass media, to influence viewers and readers is well established in academic literature. Scholars such as Stuart Hall describe the importance of media texts in the formation of social subjectivity. Literary analyses thereby direct attention to the connection between discursive practices and identity formation. For young viewers, scholars suggest that adolescence is the time when the social world of young people provides information on heteronormative expectations for romance and relationships.[84] This is a particularly vulnerable time for girls, for example, who are "just beginning to take up (and to resist) cultural coherence systems that construct gender and sexuality."[85] Furthermore, for both adolescent girls and adult women, "the notion of threat or vulnerability relates to the positioning of females as submissive, passive, and dependent within dominant cultural discourses of both heterosexuality and romance."[86] While "every decade offers an iconic bad boy who gets the girl,"[87] such as James Dean, Elvis, 50 Cent, according to Strasburger, "Hollywood producers and directors would have us believe that their products are harmless fantasy, but the communication literature indicates otherwise."[88] To ignore that power puts our culture under the CP's spell.

NOTES

1 Cary Federman, Dave Holmes and Jean Daniel Jacob, "Deconstructing the Psychopath: A Critical Discursive Analysis," *Cultural Critique* 72 (2009): 40.

2. Psychopathy primarily affects men. Figures range from about one percent to four percent of the U.S. population. See also John Seabrook, "Suffering Souls," *New Yorker,* November 10, 2008: 92, accessed December 26, 2010, http://www.newyorker.com/report

ing/2008/11/10/081110fa_fact_seabrook; Martha Stout, *The Sociopath next Door* (New York: Random House, 2005).

3. Federman, Holmes and Jacob, 36.

4. Adolf Guggenbühl-Craig, *The Emptied Soul: On the Nature of the Psychopath* (Putnam, CT: Spring Publications, 1980/2008), 94.

5. Glenn O. Gabbard, *The Psychology of* The Sopranos: *Love, Death, Desire and Betrayal in America* (New York: Basic Books, 2002), 31.

6. Maggie Wykes and Barrie Gunter, *The Media and Body Image: If Looks Could Kill* (Newbury Park, CA: Sage, 2005); Jennings Bryant and Mary Beth Oliver, *Media Effects: Advances in Theory and Research* (New York: Taylor & Francis, 2009).

7. Kismet Baun, "Stigma Matters: The Media's Impact on Public Perceptions of Mental Illness," Canadian Mental Health Association (2009), 31–33, accessed December 21, 2010, http://www.ontario.cmha.ca/about_mental_health.asp?cID=48249. See also John Coverdale, Raymond Nairn, and Donna Claasen, "Depictions of Mental Illness in Print Media: A Prospective National Sample," *Australian and New Zealand Journal of Psychiatry* 36 (2002): 697–700.

8. Otto Wahl, *Media Madness: Public Images of Mental Illness* (New Brunswick, NJ: Rutgers University Press, 1995), 182.

9. Baun, 31.

10. Federman, Holmes and Jacob, 37.

11. David J. Cooke, "Psychopathy as an Important Forensic Construct: Past, Present, and Future," in *Psychology and Law: Bridging the Gap,* eds. David V. Canter and Rita Zukauskiené (Farnham, Surrey, UK: Ashgate Publishing, 2008), 167–190.

12. Gordon Banks, "Kubrick's Psychopaths: Society and Human Nature in the Films of Stanley Kubrick," 1990, accessed December 18, 2010, http://www.gordonbanks.com/gordon/pubs/kubricks.html#fn5.

13. Banks, n.p.

14. David J. Cooke, Christine Michie and Stephen D. Hart, "Facets of Clinical Psychopathy," in *Handbook of Psychopathy*, ed. Christopher J. Patrick (New York: Guilford Press, 2007), 92.

15. Silvano Arieti, "Psychopathic personality: Some Views on Its Psychopathology and psychodynamics," *Comprehensive Psychiatry* 4 (1963): 301–312; Hervey Cleckley, *The Mask of Sanity* (St. Louis: Mosby, 1976); William McCord and Joan McCord, *The Psychopath: An Essay on the Criminal Mind* (Princeton, NJ: Van Nostrand, 1964).

16. Hervey Cleckley, *The Mask of Sanity* (St. Louis: Mosby, 1976), 338–345.

17. Robert Hare, *Without Conscience: The Disturbing World of the Psychopaths Among Us* (New York: Guilford Press, 1999), 34.

18. Robert D. Hare and Craig Neumann, "The PCL-R Assessment of Psychopathy: Development, Structural Properties, and New Directions," in *Handbook of Psychopathy*, ed. Christopher J. Patrick (New York: Guilford, 2006), 58–77.

19. Nicole H. Rafter, *Shots in the Mirror: Crime Films and Society* (New York: Oxford University Press, 2006), 94.

20. McCord and McCord, 2.

21. American Psychiatric Association, *Diagnostic and Statistical Manual of mental Disorders: DSM-IV-TR* (Arlington, VA: American Psychiatric Publishing, 2000), 702.

22. American Psychiatric Association, 702.

23. Monica A. Marsee, Persephanie Silverthorn and Paul J. Frick, "The Association of Psychopathic Traits with Aggression and Delinquency in Non-Referred Boys and Girls," *Behavioral Sciences and the Law* 23 (2005): 804.

24. Cooke, "Psychopathy as an Important Forensic Construct," 167.

25. Robert Hercz, "Psychopaths Among Us," 2001, accessed December 28, 2010, http://www.informationliberation.com/?id=26343.

26. See Cleckley; Martin Kantor, *The Psychopathy of Everyday Life: How Antisocial Personality Disorder Affects All of Us* (New York: Greenwood, 2006); Michael H. Stone, *Personality Disorderly Patients, Treatable and Untreatable* (Arlington, VA: APA Publishing, 2006), 209.

27. Robert D. Hare and Daisy Schalling, *Psychopathic Behaviour: Approaches to Research* (New York: Wiley, 1978).

28. Donald W. Goodwin, and Samuel B. Guze, *Psychiatric Diagnosis* (New York: Oxford University Press, 2010), 230.

29. Cleckley, 338–345.

30. Ibid., 343.

31. Banks, n.p.

32. Ibid.

33. David M. Buss, "Human Nature and Individual Differences: Evolution of human Personality," in *Handbook of Personality: Theory and Research,* ed. Oliver P. John, Richard W. Robins, and Lawrence A. Pervin (New York: Guilford, 2008), 52.

34. Buss, 52.

35. Ibid.

36. Cleckley, 340.

37. Adolf Guggenbühl-Craig, *The Emptied Soul: On the Nature of the Psychopath* (Putnam, CT: Spring Publications, 1980/2008), 139.

38. Guggenbühl-Craig, 130.

39. Ibid., 95.

40. Ibid., 86.

41. Ibid., 95.

42. Ibid., 105.

43. Ibid., 114.

44. Adolf Guggenbühl-Craig and James Hillman, *The Emptied Soul: The Psychopath in Everyone's Life* (Putnam, CT: Spring Publications, 1995). Audio recording.

45. Cleckley, 198–199.

46. Ibid., 332.

47. Carl G. Jung, "Psychology and Religion: West and East," trans. R. F. C. Hull, in *Collected Works, Vol. 20* (New York: Bollingen, 1966), 92.

48. Kathy Merlock Jackson, *Rituals and Patterns in Children's Lives* (Madison, WI: Popular Press, 2005), 217.

49. Katherine M. Ramsland, *The Science of Vampires* (New York: Berkley Books, 2002), 116.

50. Robert Hare, *Without Conscience: The Disturbing World of the Psychopaths Among Us* (New York: Guilford Press, 1993), xi.

51. Guggenbühl-Craig, 116.

52. Ibid., 130.

53. Cleckley, 395.

54. Ramsland, 127.

55. Julie Cresswell and Landon Thomas, Jr., "The Talented Mr. Madoff," *New York Times,* January 24, 2009, BU1.

56. Cresswell and Thomas, BU1.

57. Ibid.

58. Guggenbühl-Craig and Hillman.

59. Hercz, "Psychopaths Among Us," 2001, accessed December 28, 2010, http://www.informationliberation.com/?id=26343.

60. Michie Cooke and Hart, 167.

61. Guggenbühl-Craig and Hillman.

62. Steven E. Hyler, Glen O. Gabbard and Irving Schneider, "Homicidal Maniacs

and Narcissistic Parasites: Stigmatization of Mentally Ill Persons in the Movies," *Hospital & Community Psychiatry* 42 (1991): 1044–1048.

63. Matt DeLisi et al., "The Hannibal Lecter Myth: Psychopathy and Verbal Intelligence in the MacArthur Violence Risk Assessment Study," *Journal of Psychopathological Behavioral Assessment* 32, 2 (2009): 169.

64. Guggenbühl-Craig, 42.

65. George Simon, "'Dexter' and the Truth About What Makes a Psychopathic Personality," Counseling Resource, accessed December 31, 2010, http://counsellingresource.com/features/2010/06/02/dexter-psychopaths/.

66. Gabbard, 31.

67. See Christopher Sharrett, ed., *Mythologies of Violence in Postmodern Media* (Detroit: Wayne State University Press, 1999); David Schmid, *Natural Born Celebrities: Serial Killers in American Culture* (Chicago: University of Chicago Press, 2005).

68. "Keaton Is Evil Incarnate as Psychopath in Pacific Heights," *Baltimore Sun,* accessed December 31, 2010, http://articles.baltimoresun.com/1990-09-28/entertainment/1990271005_1_michael-keaton-drake-pacific-heights.

69. http://www.jahsonic.com/Psychopath.html.

70. Brent E. Ellis, *American Psycho* (New York: Random House, 1991), 282.

71. *Wall Street,* directed by Oliver Stone, 1975 (Hollywood, CA: Twentieth Century–Fox, 2000), DVD.

72. A. O. Scott, "Wall Street: Money Never Sleeps (2010)," *New York Times* review, accessed December 27, 2010, http://movies.nytimes.com/movie/450346/Wall-Street-Money-Never-Sleeps/overview?scp=3&sq=film%20review%20wall%20street%20money%20never%20sleeps&st=cse.

73. Stephenie Meyer, *Twilight* (New York: Little, Brown, 2005), 195.

74. Ruth La Ferla, "A Trend with Teeth," *New York Times* (July 1, 2009), E1.

75. Linda Hilburn, L., "Why Do Women Love Vampires? Paranormality," accessed December 31, 2010, http://paranormalityuniverse.blogspot.com/2008/10/why-do-women-love-vampires.html.

76. Quoted in La Ferla, 2009, E1.

77. Caitlin Flanagan, "What Girls Want," *The Atlantic,* December 2008, accessed December 31, 2010, http://www.theatlantic.com/magazine/archive/2008/12/what-girls-want/7161/.

78. Deborah Cameron and Elizabeth Frazer, *The Lust to Kill: A Feminist Investigation of Sexual Murder* (Cambridge, MA: Polity, 1987): 30–31.

79. Meyer, 273.

80. Ibid., 140.

81. Peter Picard, "Tech Abuse in Teen Relationships Study," Teen Research Unlimited, accessed December 31, 2010, http://www.loveisnotabuse.com.

82. Picard, 14.

83. Danny Wedding, Mary Ann Boyd and Ryan M. Niemiec, *Movies and Mental Illness: Using Films to Understand Psychopathology* (Cambridge, MA: Hogrefe, 2010), 1.

84. Marsha D. Walton, Ann Weatherall and Sue Jackson, "Romance and Friendship in Pre-Teen Stories About Conflicts: 'We Decided That Boys Are Not Worth It," *Discourse & Society* 13 (2002): 673–690.

85. Walton, Weatherall, and Jackson, 673.

86. Ibid., 674.

87. Nando Pelusi, "Neanderthink: The Appeal of the Bad Boy," *Psychology Today*, January 1, 2009, accessed December 31, 2010, http://www.psychologytoday.com/articles/200901/neanderthink-the-appeal-the-bad-boy.

88. Vincent C. Strasburger, "Adolescents, Sex, and the Media: Ooooo, Baby, Baby — A Q & A," *Adolescent Medicine,* 16 (2005), 276.

BIBLIOGRAPHY

American Psychiatric Association. *Diagnostic and Statistical Manual of Mental Disorders: DSM-IV-TR.* Arlington, VA: American Psychiatric Publishing, 2000.
American Psycho. Directed by Mary Harron. Hollywood, CA: Universal Studios, 2000. DVD.
Arieti, Silvano. "Psychopathic Personality: Some Views on its Psychopathology and Psychodynamics." *Comprehensive Psychiatry* 4 (1963): 301–312.
Banks, Gordon. "Kubrick's Psychopaths: Society and Human Nature in the Films of Stanley Kubrick." 1990. Accessed December 18, 2010. http://www.gordonbanks.com/gordon/pubs/kubricks.html#fn5.
Baun, Kismet. "Stigma matters: The media's impact on Public Perceptions of Mental Illness." Canadian Mental Health Association (2009), 31–33. Accessed December 18, 2010. http://www.ontario.cmha.ca/about_mental_health.asp?cID=48249.
Bryant, Jennings, and Mary Beth Oliver. *Media Effects: Advances in Theory and Research.* New York: Taylor & Francis, 2009.
Buss, David M. "Human Nature and Individual Differences: Evolution of Human Personality." In *Handbook of Personality: Theory and Research,* edited by Oliver P. John, Richard W. Robins, and Lawrence A. Pervin, 29–60. New York: Guilford, 2008.
Cameron, Deborah, and Elizabeth Frazer. *The Lust to Kill: A Feminist Investigation of Sexual Murder.* Cambridge, MA: Polity, 1987.
Cleckley, Hervey. *The Mask of Sanity.* St. Louis: Mosby, 1976.
Cooke, David J. "Psychopathy as an Important Forensic Construct: Past, Present, and Future." In *Psychology and Law: Bridging the Gap,* edited by David V. Canter, and Rita Zukauskiené, 167–190. Farnham, Surrey, UK: Ashgate Publishing, 2008.
Cooke, David J., Christine Michie, and Stephen D. Hart. "Facets of Clinical Psychopathy." In *Handbook of Psychopathy,* edited by Christopher J. Patrick, 91–106. New York: Guilford Press, 2007.
Cooke, David J., and Stephen D. Hart, "Personality Disorders." In *Companion to Psychiatric Studies.* 7th, edited by Eve C. Johnstone, David Cunningham Owens, Stephen M Lawrie, Andrew M McIntosh, and Michael D. Sharpe, 502–526. Edinburgh: Elsevier, 2004.
Coverdale, John, Raymond Nairn, and Donna Claasen. "Depictions of Mental Illness in Print Media: A Prospective National Sample." *Australian and New Zealand Journal of Psychiatry* 36 (2002): 697–700.
Cresswell, Julie, and Landon Thomas, Jr. "The Talented Mr. Madoff." *New York Times,* January 24, 2009, BU1.
Cutliffe, John R., and Ben Hannigan. "Mass Media, 'Monsters' and Mental Health Clients: The Need for Increased Lobbying." *Journal of Psychiatric and Mental Health Nursing* 8, no 4 (2001): 315–321.
DeLisi, Matt, Michael G. Vaughn, Kevin M. Beaver, and John Paul Wright. "The Hannibal Lecter Myth: Psychopathy and Verbal Intelligence in the MacArthur Violence Risk Assessment Study." *Journal of Psychopathological Behavioral Assessment* 32, no 3 (2009): 169–172.
Dexter. Television series. Executive producers Daniel Cerone, Clyde Phillips and Melissa Rosenberg. New York: Showtime, 2006–.
Ellis, B. *American Psycho.* New York: Random House, 1991.
Federman, Cary, Dave Holmes, and Jean D. Jacob. "Deconstructing the Psychopath: A Critical Discursive Analysis." *Cultural Critique* 72 (2009): 36–65.
Flanagan, Caitlin. "What Girls Want." *The Atlantic.* Accessed December 20, 2008. http://www.theatlantic.com/magazine/archive/2008/12/what-girls-want/7161/.
Gabbard, Glenn O. *The Psychology of* The Sopranos: *love, death, desire and betrayal in America.* New York: Basic Books, 2002.

Goodwin, Donald W., and Samuel B. Guze. *Psychiatric Diagnosis.* New York: Oxford University Press, 1979.

Gordon, Robert M. *Ethics and the difficult Person: The Psychopath in Film and in Your Office.* Accessed December 15, 2010. http://www.mmpi-info.com/psychology-publications/pdm-ethics-difficult-person-psychopath.html.

Guggenbühl-Craig, Adolf. *The Emptied Soul: On the Nature of the Psychopath.* Putnam, CT: Spring Publications, 1980/2008.

Guggenbühl-Craig, Adolf, and James Hillman. *The Emptied Soul: The Psychopath in Everyone's Life.* Putnam, CT: Spring Publications, 1995. Audio recording.

Hare, Robert. *Without Conscience: The Disturbing World of the Psychopaths Among Us.* New York: Guilford Press, 1999.

Hare, Robert D., and Craig Neumann. "The PCL-R Assessment of Psychopathy: Development, Structural Properties, and New Directions." In *Handbook of Psychopathy,* edited by Christopher J. Patrick, New York: Guilford, 2006.

Hare, Robert D., and Daisy Schalling, *Psychopathic Behaviour: Approaches to Research.* New York: Wiley, 1978.

Hilburn, Linda. "Why Do Women Love Vampires? Paranormality." Accessed December 21, 2010. http://paranormalityuniverse.blogspot.com/2008/10/why-do-women-love-vampires.html.

Hyler, Steven E., Glen O. Gabbard, and Irving Schneider. "Homicidal Maniacs and Narcissistic Parasites: Stigmatization of mentally Ill Persons in the Movies." *Hospital & Community Psychiatry* 42 (1991): 1044–1048.

Kantor, Martin. *The Psychopathy of Everyday Life: How Antisocial Personality Disorder Affects All of Us.* New York: Greenwood, 2006.

"Keaton Is Evil Incarnate as Psychopath in Pacific Heights." *Baltimore Sun.* Accessed December 5, 2010. http://articles.baltimoresun.com/1990-09-28/entertainment/1990271005_1_michael-keaton-drake-pacific-heights.

La Ferla, Ruth. "A Trend with Teeth." *New York Times,* July 1, 2009, E1.

Marsee, Monica A., Persephanie Silverthorn, and Paul J. Frick. "The Association of Psychopathic Traits with Aggression and Delinquency in Non-Referred Boys and Girls." *Behavioral Sciences and the Law* 23 (2005): 803–817.

McCord, William, and Joan McCord. *The Psychopath: An Essay on the Criminal Mind.* Princeton, NJ: Van Nostrand, 1964.

Merlock Jackson, Kathy. *Rituals and Patterns in Children's Lives.* Madison, WI: Popular Press, 2005.

Meyer, Stephenie. *Twilight.* New York: Little, Brown, 2005.

Pelusi, Nando. "Neanderthink: The Appeal of the Bad Boy." *Psychology Today,* January 1, 2009. Accessed December 5, 2010. http://www.psychologytoday.com/articles/200901/neanderthink-the-appeal-the-bad-boy

Picard, Peter. "Tech Abuse in Teen Relationships Study." Teen Research Unlimited, 2007. http://www.loveisnotabuse.com.

Rafter, Nicole H. *Shots in the Mirror: Crime Films and Society.* New York: Oxford University Press, 2006.

Ramsland, Katherine M. *The Science of Vampires.* New York: Berkley Books, 2002.

Rose, Diana. "Television, Madness, and Community Care." *Journal of Community & Applied Social Psychology* 8, 3 (1998): 213–228

Rotenberg, Mordechai. *Damnation and Deviance: The Protestant Ethic and the Spirit of Failure.* Piscataway, NJ: Transaction, 2003.

Schmid, David. *Natural Born Celebrities: Serial Killers in American Culture.* Chicago: University of Chicago Press, 2005.

Scott, A. O. "Wall Street: Money Never Sleeps (2010)." *New York Times* review. Accessed December 15, 2010. http://movies.nytimes.com/movie/450346/Wall-Street-Money-

Never-Sleeps/overview?scp=3&sq=film%20review%20wall%20street%20money%
20never%20sleeps&st=cse.

Seabrook, John. "Suffering Souls." *The New Yorker,* November 10, 2008: 92. Accessed
December 15, 2010. http://www.newyorker.com/reporting/2008/11/10/081110fa_fact_
seabrook.

Sharrett, Christopher, ed. *Mythologies of Violence in Postmodern Media.* Detroit: Wayne
State University Press, 1999.

Simon, George. "'Dexter' and the Truth About What Makes a Psychopathic Personality."
Counseling Resource. Accessed December 22, 2010. http://counsellingresource.com/
features/2010/06/02/dexter-psychopaths.

Stout, Martha. *The Sociopath Next Door.* New York: Random House, 2005.

Strasburger, Vincent C. "Adolescents, Sex, and the Media: Ooooo, Baby, Baby — A Q&A."
Adolescent Medicine 16 (2005), 276.

Twilight. Directed by Catherine Hardwicke. 2008. Hollywood, CA: Summit Entertainment, 2008. DVD.

Wahl, Otto. *Media Madness: Public Images of Mental Illness.* New Brunswick, NJ: Rutgers
University Press, 1995.

Wall Street. Directed by Oliver Stone. 1975. Hollywood, CA: Twentieth Century–Fox,
2000. DVD.

Wall Street: Money Never Sleeps. Directed by Oliver Stone. Hollywood, CA: Twentieth
Century–Fox, 2010. DVD.

Walton, Marsha D., Ann Weatherall, and Sue Jackson. "Romance and Friendship in Pre-
Teen Stories About Conflicts: We Decided That Boys Are Not Worth It." *Discourse
& Society* 13 (2002): 673–690.

Wedding, Danny, Mary Ann Boyd, and Ryan M. Niemiec. *Movies and Mental Illness: Using
Films to Understand Psychopathology.* Cambridge, MA: Hogrefe, 2010.

Wykes, Maggie, and Barrie Gunter. *The Media and Body Image: If Looks Could Kill.* Newbury Park, CA: Sage, 2005.

4

The Most Dangerous Deviants in America

Why the Disabled Are Depicted as Deranged Killers

SHAWN M. PHILLIPS

This essay examines the development of the depiction of individuals with congenital physical (and/or mental) disabilities as killers in American popular culture. In such character depictions, the congenital anomaly tends to be made evident as some form of physical impairment that serves as an indicator of behavioral deviancy.[1] In those popular culture depictions, the categories of disability, such as physical or mental, tend to be collapsed into a vague grouping of "deviants." The idea of embodied deviance then is employed such that a visible physical difference is present to symbolize the unspoken source of the deviant behavior.[2] This is, perhaps, best exemplified in "slasher" films and "serial killer" film and fiction. The analysis pushes beyond obvious contradictions, such as disabled killers being portrayed as near superhuman in strength, as being immune to pain, and near immortal when no evidence exists to suggest such abilities. Beyond that contradiction, the analysis considers how groups outside of the mainstream are used in entertainment to explore popular notions of the "insane," monsters, atrocities, and other themes that link together deviancy and horror. To understand popular (mis)perceptions of this cultural phenomenon, this essay considers the works of Foucault, Douglas, Simpson, and Caputi to investigate how cultural systems function to create and maintain boundaries of normalcy and the works of Simpson, Haltunnen, Urla, and Terry to examine the tandem development of gothic horror and its confluence with deviancy in contemporary American popular culture. It is concluded, aligning most closely with the works of Douglas, that drawing out the disabled as deviant killers, a story line that is rarely questioned by audiences (there is never a motive except the basis in deviancy), is an effort to maintain the boundaries of normalcy while those that violate the norms are held in disgust and derision. Thus atrocities can be observed and enjoyed from the comfortable distance of mass entertainment while boundaries are maintained between the audience, the deviant acts, and the perpetrators. Most importantly, the uniform reaction of disgust and horror confirms the normalcy of the audience against the disabled portrayed as deviants in this genre.

The Killer and Victim in American Popular Culture

There has been great interest in the slasher/serial killer genre, but, to date, only certain aspects of the genre have been examined. This analysis gives close consideration to the two strands of literature that most closely link to the assessment of the use of the disabled as killers. Philip Simpson[3] provides a thoughtful discussion on the transition from Gothic horror, vampires, were-wolves, and such, to the contemporary serial killer. In addition, Simpson includes in his analysis a lens to consider how the killer, detective, and profiler are constructed with regard to which one the audience is intended to identify with. This aspect of his work is useful in the current study as we consider how disability is used to nurture and perhaps strengthen boundaries within the popular culture medium. The other strand is the habitual use of females as victims in slasher/serial killer story lines. Such usage has rightfully come under feminist critique, most fully by Caputi,[4] for whom, similarly to Foucault, the idea of power is a central unit of analysis in the depiction of the fictional victim. More recent scholarship by Jhally[5] and Kilbourne[6] considers the gendered structure more fully and how the symbolism within such popular culture mediums provides models of masculinity and femininity. Like feminism, however, both scholars are critical, as the majority of the gendered messages, in tandem, promote violence as an aspect of the male gender and victimhood as an aspect of the female gender. Both strands of research, the development of the killer/profiler and gender, are useful when considering how disability is used in this genre and American popular culture.

Psycho (1960)[7], directed by Alfred Hitchcock, is often identified as the predecessor for the serial killer/slasher storyline.[8] In this film, however, as Philip Simpson argues, the audience is not meant to identify with any of the characters. The killer is a young, attractive, male, but he is nervous, peculiar, and violent. The woman killed in the shower leads the way to a string of subsequent brutalizations of women in this and other similar films. This storyline may not bother audiences of 21st-century America, but such actions did not endear the character to audiences in 1960. Simpson[9] suggests that since the audience is not intended to identify with any character, the film is actually designed for its shock value and as such, is less "real" or less "dangerous." From this starting point, Simpson has traced the development of the slasher genre with an eye toward which characters the audience is to identify with and which storylines are meant to seem more real, threatening, and dangerous. In this process of becoming more real and dangerous, the audience comes closer to the killer and the danger by gaining access to the psychopathological mind. Simpson uses famed author Thomas Harris's *Red Dragon*[10] as a prime example of how the audience gains entry into the mind of the serial killer. Simpson argues that the "profiler" and the "serial killer" are two alternatives to the same personality type. One manifests as a detective and the other as a deranged killer. They are of the same mind in that both are hunters, both will kill, and it takes a likeminded individual, the profiler, to be able to think like the serial killer in order to catch them. Through the profiler, who has the uncanny ability to "think" like the killer, and ultimately kills as well, the audience catches its lurid glimpse of the "serial killer mind." Such a dynamic was clearly absent from Hitchcock's original work. The horror that a killer of this type existed at all was enough for the audiences at that time.

Consider the imagery used when the audience is intended to identify with a killer. In the film version of *Red Dragon*, for example, the young, attractive Edward Norton is the profiler (and a killer) the audience identifies with, while the serial killer has a facial disfigurement that is understood, along with a difficult childhood, to have contributed to his mental state. Further along this line, a new manifestation has emerged that was nearly predicted by Simpson in the recent TV series *Dexter*,[11] directed by Robert Leiberman, in which the serial killer and forensic scientist merge into the same individual. In this storyline, the killer is a vigilante, he is young, white and attractive, and here the audience is meant to identify with the killer. Of note in Simpson's work is that if the American audience is willing to identify with serial killer characters, it is evidently not "put off" by serial killers — as long as they are attractive, 30-something white men who kill according to some socially acceptable rules. The contrast here is that when the slasher/killers are disabled, the audience is meant to identify with the victims, who always tend to be young, white, urban, attractive, and non-disabled. This becomes significant when we consider how cultural systems function to assert and maintain boundaries that include and exclude subsets of the population.

Jane Caputi has provided the most thorough feminist critique of the horror/criminal genre in her analysis of women as victims in American film and advertising.[12] Caputi's critique of the literature argues that the normalization of women as victims dehumanizes and objectifies them for the purposes of sheer entertainment. This process, then, has the effect of creating assumptions surrounding women as disposable victims of violent crimes, creating self-fulfilling prophecies not only in the treatment of women by men, but also in the gender construction of what women are to expect of themselves. Though Caputi's work is dated, the use of women as victims in the genre has changed very little. A simple test of this is the question: How many of the killers are women? Very few, and the majority of victims in such films remain women. A challenge of Caputi's work is to question what happens when victims are male and the violence against them is sexualized. Famed author Joyce Carol Oates produced *Zombie*,[13] a chilling, award-winning novel in which the victims are sexually brutalized males. Unlike other "classic" works in the genre that depict females as sexualized victims, the book actually slipped out of print soon after printing for a few years, but due to Oates's popularity and appeal, it is again in print. Clearly, gender influences greatly who is to be in the killer and victim roles for the cultural tastes of the serial killer/slasher genre.

A gendered analysis (beyond feminist critique) of the depiction of male and female roles in "slasher" film and fiction provides an interesting glimpse into the storylines popular in contemporary America. Jhally[14] examines the extent to which violence and masculine identity are increasingly linked together in mainstream media. Kilbourne[15] details how the mainstream media, advertising in particular, portrays the female image as passive, sexualized, and accommodating. Both sets of researchers reveal the link between gender construction and sexualized violence — where storylines geared toward adolescent males create situations to prod sexual interest and then conclude the scene with a violent slaughter of the female by a male. Where Jhally argues that violence is being engendered as part and parcel of the expected male identity, Kilbourne asserts that aspects of pornography that portray sexualized violence against women are now mainstream popular culture. Examples that merge their views are present in the slasher films of director Rob Zombie, which provide perhaps the clearest mainstream examples of a relatively new facet of the genre deemed "torture porn." In torture porn, a female character will writhe in orgasmic ecstasy while being tortured and mutilated until death. In this work, close attention is given to the gendered roles of the characters, especially with regard to the characters the audience are meant to identify with and those whom the audience are meant to despise. This depiction of a sexually pathologized female harkens back to the Victorian period in which any sexual desire in a female was deemed pathological.[16] The persistence of the notion of female sexuality as pathological appears to be current in the mainstream gender construction. The purity in which the kernel idea of the sexually pathological female has been maintained from the Victorian era, especially since sexuality has always been a central aspect of the normal male, is somewhat alarming. Still, how the gender construction of killer and victim are used in American popular culture serve the current study as we consider how this cultural aspect is used to maintain cultural boundaries and provide depictions of what is and is not acceptable based on with whom the audiences are intended to identify in the storylines.

Power, Gothic Horror, and the Deviant Killer

The depiction of the disabled as killers and slashers in mainstream contemporary film and fiction stretches back to the 1960s in American pop culture. Although prodigious efforts have been put forth to interpret the serial killer/slasher genres, none have devoted attention to the common use of the disabled as killers in such storylines. This essay examines those depictions and how they have changed in recent decades. I first became interested in the notion of deviancy and the power of that label several years ago while researching a nineteenth-century study of the treatment and care of the mentally ill and disabled at a custodial asylum.[17] Psychological thought at the time was to use "labor therapy" as the primary mode of treatment. Labor therapy was a gender-based regimen in which both sexes performed arduous labor throughout the day with the hopes that if they recovered from their ailment, they would be ready to rejoin mainstream society. The inmates seemed to be trained in the most rudimentary of tasks. Even if someone had been cured, which never occurred at this asylum, they never entered the workforce. If they did, they would have entered at the very bottom where the newly recovered would have been unlikely to have been able to secure a living wage. This system did not appear to hold true to the benevolent promises that its developers proclaimed. In such cases, the diagnosis of mental illness would always serve to overlay the patients' experience, even if they were deemed "cured."

Foucault offers some clarity regarding the question of the treatment of the mentally ill and why their treatment only took the form of training in menial tasks. And his work speaks to the broader dilemma of how the medically labeled "deviant" is regarded in mainstream popular culture. In "*Madness and Civilization*,"[18] Foucault explained the interplay of his unit of analysis, "power," and its relation to medical authority. In that view, the authority to define and label groups, classifying and thus separating the "deviants" from the normal, ultimately confers the power to control such groups by those in authority. Any group outside of the mainstream can be subject to societal authority, whether it is through the edicts of law, medicine, or academia, or through the power of knowledge and the labeling process. In the example of the asylum, it seems clear that once the inmates had been labeled with any form of deviancy, even the process of rehabilitation ensured they would remain outside the boundaries of the mainstream consciousness. The works of Douglas,[19] Gilman,[20] Simpson,[21] Levi-Strauss,[22] and Caputi[23] are particularly informative in this regard. The work of these theorists provides a unique lens through which depictions of the disabled in fictional "serial killer/slasher" is brought into sharp focus.

In addition to the iconic films such as *Deliverance* (Boorman*)*, *Texas Chainsaw Massacre* (Hooper), or *The Hills Have Eyes* (Craven), consistent themes persist in the horror genre that depict the disabled as mentally ill slashers who are set up to disgust and horrify the audience while simultaneously permitting a voyeuristic glimpse into the inner world of their deviance. For example, the fictional novels *The Woods are Dark* (1981),[24] *Depraved* (2009),[25] and the *X-Files* episode "Home" (1996)[26] all are considered "classic" horror in their separate mediums. That spans nearly thirty years. The common element in these storylines is that inbred generations of disabled country folk have degenerated into cannibalistic killers set on the capture of any normal folk that happen to pass through their territory. The usage of this concept exemplifies the "othering" process. "Othering" is the process by which a group excludes others based on differences between those inside the group and those perceived as different. The elements present in the themes indicated above suggest the film is made for young urban audiences. Furthermore, all three mediums, from recent decades, demonstrate the consistent use of disability as a means to disgust the audience, reaffirm their normalcy, and titillate their fears with the entertainment of the mindless killers. Clearly, given its popularity, this paradigm of deviancy and the process of othering represent a comfort zone in American popular culture.

Philip Simpson, although he does not directly address the facet of killers depicted as disabled, argues that the serial killer/slasher genre is an extension of the Gothic/Horror storyline.[27] The origin of the Gothic style is interesting in that it represented a cultural shift in how murder was understood in the mainstream populace. The Gothic style developed in the late eighteenth/early nineteenth centuries, largely, as argued by Haltunen, as a shift in the explanation of murder.[28] Prior to the emergence of the "Gothic" symbolic discourse, murder, in secular literature, was explained as a sin, that any sinner might commit if he continued long enough down the wrong path. The shift in the Gothic style is linked with an othering process in which readers differentiate themselves from the killer on moral grounds. Halttunen argues that a significant convention of the Gothic style is "horror." Horror writing, as a convention of the Gothic style, especially non-fictional accounts of murder, developed to shock the reader and trigger an emotional state that linked hatred and disgust with fear of the act and the offender. Along with the othering process, the readers were able to use the experience of horror to confirm their own normalcy. Although the Gothic style and the convention of horror originally developed as a means to explain "murder," the discourse was always a cultural construction that served to differentiate deviancy from the norm.

Disability, Difference, and Deviancy in American Popular Culture

Representations of the body, it is argued by many, are a means to establish and filter dynamic cultural meanings, construct social interaction, and determine how power is utilized among disparate social groups.[29] The idea of embodied deviance, and the binarist track of Western thought,[30] aids in the use of the disabled as mentally ill killers since it cogently uses the tool of horror to distinguish the normal — and the audience — from the deviant. In this paradigm, no one questions how or why the deviants kill or cannibalize; the fact that they are represented with embodied deviance is enough to preclude any further explanation. Of concern, however, is how the boundaries of acceptable normalcy have narrowed in this contemporary narcissistic and isolationist context. In several popular culture mediums, several "other" groups are co-conspirators with the disabled deviants. The obese, elderly, physically disabled (i.e., distinguished from the congenitally disabled), and foreign have joined the ranks of deviants that are depicted as railing against the attractive, normal urban folks who are generally depicted as just looking to have a good time.

Along similar lines, fiction novelist Patricia Cornwell produced a nonfictional account in which she claims to have identified the murderer in the infamous "Jack the Ripper" case.[31] Cornwell explains that she applied the powerful tool of forensic science and identifies a candidate. In this account, forensic science is used as a form of authority that gives Cornwell the power to identify the individual. Her actual forensic efforts; however, are questionable.[32] That issue aside, Cornwell attempts to convince the audience that the individual she identifies as the killer had a penile disability[33] that would have rendered him impotent. Although Cornwell admits to having no evidence that he had such an anomaly and no medical records exist for this individual, she uses graphic language to disgust the reader with how such an anomaly would have been surgically corrected in nineteenth-century Europe. This disability and the ensuing pain from surgeries, she argues, forged in him a shame of his lack of manhood and a fulminating hatred of women. For example, she states:

> Sickert was born with a deformity of his penis requiring surgeries when he was a toddler that would have left him disfigured if not mutilated. He probably was incapable of an erection. He may not have had enough of a penis left for penetration, and it is quite possible he had to squat like a woman to urinate.[34] (p. 5)

Again, although Cornwell uses such graphic descriptions as her basis of evidence, she admits throughout the book that there is no way to know what the nature of Sickert's early health issue was, nor whether he was indeed treated medically. Here, in this nonfictional account, as in serial killer/slasher fiction, disability itself is understood as motivation to be a brutal psychotic killer. An important lesson from this work is the extent to which the notion of disability can be utilized, as Haltunnen explains with gothic horror,[35] as evidence of embodied deviance from which much conjecture can seamlessly wed physical impairment with mental derangement and murderous tendencies. Clearly, the audience is meant to join in the vilification of the culprit Cornwell identifies based on repeated graphic descriptions of his conjectured disability. And as Haltunnen explains, the purpose of the horrified response is to confirm the normalcy of the audience,[36] which, in examples such as Cornwell's work, demonstrates the seamless connection in American popular culture between physical disability and deviancy.

The Use of "Othering" to Maintain Moral Order

Up to this point, this essay has applied Foucault's perspective on deviance as a means to see how the disabled are defined as killers and understood within the mainstream consciousness and, via Simpson, how the audience can be accepting of killers (somewhat tied to their appearance). Moving next to the work of structural theorist Mary Douglas, we see how cultures use dichotomized concepts to maintain a "moral order" (i.e., societal norms).[37] This concept is useful to this study as a unit of analysis that demonstrates a process for the manner in which cultural systems function. With Douglas's work, it is possible to question how and why the disabled are depicted as murderous deviants in the slasher character construction. Following Douglas's approach, to understand how the "moral order" is maintained in a cultural study, one must monitor for "behavioral boundary" violations — this occurs when an individual violates norms and threatens the moral order. Douglas explains this interplay as a process where dichotomies establish boundaries which are the foundation of the "structuralist" thought of Western civilization.

Below are listed examples of such dichotomized boundaries that are commonly violated in the slasher genre:

Normal	Abnormal
Urban	Rural
Clean	Dirty
Attractive	Ugly
Young	Old
Sexual	Asexual
Thin	Obese
Eat food	Cannibalize

This list of dichotomized characteristics tends to be consistently present between the two groups of characters depicted in most slasher horror storylines that depict the disabled as killers. The victims are generally a group of young adults (i.e., normal, urban, clean, attractive, etc.) traveling through a rural area who encounter and are impeded in their journey by the "slasher" (abnormal, rural, dirty, ugly, etc.).

In Douglas's view, one can observe how the depiction of the disabled in this genre continually places them on the wrong side of the dichotomy. Douglas argues that such a slippery slope can occur once an individual or a group is identified as violating a boundary, at which point, they can potentially be guilty of any boundary violation. This perhaps explains how the notions of horror and deviance replace the need for substantial issues such as motive. If the disabled can be classed as deviants, then we need know nothing more about them because their boundary violation is sufficient. The audience's entertainment rests in the pleasure of the normalizing experience of identifying with the "normal" characters that are threatened by the deviants.

When considering the use of disability and Douglas's framework, an interesting transition took place since the original 1974 *Texas Chainsaw Massacre* and the recent 2004 screen version. In the original, among the group of victims was a disabled, wheelchair-bound man. In the 21st-century version, however, none of the victims are disabled, but among the "killers" is a wheelchair-bound, legless man. He is old, dirty, ugly, and his only apparent disability (his missing legs) is used to disgust the audience. As his chair turns, the audience gets a close up view of a bloody stump of his missing legs wrapped in dirty bandages. Here we can see that now, no form of disability is tolerated (congenital or accidental) and a variety of images are consistently used to disgust the audience to reinforce the boundary between the disabled and the mainstream.

In several films, *Wrong Turn*, directed by Rob Schmidt (2004) and *The Hills Have Eyes*, directed by Wes Craven (2006), for example, images of fetuses and neonates with congenital anomalies in medical specimen jars are displayed in the opening credits with the intention of frightening and disgusting the audience. Those images flash quickly, interspersed with scientific papers with titles that include the words "congenital," "abnormal," "mutation," etc. Images of newspapers also flash, interspersed with titles that include the words "family killed," "hikers missing," "generations of inbreeding," etc. Clearly the audience is intended to link disability with mindless killing. This linkage easily asserts the boundary between the dangerous deviants and the normal victims. Rob Schmidt, director of *Wrong Turn*, addresses the use of such imagery in an interview that accompanies the DVD release. Schmidt states that he used the imagery to make the threat "real." Schmidt asserts that if the audience knew that such disabilities/monstrosities were real, then the story would be all that more horrifying. The paradigm also removes the need for developing a motive; if they are different/deviant, that is all that is really needed to know about them. They are not like Dexter, whom the audience identifies with and who kills as a self-righteous vigilante.

The depiction of the disabled as killer was presented with new facets n the 2001 *X-Files* episode "Badlaa." In this episode, a disabled East Indian man kills traveling American parents, controlling their corpses by crawling into them and then breathing through their anuses. The killer's primary motivation is to kill American parents who he observes are able to protect their children. Presumably, he lost his family in a chemical explosion. Still, in this episode, disability is the primary means of "othering" the killer. Disability is accompanied by a filthy appearance, a hateful disposition, unclear powers/abilities, and a basic hatred of the "normal" for who they are. The character clearly crosses many behavioral boundaries while developing a new category of feared deviant — rather than the rural, the killer deviant is ethnic/foreign. The use of disability/deviancy perhaps exposes currents in cultural tensions with regard to job loss and other economic concerns and is a variation on a theme of othering any group that threatens the urban white norm.

Conclusion

The goal of this chapter was to demonstrate how a dominant culture can function to maintain boundaries through assumptions in the mainstream consciousness. This process is potentially revealed in a variety of ways. Through Foucault it is possible to establish how the authority of medical knowledge is used to define the disabled as abnormal to assert their place outside of normalcy. With Simpson, we can see that it is not really murderers, slashers, or serial killers per se that society disdains if they are depicted as otherwise attractive personages. Finally, with Douglas's view, it is possible to retrieve the variety of categories that are unacceptable to the mainstream — the categories that violate expectations of societal norms. *Deliverance*, as some have argued, revealed societal tensions between urban and rural populations — with urbanites being on the "correct" side of the dichotomy. What tensions does the harsh view of the disabled reveal? One suggestion might be that in the downward economic spiral of the past 15 years, the definition of normalcy has become more limited and less tolerant. Another interpretation could be that as beauty standards have become more restrictive, any form of physical deviance is less tolerated. Of note on this topic is a fairly new wrinkle in the depiction of the disabled as not only dirty, ugly, old, non-speaking, asexual killers — but also as foreign. Just as a new glut of American jobs were lost to India through outsourcing beginning in the late 1990s, a new tension was exposed in the form of our first East Indian serial killer portrayed in the fictional genre. But we shall leave this for another time.

NOTES

1. Since American popular culture is being referenced broadly here, see examples from film, *Texas Chainsaw Massacre* (1974; 2003), television, *X-Files: Home* episode (1996), and fiction, Richard Laymon's, *The Woods are Dark* (1981) and Bryan Smith's *Depraved* (2009) for examples of the consistent popularity of the coupling of disability and deviancy in which the apparent primary motive for killing rests in the physical embodiment of difference from the norm.

2. See Jennifer Terry and Jacqueline Urla, eds., *Deviant Bodies: Critical Perspectives on Difference and Science in Popular Culture* (Bloomington: Indiana University Press, 1995), for a discussion on embodied deviancy and how this concept can work to systematically maintain boundaries of normalcy and pathologize those who fall outside standards of the norm.

3. Philip Simpson, *Psycho Paths: Tracking the Serial Killer through Contemporary Film and Fiction* (Carbondale, IL: Southern Illinois University Press, 2000), 2–3.

4. Jane Caputi, *The Age of Sex Crime* (Bowling Green, OH: Bowling Green State University, 1987), 1–13.

5. Sut Jhally, *Wrestling with Manhood: Boys, Bullying, and Battering* (Northampton, MA: Media Education Foundation, 2003), DVD.

6. Jean Kilbourne, *Killing Us Softly* (Northampton, MA: Media Education Foundation, 2010).

7. *Psycho*, directed by Alfred Hitchcock (Universal City, CA, 1960).

8. Caputi, *Age of*; Simpson, *Psycho Paths*.

9. Philip Simpson, *Psycho Paths*.

10. Thomas Harris, *Red Dragon* (New York: Dell Press, 1981).

11. *Dexter*, Showtime Entertainment (2006).

12. Caputi, *The Age of Sex Crime*.

13. Joyce Carol Oates, *Zombie* (New York: Ecco Press, 1996).

14. Jhally, *Wrestling with Manhood*.

15. Kilbourne, *Killing Us Softly*.

16. Carol Groneman, "Nymphomania: The Historical Construction of Female Sexuality," in *Deviant Bodies: Critical Perspectives on Difference in Science and Popular Culture*,

ed. Jennifer Terry and Jacqueline Urla, 219–250 (Bloomington: Indiana University Press, 1995).

17. See Shawn Phillips, "Inmate Life in the Oneida County Asylum: A Biocultural Analysis of the Skeletal and Documentary Records" (PhD diss., Department of Anthropology, SUNY Albany, 2001), 1–8; "Worked to the Bone: Biomechanical Consequences of Labor Therapy," in *Human Biologists in the Archives*, eds. Swedlund and Herring (Cambridge University Press, 2002), 96–98; "County Institutions as Crucibles of Social Judgment: Bioarchaeological Evidence of the Consequences of Disease and Social Stigma," *Northeast Anthropology* 61 (2001): 27–47.

18. Michel Foucault, *Birth of the Clinic* (New York: Pantheon Books, 1963), 3–9; Michel Foucault, *Madness and Civilization* (New York: Pantheon Books, 1961), 4–7.

19. Mary Douglas, *Purity and Danger* (New York: Routledge University Press, 1966), 2–6.

20. Sander Gilman, *Disease and Representation: Images of Illness from Madness to AIDS* (Ithaca, NY: Cornell University Press, 1988), 1–49.

21. Simpson, *Psycho Paths.*

22. Claude Levi-Straus, *Structural Anthropology* (New York: Basic Books, 1963), 132–163.

23. Caputi, *The Age of Sex Crime.*

24. Richard Laymon, *The Woods Are Dark* (New York: Leisure Books, 1981).

25. Bryan Smith, *Depraved* (New York: Leisure Books, 2009).

26. This episode, which aired in 1996, ranks among the top five for the popular series and is considered classic horror despite the unsavory and voyeuristic nature of the subject matter.

27. Simpson, *Psycho Paths.*

28. Karen Halttunen, *Murder Most Foul: The Killer and the American Gothic Imagination* (Cambridge, MA: Harvard University Press, 1998), 5–7.

29. Jennifer Terry and Jaqueline Urla, *Deviant Bodies: Critical Perspectives on Difference in Science and Popular Culture* (Bloomington, IN: Indiana University Press, 1995), 3–7.

30. This refers to the dichotomized pattern of thought present in Western and other cultures. Binarist thinking is a unit of analysis in Structural Theory and is a foundation of theorists such as Levi-Straus, Douglas, and Foucault. In this essay, the deviancy/normalcy dichotomy is central to understanding how disability is used in American popular culture.

31. Patricia Cornwell, *Portrait of a Killer: Jack the Ripper Case Closed* (New York: Putnam's, 2002).

32. n.b. My view on Cornwell's application of forensic science is not new and is by far in the majority. I have not found a source that does not critique her harshly on all fronts in her investigation.

33. Again, the evidence for this is grossly speculative. Cornwell goes so far as to claim his penile impairment forced him to his impotence drove his rage yet she acknowledges he was married on more than one occasion.

34. Cornwell, *Portrait of a Killer,* 5.

35. Halttunen, *Murder Most Foul.*

36. *Ibid.*

37. Mary Douglas, *Purity and Danger.*

BIBLIOGRAPHY

"Badlaa." *X-Files, Season 8.* Twentieth Century–Fox for Television. January 21, 2001. DVD.
Caputi, Jane. *The Age of Sex Crime.* Bowling Green, OH: Bowling Green State University, 1987.

Cornwell, Patricia. *Portrait of a Killer: Jack the Ripper Case Closed.* New York: Putnam's, 2002.

"County institutions as crucibles of social judgment: Bioarchaeological evidence of the consequences of disease and social stigma." *Northeast Anthropology* 61 (2001) 27–47.

Deliverance. Directed by John Boorman. Warner Brothers, 1969. DVD.

Dexter. Showtime Entertainment, 2006. DVD.

Douglas, Mary. *Purity and Danger: An Analysis of Concepts of Pollution and Taboo.* New York: Routledge University Press, 1966.

Foucault, Michel. *The Birth of the Clinic: An Archaeology of Medical Perception.* New York: Pantheon Books, 1973.

_____. *Madness and Civilization: A History of Insanity in the Age of Reason.* New York: Pantheon Books, 1965.

Gilman, Sander. *Disease and Representation: Images of Illness from Madness to AIDS.* Ithaca, NY: Cornell University Press, 1988.

Groneman, Carol. "Nymphomania: The Historical Construction of Female Sexuality." In *Deviant Bodies: Critical Perspectives on Difference in Science and Popular Culture,* eds. Jennifer Terry and Jacqueline Urla, 219–250. Bloomington, IN: Indiana University Press, 1995.

Halttunen, Karen. *Murder Most Foul: The Killer and the American Gothic Imagination.* Cambridge, MA: Harvard University Press, 1998.

Harris, Thomas. *Red Dragon.* New York: Dell Press, 1981.

The Hills Have Eyes. Directed by Wes Craven. Fox Searchlight, 2006. DVD.

"Home." *X-Files, Season 3.* Twentieth Century–Fox for Television. October 11, 1996. DVD.

Jhally, Sut. *Wrestling with Manhood: Boys, Bullying, and Battering.* Northampton, MA: Media Education Foundation, 2003.

Kilbourne, Jean. *Killing Us Softly: Advertising Image of Women.* Northampton, MA: Media Education Foundation, 2010.

Kimmel, Michael. *The Gendered Society.* New York: Oxford University Press, 2004.

Laymon, Richard. *The Woods Are Dark.* New York: Leisure Books, 2008, 1981.

Levi-Strauss, Caude. *Structural Anthropology.* New York: Basic Books, 1963.

Oates, Joyce Carol. *Zombie: A Novel.* New York: Ecco Press, 2009.

Phillips, Shawn. *Inmate Life in the Oneida County Asylum: A Biocultural Analysis of the Skeletal and Documentary Records.* Dissertation, Department of Anthropology, SUNY Albany, 2001.

_____. "Worked to the Bone: Biomechanical Consequences of Labor Therapy." In *Human Biologists in the Archives: Demography, Health, Nutrition, and Genetics in Historical Populations,* edited by D. Ann Herring and Alan Swedlund, 96–129. Cambridge: Cambridge University Press, 2002.

Psycho. Directed by Alfred Hitchcock. Universal City, CA: 1960.

Red Dragon. Directed by Brett Ratner. Universal City: Universal Films, 2003. DVD.

Simpson, Philip. *Psycho Paths: Tracking the Serial Killer Through Contemporary Film and Fiction.* Carbondale: Southern Illinois University Press, 2000.

Smith, Bryan. *Depraved.* New York: Leisure Books, 2009.

Terry, Jennifer and Jacqueline Urla, editors. *Deviant Bodies: Critical Perspectives on Difference in Science and Popular Culture.* Bloomington, IN: Indiana University Press, 1995.

Texas Chainsaw Massacre. Directed by Marcus Nispel. Newline Cinema, 2003. DVD.

Texas Chainsaw Massacre. Directed by Tobe Hooper. Bryanston Pictures, 1974. DVD.

Wrong Turn. Directed by Rob Schmidt. Paramount Pictures, 2004. DVD

5

Off Their Rockers

Representation of Postpartum Depression

LAURA TROPP

Britney Spears is as famous for her public image troubles as she is for her music — whether she is drinking too much, having lapses of judgment such as driving her car with her child in her lap, or behaving erratically, as in shaving her head. Devoted fans and casual gawkers have begun to explain her behavior with rumors that Spears suffers from postpartum depression (PPD), a mood disorder that affects women following childbirth. Media coverage of PPD brings about extreme reactions in the public as they attempt to understand this mental illness.[1] From Brooke Shields's battle with Tom Cruise over how to "fix" her suffering, to reality television stars' silent struggles, to fictional television characters' extreme behavior after giving birth, popular television's representation of PPD is confusing at best and a gross mischaracterization at worst. This chapter examines the problematic constructions of PPD through a framework that explores how motherhood myths, the lack of consensus about the diagnosis and treatment of PPD among medical and feminist communities, and the limitations and biases of media technologies all contribute to PPD coverage and its social construction.

PPD and the Mommy Myth

Problematic mediated depictions of PPD arise partly from the nature of the disorder. Despite its identification as a specific condition only recently, historical anecdotes suggest that PPD has always affected women. Its related condition, postpartum psychosis, may be an explanation for ancient myths of infanticide.[2] Yet, despite its omnipresence, PPD also has been a silent disease. Afraid of compromising their maternal identity, as well as the real threat of being labeled unfit for motherhood, women have often kept silent about their feelings. Even when recognized as a condition in the mid-twentieth century, psychoanalytic theory blamed PPD on a woman's inability to adjust to her duty to desire and raise children.[3]

Conflicting representations of PPD in popular culture mirror similar conflicts within the mental health community. Historian Verta Taylor notes that medical texts did not treat PPD as a medical condition separate from general depression or psychosis in the United States until the 1990s.[4] More recently, growing numbers of female physicians and nurses have advocated affixing a medical label to the condition and offer a physiological explanation for its symptoms. However, not everyone welcomes the medical diagnosis of PPD as a mental illness. Phyllis Chesler, in her now classic book *Women and Madness*, frames the discourse surrounding the construction of mental illness as a feminist issue. Chesler writes, "It is clear that for a woman to be healthy she must 'adjust' to and accept the behavioral norms for her sex even though these kinds of behavior are generally regarded as less socially desirable."[5] Because women have less power in a patriarchic society, their bodies are thought of as less resilient, and they are more likely to be labeled and then treated for mental illness. For these critics, the medical label of PPD prevents constructive discussion of social, economic, and political factors that could contribute to the condition. This problem of representation reflects the ongoing societal conflicts between biological explanations and those that involve the construction of social power.

Adding to this conflict is the fact that PPD is at odds with the primary social ideology of motherhood. A mother's love and instinct for her children is assumed by many to be an ideal and basic instinct; by acknowledging that women suffer from PPD, the Madonna myth is thrown into question. Rather than acknowledge the fact that some women experience sadness and anxiety after childbirth, many hold on to the myth, choosing instead to ignore symptoms and stigmatize those who suffer PPD as not "real" mothers. In fact, the "good" mother is a relatively modern concept. Historically, as Shari Thurer writes in *The Myths of Motherhood*: "Children may not have been precious when they competed with their parents for limited food and resources or were evidence of their mothers' 'immoral' behavior." [6] In contrast, the modern mom, as constructed by popular media, accepts her children unconditionally and is thankful for her role. Susan Douglas and Meredith Michaels, in their book *The Mommy Myth*, label this construction as "the 'new momism': the insistence that no woman is truly complete or fulfilled unless she has kids, that women remain the best primary caretakers of children, and that to be a remotely decent mother, a woman has to devote her entire physical, psychological, emotional, and intellectual being, 24/7, to her children."[7] This popular representation of motherhood makes PPD difficult for many people to understand. Since it often leaves women with conflicted feelings about being mothers, the condition diverges from the mommy myth, closing off possibilities for its recognition, let alone open discussion.

PPD & Medium Theory

The media through which characterizations of PPD are communicated magnify the problems of representations of this condition. In his well-known book *Understanding Media*, Marshall McLuhan warns, "Any medium has the power of imposing its own assumption on the unwary."[8] McLuhan illustrates how the inherent characteristics and limitations of each medium define its use. His work has been expanded by scholars such as Neil Postman, who focused on the entertainment bias of television. "Entertainment is the supraideology of all discourse on television," Postman asserted.[9] The commercial demand of television to be entertaining in order to attract and retain audiences simply may not be compatible with the subject material that the medium is covering. Television representation of PPD provides a vivid example of this disconnect. The condition, clearly not a topic that offers many opportunities for appealing visuals, sets up a problem for producers of both narrative and nonfiction television content. Moreover, its conflict with the motherhood ideology troubles advertisers, who prefer to have content wash over viewers. In "Television News Coverage of Postpartum Disorders and the Politics of Medicalization," Tasha Dubriwny examines the limited way in which PPD is presented in news stories. These stories refer to expert psychiatrists who frame the issue of PPD as exclusively biological, and they showcase personalities (often white) that conform to the myth of the good mother. Dubriwny concludes: "The potential for postpartum disorders to disrupt the hegemonic discourse of essential/good motherhood disappears in television news coverage, largely because of the reports' use of common news routines to frame the information about postpartum disorders"[10] The distortions created by news media as noticed by Dubriwny appear in even more stark relief when comparing televised drama and reality programming that refer to PPD and tabloid coverage of celebrities with the disorder.

The Extreme as the Everyday on Narrative Television

Private Practice, a televised medical drama, depicted PPD twice during its three completed seasons on air. After one episode showed a woman supposedly suffering from PPD nearly drowning her child, the program offered a poll on its website: "Should a woman undergoing psychiatric treatment after nearly drowning her child be allowed to see the baby?" Possible answers were limited to: "Yes, it will motivate her to get better," or "No, She can't be trusted right now."[11] Both the episode and the poll reflect a lack of understanding about PPD and the way that narrative television favors the most extreme representations of the disorder in order to generate excitement and entertainment.

Some prime-time programs that have included a PPD story arc are *Judging Amy*, *Rescue Me*, and *Private Practice*. Each show features a new mother who has failed to bond with her newborn. In *Judging Amy*, Gillian gives birth while in a coma, missing the beginning of her child's life.[12] When she regains consciousness, she finds herself unable to attach to her baby. In the fourth season of *Rescue Me*, Janet suffers from PPD and does not bond with her new baby, whom she is unable to comfort.[13] At one point, she becomes jealous that her husband seems to prefer the baby to her. The plot is complicated by the fact that the baby may be the biological child of her husband's now-deceased brother, with whom she had been carrying on an affair. Even more dramatically, *Private Practice* has a mentally unbalanced assailant kidnap single and pregnant Violet and unflinchingly cut the baby from her stomach, leaving her for dead.[14] Violet and her baby survive the attack, but she finds herself unable to attach to her child.

In each of these programs, new mothers have trouble bonding to their babies, which is a symptom of PPD. However, in each case, the shows offer an external explanation for this lack of bonding. In *Judging Amy*, Gillian's lack of connection comes from her coma. In *Rescue Me*, it is Janet's guilt over her affair and her grief over the death of her brother-in-law. In *Private Practice*, it is the brutal attack Violet endured. In reality, many mothers who suffer from PPD have difficulty bonding with their babies, but these depictions are missing from these shows. These story arcs seem to imply that symptoms of PPD occur only after something incredibly bizarre happens. They create a mindset that the act of birth itself cannot bring on PPD.

These stories may be influenced by the medical debate over PPD. Currently, the condition does not appear as a separate category in the *Diagnostic and Statistical Manual of Mental Disorders—Fourth Edition* (*DSM-IV-TR*) (2000), but merely grouped under the more general category of depression. The onset of depression associated specifically after giving birth is not seen as a condition that warrants extra attention. For feminists and some medical professionals, this is problematic not only when diagnosing the condition, but also for the legal and economic ramifications that follow.

The programs further magnify their misrepresentation of PPD with the effects resulting from the problem. *Judging Amy* offers the mildest consequence, which involves Gillian questioning her marriage and separating from her husband for some time, as she realizes her bonding issues are not with her child, but with her husband. In *Rescue Me*, Janet's husband plots to steal and give away the baby to his brother's widow. *Private Practice*'s Violet feels guilt and remorse after abandoning her baby. The other doctors at first try to understand her feelings but then think of her as selfish and cannot fathom her lack of interest in her baby. The program is set in the medical establishment, yet the doctors' understanding and empathy will only go so far. Eventually, when Violet does feel better, she has to go through a custody battle to regain contact with her son. In each of these shows, the outcome is extreme and involves a threatened or actual loss of the baby or the family unit. Each story arc frames the women, in part, as selfish for their inability to get over themselves and go on about their lives.

An earlier episode of *Private Practice* goes further in its misrepresentation of PPD by incorrectly diagnosing its symptoms.[15] Doctors believe a patient who attempted to kill her newborn by drowning it in a bathtub is suffering from PPD, and Violet, in her role as therapist, must decide whether to allow the woman to keep her child. As the doctors debate, the program never differentiates between PPD and a separate and more rare disorder of postpartum psychosis. Nicole Hurt, in her study of media coverage of PPD, asserts: "Instead of making the distinction between postpartum depression and psychosis, most popular discourse relays stories about women who suffered from the more severe postpartum psychosis while mistakenly describing it by the term 'postpartum depression.'"[16]

Viewers who are experiencing symptoms of PPD may infer from this episode that they too may succumb to this danger. Postpartum Support International, an organization dedicated to raising awareness and support for this disorder, was particularly angry about this misrepresentation. The PR chair for the organization, who was commissioned by ABC to write a public service announcement that follows the episode, explained:

> It was my responsibility to write the text of ABC's public service announcement. I happily did so because I was excited about the opportunity to educate millions of people, and I wrote it about postpartum depression because that is the direction I was given. Had I been given more truthful information up front, I could have written something completely different and more appropriate to the episode. Since I didn't, the PSA just continues to blur the lines between postpartum depression and postpartum psychosis as if they are one in the same.[17]

Neglecting an opportunity to demonstrate how proper therapy can help a mother suffering from PPD, instead the episode concludes with the father finally arriving, which reassures the doctors that he will protect the baby from the mother. Again, an external solution is privileged over dealing with the disorder.

The television medium encourages this framing of PPD by forcing narrative programming to conform to an entertainment standard that promotes exaggeration, extreme danger, and simplification. While viewers may well expect some divergence from reality in television programming, so few programs depict PPD at all that women have only these distorted examples to use as points of reference to understand the disorder. When these depictions imply that PPD results in the loss of one's child and one's mind, the path to diagnosis and treatment becomes obscured.

Silent Suffering and Reality Television

Blogs were awash in excitement in the fall of 2010 over a storyline on ABC's *Desperate Housewives*. The hit program included a story arc about PPD in its seventh season. The biggest surprise, though, was the twist that the program took. The character suffering from PPD was not the housewife Lynette, but her husband Tom. This revelation was emblematic for a show that prides itself on critiquing the modern housewife and surprising its audiences with unexpected plot twists. However, to scholars interested in the media coverage of mental health issues, what makes this twist peculiar is that the program had never acknowledged the possibility that Lynette herself suffered symptoms of PPD. In fact, in the show's first season, Lynette, having just given birth to her fourth child, often seemed overwhelmed and depressed. Her mood brightened only when she hired a nanny, found work and changed her feelings of self-worth. It would seem clear that Lynette may have been suffering from PPD, but if that is the case, she was a silent sufferer. This is an image all too pervasive in tracking televised coverage of postpartum depression.

One may expect to find that characters in fiction programs suffer from the most extreme mood disorders in service of sensational plots, limited by only whatever a writer can dream up. Reality television, in contrast, is constrained by the real lives of the subjects the cameras follow. To be sure, most viewers understand that the presentation of some events is constructed by both reality show producers and the stars themselves. However, a basic tenet about reality television assumes that real people who are experiencing their lives are presented, and their experience bears at least some resemblance to everyday life. In fact, one may argue that part of the draw of reality programming is the ability to share common life experiences with the stars of the program. These days, one can turn on the television to watch people struggling to overcome obesity (*The Biggest Loser*), competing as professional chefs (*Top Chef*), or coming to terms with their obsessive-compulsive disorder (*Hoarders*). Vicariously watching celebrities cope with everyday life experiences is a subset of the reality genre, and two successful examples are *Bethenny Getting Married*, featuring *Real Housewives* reality star Bethenny Frankel, and *Kendra*, starring former Playboy Playmate Kendra Wilkinson. In both programs, each star gives birth to a child and subsequently seems to suffer from feelings of anxiety and discomfort when they return home, yet neither PPD nor the milder term "baby blues" is ever mentioned within either program.

In *Bethenny Getting Married*, Frankel becomes pregnant, plans her wedding, and has a baby all within the same season.[18] During most of her pregnancy, the show keeps its focus on the minutiae of planning for the wedding and reception. Only after the wedding is over, when Bethenny and her newlywed husband are on their honeymoon and just before she gives birth, does she first express some nervousness about having a baby so soon after getting married. Her feelings are resolved, however, by the end of the episode, and she does not express her uncertainty about being a mother again until she brings her new baby home. After she returns from the hospital, Bethenny meets with her therapist, Dr. Amador, who appears frequently in the program. She confides that she is nervous about something happening to her baby and admits, "Like, I have weird thoughts happening in my head." She dismisses these thoughts, and when she says, "I became a crybaby lately," she looks for reassurance that she is merely hormonal, providing a biological explanation for her atypical behavior. The therapist, though, avoids a physiological diagnosis and tells her, "It seems to me you're doing a lot of crying because you're happy," reinforcing the myth of the good mother by not acknowledging that she could be feeling anything other than joy. Bethenny, on the other hand, discusses the investment and cost of motherhood. She talks about her own dysfunctional relationship with her mother and worries that her baby is not guaranteed to grow to become a happy and fulfilled adult. Yet her therapist minimizes these reasonable concerns when reframing her discussion to center around her extreme joy.

The title character in the reality program *Kendra* has traded in her relationship with Hugh Hefner for a new husband and son.[19] Soon after giving birth, Kendra invites her friends out for a much-needed girls' weekend. As she gets ready, she worries about her post-partum figure. She breaks down crying and says she just does not feel good about herself. She walks over to her husband and cries, "Babe, I just, I don't feel, I don't feel pretty right now." She debates whether she should cancel her plans. "I just feel like I don't want to go out tonight," she confides. "I feel like it's just going to kill me." Her husband, to his credit, takes her concerns seriously and tries to understand them. Like *Bethenny Getting Married*, however, *Kendra* never offers the baby blues as an explanation of why she may be feeling this way. Instead, the show frames her feelings as a concern about her body image. Appearing on the talk show *Chelsea Lately*, Kendra acknowledges feeling depressed after having her baby.[20] She admits that her cure was "forbidden" sexual relations with her husband: having sex before the medically advised six week waiting period was over. It may not be surprising that a former Playmate advocates sex as a cure for depression, but the fact that Kendra can discuss her depression only when coupling it with a lighthearted reference to sex demonstrates the difficulty of having a substantive discussion of PPD on television.

These shows are constrained by the traditional television plot. Characters face a challenge or conflict: How will a baby disrupt their lives? The solution quickly follows; their fears were unfounded, and they love their babies. Even when real life intervenes, such as Bethenny's and Kendra's crying spells, to contradict this narrative, viewers are reassured that other, more legitimate reasons than PPD explain the behavior. Though these reality shows do not use the fiction plot device of characters facing extreme obstacles to explain the onset of PPD, they do use the frame of alternative explanations for justifying the symptoms that could have been attributed to PPD. The difficulty in representing PPD on television arises from the dichotomy separating birth and loss. These shows present pregnancy as providing a "gift" of the baby, when in reality giving birth sometimes includes anxiety and feelings of grief over this life change. The medium of television precludes discussion of these complex and sometimes conflicting issues in favor of narrative structure that is easily resolved.

A Woman's Problem

"My wife is getting all postpartum depression-y on me," Turk, a doctor and new dad on the medical sitcom *Scrubs*, says in exasperation as he pleads for help in dealing with his wife, Carla, who has recently given birth and is exhibiting symptoms of PPD.[21] This quote illustrates the challenges faced in television representations of medical conditions. *Scrubs* sincerely attempts to explore the realities of PPD, but, as a television comedy, jokes are its building blocks. As a result, PPD becomes a setup to a punch line.

Scrubs successfully uses PPD to critique the Mommy Myth. Carla wants to be the perfect mother to her newborn baby, Isabella, but is frustrated when she has difficulty breastfeeding because she cannot latch the baby. After receiving so much help at the hospital, she is afraid to be home alone with her baby. Unlike other television programs, this series acknowledges the difficulties of becoming a new mother, including the fear of the dependence of a new life and the difficulties of living up to the perfection that seems to be required of motherhood. The program also reveals the stigma attached to these feelings of helplessness and depression. Carla works hard to keep her feelings hidden but appears depressed to the others in the program, including her husband. None of his efforts to help work, bringing him to a comic and desperate appeal for help.

In response, a fellow doctor has his own wife, Jordan, who is pregnant with her second child, talk to Carla. Jordan tells Carla that she understands her feelings, even when they seem so extreme. Jordan treats the illness as no big deal. She says matter-of-factly that Carla has PPD. Resisting, Carla replies, "No, I just have the weepies." To show her that she is not alone, Jordan admits to her own feelings of wanting to throw her newborn out the window. Carla identifies: "I wanted to throw Isabella out the window. We just had our apartment repainted, and all the windows were sealed shut, so I just wanted to drop her off the roof." Jordan treats these feelings as normal and typical. In contrast, the cameras pan to Turk, who clearly sees the "crazy" in Carla's admission. The blocking of the scene uses Turk as a proxy for a society unaware of the symptoms and treatment of PPD.

Despite its enlightened take on PPD, the program suggests that only women can understand the disorder. When Turk tries to participate in the conversation, he immediately is hushed by Jordan: "You have no lines in this play." Echoing *Private Practice*, it is ironic that Carla is a nurse, surrounded by medical professionals, but they are unable to diagnose or treat her condition. Only someone from outside the medical profession can help. Increasingly, supportive self-help groups run by women are becoming a solution to helping women deal with PPD. Verta Taylor, tracing the history of postpartum support groups, explains:

> An important element of self-help consciousness in the postpartum support group movement is the recognition and reevaluation of the negative side of motherhood. In attempting to understand why so many women find themselves unable to live up to society's image of what constitutes a good mother, the founders of the postpartum support group movement sought to remove women's experiences and self-definitions from the deviant clinical realm and to place them in the somewhat more acceptable feminist arena.[22]

Women may be most empowered when surrounded by other women to tackle a problem, but at what cost? With Turk left on the fringe of the conversation, the program presents PPD as a strictly female problem, leaving out larger societal obligations to help address it.

Despite its depiction of some realistic symptoms of PPD, *Scrubs* is constrained by the limits of the medium. As a half-hour sitcom, Carla's problem is diagnosed and addressed by the end of the episode. In future episodes, Carla moves on to her next dilemma: should she go back to work or stay at home with her baby, clearly having moved on from her PPD. In addition, the show uses Turk's exclusion for comic effect, rather than finding a way to include men in supporting women suffering from PPD.

PPD and the Celebrity Image

To help the many women who may be silently suffering with PPD, some celebrities are raising awareness by "outing" themselves as recovered or recovering victims of the disorder in celebrity gossip websites and magazines. Monica Danger, from the reality show *For the Love of Ray J,* talked about her suffering in an interview on VH1: "People don't understand that when you come from a tough past, and you have a child and you have postpartum depression, a lot hits you at once."[23] Gwynth Paltrow not only openly discusses her own experiences but also has created a blog that collects other mothers' stories as well. She writes:

> When my son, Moses, came into the world in 2006, I expected to have another period of euphoria following his birth, much the way I had when my daughter was born two years earlier. Instead I was confronted with one of the darkest and most painfully debilitating chapters of my life.[24]

OnTheRedCarpet.com reports that Bryce Dallas Howard of *Twilight* fame likens her experience with postpartum depression to surviving a *Star Trek* alien abduction.[25] Gena Lee Nolin, a former star of *Baywatch*, is writing a book about her experiences suffering from PPD. She joins other celebrity moms like Brooke Shields and Marie Osmond, fellow sufferers turned authors.[26] These women have created a new wave of celebrity activism, determined to fight the stigma of PPD and to disassociate victims from the label of bad mothers. Yet at times, media coverage of these celebrities and their activism distracts audiences from receiving the message.

Surprisingly, scholarly research suggests that celebrity activism may not have as powerful an influence on mainstream news coverage than expected. One such study argues, "Thanks to the limits of the public's attention span and the mainstream media's restless search for the next big thing, even the most influential groups are at the mercy of a constantly shifting political and media agenda."[27] Despite the challenge of maintaining news coverage, celebrities are often influential in mobilization and building an infrastructure for their cause.[28] The questionable effectiveness of mediated celebrity activism is reflected in how little coverage of PPD is sustained once a celebrity's book or story has been revealed. Because of the biases of the medium, most coverage tends to be dramatic and focuses on celebrities, while it shies away from delving into substantive issues. The celebrities that discuss the PPD may find that they are raising public awareness, but it is not sustained awareness and tends to focus on personal stories rather than social and political consequences.

The now infamous feud between Brooke Shields and Tom Cruise regarding her diagnosis and treatment of PPD illustrates this bias. In her book *Down Came the Rain*, Shields describes her public appearances while secretly suffering from PPD:

> It was if I'd been in an awful, freak car accident, one where I flew headfirst into the windshield through which I had viewed my life for the past thirty-seven years.... Somehow I felt responsible for the predicament I was in, but I also felt it was futile to attempt to improve my situation. I was too unhappy to believe it could ever get better.[29]

Upset with both the stigma she felt and the lack of public awareness about the disorder, she went public with her cause by writing and promoting her book. Tom Cruise, a devout member of Scientology, which rejects the legitimacy of psychiatry, went public with his opposition to her promotion of antidepressants as a solution for PPD. "All the drugs just mask the problem," Cruise told *Today Show* host Matt Lauer. "If you understand the history of it, it masks it. You aren't getting to the reason why. There is no such thing as a chemical imbalance."[30] Brooke Shields answered Cruise in the *New York Times*:

> In a strange way, it was comforting to me when my obstetrician told me that my feelings of extreme despair and my suicidal thoughts were directly tied to a biochemical shift in my body. Once we admit that postpartum is a serious medical condition, then the treatment becomes more available and socially acceptable. With a doctor's care, I have since tapered off the medication, but without it, I wouldn't have become the loving parent I am today. So, there you have it. It's not the history of psychiatry, but it is my history, personal and real.[31]

News media labeled this exchange a "War of the Words," replayed and retold on several morning and evening news programs. This framing of the issue as a personal battle deflected serious discussion about the basis of their disagreement. Television used the common narrative structure of hero and villain for this story, and Cruise played the part of the bad guy. Lauer critiqued him harshly on the *Today Show*, implying Cruise was merely promoting his agenda of Scientology. *Scrubs* reinforced this narrative thread when Jordan comforts Carla by saying, "Look, you can't get rid of this by sheer force of will or positive thinking or taking advice from a big Hollywood movie star and the dead science fiction writer he worships." In the process of vilifying

Cruise, most televised media missed that his argument, whatever his motivation, reflects the ongoing battle between feminists and the medical community regarding the treatment of this illness. Both Cruise and feminist critics articulate the problem of constructing the illness as a purely medical one. Within the hero/villain frame, however, mediated coverage of these celebrities focused on the drama of the conflict rather than the debate of the issue.

Conclusions: PPD and New Media Environments

Representing PPD in popular culture is difficult not only because of the complexities and disagreements over understanding the illness but also because of the constraints of commercial media. These depictions demonstrate that the television medium, with its focus on the extreme, the entertaining, and the comedic, offers simplistic and sometimes troubling views of PPD.

New changes in the media environment have the potential to shift representation of PPD. Websites and blogs encourage women to post their opinions of representations on these shows. When *Private Practice* aired its disturbing episode conflating PPD and psychosis, mommy bloggers and PPD activists responded in force.[32] However, it is an open question whether this response merely allowed women to vent or if it promoted any real change. After a woman in South Carolina drowned her children, news media debated whether or not the woman suffered from PPD. One article on the AOL News website included a quote from criminal profiler Pat Brown:

> Most women who suffer depression after their children are born are suffering from post-how-did-I-get-stuck-with-this-kid, this body, this life? They may be depressed, but it is their situation and their psychopathic personality that brings them to kill their children, and not some chemical malfunction.[33]

The outcry throughout the mommy blogs led to AOL eventually removing that particular quote from their story.[34] In this case, women speaking through new media were able to change coverage of PPD within new media. Because Internet content can be revised, this was possible. In contrast, traditional broadcast media tend to remain in fixed form once produced.

A more realistic representation of PPD can be found on blogs that chronicle the experiences of women suffering from the disorder. The blog His Boys Can Swim was started by anonymous expectant parents who posted about their pending arrival.[35] They live-tweeted the birth of their child, and their followers were quick to rejoice. However, the new mom began to suffer from PPD, and her unhappy posts reflected it. Their blog-in-progress does not require a happy ending, unlike the television shows, which are dependent on a narrow narrative structure. While Shields and Cruise had little control over how their feud was framed in the media, celebrity moms like Gwyneth Paltrow can use the Internet to promote their stories without a filter. Unfortunately, this empowerment is tempered by the lack of media attention, which seeks out dramatic conflict over useful information.

Rather than simply blame producers for distorted representations of PPD, it may be more productive to understand how the limitations of the media environment in which these stories are produced shape these representations. The powerful ideology of the Mommy Myth, the limitations of commercial media, and the disagreement among the medical community over how to label and treat PPD all conspire to reinforce problematic representation of the disorder. Without an active resistance against these influences, the sad mommy will continue to be labeled the bad mommy.

NOTES

1. Different groups contest the designation of PPD as a "mental illness," a conflict that is explored throughout this chapter.

2. Margaret G. Spinelli, "Maternal Infanticide Associated with Mental Illness: Prevention and the Promise of Saved Lives," *The American Journal of Psychiatry* 161 (September 2004): 1548.

3. Shari L. Thurer, *The Myths of Motherhood: How Culture Reinvents the Good Mother* (New York: Penguin Books, 1995).

4. Verta Taylor, *Rock-a-by Baby: Feminism, Self-Help, and Postpartum Depression* (New York: Routledge, 1996), 48.

5. Phyllis Chesler, *Women and Madness* (New York: Doubleday, 1972), 69.

6. Thurer, *The Myths of Motherhood*, xxv.

7. Susan J. Douglas and Meredith W. Michaels, *The Mommy Myth: The Idealization of Motherhood and How It Has Undermined Women* (New York: Free Press, 2004), 4.

8. Marshall McLuhan, *Understanding Media: The Extensions of Man* (Cambridge: MIT Press, 1995), 15.

9. Neil Postman, *Amusing Ourselves to Death: Public Discourse in the Age of Show Business* (New York: Penguin Books, 1986), 87.

10. Tasha N. Dubriwny, "Television News Coverage of Postpartum Disorders and the Politics of Medicalization," *Feminist Media Studies* 10, no. 3 (2010): 297. doi: 10.1080/14680777.

11. Katherine Stone, "ABC Television Should Be Ashamed of 'Private Practice' Postpartum Psychosis Treatment," February 13, 2009, Postpartumprogress.typed.com.

12. *Judging Amy*, "Motion Sickness," no. 1, Season 5, first broadcast September 23, 2003, by CBS, directed by James Frawley and written by Alex Taub.

13. *Rescue Me*, "Babyface," no. 40, season 4, first broadcast on June 13, 2007, on FX, directed by Peter Tolan and Denis Leary and written by Peter Tolan.

14. *Private Practice*, episodes 1–23, Season 3, first broadcast 2009–2010.

15. *Private Practice*, "Ex-Life," episode no. 16, Season 2, first broadcast February 12, 2009, by ABC, directed by Jon Cowan, Robert Rovner, Krista Vernoff, and Debora Cahn and written by Mark Tinker.

16. Nicole E. Hurt, "Disciplining Through Depression: An Analysis of Contemporary Discourse on Women and Depression," *Women's Studies in Communication* 30 (2007): 19.

17. Stone, "ABC Television Should Be Ashamed of 'Private Practice' Postpartum Psychosis Treatment."

18. *Bethenny Getting Married,* "Bryn There, Done That," first broadcast July 29, 2010, by Bravo.

19. *Kendra,* "Here Comes Baby," episode no. 1 Season 2, first broadcast December 20, 2009, on E! Channel.

20. Kendra Wilkinson, interview with Chelsea Handler, *Chelsea Lately,* first broadcast March 3, 2010, by E! Channel.

21. *Scrubs,* "My Friend with Money," episode no. 122, first broadcast January 11, 2007, by NBC, directed by John Michel and written by Gabrielle Allan.

22. Taylor, *Rock-a-by Baby,* 139.

23. Hilton Hater, comment on Danger, "Monica Danger Denies Breakdown, Admits to Depression," *The Hollywood Gossip* (Blog), December 19, 2009, http://thehollywood gossip.com/2009/12.

24. www.goop.com, retrieved November 16, 2010.

25. Corinne Heller, "Bryce Dallas Howard of 'Twilight' Had Postpartum Depression," July 23, 2010.

26. www.breezymama.com, retrieved November 16, 2010.

27. A. Trevor Thrall et al., "Star Power: Celebrity Advocacy and the Evolution of the Public Sphere," *The International Journal of Press Politics* 13 (2008): 376, doi: 10.1177/ 1940161208319098.

28. Thrall et al., 381.

29. Brooke Shields, *Down Came the Rain: My Journey through Postpartum Depression* (New York: Hyperion, 2005), 216.

30. Tom Cruise, interview by Matt Lauer, *Today Show,* first broadcast June 24, 2005, on NBC.

31. Brooke Shields, "War of Words," *The New York Times.* July 1, 2005, www.nytimes. com.

32. postpartumprogress.typepad.com.

33. Lauren Hale, "Media Sensationalism, AOL, and Postpartum Mood Disorders," *My Postpartum Voice (Blog),* August 16, 2010, www.mypostpartumvoice.com.

34. David Lohr, "Police: Mom Charged in Kids' Deaths 'Just Wanted to Be Free,'" August 18, 2010, AOL News, www.aolnews.com/2010/08/18.

35. "Jane and Tarzan's blog," last updated December 27, 2010, HisBoysCanSwim. Com.

BIBLIOGRAPHY

Bethenny Getting Married. "Bryn There, Done That." Broadcast July 29, 2010. Bravo.

Cruise, Tom. Interview by Matt Lauer. *Today Show.* First broadcast June 24, 2005. NBC.

Chesler, Phyllis. *Women and Madness.* New York: Doubleday, 1972.

Dubriwny, Tasha N. "Television News Coverage of Postpartum Disorders and the Politics of Medicalization." *Feminist Media Studies* 10, no. 3 (2010): 285–303.doi: 10.1080/14680777.

Douglas, Susan J., and Meredith W. Michaels. *The Mommy Myth: The Idealization of Motherhood and How It Has Undermined Women.* New York: Free Press, 2004.

Hale, Lauren. "Media Sensationalism, AOL, and Postpartum Mood Disorders." *My Postpartum Voice.* August 16, 2010. http://www.mypostpartumvoice.com.

Hater, Hilton. Comment on Danger, "Monica Danger Denies Breakdown, Admits to Depression." *The Hollywood Gossip* (blog). December 19, 2009. http://thehollywood-gossip.com/2009/12.

Heller, Corinne. "Bryce Dallas Howard of 'Twilight' Had Postpartum Depression." July 23, 2010. http://OnTheRedCarpet.com.

Hurt, Nicole E. "Disciplining Through Depression: An Analysis of Contemporary Discourse on Women and Depression." *Women's Studies in Communication* 30, no. 19 (2007): 284–309.

"Jane and Tarzan's blog." HisBoysCanSwim.com.

Judging Amy. "Motion Sickness." Episode 1, Season 5. Broadcast September 23, 2003. CBS. Directed by James Frawley. Written by Alex Taub.

Kendra. "Here Comes Baby." Episode 1, Season 2. Broadcast December 20, 2009. E! Channel.

Lohr, David. "Police: Mom Charged in Kids' Deaths 'Just Wanted to Be Free.'" *AOL News.* Accessed August 18, 2010. www.aolnews.com.

McLuhan, Marshall. *Understanding Media: The Extensions of Man.* Cambridge: MIT Press, 1995.

Postman, Neil. *Amusing Ourselves to Death: Public Discourse in the Age of Show Business.* New York: Penguin Books, 1986.

Private Practice. Episodes 1–23, Season 3. Broadcast 2009–2010. ABC.

Private Practice. "Ex-Life." Episode 16. Broadcast February 12, 2009. ABC. Directed by Jon Cowan, Robert Rovner, Krista Vernoff, and Debora Cahn. Written by Mark Tinker.

Rescue Me. "Babyface." Episode 40, Season 4. Broadcast June 13, 2007. FX. Directed by Peter Tolad and Denis Leary. Written by Peter Tolan.

Scrubs. "My Friend with Money." Episode 122. Broadcast January 11, 2007. NBC. Directed by John Michel. Written by Gabrielle Allan.

Shields, Brooke. *Down Came the Rain: My Journey through Postpartum Depression.* New York: Hyperion, 2005.

Shields, Brooke. "War of Words." *The New York Times.* July 1, 2005. http://www.nytimes.com2005/07/01/opinion/01shields.html.

Spinelli, Margaret G. "Maternal Infanticide Associated with Mental Illness: Prevention and the Promise of Saved Lives." *The American Journal of Psychiatry.* 161, no. 9 (2004): 1548–1557.

Stone, Katherine. "Postpartum Progress." Last modified December 22, 2010. http://postpartumprogress.typepad.com

Taylor, Verta. *Rock-a-by Baby: Feminism, Self-Help, and Postpartum Depression.* New York: Routledge, 1996.

Thrall, A. Trevor, Jaime Lollio-Fakhreddine, Jon Berent, Lana Donnelly, Wes Herrin, Zachary Paquette, Rebecca Wenglinski, and Amy Wyatt. "Star Power: Celebrity Advocacy and the Evolution of the Public Sphere." *The International Journal of Press Politics* 13 (2008): 362–385. doi: 10.1177/1940161208319098.

Thurer, Shari L. *The Myths of Motherhood. How Culture Reinvents the Good Mother.* New York: Penguin Books, 1995.

Wilkinson, Kendra. Interview with Chelsea Handler. *Chelsea Lately.* Broadcast March 3, 2010. E! Channel.

6

Lesbianism and the Fourth Dimension

The Psychotic Lesbian

Julian Vigo

In cinema theory, Laura Mulvey identifies the *male gaze* in parallel to the Lacanian notion that "woman is a symptom of man.[1] This theory of "woman as symptom," that femininity is a social construct, has been critiqued by feminist and psychoanalytic scholars since the 1970s (e.g., Irigaray, Silverman). Essentially, "woman as symptom" renders the feminine as object (the object *petit a)*, the object of desire, thus constituting the male lack and the male's "positive identity." Such theories gave birth to various cultural and media studies terms for how the female is "seen" both as a political and symbolic subject. However liberating Mulvey's work seemed at the time, her notion of the "male gaze" has been under scrutiny from scholars of feminist and queer theory who argue that power and visibility are not necessarily unidirectional, nor strictly manifested from a male subject to a female object.

Bracha Ettinger criticizes this notion of the male gaze in *Matrixial Gaze* (1995) by suggesting that the question of positing a subject versus an object is no longer a valid relationship of power, nor is the question of two figures looking at each other, effectively constituting a double gaze. Ettinger constructs the "matrixial gaze" as that which dismantles the notion of male/female dichotomizations wherein one constitutes the other residually from this "lack." In fact, her construction of the "matrixial gaze" undoes the opposition of male/female, and in so doing she dismembers the phallus as a central symbolic point of this opposition, replacing the phallic with a hybrid, floating, matrixial gaze.[2] Ettinger's work, however, was just the beginning of understanding the relationship between subject/object relations of power and desire, since cultural models have evolved various vehicles in the past twenty years for understanding desire as related to a gaze that is very much unrelated to specific gendered and sexed bodies. First, we need to understand the relationship between the gaze and the development of desire.

In his 1951 article, "Some Reflections on the Ego," Lacan wrote: "[The mirror stage is] a phenomenon to which I assign a twofold value. In the first place, it has a historical value as it marks a decisive turning-point in the mental development of the child. In the second place, it typifies an essential libidinal relationship with the body-image."[3] Lacan further develops the mirror stage concept, focusing less on its historical value and more on its structural value. ("Historical value" refers to the mental development of the child and "structural value" to the libidinal relationship with the body image.) In Lacan's fourth Seminar, *La relation d'objet*, he states that "the mirror stage is far from a mere phenomenon which occurs in the development of the child. It illustrates the conflictual nature of the dual relationship."[4] This conflict is born from the process of identification born from the mirror stage. The mirror stage, Lacan hypothesizes, shows that the Ego is the product of misunderstanding — Lacan's term "méconnaissance" implies false recognition. In essence, the mirror stage is where the subject becomes alienated from itself, and where it is introduced into the Imaginary order. Specifically, the mirror stage refers to the formation of the Ego via the process of identification; thus the Ego is the result of identifying with one's own specular image.

Lacan's work on the mirror stage essentially posits that human identity is decentered, a correlative to post-structuralist doctrines of the twentieth century. This recognition comes about from the individuation of the subject which develops in infants between six and eighteen months when the child recognizes itself in the mirror and comes to understand that she and Other are separate entities as she gradually gains more motor capacity and physical independence. Lacan maintains that the child sees its image as a whole, yet this lies in stark contrast to the lack of coordination of the body, leading the child to perceive its body as fragmented. This conflict between the perception of the body and the lack of coordination thereof, according to Lacan, is first felt by the infant as a struggle with its image, because the entirety of the image threatens it with fragmentation. In this way the mirror stage gives rise to an aggressive tension between the subject and the image. In order to eliminate or subdue this aggressive tension, the subject identifies with the image: the primary identification with the counterpart is the foundation of the Ego. The moment of identification is that of jubilation, according to Lacan, since it leads to an imaginary sense of mastery.[5] Yet, the jubilation may also be accompanied by a depressive reaction, when the infant compares his own precarious sense of mastery with the omnipotence of the mother (*la relation d'objet*). This identification also involves the ideal ego, which functions as a promise of future wholeness, sustaining the Ego in anticipation.

Jacque Lacan links the concept of the gaze to the development of individual human agency. Essentially he transforms the gaze to a dialectic between the Ideal-Ego and the Ego-Ideal. The ideal-ego is the *imagined* self-identification image — whom the person imagines herself to be or whom she aspires to be. Lacan further develops his concept of the gaze, saying that it does not belong to the subject but, rather, to the object of the gaze. In *Seminar One*, Lacan told the audience: "I can feel myself under the gaze of someone whose eyes I do not see, not even discern. All that is necessary is for something to signify to me that there may be others there. This window, if it gets a bit dark, and if I have reasons for thinking that there is someone behind it, is straight-away a gaze."[6] Lacan would argue that the "gaze" exists within the mind of the person who feels the gaze cast on him. This statement implicates, in effect, that perception supersedes reality, that reality is false, and most importantly, that *only* the interlocutor is real. This sentence would throw a wrench into the dialectic between recognition and false recognition, operating in much the same way that Derrida's infamous formula of textual interpretation functions — his claim in "Plato's Pharmacy" that writing removes the text from the author, from the truth, thus opening up the text to interpretation and misinterpretation.[7] But Lacan's play of the gaze goes much further and marginalizes, at the very point of experiential knowledge everyone *but* the interlocutor. So how do we address the problems of recognition, false recognition and desire that are reproduced in popular culture from the social to the cultural levels of reading?

Pursuant to identification is desire, since the child, from a very early age, attempts to satisfy its basic biological needs and it gets caught up in the dialectics of exchanges with others. Because the child's sense of self is fabricated from these identifications with the images of the others, Lacan argues that it is particular to humans to desire directly or to desire through another or others. Our sense of desire, according to Lacan, is no longer separable from the biological needs of the individual, and there is a subordinate need for the recognition of love of other people. Hence, the object of desire becomes more desirable if others desire the object as well; less desire is manifested if the masses withdraw their desire. Hence, the subject's own relationship to desire is decentered by the other. In essence, Lacan maintains that the ego is, at its fundamental core, an object. Moreover, this notion constructs a sense of subject which is not "organic" or "natural," but rather the I is an identification with the other consistently throughout the individual's life. It is this identification with the self which takes place through the other.

Lacan writes that "desire is neither the appetite for satisfaction nor the demand for love, but the difference that results from the subtraction of the first from the second." He adds that "desire begins to take shape in the margin where demand becomes separated from need." In this way, desire can never be satisfied, or as Slavoj Žižek states: "Desire and jouissance are inherently antagonistic, exclusive even. Desire's raison d'être is not to realize its goal, to find full satisfaction, but to reproduce itself as desire."[8] Indeed, even though psychoanalysis has taught us is that desire is not a relationship to an object, but rather a relationship to a lack (*manque*), the subject often mistakes desire for need to possess that object. So what are the repercussions for desire if desire is not to be realized, wherein the subject must maintain her object of desire in a state of limbo and must, in order to keep this longing alive, *not* achieve this desire as such? What are the vehicles for maintaining desire wherein its object will always be alive and accessible?

Lesbian Desire

Lesbian desire replicates this narrative of false recognition, of "méconnaissance." But what is the symbolic dimension of lesbian desire? Might there be an attempt to recuperate the narratives of power and possession, a long held trope for heterosexual desire, a stereotype that perhaps can no longer be said to apply from the male gaze to the female subject/object? It would seem, given the plethora of narratives of lesbian desire present in recent cinema and culture, that lesbian desire might very well be no different than any other sort of eroticized or intellectualized desire. What if all desire is about the framing of the subject, more specifically, the inescapability of the subject from recognizing its own artificial projection of subjective wholeness modeled upon others whom the subject encounters in the world? More relevant, perhaps, in the late twentieth century and early twenty-first century, when desire would seem more linked to iterability, to repetition, than it is to the mirroring of the other, how can we understand subjective desire when desire today would seem to be more integral to a social process of *identification as* rather than *identification with*? Indeed, the answers to this question of desire begin to unravel through psychoanalytic theory, but their ends pour into the modalities of theories of deconstruction, as there is a need to understand the space between the reproduction of desire common to psychoanalysis and the (re)iterability of desire developed through deconstruction.

Laying the ground for the politicization of Derrida's work, Gayatri Spivak analyses "Limited Inc.: abc."[9] Herein, Spivak cautions the reader that deconstruction alone cannot found political actions: "A mere change of mindset, however great, will not bring about revolutions. Yet without this revolutionary change of mind, revolutionary 'programs' will fall into the same metaphysical bind of idealized and repeatable intention and context that Derrida plots in speech act theory."[10] Central to Spivak's argument here is that iterability — and not repetition — lays the foundation for identity formation which is integral in fomenting revolutionary or individual discourses of identity:

> But repetition is the basis of identification. Thus, if repetition alters, it has to be faced that alteration identifies and identity is always impure. Thus iterability — like the trace structure — is the positive condition of possibility of identification, the very thing whose absolute rigor it renders impossible. It is in terms of iterable (rather than repeatable) identities that communication and consensus are established.[11]

Herein we see how identity, when iterated, is always "polluted," and thus identity is established through a conterminous replication and impurity of this act. The re-marking of the self must pass through the other vis-à-vis an idealization of this object/other, hence rendering this object through the subject's body and performance. There is absolutely no contradiction in terms of the original or the replica. Iterability keeps both alive perpetually, as the object of desire can be retained through the re-performance of the subject, who constantly recasts this object of desire in the present terms of time and space.[12] Spivak's analysis of Derrida takes critical discourse and attempts to lay bare the authoritative analysis of such constructions whereby "authority" per se renders visible the skeleton of authority whose power rests upon its own iterability and citation within an academic scene.[13] But what if this field of production of "knowledge" might also be the theatre for the production, containment, and nurturing of desire? And how might this desire be interpreted when desire is assumed to be part and parcel of the psychotic moment of the subject who loses herself in the other?

I will now turn to a genre of cinema and cultural studies which, although not formally labeled, I will call "lesbian psychosis." "Lesbian psychosis" is a leitmotif not uncommon in cinema and cultural studies; however, in recent years the "psychotic lesbian" has entered into the cultural economy of the social and Internet: as a field of production of iterability, as social construction, and as a reaffirmation of the object of desire wherein the description of that discourse is one of mirroring, un-writing, undoing. The un-writing takes the form of verbal play, of oral/aural productions of desire in parallel to the psychoanalytic model. Similarly, the space of desire is reduced to pure language whereby "nothing happens" and the psychotic event lies not in what happened, *but instead in what did not.* Desire and the real as symbolic are forever intertwined, and the subject's inability to bring about a real body based on the perceived desire reproduces what could be called the "mirror stage of lesbianism" through which the psychotic scenario and subject unfold. The only way to capture the other, to arrive at one's desire, is through a reproduction of the description of desire — through writing, storytelling, and, when language fails, through the somatic reproduction of desire or of that specific object of desire.

Vito Russo's *Celluloid Closet* marks a clear critique of the genre of perceived homophobic plots within ostensibly gay cinema by noting the many films in which the protagonist commits suicide (e.g., *The Children's Hour*, 1961), where homosexuals are the object of a mass murder (e.g., *Cruising*, 1980) and where homosexuals are themselves murderers (i.e., *Silence of the Lambs*, 1991, and *Basic Instinct*, 1992).[14] Many of the films were the objects of massive protests as their production was disrupted and/or their release in movie theatres thwarted since gay activists identified certain of these films as a type of cinema which "negatively portrays" homosexual characters. Due to the paucity of gay characters in cinema, these critiques would seem well-founded given that the few roles to be filled would end in the subject's death or inevitable psychosis. Yet the problem with such critiques is that the notion of "negative" and "positive" representations can never really be established as a sort of democratically evolved consensus, and, admittedly, all sorts of people become — both in reality and on screen — psycho killers and obsessive lovers.

Yet the one prototype in popular culture which seems to function as both trope of this mirror stage to transference of desire in both popular cultural models of cinema, within the social and in the realm of the cyber-social, is that of the "psychotic lesbian." The trope of the psychotic lesbian functions as both a model of the cinematic roles formerly assigned to lesbian characters — for we must not forget that Shirley McClaine's character in *The Children's Hour*, although she kills herself, is rendered "psychotic" by her desire for Audrey Hepburn's character. Let's not forget that in films where the lesbian is "psychotic" she is generally both an assumed psychotic of a given social reality and one of a narrative vehicle, which adds to the mystery of the plot, confuses the roles that various characters play, and ultimately plays with the dissonance between reality and fiction on many levels within the film and from within cultural tropes within the social.

For instance, in *Basic Instinct*, the murder suspect and mystery writer, Catherine, becomes the object of inquiry and desire for Nick, the San Francisco Police detective, who ends up becoming more like Catherine, imitating her words and becoming a psychological subject of study for her forthcoming novel. Catherine is also the doppelganger for Beth (a police psychologist) as Beth is for Catherine — Nick's desire for both women becomes that of the patient for the psychoanalyst, and the "breakthrough" Nick seeks is nothing other than to resolve the mystery. The mystery could likewise be said to be two-fold: that of the murders and that of his own desire. Similar to *Rear*

Window, wherein the same type of drama unfolds as each character plays a role made to fit into the "frame of desire," Žižek describes this play of desire that is manifested through the actions of Grace Kelly: "By literally entering the frame of his fantasy; by crossing the courtyard and appearing 'on the other side' where he can see her *through the window.* When Stewart sees her in the murderer's apartment his gaze is immediately fascinated, greedy, desirous of her: she has found her place in his fantasy-space."[15] Yet in *Rear Window,* it is James Stewart who reduces Grace Kelly's character to object of desire as she becomes his physical surrogate while he lays helpless in a wheelchair, while in *Basic Instinct,* although she is not paralyzed, it is Catherine who commands Nick into her frame of desire, as he plays a role for her novel and as her psychological subject. Although Žižek attributes this to the gaze of a decentered, male chauvinist subject, I would argue that this gaze of desire is not uniquely male chauvinist. In fact, I would say that the gaze of desire by the subject desiring her object is often caught within the trap of enacting that desire — should she be wheelchair-bound, closeted, or fearful of engaging that desire for any number of reasons, the incapacity to reach that goal, that aim of expressing desire sets into motion a totally different interplay wherein the subject attempts to control and manipulate the actors within her frame of desire in order to envisage something approximating desire, something akin to the fantasy space she imagines but cannot have. Control, drama, and manipulation take over where the subject can no longer exercise control over her own life. *Basic Instinct* essentially takes the powerful woman (lesbian, bisexual or heterosexual — we never really learn) and turns around the gaze of desire and roles of power through narration and writing. The "psychotic lesbian" was an utter invention of the protesting masses which reduced this film to homophobia rather than unravel the levels of sexual play between men and women that this movie directly addresses.

Not discussed frequently amongst scholars of queer theory, sociology, psychology, and cultural studies is the "psychotic lesbian," who is a common figure of anxiety amongst lesbians who chronicle their stories on dating and social networking sites. Likewise, the "psychotic lesbian" is also a trope, an "inside joke" of sorts, that has fairly or unfairly been stereotyped. On okcupid.com you can find hundreds of profiles which attempt to warn off the "potential psycho" through the built-in narrative which allows all viewers to be warned: "You should message me if: [y]ou have a sense of humor and can roll with the punches! Oh. And if you are not a psycho. Although many psychotic-types I have met tend to think they are perfectly sane, so I suppose that is a pointless request." Many others get right to the point: "Write me if you are not psychotic." What is most interesting is how this trope of psychosis functions as a means of interpreting desire and identity *from within* and *from without* the "lesbian community," for perceived psychosis can be a fear in any context, in any community; yet the narrative of psychosis also flows from the very subjects who maintain a politics which resists homophobia. Has the "psychotic lesbian," within lesbian culture specifically, become the "n-word" of gansta culture wherein recognition, permissibility and even desire regain their legitimation from the widely circulated vehicles of the lesbian as the iterative of persona and desire?

Cinema is replete with tropes of identification and desire which go terribly awry; yet as gay rights came to the fore of discussions in popular culture, mass media, politics and cinema, the lesbian psycho killer was not ignored in the proliferating roles written for the big screen. Here I will focus upon two films which examine the psychotic lesbian through the mirroring of individual identity and the construction desire which most often take the form of iterability by the central "psychotic lesbian" figures: *Single White Female* (1992)[16] and *Chloe* (2009).[17]

Single White Female and the Mirror of Desire

In *Single White Female*, Allie breaks up with her boyfriend and needs to find a flatmate with whom to share her expensive New York City rent. Enter Hedy, the maladjusted young newbie to the city who wins over Allie in her interview for the flat. The two begin a happy co-existence which we are shown as a mise-en-scène very reminiscent of the "falling in love" scenes of Hollywood romantic comedies: lilting flute music accompanying the scenes of Allie helping Hedy move into their home; Hedy finds an old lamp which Allie repaints for her; they move furniture around, spilling items from a table on the floor; Hedy finds a silver platter under the sink and polishes it to reveal Allie looking at their reflection together; Hedy screen's Allie's ex-boyfriend's phone calls; they stroll the streets of New York eating ice cream. As a friendly gesture to Hedy, who seems interested in learning about dressing nicely, Allie helps Hedy to gain fashion sensibility as they spend all their free time together in their first weeks together. They fall asleep on the bed watching *In a Lonely Place* (1950), a film which foreshadows the anger and madness of Hedy as Hedy attempts to take the place of Allie's ex-boyfriend, Sam.

As the film progresses, Allie discovers that Hedy has been stealing Sam's letters from the postbox, and things get markedly worse when Sam and Allie reunite. Hedy goes to even greater lengths to stay in the picture, as it is eventually revealed that they want to move back in together and that Hedy needs to find another flat. At this point, Hedy ends up looking more and more like Allie as Hedy's obsession with her dead twin sister is externalized through her iteration of Allie's body and sexuality. Sister, friend, flatmate, lover — all the social roles are confused, as are the distinctions between the movie we are watching and the movies cited within *Single White Female*. These movies serve to further mirror Hedy's desire for Allie, as we see in *Bell, Book and Candle* the possibility of love is discussed:

> JIMMY STEWART: I know it doesn't make sense, but ... I have an idea I must be in love with you.... Would you like it to go on for always?
>
> KIM NOVAK: Does anything go on for always?
>
> JIMMY STEWART: Well, one likes to think some things do.[18]

This scene is followed by Allie's return after a 24-hour absence: Hedy, in Allie's bed with their dog, exclaims that the dog missed Allie, hence Hedy had to go to her bed to comfort the dog. Hedy scolds Allie as if a child, mimicking the words of a parent in a string of clichés, "Where the hell have you been? I've been waiting since six o'clock last night to hear from you. I've been worried sick.... There's such a thing as a phone, you know?" The romantic and sisterly love becomes distorted and the jealousy of Sam's new insertion into Allie's life is of great concern to Hedy when she learns that they are now engaged and her tenure in the apartment is threatened. The rest of the film is dedicated to Hedy's intensified mirroring of Allie as she imitates Allie's dressing style, her sexual habits, and, in the most intense scene of verisimilitude, Hedy's descent down the hair salon's white and steel staircase sporting an exact replica of Allie's hair. The psychotic moment is revealed and Allie finally begins to understand that something about Hedy is amiss as she says, upon seeing Hedy's new haircut, "You have got to be kidding." Hedy works to emulate Allie sexually as she escalates her iteration of Allie: she masturbates while Allie catches a glimpse, and in a later scene Hedy sneaks into Sam's bed, pretending to be Allie. The sex with the self is made to iterate that of the other, and through Allie's absence Hedy is able to keep hold of her desire for her sister/flatmate/lover. Hedy, as Allie announces to herself in the mirror, admiring her new haircut, "I love myself like this." The object of desire is multiple — it is Allie, it is Hedy mirroring Allie, but it is never Hedy.

The sexual tension and identity confusion reach their apex when Allie confronts Hedy after learning of Sam's murder:

> ALLIE: I know you weren't yourself when you did this, Hedy.
>
> HEDY: I know. I was YOU.

The mirroring of Allie results in a series of psychotic episodes that leave everyone in Allie's life dead. The production of lesbian desire and identity in this film takes place through the reproduction of the other somatically and ultimately, the repositioning of characters through their elimination and the weaving together of narratives from Hedy's past and Hollywood cinema. The mirror is shattered when Hedy says: "Did you know that identical twins are never really identical? There's always one who's prettier ... and the one who's not does all the work.... She used me, then she left me — just like you." Allie responds, "I'm not like your sister, Hedy. Not any more. I'm like you now." Hereafter the roles become re-reversed: Hedy becomes Allie and Allie becomes Hedy. In looking for Allie, Hedy reverses who ought to be frightened of whom, as Hedy is on a psychopathic rampage and calls out to Allie, who is hiding from her: "Allie? Allie, come out of hiding now! I'm scared!" The cross-identifications and mis-identifications are multiple and constantly in the process of construction and fracture. Desire is attained only through the suspense that keeps these two women apart, for their union brings about the death of desire and somatic death. The female gaze of this film is always dual: that of Allie who is initially curious about Hedy, and as the film progresses, her curiosity grows to concern, while Hedy's gaze is constantly eroticized, associated with desire, insanity, and aggression.

Chloe and the Iterability of Desire

Chloe, by Atom Egoyam, takes the story of a couple, Catherine, an OB/GYN, and David, a university professor, whose marriage is in a lull. Chloe, a young prostitute, hits on Catherine one night at a bar; her response is to hire Chloe to test her husband, whom she has suspected of cheating. As the story unfolds, Chloe comes to Catherine with her erotic narratives of what she did with David. Catherine grows closer to her husband through these stories, while Chloe's attraction grows for Catherine, and eventually Catherine gives in to Chloe's advances, for a night. Her eventual refusal of Chloe, her "return to heterosexuality," brings about the continuance of Chloe's psychotic break. For as we learn, the affair she was paid to have with David never occurred — Chloe's fictional relationship was merely an aphrodisiac for Catherine, both of whom feed upon this fiction in order to fulfill their relationships: Catherine with David, and Chloe with Catherine. The psychotic lesbian in this film is embodied by Chloe, but the manner of seduction takes place through words, stories, truths, and lies. Chloe, though extremely young, is perspicacious about matters of sexuality and very early on in the film states: "I guess I've always been pretty good with words. In my line of business, it's as important to be able to describe what I'm doing as it is to do what I'm doing. When to say what. What words to select."

Thusly Chloe weaves her narrative of desire for Catherine, who feeds off this faked romance with Catherine's husband that Chloe has created just for her to bring her lover pleasure and eventually to seduce her lover. Chloe is aware of the power of words and body and the choreography of each: "Some men hate to hear certain terms. They can't stand specific moves and then they can't live without others. It's part of my job to know where to place my hand, my lips, my tongue, my leg and even my thoughts." Yet, Chloe is aware that the stories and words she weaves for her clients are but one part — there is the other facet of fantasy into which she plays and then, suddenly, as all fantasies do, finish, "disappear": "Am I your secretary or am I your daughter? Maybe I'm your seventh grade math teacher you always hated. All I know is that if I do it just right, I can become your living, breathing, unflinching dream, and then I can actually disappear." This line foreshadows the film's end as she ultimately fulfills the dreams of all involved, including her own, and then she does indeed disappear.

Representing sex with men as formulaic, a science of what to do, what not to do, Chloe evokes for Catherine the young escort who can help fix her marriage. Little does Catherine suspect that Chloe has fallen in love with her, becoming fixated on her, obsessed with entering her life. After their sexual encounter, Catherine breaks it off. In retaliation, Chloe uses Catherine's son as access to his mother by having sex with him in Catherine's bed. The story ends tragically, with Catherine confronting Chloe in her house, Chloe turns the role of prostitute/pimp around, telling Catherine that she cannot be bought off. When Catherine asks Chloe what she wants, Chloe responds, "A kiss," and Catherine complies; however, while kissing Chloe, Catherine sees her husband watching her. Catherine panics and pushes Chloe back, causing the bedroom window to shatter. Chloe safely catches the window frame, for a moment — she then smiles and lets go of the window, plunging to her death. The last scene in the movie is of the happy couple attending their son's graduation party, and Catherine is wearing the hairpin that Chloe gave her.

The oral stories that Chloe creates and Catherine demands of her fabricate a very odd picture of desire and fantasy, of how the self mirrors the other through the narratives she needs to hear, and how the storyteller's lies might just be the fantasy of truth for the listener. The psychotic lesbian in this film is more complex to interpret, since Chloe is ultimately a young woman with no experience in emotions — she knows how to handle sex, desire and eroticism, but not love. Chloe is also, it would appear, extremely vulnerable. Catherine, on the other hand, is more adept at handling love but craves the sexual and erotic which Chloe offers, initially as narrative and ultimately as performance. When Catherine realizes that the sexual performance is not what she wants and that the narrative of her husband's infidelity with Chloe was a hoax, she wants out and stops the action. Catherine had presupposed that money would buy her confirmation of her husband's infidelity, and instead of receiving this confirmation or negation, she ended up having an erotic encounter through a fictionalized narrative, styled by the prostitute she hired. Money buys Catherine what she wants, a story, but she is ultimately denied the truth behind the narrative she wants to believe. Chloe, on the other hand, is a master of words and of storytelling more than she is of sex. She understands what it takes to seduce a man but falls in love with the woman who pays her for her for her words — for Chloe does not make the distinction between the somatic and linguistic — hence this storytelling that she performs for Catherine is an incredibly sexual act. In the end, it becomes clear that Chloe (whose sexuality is at the very least bisexual and perhaps homosexual) is in love with Catherine and cannot continue to dominate this discourse of love with Catherine.

Once the fantasy of Chloe and David has been defused, the only way that Chloe can "have" Catherine is through her own death. Chloe is the psychotic lesbian in search of her object of desire, for certain; but she is also a figure who is tragically romantic. Catherine, on the other hand, disassociates from Chloe with a certain ease that is uncanny — she commands Chloe about *as a prostitute*, she later "experiments" with Chloe, then kills her "accidentally." But the "accident" could be read as one of homosexual panic — for the fear Catherine felt when her husband saw her kissing Chloe led her to push Chloe to her near-death. Yet within this film, the spectator is not initially led to question this death, not forced to postulate Catherine's potential psychosis, simply because Chloe's death returns the alienated couple to their "happy ending" at their son's graduation party. It would seem that Chloe remains incidental to this couple's married life as they present the image of being happily married in this last scene. The true force of this film lies in Chloe making Catherine see that fiction can be — and often is — better than reality. What is really true in this final scene? Are we witnessing the happy couple or the placated, passionless couple making an appearance? In the last scene of the film we see that Catherine has retained the trace of her experience with Chloe in her hair (the hairpin). This final image evidences to the viewer that perhaps Catherine is not purely heterosexual after all, and that she might even be less mentally stable.

Stranger Than Fiction: "I wasn't a lesbian.... I was psychotic!"

These three films contain the tropes of the psychotic lesbian that are played out in a not so atypical manner. I say "not so atypical" because in general at the end of Hollywood films, the "bad guy" dies. So ought we to be surprised when the "psychotic lesbian killer" meets her horrid death? What is most interesting is how the protests regarding cinema extend to real life dramas of lesbians who fall out of love, out of glamour and go out of their minds. In fact, some stories are simply much stranger than fiction. I turn here to a report published on August 21, 2000, which describes the end of one of America's most famous lesbian relationships in terms of mental illness:

> Just hours after announcing her separation from longtime partner Ellen DeGeneres, Anne Heche was hospitalized Saturday after she wandered to a rural home near Fresno (yes, we said Fresno), California, appearing shaken and confused, and began making strange statements to the homeowners.
>
> Heche, 31, reportedly parked her car along a highway and then walked about a mile to a house in Cantua Creek, located near Highway 33 in rural western Fresno County in Central California. Sheriff's deputies were called to the home around 4:30 P.M. They said the star of such films as *Six Days, Seven Nights* and 1998's *Psycho* cooperated with them and then asked for an ambulance.
>
> According to a deputy's report obtained by Fresno's NBC affiliate, KSEE-TV, Heche (who, according to witnesses, was wearing just a bra, shorts and shoes) told the deputy "she was God and was going to take everyone back to heaven with her ... on some sort of spaceship."[19]

This event put Anne Heche in the uncomfortable spotlight of the "bizarre." Yet, this running about Fresno in her underwear was not nearly as offsetting as her re-entry into Hollywood. ABC's *20/20* screened on September 5, 2001, an interview of Anne Heche with Barbara Walters. Presenting her Fresno episode from the year before and her book, *Call Me Crazy*, this interview re-presented Heche to the American public as a newly formed subject, who returned from an otherworld of psychosis within the framework of "normalcy," a Barbara Walters interview. Though both media coverage and Heche as well made herself out to be "psychotic," her rendering of her insanity and the recuperation of her "self" reveal the liminal space of sexual identification and (in)sanity in our culture today — both how they evidence themselves in popular culture and how they symbiotically feed each other. In fact, I would argue that this particular Hollywood story exemplifies perfectly the trope of sexuality in American culture wherein the modality for finding oneself is first through losing the self (i.e., "insanity," "craziness") and secondly through this evolution of a mirror stage of an adult "rediscovery" of sexuality.[20] In the year following her breakup with Ellen DeGeneres, Heche "recuperated" her sanity by abandoning her abusive childhood, distancing herself from her lesbian past, and by shedding the skin of her other constructed person, Celestia, who resides in what Heche called the "Fourth Dimension."

In the Barbara Walters interview, Heche presents her story and her book, whose title invites the viewer/reader to "call her crazy"; yet, this interview exemplifies how Heche had bubble-wrapped her insanity in the rhetoric of a split persona. Infused within this oral and written narrative are the tropes for sexual and spiritual rebirth whereby the finding of one's sexuality and God are interwoven. Heche summarizes her story to Walters: "I had another personality. I had a fantasy world. I called my other personality Celestia. I called the other world that I created for myself the Fourth Dimension. I believed I was from another planet. I think I was insane." From here, Anne Heche attempts to describe the degeneration of her person throughout her life — from the sexual abuse of her father, her mother's negation of this abuse, her father's homosexuality and eventual death resulting from AIDS and the residual "splitting of the self" as she terms it. Heche claims to have existed as two people mirroring a Jesus who could not and who did not save her while embodying the damaged woman who delved into her work and sex to reconstruct herself. This description of Heche's embodiment of a God figure was not the "insanity" for Heche, but rather the sign of a greater insanity: her life of 31 years. As she discusses her life her interlocutor, Walters, is presented as the figure of "normalcy" and in turn we hear Walters respond with incredulity to Heche's descriptions of alterity:

> ANNE: I told my mother at about the seventh year of therapy that I had been abused sexually by my father and she hung up the phone on me. To have gone through so much work to heal myself, and have my mother not acknowledge in any way that she was sorry for what had happened to me, broke my heart. And in that moment I think I split off from myself. So Anne, this girl who had just confronted her mother, shrunk, and out came Celestia, where I was literally thrown to the ground, and I'm not kidding, in New York City, thrown to the ground and heard the voice of God, and thought I was absolutely insane. I had no idea what to do. I was existing as two people.
>
> BARBARA: So even though you thought you were Jesus, or Celestia, you also at the same time knew this was an aberration.
>
> ANNE: Absolutely. That's the thing about going crazy. You are absolutely aware — at least, I was — that I was Anne Heche, an actress, *that I had friends*, there were people who would think I was crazy if I was ever going to talk about this. And at the same time I'm hearing God talk to me saying 'You are basically from Heaven....
>
> BARBARA: You go in your trailer and you're another person. You close the door and you're another person. You're Jesus.
>
> ANNE: I'm Celestia.
>
> BARBARA: And Celestia is also Jesus?
>
> ANNE: No. Celestia, as I was told, is the reincarnation of God, here [on earth].

Heche presents her schism as one of illness and, conterminously, as one of a breaking point, the return to herself. Heche's personification of the heterosexual "turned lesbian" who becomes possessed by *God as a woman* enacts one of the most bizarre of Hollywood stories, for certain; however, this story also feeds the image of lesbian identification as the "final phase" in returning to the "saner self." This identification of self for Heche and the conterminous desire for the other (DeGeneres) is evidenced within Heche's autobiography:

> By the time I finished shooting *Six Days Seven Nights* I felt like three completely different people, all existing at the same time. I was Anne-n-Ellen, the second half of the most famous gay couple in the world. I was Anne Heche, the closeted abuse victim with a burning desire to be a successful actress, writer, and director. And I was Celestia, a spirit being from the fourth dimension here to teach the world about love. The fight to keep all of me alive over the next three and a half years almost killed me.[21]

The mirror identification for Heche results in both jubilation and horror — though Heche disavows her relationship with DeGeneres as one of experimentation — it is clear that on a super-sexual level the heterosexual turned gay actress had a conflictual relationship with many dualities she embodied: her heterosexuality and homosexuality; her destructive past and her healing present; and her insanity as symptom and her insanity as remedy. Born from her identification to the last three and a half years of her life which "almost killed" her, lesbianism could be said to have both rendered her insane and killed her; likewise it could have been the trigger to understanding her problems while it might have also been part of the problem. Or was she, as many web entries attest, just another "psycho lesbian?"

What is clear from Heche's interview with Walters and her autobiography is that her relationship to DeGeneres was part of a larger "journey" — a voyage of love, of sexual discovery, of self-discovery and of the "psychotic." She tells Walters, "Fresno was the culmination of a journey. Of a world that I thought I needed to escape to in order to find love. So in the pain I think what triggered the pain of my breakup with Ellen, was a bottoming out of 'there's no love here, I'm going to go get love.'" So from Fresno where her journey ended, Heche was instructed to meet a spaceship, to board the spaceship and "take a hit of ecstasy." As Heche describes, it was then that she realized that she did not have "to leave the world to get love." Heche, the mirror of her lesbian lover, of God, and of sanity was finally "cured" through a psychotic terrain of spaceships, ecstasy and Fresno — not to mention a night in a mental hospital.

Between 2000 and 2001, the Internet was rife with postings which complained that Heche gave lesbians a "bad reputation" while others accused Heche of being a Hasbian (essentially, "a former lesbian who is now in a heterosexual relationship."[22] Slowly, Heche's name soon developed into its own definition whereby "pulling an Anne Heche"[23] is now a synonym of Has-bian. Since Heche's "coming out" *to sanity* in 2001, her narrative serves as a compelling introduction regarding how psychosis and lesbianism are strung together and spun in the media by everyone including *those in the gay and lesbian community*. Many people in the gay community were angry with Heche, misquoting her interview frequently, rephrasing her words, to say something she did not in fact state: "I wasn't a lesbian.... I was psychotic!" This phrase became a current rejoinder for those referring to Heche as the "sell-out" or budding starlet using a more well-known celebrity to climb the wall of fame. But what does the "psychotic lesbian" say for those of us who are acutely aware of the troubles of speaking about very real problems within the community that do include various "psychoses": incidents of stalking, obsessive behavior within relationships, high rates of domestic violence, serious drug and alcohol abuse and then the common references to "U-Haul lesbians?"[24]

Derrida writes on the language of life and death, a modality which can be applied to this problem of representation of the truths and fictions of psychosis — the ability to discuss reality by taking part in the distinction between writing science and writing life.[25] Lesbian desire as "psychotic" is caught between the thanatological and thanatographical, between life/death and writing. Lesbian desire could be said to be the reproduction through these narratives which reframe life as death, death as life, and identity as iterability. The tropes through which we had heretofore collided with the hegemony of mass media, for instance, are also the tropes through which we have come to understand ourselves in the polysemous manifestations and language of identity politics. Ultimately, the "psychotic lesbian" might be best understood as an implosion of identity politics upon itself wherein the sexuality of a person/character can never be precisely represented or deciphered. Likewise, the trope of the "psychotic lesbian" manifests an aporetic space wherein the scope of identity as a mirroring of the other takes its toll on the social when iteration upon iteration becomes imitation and renders sexual identity and desire a house of mirrors wherein desire moves the unknown real and the projection of a fiction which, in the end, disappoints.

NOTES

1. Laura Mulvey, "Visual Pleasure and Narrative Cinema," in *Film Theory and Criticism: Introductory Readings,* eds. Leo Braudy and Marshall Cohen (New York: Oxford University Press, 1999), 833–44.

2. Bracha Ettinger, *The Matrixial Gaze* (Leeds: University of Leeds, 1995).

3. Jaques Lacan, "Some Reflections on the Ego," *International Journal of Psychoanalysis* 34, 1 (1953): 11–17.

4. Ibid, 17.

5. Jacques Lacan, "The Mirror Stage as Formative of the Function of the I," *Écrits: A Selection*, trans. Bruce Fink (New York: W. W. Norton, 2002), 1–7.

6. Jacques Lacan, *The Seminar of Jacques Lacan: Book 1, Freud's Papers on Technique 1953–1954*, trans. Alan Sheridan (New York: Cambridge University Press, 1988), 215.

7. Jacques Derrida, "Plato's Pharmacy," *Dissemination*, trans. Barbara Johnson (Chicago: University of Chicago Press, 1982).

8. Slavoj Žižek, A Plea for Ethical Violence, *Umbr(a)* 1 (2004): 7591.

9. Limited Inc abc..., *Glyph* 2, trans. Samuel Weber (Baltimore: Johns Hopkins Press, 1977), 162254.

10. Gayatri Chakravorty Spivak, "Revolutions That as Yet Have No Model: Derrida's *Limited Inc,*" in *The Spivak Reader: Selected Words of Gayatri Chakravorty Spivak* (New York: Routledge, 1996), 87.

11. Ibid, 87.

12. Here Spivak elaborates this point of iterability further:
Iterability "itself" cannot be privileged as a "transcendental condition of possibility" (72–244) for fiction, theater, parasite, citation, and the like. Whereas repetition pre-supposes a full idealization (repeatability as such), iterability entails no more than a minimal idealization which would guarantee the possibility of the re-mark. But since "the iterability of the mark does not leave any of the philosophical oppositions which govern the idealizing abstraction intact (for instance, serious/non-serious, literal/metaphorical or ironic, normal/parasitical, strict/non-strict, etc." (42, 209–10), this is an impure idealization, a contradiction in terms, which cannot be caught within the either-or logic of noncontradiction. "No processor project of idealization without iterability, and yet no possible idealization of iterability" (42–43, 210). In order to work with a non-transcendental, non-logical (non)-concept (or graphic) such as iterability, one must think a great change of mindset (Ibid, 88).

13. "Material objects, and seemingly non-textual events and phenomena would have to be seen not as self-identical, but as the space of dispersion of such 'constructions,' as the condition or effect of interminable iterations. Yet, since iterabilty fractures intention as well, a simple stockpiling of 'authoritative analyses from this point of view' without intervention in enabling and disabling auto- and disciplinary critiques would be beside the point" (Ibid, 90).

14. *Basic Instinct*, directed by Paul Verhoeven (Los Angeles: Columbia Tristar, 1992), DVD.

15. Slavoj Žižek, *The Sublime Object of Ideology* (New York: Verso Books, 1989), 199.

16. *Single White Female*, directed by Barbet Schroeder (Los Angeles: Columbia Pictures, 1992), DVD.

17. *Chloe*, directed by Atom Egoyam (Toronto: Sony Picture Classics, 2009), DVD.

18. *Bell, Book and Candle*, directed by Richard Quine (Los Angeles: Sony Pictures Home Entertainment, 1958), DVD.

19. Mark Armstrong, "Anne Heche Hospitalized," *E!Online,* August 21, 2000, http://www.eonline.com/uberblog/b40331_anne_heche_hospitalized.html.

20. 21. Anne Heche, *Call Me Crazy: A Memoir* (New York: Scribner, 2001), 224.

22. "Hasbian," Urban Dictionary, last modified November 30, 2003, http://www.urbandictionary.com/define.php?term=hasbian.

23. "Anne Heche," Urban Dictionary, last modified August 1, 2008, http://www.urbandictionary.com/define.php?term=anne+heche.

24. "U-Haul lesbians" is a reference to the popular joke which not so subtly described the problems of lesbians who move very quickly from dating to a live-in relationship. The joke goes as such: QUESTION: "What type of car does a lesbian bring on the first date? ANSWER: "A U-Haul." (U-Haul is a rental self-moving company.)

25. In Jacques Derrida's *The Ear of the Other: Otobiography, Transference, Translation:*

Texts and Discussions with Jacques Derrida (Lincoln: Nebraska University Press, 1982), 4–6, he writes:

> What one calls life — the thing or object of biology and biography — does not stand face to face with something that would be its opposable ob-ject: death, the thanatological or thanatographical. This is the first complication. Also, it is painfully *difficult* for life to become an object of science, in the sense that philosophy and science have always given to the word "science" and to the legal status of scientificity. All of this — the difficulty, the delays it entails — is particularly bound up with the fact that the science of life always accommodates a philosophy of life, which is not the case for all other sciences, the sciences of nonlife — in other words, the sciences of the dead.... A discourse on life/death must occupy a certain space between logos and gramme, analogy and program, as well as between the differing senses of program and reproduction. And since life is on the line, the trait that relates the logical to the graphical must also be working between the biological and biographical, the thanatological and thanatographical.

BIBLIOGRAPHY

"Anne Heche." Urban Dictionary, last modified August 1, 2008. http://www.urbandictionary.com/define.php?term=anne+heche.

Armstrong, Mark. "Anne Heche Hospitalized." *E!Online*. August 21, 2000, http://www.eonline.com/uberblog/b40331_anne_heche_hospitalized.html.

Basic Instinct. Directed by Paul Verhoeven. Los Angeles: Columbia Tristar, 1992. DVD.

Bell, Book and Candle. Directed by Richard Quine. Los Angeles: Sony Pictures Home Entertainment, 1958. DVD.

Chloe. Directed by Atom Egoyam. Toronto: Sony Picture Classics, 2009. DVD.

Derrida, Jacques. *The Ear of the Other: Otobiography, Transference, Translation: Texts and Discussions with Jacques Derrida*. Lincoln: Nebraska University Press, 1982.

Derrida, Jacques. "Limited Inc abc...." *Glyph* 2. Translated by Samuel Weber. Baltimore: Johns Hopkins Press, 1977.

Derrida, Jacques. "Plato's Pharmacy." *Dissemination*. Translated by Barbara Johnson. Chicago: University of Chicago Press, 1982.

Ettinger, Bracha. *The Matrixial Gaze*. Leeds: University of Leeds, 1995.

Freud, Sigmund. *Beyond the Pleasure Principle* in *The Standard Edition of the Complete Works of Sigmund Freud*. London: Psychoanalysis, 1953–1974.

Freud, Sigmund, "The Theory of Instincts." In *An Outline of Psychoanalysis*. Eds. Clara Thompson, Milton Mazer, and Earl Witenberg. New York: Random House, 1955.

"Hasbian," Urban Dictionary, last modified November 30, 2003. http://www.urbandictionary.com/define.php?term=hasbian.

Heche, Anne. *Call Me Crazy: A Memoir*. New York: Scribner, 2001.

Lacan, Jacques. "The Mirror Stage as Formative of the Function of the I." *Écrits: A Selection*. Translated by Bruce Fink. New York: W. W. Norton, 2002.

Lacan, Jacques. *The Seminar of Jacques Lacan: Book 1, Freud's Papers on Technique 1953–1954*. Translated by Alan Sheridan. New York: Cambridge University Press, 1988.

Lacan, Jaques. "Some Reflections on the Ego." *International Journal of Psychoanalysis* 34, 1 (1953): 11–17.

Mulvey, Laura. "Visual Pleasure and Narrative Cinema." *Film Theory and Criticism: Introductory Readings*. Edited by Leo Braudy and Marshall Cohen. New York: Oxford University Press, 1999.

Single White Female. Directed by Barbet Schroeder. Los Angeles: Columbia Pictures, 1992. DVD.

Spivak, Gayatri Chakravorty. "Revolutions That as Yet Have No Model: Derrida's *Limited Inc.* In *The Spivak Reader: Selected Words of Gayatri Chakravorty Spivak.* New York: Routledge, 1996.
Žižek, Slavoj. A Plea for Ethical Violence. *Umbr(a)* 1 (2004): 7591.
Žižek, Slavoj. *The Sublime Object of Ideology.* New York: Verso Books, 1989.

7

"The Veteran Problem"

Examining Contemporary Constructions of Returning Veterans

Alena Papayanis

This chapter examines how war trauma is negotiated around the contemporary image of the "damaged" war veteran. With the Wars in Iraq and Afghanistan resulting in unprecedented numbers of veterans suffering from traumatic brain injuries (the "signature injury" of these wars), increased suicide rates, and problematic behaviour (even gaining the reputation as "a new and dangerous class of offender"[1]), unique challenges to conceptualizing, treating, and managing war veterans are arising and pushing the veteran figure into cultural prominence.

The idea of veterans as a dangerous population is not new; in fact, the "veteran problem" has a long history. For example, in Tudor England, returning soldiers caused significant social problems, such as increased crime and murder, and provided the impetus for the Tudor Poor Laws in order to control these former soldiers. John Pound tackled this subject in *Poverty and Vagrancy in Tudor England* (1971), as did Rory Rapple more recently in *Martial Power and Elizabethan Political Culture* (2009). The problems of veterans has provided a rich theme in many cultural contexts, from the issue of homelessness (within the Civil War veteran population, for example), to Siegfried Sassoon's "Aftermath" poetry, to the anti-war writing of Dalton Trumbo in *Johnny Got His Gun* (1939). How the "veteran problem" has been popularly constructed within a selection of contemporary American films is addressed in this chapter.

Kenneth Hyams, epidemiologist at the U.S. Naval Medical Research Institute in Rockville, Maryland, claimed that if "history teaches us anything, it is that men and women are changed by war."[2] "No one returns from war unaffected by the experience," he explained, and some veterans "can be expected to have chronic, difficult-to-explain health problems because the wounds of combat are not always visible."[3] According to this logic, it was normal for veterans to show signs of psychological disturbance, invisible wounds caused by the war that the medical profession could find and diagnose. My research will demonstrate how these veterans, who can be referred to using sociologist Jerry Lembcke's phrase, "the 'right stuff' gone wrong,"[4] are publicly constructed in relation to the medical understanding of war trauma.

Popular images of veterans reflect the cultural and political attitude towards a nation's current conflicts, resilient cultural stereotypes and tropes about warriorhood, and the current medical understanding of war-related illnesses, war trauma in particular. Do we expect our men[5] to be traumatized by war or to return unfazed? When they do return home "sick" or changed, who or what is the cause? How does the image of the particular war influence the ways in which a veteran's illness is understood and represented? This chapter examines these questions in relation to depictions of contemporary "damaged" war veterans in films, including those representing Vietnam veterans (*Rambo: First Blood*, *The Deer Hunter*, and *Coming Home*), Gulf War veterans (*The Jacket* and *Thanks of a Grateful Nation*), and veterans of the more contemporary wars in Iraq and Afghanistan (*The Hurt Locker*, *Brothers*, and *In the Valley of Elah*). It argues that these films reflect contemporary medical understanding of, and debates around, war-related illnesses particular to each of these contemporary wars, beginning with the Vietnam War. In addition, this chapter traces concepts that constructed the popular understanding of post–Vietnam Syndrome (later post-traumatic stress disorder) through to the present day, such as the "flashback" and the notion of veteran alienation.

Revisiting the Vietnam Veteran Stereotype: Perpetrator or Victim?

The Vietnam War played a significant role in dramatically altering the popular image of the war veteran within American popular culture. The Vietnam veteran became a stereotype as a psychologically damaged and socially isolated character. Public narratives about the Vietnam War often centered on a Vietnam veteran figure as an unstable perpetrator who lacked the "heroic, sacrificial mould" that many critics have argued was disrupted by the atrocities of the Vietnam War,[6] such as the My Lai massacre. The massacre involved the mass murder of hundreds of unarmed South Vietnamese civilians, many of whom were women and children, by a unit of the U.S. Army on March 16, 1968.

Atrocity had entered the public narrative of the war, transforming the Vietnam veteran into a volatile and violent character. After 1975, "a covert narrative of violence brutally burst into the public arena,"[7] argued cultural historian Joanna Bourke, one that created "a collective narrative that circled in a fixated fashion around My Lai–type incidents. No 'grade–B melodrama' based on the Vietnam War was complete without its "standard vet — a psychotic, axe-wielding rapist."[8] However, these post-1975 films "graphically portrayed acts of killing and being killed in the context of a celebration of survival-against-horrific-odds and comradeship," with minimal (or no) sense of the "cause."[9] Viewers were presented with the "private motivations and goals of the individual soldier" as justification.[10] Violence was constructed in relation to personal, and often masculine considerations rather than political ones, providing an aura of necessity to the violent narrative. Thus, the Vietnam veteran figure that broke into popular culture was unstable and violent, but directed his rage at seemingly justified targets.

Drawing on the example of the Vietnam veteran, Simon Wessely, Professor of Epidemiological and Liaison Psychiatry at the Institute of Psychiatry at King's College London, noted how veteran illness had become a political issue. He explained how the traumatized Vietnam veteran had become a political symbol exploited by opponents of the war, such as Robert Jay Lifton and Chaim Shatan, to create an "image of the disturbed veteran as a symbol of the insane war to crystallize opposition."[11] "Psychiatry was politicized," he concluded, "and out of it came a new stereotype of the Vietnam vet."[12] Antiwar psychologists who worked with Vietnam veterans popularized the issue of post-traumatic stress disorder (PTSD) and gained its inclusion into the *Diagnostic and Statistical Manual of Mental Disorders-Fourth Edition-Text Revision* (DSM-IV-TR), which is the document that establishes "what it is possible to suffer in the way of problems psychiatrists recognize and treat."[13] Based on the resulting Vietnam veteran figure that gained notoriety within popular culture, it was apparent that the public, or perhaps the U.S. administration, was more comfortable with "sick" veterans than angry or subversive ones, which the inclusion in the DSM-IV-TR also indicated.

Over time, a more powerful narrative came to dominate, one that portrayed Vietnam veterans as victims. According to these narratives, the injuring party was the public who had greeted veterans with hostility upon their return (this is popularly known as the "spat-upon veteran myth"), or the war itself, which had left them physically and mentally destroyed and alienated from the home front (for example, *The Deer Hunter* [1979] and *Coming Home* [1978] received critical acclaim for their powerful depictions of veterans who were mentally and physically incapacitated from the war). Despite its fictional origin,[14] the idea that Vietnam veterans felt alienated upon their return shaped how the effects of post-traumatic stress disorder were constructed within the medical profession, as well as popular culture. Lembcke argued that alienation "wasn't so much a social psychological condition *found* through the study of veterans as it was a paradigm through which mental health professionals interpreted the post-war experience of former GIs"[15] and, as a result, was a concept that shaped "the very content of PTSD."[16] In other words, alienation was used to conceptualize post-traumatic stress disorder, both in theory and in substance, rather than a condition that was first organically found amongst the Vietnam veteran population.

Robert Jay Lifton, in the preface to his 2005 edition of *Home from the War: Learning from Vietnam Veterans* (2005), explained that he and his colleagues, working with Vietnam veterans in the early 1970s, used the term "'post–Vietnam syndrome' to emphasize not only their pain but their profound sense of alienation that rendered them different from veterans of other wars."[17] Similarly, Wessely asked, "was the cause of what soon became the 'Vietnam syndrome' not the jungles of Vietnam, but the atmosphere of an America turning against the military in general and the war in particular?"[18] Although veterans of previous wars have described a similar sense of alienation from the public upon returning, this experience was popularly attributed to the Vietnam generation. Historian Michael C. C. Adams acknowledged this misleading image in *The Best War Ever: America and World War II*, where he explained that

> Contrary to the popular myth that dumps all negatives on Vietnam, the worst war we had.... The majority of returning soldiers [from World War II] got no parades. James Jones, a veteran, noted that wounded men repatriated to the United States were treated as though diseased, and people rushed to wash their hands after greeting him.[19]

Adams discredited the popular idea that the Vietnam generation experience was unique, and connected it to a longer history of veteran treatment. However, the myth remains strong within popular cultural narratives.

The Alienation, Traumatization, and Exhilaration of War: Negotiating the Experience of War and its After Effects

More contemporary representations of returning veterans continue to present homecoming as an alienating experience. For example, in *The Hurt Locker, In the Valley of Elah,* and *Brothers,* characters who have recently come back from the war express a desire to return shortly thereafter. *In the Valley of Elah*'s character Private Second Class Robert Ortiez admitted,

I hated it over there. Sleep in fucking tents, no toilets, no showers, no toilet paper, gotta use your hand — and you never know where the bullet is coming from. I couldn't wait to get out. And after two weeks here, all I want to do is go back, 'cause somehow that makes sense. How fucked is that?[20]

Despite how much he had wished to escape the war, Ortiez found being home more difficult. In the end, war was where he was comfortable; home had become an unfamiliar environment that he felt alienated from.

According to the DSM-IV-TR, this feeling of alienation ordiminished responsiveness to the external world, referred to as "psychic numbing" or "emotional anesthesia," usually begins soon after the traumatic event. The individual may complain of having markedly diminished interest or participation in previously enjoyed activities, of feeling detached or estranged from other people, or of having markedly reduced ability to feel emotions.[21]

Alienation drives much of the post-war experience of Sam Cahill in *Brothers*, a film that portrays the story of two brothers, Sam, a successful captain in the Marines and Tommy, an ex-convict recently released from jail. Sam was deployed to Afghanistan where he was captured after his helicopter had been shot down. He was taken as a prisoner of war (POW), along with one other Marine; however the military wrongly presumed them dead. Sam suffered numerous beatings and psychological assaults and resisted demands by his captors to record anti–American statements. However, he ultimately succumbed and killed his fellow Marine with a baton after his captors demanded that he do so. At that moment, it is clear that he had reached his psychological breaking point. The Americans eventually find Sam, unresponsive, within the encampment and return him to the United States and to his family, who had already mourned his death and grown closer together, and to Sam's brother Tommy.

When Sam returns to his family, he is no longer the same upbeat and loving father who left for Afghanistan. Instead, he is distant, cold, and paranoid about his wife's fidelity (and suspects his brother Tommy in this affair). Whereas Sam used to be involved with his daughters, he is now disengaged, preferring to watch his wife and daughters interact amongst themselves and with Tommy, who became a father figure in his absence. Although "home" had physically changed and developed while Sam was away — for example, Tommy redid the kitchen and is now a staple in the family's life — it is Sam who has changed drastically. He is psychologically locked into his experience as a prisoner of war, and his family is unable to integrate this changed man into their lives. This behavior falls into the DSM-IV-TR's diagnostic criteria for PTSD that refers to "numbing of general responsiveness (not present before the trauma), which includes "markedly diminished interest or participation in significant activities," feelings of "detachment or estrangement from others," and "restricted range of affect," which is the inability to have loving feelings.[22] Sam's family lamented his changed personality and emotional numbness, and his older daughter admitted that she wished her father actually had died in Afghanistan; they felt alienated by, and from, him.

It is important to note that Sam's anguish revolved around what he did to his fellow Marine, rather than what his captors did to him. Although his wife assumes that he is traumatized by the latter, and begs him repeatedly to tell her what *they* did to *him*, Sam is anguished over *his act* of perpetration. However, Sam's violence was contextualized within his position as a POW and was thus more easily justified. Did his position as a victim justify his perpetration? What emotion or compulsion did Sam kill with? Does it make a difference to our perception of his fatal act? These are all important questions to consider, although the DSM no longer makes these distinctions. Interestingly, guilt events "based on pleasure rather than necessity" were affixed to the traumatic memory after the Vietnam War, the publication of the DSM-III, and the adoption of PTSD by the VA as "a service-connected disability."[23] Thus, guilt felt for committing an act merely for pleasure rather than necessity, such as mutilating a dead corpse rather than killing an attacking enemy soldier, was brought into the framework of PTSD.

Sam represents an attempt to negotiate atrocity in light of revelations of torture and prisoner abuse at Abu Ghraib by American soldiers, which has left the military's reputation tarnished and continually vulnerable to further damaging disclosures. Interestingly, PTSD specialists are beginning to study the effects of killing on soldiers, and one recent study entitled "The Impact of Killing on Mental Health Symptoms in Gulf War Veterans" (2009) concluded that "taking a life in combat is a critical ingredient in the development of postdeployment mental health concerns."[24] However, diagnostic features of PTSD listed in the DSM do not include perpetration and rather, require that a person experiencing a traumatic event feel "intense fear, helplessness, or horror."[25] Yet, the fact sheet for the National Center for PTSD outlining the experience of returning veterans of the Iraq War emphasized that "the trauma of war is colored by a variety of emotional experiences, not just horror, terror, and fear. Candidate emotions are ... guilt about personal actions or inactions."[26] Thus, contemporary attempts to negotiate the relationship of perpetration to the mental health of veterans, and to other experiences of soldiers during wartime, are only beginning to be discussed.

The Hurt Locker acknowledges a variety of emotional experiences of wartime, including terror and fear; most interestingly, however, it addresses exhilaration. The final two scenes of the movie solidify this message, which was expressed at the start of the film when the following quotation appeared: "The rush of battle is often a potent and lethal addiction, for war is a drug."[27] These final scenes show Sergeant First Class William James, the main character in the film, returning home after his tour in Iraq and feeling out of place. While chatting in the kitchen and preparing dinner, James attempted to tell his wife a war story, but it was clear that she was not interested in hearing it, and she instead asked him to cut up some vegetables. Similar to Sam Cahill in *Brothers*, James's wife did not understand her returning husband, a fact that allegedly exacerbated feelings of dissociation.

In the scene that followed, James was playing with his one-year-old son, who was happily enjoying his toys, and he gave the following telling speech:

> You love playing with that.... You love everything, don't you? Yeah. You know what, buddy? Once you get older, some of the things that you love might not seem so special anymore. Like your jack-in-the-box. Maybe you realize it's just a piece of tin and a stuffed animal, and then you forget the few things you really love. And by the time you get to my age maybe it's only one or two things. With me I think it's one.

The one thing that James loves is war, and in the next scene he is shown disembarking the military plane that has brought him back to Iraq. He is greeted by the words "Welcome to Delta Company — Sergeant." James feels comfortable and as though he belongs in the war rather than his home. At home, his wife did not understand his experience or the perspective he had gained through war.

James was not traumatized by his wartime experience, but rather was exhilarated by it.[28] Some experts have uncovered the positive experiences of soldiers in war, although much medical and psychological literature emphasizes its traumatizing nature. For example, cultural historian Joanna Bourke powerfully demonstrated in *An Intimate History of Killing* (1998) that killing was a multifarious experience for soldiers and revealed conflicting emotions, such as fear, empathy, rage and exhilaration,[29] and even provided them with moments of "spiritual resonance and an aesthetic poignancy."[30] This contrasted to one of the fundamental notions guiding the inclusion of post-traumatic stress disorder (PTSD) in the *Diagnostic and Statistical Manual of Mental Disorders*, which was that it is naturally traumatizing.

The Harmony of Delusions: Flashbacks, Trauma, and Treatment

The "flashback" came to symbolize the Vietnam veteran's traumatic experience in filmic representations, a visual technique that was then incorporated into the medical construction of PTSD. Sociologist Jerry Lembcke observed that it is difficult to pinpoint when writers on the problems of Vietnam veterans first began to refer to "flashbacks," because no references were found in early literature on PTSD, such as the articles and testimonies collected by the Veterans Administration for *The Vietnam Veteran in Contemporary Society* (1972) or Robert Jay Lifton's 1973 book *Home from the War*. Instead, Lembcke supported the argument that since it did not appear in the PTSD literature until the 1980s, was not published in the DSM until DSM-III-R in 1987, and had "no prior history of use to describe behavioural or psychological disorders.... [the flashback] was derived from popular culture."[31]

In *Rambo: First Blood* (1982), flashbacks are precursors to Rambo's violence, which fits with the DSM-IV-TR's causal explanation of the episode. The DSM entry for PTSD describes how, when a person is "exposed to triggering events that resemble or symbolize an aspect of the traumatic event," they can experience "intense psychological distress or physiological reactivity."[32] "In rare instances," the DSM states, "the person experiences dissociative states that last from a few seconds to several hours, or even days, during which components of the event are relived and the person behaves as though experiencing the event at that moment."[33] Thus, according to the DSM, dissociative or violent reactions can be elicited by events that literally or metaphorically resemble a traumatic moment.

In Rambo's case, while wandering through a small town called Hope after returning from Vietnam, he was confronted by the town's sheriff, who attempted to drive him out of town. When Rambo defied the sheriff's wishes and immediately headed back into town, he was arrested and taken into the local station. When Rambo entered the station and saw the bars, he had a flashback to his time as a POW in Vietnam. He recalled being held captive in a hole with bars above him; in his memory, the Vietnamese were pouring feces over him. A moment later, one of the officers touched him and Rambo reacted violently, requiring restraint by a number of officers.[34] Later, when an officer attempted to dry-shave Rambo before processing him, Rambo had flashbacks and heard the sound of a razor being sharpened by one of his Vietnamese captors, who then proceeded to cut Rambo's chest. Rambo reacted explosively to this memory, attacking the police officers in the station and escaping into the nearby mountains. A manhunt ensued, but Rambo became the hunter in this situation, severely injuring the deputies in pursuit of him.[35]

The flashbacks in *Rambo: First Blood* are visual and sensory connectors between Rambo's traumatic wartime experience and his violence in the present. The desire to connect present problematic behavior to a past experience was a primary focus of the diagnostic process for PTSD, which attempted to "get traumatic time to run in the right direction: *from* the etiological event *to* the post-traumatic symptoms."[36] Anthropologist Allan Young explained how the patient's current anguish, "either his expressed emotion (grief, guilt, etc.) [*sic*] or his embodied distress, is projected back, over time, to the traumatic moment" in a way that "infuses and connects the morally and experientially heterogeneous events ... with a new and homogeneous meaning."[37] This sense of time attached to PTSD, which Young argued is "an achievement, a product of psychiatric culture and technology," is reflected in the DSM, where it is "taken for granted that time and causality move *from* the traumatic event *to* the other criterial features and that the event inscribes itself on the symptoms."[38] Visual flashbacks attempt to use a previous experience in the war to explain their present actions and feelings, which, essentially, gives them meaning. This sense of time, and connection between a stressful event in war and post-war violence, is made in films through the use of flashbacks.

However, this simple sense of time is complicated in *The Jacket*, which tells the story of Gulf War veteran Jack Starks. Early in the film, there is a scene that is reminiscent of the scene from *Rambo: First Blood* where Rambo wandered through the town of Hope, a narrative connection that evokes a similar image of a "lost" veteran. Starks came back to life after dying from a gunshot wound to the head inflicted by an Iraqi child and was sent back to the United States. Months later, he is seen walking down a snowy highway in Montana carrying nothing but a backpack, and with no apparent destination in mind. He comes across a young girl and her mother whose truck had broken down and stops to help. After fixing the truck, Starks leaves and begins to hitchhike. He is picked up by a man who, when their car was later pulled over by the police, fatally shoots the officer multiple times. One bullet ricochets off of the car and incapacitates Starks, and the driver leaves the scene of the crime in a state that implicates the wounded Starks in the murder.

Suffering from amnesia, Starks does not recall the fatal incident or the moments leading up to it, except for the girl and mother that he had assisted earlier that day. The court ruled that although Starks committed the crime, he was not criminally responsible because he was suffering from a delusional disorder. Although labeling Starks with a delusional disorder fit within the understanding of war-related symptoms, the fact that Starks was *wrongly* considered delusional suggests a fundamental failure of the medical profession to understand and properly care for its veterans. According to the doctors, Starks's memory was fabricated in order to suppress his crime, a crime that was perhaps connected to his traumatic shooting in the war. This inability to "recall an important aspect" of a trauma is one symptom for the criteria of "persistent avoidance of stimuli associated with the trauma" required for a diagnosis of PTSD.[39]

This skepticism shown towards Starks's claims reflected the discourse that first governed the medical profession and administration's reaction to Gulf War Syndrome. This stance held that the symptoms claimed by veterans were fabricated or merely psychosomatic, rather than authentic physical reactions with a causal explanation originating with their service in the Gulf. Although debate still exists around GWS into the present day, and the medical profession has yet to diagnose specific causation for the symptoms suffered by many Gulf veterans, James P. Terry noted how Congress "has judiciously bridged the gap and has provided presumptive relationships that ensure equitable disability determinations for these veterans,"[40] essentially recognizing Gulf War Syndrome as a unique disorder. Moreover, major legislation passed in 1994, 1998, and 2001 guaranteed that illnesses claimed by veterans who were deployed to the Gulf, exhibit one or more listed symptoms, and were exposed to at least one listed agent (a toxic agent, an environmental or wartime hazard, or a preventative medication or vaccine), "*are presumed* to be service connected."[41]

This scepticism towards Gulf War Syndrome was also reflected in the reliability attributed to Starks's statements both in court and in his subsequent diagnosis as delusional. At his murder trial, the prosecutor challenged Starks's only memory of the evening, asking him "Are you aware that we have no last name, no place of residence, and no record of any physical presence for these *friends* of yours?"[42] The prosecutor assumed that because there was no physical evidence to support his account, Starks had fabricated these people in his mind. A psychologist at the trial testified that "Jack Starks could be blocking the incident [the murder]. That would explain his well-conceived plan about the little girl and her mother. I have heard of Gulf War Syndrome."[43] The fact that Starks could not remember the shooting stood as evidence of his repressed trauma (a "secret"), and his story was allegedly his mind's attempt to compensate for the experience.

Anthropologist Allan Young traced the history of the traumatic memory as a "pathogenic secret" in *The Harmony of Illusions: Inventing Post-Traumatic Stress Disorder* (1995). The memories are pathogenic because they reportedly caused psychiatric disorders, and they were considered "secret" because they were "acts of concealment."[44] Young explained that two kinds of concealment were considered possible. In one, "the owner wants to hide the contents of his recollection from other people. In addition, he wants to forget the memory himself or, failing this, he wants to push it to the edges of awareness."[45] The second kind of concealment involved the owner hiding the memory from him- or herself. "He knows that he has a secret memory, because he senses its existence," Young explicated, "but he is unable to retrieve it; or, what is more common, he does not remember that he has forgotten and has to learn about his memory from someone else, typically a therapist."[46] Thus, in a diagnosed patient, such as Starks in *The Jacket*, his or her inability to recollect such a distressful memory was seen as evidence of its successful repression.[47]

Starks's therapists insisted on their diagnosis despite his claims, and when Starks proclaimed that he was not "crazy," one doctor clarified that the delusional disorder "doesn't mean you're crazy, it just means you're confused."[48] She began to tell Starks that his "mind's ability to distinguish between delusions and the real events that have happened" to him was failing when he interjected and screamed, "The real events are fucked up, not my mind!"[49] These sentiments pointed to the improper treatment of veterans, whose claims were met with disbelief, and in this case, led to emotionally traumatic experiences.

Starks underwent extreme therapy used on only the worst offenders. The experimental use of drugs on Starks reflects the accusation alleged against the U.S. military that although they forced Gulf soldiers to take a number of pills for preventative purposes, that these pills in fact made them sick. The treatment involved administering drugs and putting him, while restricted by a straight jacket, into a shelf in the morgue for hours at a time. During these periods of isolation and sensory deprivation, Starks experienced both flashbacks to moments from his past, including his death, and also, unexplainably, traveled into the future (to the year 2007). Flashbacks were central to his treatment, forcing him to confront not only his actions and experiences in the past, but also the knowledge of his impending death (which he was made aware of in the "future"). *The Jacket* points to the medical establishment's inability to properly understand and treat Gulf War veterans; in fact, treatment is seen as exacerbating the veteran's existing problems, or even acting as a traumatic experience itself.

The Politics of Diagnosis: (Ma)Lingering Debate over the Gulf and its Veterans

Debate over GWS is reflected in the way it is represented in films;[50] they question the reliability of veteran's accounts as well as the medical establishment's handling of suffering veterans. The United States emerged from the Gulf War relatively unscathed and brimming with a sense of renewed strength, national identity, and hope. Images of Gulf veterans suffering from a range of acute and chronic symptoms (such as fatigue, joint pain, memory problems, skin rashes, birth defects, and immune system problems) departed from the popular and desirable image of the war. Unlike Vietnam veterans, whose "sickness" came to popularly represent the nature of the war itself, the symptoms suffered by Gulf veterans could not be taken up by the public narrative of the war in a way that reinforced popular sentiment about the conflict. Representations of Gulf War veterans reflect the intense and unresolved debate surrounding Gulf War Syndrome and its contrast to the image of the war as relatively casualty-free. Interestingly, rather than appear in popular cultural representations as perpetrators of violence as Vietnam veterans were, they often appeared as uncompensated and even mistreated victims of Gulf War–related symptoms; similar to Vietnam veterans, they appeared as a misunderstood, and often victimized, population.

The military and medical establishment's reluctance to acknowledge Gulf War Syndrome as a unique and authentic disorder is depicted in the movie *Thanks of a Grateful Nation* (1998). In the film, retired U.S. Secret Service agent Jim Tuite proclaimed a desire to get "the President to ... admit it. That's what the guys [Gulf veterans] want most. They want to be told they're not crazy, that they're not malingerers, that their country cares about them for God's sake!"[51] Tuite represented the desire of sick Gulf veterans for the medical establishment and the U.S. administration to admit not only that the veterans' symptoms were not merely "in their heads," but also that they were not being fabricated in order to gain compensation. His last sentiment, that the country should prove its gratitude and support for Gulf soldiers by addressing their issues, points to the intended irony in the title of the film.

The film also depicts Gary Wall, president of the Vietnam Veterans of America's New Jersey chapter, testifying at a House Subcommittee on Compensation, Pension, and Insurance for Veterans Affairs. Wall proclaimed,

> The experience of the Vietnam generation has proven that the government simply cannot be trusted to come forward with answers on its own. Someone needs to explain to the families and the veterans themselves why it is that they were financially destroyed and emotionally destroyed while waiting for someone to diagnose what it is that is slowly killing them.[52]

Wall referred to the experience of Vietnam veterans, particularly those claiming illnesses related to Agent Orange exposure, and implied that Gulf veterans could experience similar difficulty regarding diagnosis and treatment. He suggested that, like Vietnam veterans and their supporters did, Gulf veterans will have to mobilize in order to uncover answers for themselves.

Similar to *The Jacket*, the position of the administration and medical establishment in *Thanks of a Grateful Nation* reflected the debate over "Gulf War Syndrome" when it first began to surface. In the film, a head doctor expressed his scepticism, remarking,

> We sent 700,000 people to war and everybody thought it was a cakewalk. Mystery illness, I don't know where it started. [It] had a great allure, government conspiracy. There was some connection to Vietnam, Agent Orange

paranoia, and it's taken on a life of its own. There's no evidence ... to date of anything.[53]

Referring to GWS as a "mystery illness" and associating it with "Agent Orange paranoia" attempted to discredit the validity of the disorder. Here, the claims of Vietnam veterans to contamination by Agent Orange during their service were used as evidence against Gulf War veterans, suggesting that Gulf War veterans were making claims based on paranoia rather than physical evidence.[54]

Scepticism surrounding GWS was also based on the image of the Gulf War as a relatively "casualty-free" and straightforward success. One doctor in *Thanks of a Grateful Nation* exemplified this sentiment when he criticized that in the Gulf War, "The most important event is that there was no major event. No world war one, no catastrophe."[55] A PTSD diagnosis requires exposure to an "extreme traumatic stressor," such as witnessing an event that involves death or injury (among others), and the Gulf War's sanitized image hid the carnage that took place and was witnessed by many soldiers in the Gulf. With no causal event to precipitate the symptoms of sick Gulf veterans, the understanding of the effects of war on the minds and bodies of Gulf veterans had to be re-examined, a complex issue that these Gulf War films reflect.

Conclusion

Contemporary representations of "sick" American war veterans are a complicated breed of fiction and fact, blending together the medical understanding of war's effects with cultural tropes about war and warriorhood, and also reflecting the politico-cultural climate of the war being considered. As a whole, the films examined in this chapter tell us that war-related illnesses are not the result of problems with our soldiers (their mental or moral aptitude or their training for example), but that they are indicative of more systematic problems, such as a divisive or unclear war, an unsupportive home front, or a misguided medical establishment. In other words, they tell us that the real problem is what is being done to soldiers (in the war or through their treatment) or what is not being done for them, rather than what they are doing. In many cases, this is not problematic; however, now more than ever before, soldiers are returning from war and becoming violent on the home front, either taking their own lives or, worse yet, taking the lives of others, primarily their wives and children.

This tragic fact makes it increasingly important to examine how the contemporary veteran is popularly represented, and how these images relate to the real experiences and actions of America's actual veterans. By deconstructing images of veterans, this chapter has provided questions for viewers to ask in order to critically examine popular cultural representations of war and its warriors. How do they represent the connection between service in the military and problematic post-war behavior on the home front? In what ways are veterans constructed in relation to victimhood and perpetration? Do these images obstruct our view of other victims of their war, such an "enemy" civilians? What do these representations lead us to believe about war and its effects? By no means does this chapter attempt to minimize the very real symptoms suffered by veterans, but instead, it aims to create a critical perspective from which to view the contemporary construction of our returning veterans.

NOTES

1. David Bruser, "A Soldier's Rage," *Toronto Star*, June 13, 2009.

2. Kenneth C. Hyams et al., "Protecting the Health of United States Military Forces in Afghanistan: Applying Lessons Learned Since the Gulf War," *Clinical Infectious Diseases 34, Supplement 5. Afghanistan: Health Challenges Facing Deployed Troops, Peacekeepers, and Refugees,* June 15, 2002, S212, accessed October 30, 2010, http://www.jstor.org/stable/4461995.

3. Ibid.

4. Jerry Lembcke, "The 'Right Stuff' Gone Wrong: Vietnam Veterans and the Social Construction of Post-Traumatic Stress Disorder," *Critical Sociology* 24, no 1–2, (1998): 52.

5. I will refer mainly to men because women's proximity to combat is largely unrecognized and thus, their experiences with post-traumatic stress disorder (which, it is important to note is often due to military sexual trauma) are only beginning to gain attention.

6. Joanna Bourke, "'Remembering' War," *Journal of Contemporary History*, Vol. 39, no. 4 (2004), 480.

7. Ibid.

8. Ibid.

9. Ibid., 481.

10. Ibid.

11. Simon Wessely, "Twentieth-Century Theories on Combat Motivation and Breakdown," *Journal of Contemporary History* 41, no. 2 (2006): 280, accessed November 1, 2010, http://www.jstor.org/stable/30036386.

12. Ibid.

13. Wilbur J. Scott, "PTSD in DSM-III: A Case in the Politics of Diagnosis and Disease," *Social Problems* 37, no. 3 (1990): 294.

14. Lembcke found that Vietnam veterans felt generally accepted by their peers. A Harris poll of Vietnam-era veterans taken in August 1971 and published by the Senate Committee on Veteran's Affairs found that 94 percent of veterans felt their reception home by their peers was friendly and that only 3 percent rated their homecoming "not at all friendly." The same poll asked veterans whether they agreed with the statement, "Those people at home who oppose the Vietnam War often blame veterans for our involvement"; 75 percent of Vietnam-era veterans disagreed.

15. Lembcke, 49.

16. Lembcke he suggested that alienation was the behavioural characteristic with the longest history within PTSD literature. Lembcke, 58. Emphasis in original.

17. Robert Jay Lifton, *Home from the War: Learning from Vietnam Veterans* (New York: Other Press, 2005, 1973), x.

18. Wessely, 280.

19. James Jones, *WWII* (New York: Grosset & Dunlap, 1975). Quoted in Michael C. C. Adams, *The Best War Ever: America and World War Two* (Baltimore: Johns Hopkins University Press, 1994), 7.

20. *In the Valley of Ellah*, directed by Paul Haggis, 2007 (Burbank, CA: Warner Independent Pictures, 2008), DVD.

21. *Diagnostic and Statistical Manual of Mental Disorders, Fourth Edition* (Washington, DC: American Psychiatric Association, 1994), 425.

22. Ibid., 428.

23. Allan Young, *The Harmony of Illusions: Inventing Post-Traumatic Stress Disorder* (Princeton, NJ: Princeton University Press, 1995), 126.

24. Shira Maguen et al., "The Impact of Killing on Mental Health Symptoms in Gulf War Veterans," *Psychological Trauma: Theory, Research, Practice and Policy,* October 4, 2010: 4, doi: pen.1037/a0019897.

25. *Diagnostic and Statistical Manual of Mental Disorders, Fourth Edition*, 424.

26. Brett Litz and Susan M. Orsillo, "The Returning Veteran of the Iraq War: Background Issues and Assessment Guidelines," *National Center for PTSD*, accessed October 29, 2010, http://www.ptsd.va.gov/professional/pages/vets-iraq-war-guidelines.asp.

27. Chris Hedges, *War Is a Force that Gives Us Meaning* (New York: Public Affairs, 2002), 2–3. Quoted in *The Hurt Locker*, directed by Kathryn Bigelow, 2008 (Seattle, WA: First Light Production, 2010), DVD.

28. One could argue that the audience is comfortable with his exhilaration because rather than kill enemies (or Iraqis who pose a perceived threat), James' job is to dismantle inordinate explosive devices (IEDs). He not only saves people's lives by risking his own, but part of his motivation for returning to war is to avenge the death of an Iraqi child.

29. Joanna Bourke, *An Intimate History of Killing: Face-to-Face Killing in Twentieth Century Warfare* (London: Granta Books, 1999), 1.

30. Ibid., 14.

31. Lembcke, 53.

32. *Diagnostic and Statistical Manual of Mental Disorders, Fourth Edition Text Revision* (Washington, DC: American Psychiatric Association, 2000), 464.

33. Ibid.

34. *Rambo: First Blood*, directed by Ted Kotcheff, 1982 (Beverly Hills, CA: Carolco Pictures, 1998), DVD.

35. Ibid.

36. Young, 141. Emphasis in original.

37. Ibid., 126.

38. Ibid., 115. Emphasis in original.

39. *Diagnostic and Statistical Manual of Mental Disorders, Fourth Edition,* 428.

40. James P. Terry, "Gulf War Syndrome: Addressing Undiagnosed Illnesses from the First War with Iraq," *Veterans Law Review* 1 (2009), 181.

41. Ibid. Emphasis in original.

42. *The Jacket*, directed by John Maybury, 2005 (Burbank, CA: Warner Bros., 2005), DVD.

43. Ibid.

44. Young, 28.

45. Ibid.

46. Ibid., 29.

47. Ibid., 67.

48. *The Jacket.*

49. Ibid.

50. *The Manchurian Candidate* (2004) is another example of a film that addresses

the mystery surrounding GWS. Due to space limitations, this chapter could not examine this film.

    51. *Thanks of a Grateful Nation* (also known as *The Gulf War*), directed by Rod Holcomb, 1998 (New York City: Showtime Studio, 1998), DVD.

    52. Ibid.

    53. Ibid.

    54. However, more recent U.S. government actions, such as the Agent Orange Act of 1991, demonstrate that Agent Orange "paranoia" is being redressed. Suffering veterans are now eligible to receive treatment and compensation.

    55. *Thanks of a Grateful Nation.*

BIBLIOGRAPHY

Adams, Michael C. C. *The Best War Ever: America and World War Two.* Baltimore: Johns Hopkins University Press, 1994.

Bourke, Joanna. *An Intimate History of Killing: Face-to-Face Killing in Twentieth Century Warfare.* London: Granta Books, 1999.

Bourke, Joanna. "'Remembering' War." *Journal of Contemporary History*, Vol. 39, 4 (2004): 473–485.

Bruser, David. "A Soldier's Rage." *Toronto Star*, June 13, 2009.

Diagnostic and Statistical Manual of Mental Disorders, Fourth Edition. Washington, DC: American Psychiatric Association, 1994.

Diagnostic and Statistical Manual of Mental Disorders, Fourth Edition Text Revision. Washington, DC: American Psychiatric Association, 2000.

Hedges, Chris. *War Is a Force that Gives Us Meaning.* New York: Public Affairs, 2002.

The Hurt Locker. Directed by Kathryn Bigelow. 2008. Seattle, WA: First Light Production, 2010. DVD.

Hyams, Kenneth C., James Riddle, David H. Trump, and Mark R. Wallace. "Protecting the Health of United States Military Forces in Afghanistan: Applying Lessons Learned since the Gulf War." *Clinical Infectious Diseases 34, Supplement 5. Afghanistan: Health Challenges Facing Deployed Troops, Peacekeepers, and Refugees,* June 15, 2002: S212. Accessed October 30, 2010. http://www.jstor.org/stable/4461995.

In the Valley of Elah. Directed by Paul Haggis. 2007. Burbank, CA: Warner Independent Pictures, 2008. DVD.

The Jacket. Directed by John Maybury. 2005. Burbank, CA: Warner Bros., 2005. DVD.

Jones, James. *WWII.* New York City: Grosset & Dunlap, 1975.

Lembcke, Jerry. "The 'Right Stuff' Gone Wrong: Vietnam Veterans and the Social Construction of Post-Traumatic Stress Disorder." *Critical Sociology* 24, no. 1–2, (1998): 37–64.

Lifton, Robert Jay. *Home from the War: Learning from Vietnam Veterans.* New York: Other Press, 2005, 1973.

Litz, Brett, and Susan M. Orsillo. "The Returning Veteran of the Iraq War: Background Issues and Assessment Guidelines." *National Center for PTSD,* accessed October 29, 2010. http://www.ptsd.va.gov/professional/pages/vets-iraq-war-guidelines.asp.

Maguen, Shira, Dawne S. Vogt, Lynda A. King, Daniel W. King, Brett T. Litz, Sara J. Knight, and Charles R. Marmar, "The Impact of Killing on Mental Health Symptoms in Gulf War Veterans." *Psychological Trauma: Theory, Research, Practice and Policy* Vol. 23, 1 (2010): 1–6.

Rambo: First Blood. Directed by Ted Kotcheff. 1982. Beverly Hills, CA: Carolco Pictures, 1998. DVD.

Scott, Wilbur J. "PTSD in DSM-III: A Case in the Politics of Diagnosis and Disease." *Social Problems 37*, no. 3 (1990): 294–310.

Terry, James P. "Gulf War Syndrome: Addressing Undiagnosed Illnesses from the First War with Iraq." *Veterans Law Review* 1 (2009): 167–182.

Thanks of a Grateful Nation (also known as *The Gulf War*). Directed by Rod Holcomb. 1998. New York City: Showtime Studio, 1998. DVD.

Wessely, Simon. "Twentieth-Century Theories on Combat Motivation and Breakdown." *Journal of Contemporary History* 41, no. 2 (2006): 268–286, Accessed November 1, 2010. http://www.jstor.org/stable/30036386.

Young, Allan. *The Harmony of Illusions: Inventing Post-Traumatic Stress Disorder*. Princeton, NJ: Princeton University Press, 1995.

SECTION TWO

Popular Culture Genres and Mental Illness

8

Musical Storm and Mental Stress

Trauma and Instability in Contemporary American Musical Theater

Esther Terry

In the latter decades of the twentieth century, some contemporary musicals have contained characters struggling with Post-Traumatic Stress Disorder (PTSD) without naming the disorder directly.[1] These musicals, *The Who's Tommy* (1992), *Pippin* (1972), *Sweeney Todd: The Demon Barber of Fleet Street* (1979), *Passion* (1994), and *Miss Saigon* (1989),[2] utilize characters' traumatic pasts to show paths to destruction and paths to healing. That is, these musicals illustrate the immense struggle to find a type of normal after experiencing a traumatic event. In *Pippin*, the title character moves restlessly between sex and violence, in order to assuage his emptiness which is augmented by an early war experience. Stephen Sondheim portrays Lucy in *Sweeney Todd* and Signora Fosca in *Passion* as damaged women dealing with the trauma of rape and deceptive lovers, respectively. Kim from *Miss Saigon* struggles with post-traumatic stress from her village's destruction and also the Fall of Saigon. Finally, *The Who's Tommy* follows young Tommy's post-traumatic deafness, muteness, and blindness into his freedom as a young man.

Taken together, these musicals span a wide range of traumatic events and post-traumatic responses. In their choice of back stories, secrets, and obstacles for these characters, the composers and writers of these musicals use damaged characters in order to explore their attempt to overcome a traumatic past. The threats of suicide and self-destruction linger over all of these characters in their individual struggles to find their way back to a type of normal. Additionally, these musicals portray the characters re-experiencing their individual traumas and taking actions of avoidance. In effect, these musicals illus-

130

trate the liminality of PTSD and the challenges presented by characters existing in states of incompleteness. The characters stand as neither fully devastated nor fully healed, in need of closure and support in order to have a chance at recovering and returning to a sense of normalcy.

Post-Traumatic Stress Disorder

According to the DSM-IV-TR,[3] the American Psychiatric Association's system of classifying mental disorders, the diagnosis of PTSD describes a patient who develops characteristic symptoms following exposure to an extreme traumatic stressor. The stressor may include any event threatening death or serious injury to the patient, his or her person, or a person with whom the patient is very close (e.g., family member, coworker, fellow student, etc).[4] Traumatic events include, but are not limited to, war or any related activities (e.g., torture, being a prisoner of war, combat), sexual assault, being the victim of a kidnapping, natural disasters, and severe accidents. In addition, the patient must experience related symptoms for a period longer than one month, and the symptoms must interfere significantly with his or her everyday activities.

Characteristic symptoms include the patient re-experiencing the trauma, avoiding places or people who remind him or her of the traumatic event, and a general numbing towards external stimuli.[5] Re-experiences can take the form of dreams, "intrusive recollections," or flashbacks, lasting from a few minutes to several hours. The patient avoids places and people who may remind him or her of the trauma, because s/he has a heightened sensitivity towards these triggers and fears setting off a flashback or recollection. Towards his or her life, including social events, family, and friends, the patient often describes a general numbing or diminished interest, even though these previously mattered to him or her. These symptoms cause a person with PTSD to struggle in maintaining normative behavior and activities and may even drive some to consider committing suicide.

In the selected musicals, the characters do not necessarily follow the described symptoms and behaviors exactly as denoted in the DSM-IV-TR. The composers, book writers, and lyricists take creative license in manipulating their characters' objectives, obstacles, and overall narrative and trajectory. Yet, these character constructions present sufficient corroborating characteristics so that using the label of PTSD to describe their struggles does not reduce them to a clinical diagnosis or case study. Instead, applying the symptoms and struggles associated with PTSD, their musical portrayals underscore the thin line between recovery and permanent damage associated with this clinical condition.

Pippin: Depression, PTSD, and Manipulation

Within *Pippin*, the portrayal of PTSD echoes within the actions taken by the Players who surround Pippin through his trials and tribulations. The Players vary between giving information to the audience, providing ensemble extras in larger scenes, and interacting with or guiding Pippin along his way. In this third function, they illustrate the difficulty for a person to silence voices of torment or despair that may manifest in nightmares, recollections, or flashbacks. In essence, they showcase the difficulty for people suffering from PTSD to move beyond their liminal state. Pippin's journey begins with his departure from university studying and his declaration, "I promise not to waste my life in commonplace, ordinary pursuits."[6] Determined to find his "Corner of the Sky,"[7] Pippin then returns home, as the primary heir to the Holy Roman Empire and the throne of Charlemagne, but shorter in height and less accomplished in battle than his stepbrother and rival for the throne.

Coming directly after shouts for war and glory, the Leading Player tempts Pippin to yearn for warrior status. He proffers a sword and then patronizingly rescinds it, "Oh, excuse me. I thought you were a warrior."[8] Pippin, apparently overcome by all the talk of battle and glory, insists on keeping the sword. Then, he convinces his father to let him join the campaign against the Visigoths. But he quickly finds out that the glory he imagines, "Hark! The blood is pounding in our ears/Jubilations! We can hear a grateful nation's cheers,"[9] does not match the bloody reality of war. He converses with a severed head from the enemy's ranks. The head describes the mundanity of battle to the young prince and sarcastically expresses its gratitude for the honor of fighting for his king and his journey to Valhalla. After this disconcerting encounter, Pippin finds himself unable to join in the raping and pillaging: "Sorry, Father. You'll have to get used to victory celebrations without me," and continues on his quest for fulfillment and extraordinariness.[10]

After this depressing venture, Pippin then decides, at the urging of the Players, to try various sexual exploits.[11] The war excursion provides the Players with the chance to exploit the breach in Pippin's psyche and augment his depression by playing on his desire for greatness.[12] When the sexual adventures leave him exhausted and empty as ever, the Players urge Pippin to examine the corruption in his father's kingdom. Still searching for meaning, Pippin takes on this cause; he then decides to assassinate his father and replace him as king.[13] This attempt turns out as poorly as the previous ones: Pippin resurrects his father, and the Players encourage Pippin to continue, "You're on the right track!"[14] But after burning through art and religion, Pippin winds up homeless and destitute on the side of a road. In his final venture, entitled "Hearth," Pippin settles with a young widow and her son. He ends up feeling trapped in ordinary happiness and leaves her to find fulfillment: the Players stand ready and waiting.

From the beginning, then, the Players goad Pippin into various ventures to enhance his feeling of purposelessness. First, they encourage the young prince into the glory of war. Then, they have exploits ready and waiting when Pippin stands empty and traumatized from participating in killing, as well as observing the raping and pillaging. After that, the only time when Pippin reaches a semblance of normalcy and happiness is with the widow and her son. But by that late point in the play, influenced by his own dreams and the Players' constant insistence, Pippin believes himself to be destined for greatness; that is, he thinks he is above ordinary happiness. Once again, when Pippin ends this venture, the Players stand ready and waiting. This time, they present their final solution for Pippin's search for meaning and fulfillment: suicide by fire. They entice Pippin into the flame, just as they drew him into his previous ventures:

> A PLAYER: You will step into that flame, Pippin....
>
> LEADING PLAYER: Become part of that flame....
>
> A PLAYER: Be engulfed by that flame....
>
> A PLAYER: Become flame itself....
>
> LEADING PLAYER: And for one moment shine with unequalled brilliance....[15]

When Pippin asks why they don't jump into the fire, the Players invoke his greatness:

> LEADING PLAYER: Look, we're just ordinary run-of-the-mill people ... hell, we're nothing.... But you, Pippin, you're an extraordinary human being ... with extraordinary aspirations and dreams.[16]

In essence, all along, Pippin stumbles along a journey of increasing depression and PTSD, facilitated and enabled by the Players.[17] Other than assassinating his father, which he quickly reverses to resurrect the king, Pippin avoids violence and war at all costs. He seeks most of his support from the surrounding Players, instead of from any close family or friends. The Players assist Pippin's endless search for fulfillment, knowing that he will eventually end up worse than when he began, asking rhetorically at the end, "Nothing has been completely fulfilling now, has it, Pippin? Has it?"[18] They manipulate his desires for greatness, so that suicide ends up appearing as the only viable option for Pippin to make meaning out of his life. At this final, crucial moment, however, the Players fail to complete their objective. Instead, the widow and her son enter, ready to help Pippin and take him back into their lives.

Faced with death as his alternative, Pippin chooses an ordinary life with ordinary happiness above suicide. The Players, irritated by Pippin's choices, remove all the magic from the stage. They turn off the colored lights; take the costumes off Pippin, the widow, and the son; remove the sets; and basically leave them with the bare possibility of real life.[19] This final reaction by the Players reveals their game all along: fooling Pippin into a trajectory that leads to suicide. All of the lights, fun, and song provided by the Players contained a dark promise of eventual failure, a magical manipulation to achieve a live, grand finale of suicide by fire.[20] Pippin finally sees their magic manipulation for what it was and what it is, realizing that ordinary happiness stands as more fulfilling than all the promises of extraordinariness that only brought him trauma and scars.

Sweeney Todd and *Passion*: Two Sondheim Women Barely Hanging On

In *Sweeney Todd* and *Passion*, Stephen Sondheim presents two female characters struggling with emotional trauma and psychological damage from past sexual relationships.[21] In *Sweeney Todd*, the corrupt Judge Turpin publicly raped Lucy at a masquerade ball just after he shipped her husband to Australia. In the play, she lives a destitute life on the streets begging for money and offering sexual favors. Signora Fosca, in *Passion*, wastes away in a military encampment headed by her cousin. She obsesses over a young military man, Giorgio, and suffers from a debilitating illness brought on by a fake Count who married her to steal all her money and her parents' money. Sondheim portrays the traumatic pasts of each woman onstage in the form of flashbacks narrated by another character. He highlights how both Lucy and Fosca hover between destruction and healing by emphasizing their self-destructive tendencies.

When the audience and Sweeney first meet Lucy, she is the Beggar Woman who solicits money first, and then sex.[22] Although neither new audience members nor Sweeney himself realize it, soon after the Beggar Woman's solicitations, Mrs. Lovett reveals why the Beggar Woman acts as she does: after being raped by Judge Turpin, Lucy attempted to commit suicide by drinking arsenic.[23] What Mrs. Lovett conceals from Sweeney and the audience is the failure of this suicide attempt. In point of fact, Lucy lives on in the form of the Beggar Woman. This secret leads Sweeney to believe his wife has died, which hastens Sweeney into his revenge as the Demon Barber of Fleet Street.

Lucy's suffering from the double trauma of rape and a suicide attempt comes out in her seemingly unbalanced actions: sweetly begging for alms and then bawdily soliciting for sex[24]; kindly giving advice to Anthony Hope on Johanna and then, again, bawdily soliciting for sex[25]; sniffing suspiciously around the cannibalistic pie shop and then crying out City on Fire when no one else realizes Mrs. Lovett and Sweeney make their meat pies from human flesh[26]; and, lastly, giddily rocking a pretend baby in the barber shop, then trying to warn Sweeney about Mrs. Lovett's wiles before he kills her.[27] Through this nuanced behavior, Sondheim showcases a female character on the brink of insanity, never quite revealing the depth of her comprehension because she cannot fully access it herself. Lucy's presence gives Sondheim a stunning secret for Sweeney's character in the final scene, but also reveals the depths of self-destruction made possible by her double traumas.

In effect, Lucy acts as a type of foil to the other characters also seeking happiness and/or closure to their own personal traumas. Sweeney seeks bloody revenge to avenge his wife and child, and embraces the downward spiral into murderous barber and facilitator of cannibalistic tendencies in pie shop customers. Mrs. Lovett manipulates Sweeney Todd into being her business partner and potential lover. Johanna makes every effort to break out of the Judge's home and seek a happy life with Anthony. Lucy, however, can only just get along. She does not dream of any happiness or closure, but merely lives with the effects of both traumas, scraping by on the street. Lucy lives in the liminal state of recovery from a traumatic event: neither fully healed nor fully destroyed. Her trajectory reveals the third unspeakable option for the other characters: living with the reality of trauma, but unable to heal it or close it through suicide.

In contrast, despite her own debilitating and liminal post-traumatic state, Signora Fosca in *Passion* finds a sense of normalcy and solace to her trauma by the end of the play. Captain Giorgio Bachetti first meets Fosca through her unsettling screams and elegant piano playing that disturb the officers' mess.[28] The other officers assure him not to worry, the sounds coming from Fosca's room and her inattendance at meals are a regular occurrence. Giorgio offers to lend the woman some of his books, to assuage her loneliness, and asks the doctor about the exact nature of Fosca's condition. The doctor replies, "She is a kind of medical phenomenon.... One might say that her nerves are exposed, where ours are protected by a firm layer of skin.... Her body is so weak that it doesn't have the strength to produce a mortal disease."[29]

In this way, Sondheim places Fosca in the same liminal condition as Lucy in *Sweeney Todd*, but with Giorgio's presence he gives Fosca the ability to move towards a place of healing and recovery. Due to Giorgio's kindness in lending her books, Fosca quickly latches onto him and makes him the object of her affection. She gives flowers to him, finds times to walk and talk with him, pleads with him to be her friend, and bares her dark thoughts to his confidence. She reveals that she does not dream because they are painful. Then at a cemetery, she comments, "It's good to know that the dead here — can go to their graves..." and collapses.[30] Later, when Giorgio speaks of intoxicating love between two people, Fosca verbally lashes out at him, calling him cruel, and then seems to instantly become feverish and more ill.[31] In these moments, Fosca shows herself as fragile, cynical, lonely, broken, and emotionally dead inside. Still, Giorgio does not know why she acts this way.

In between Fosca's times of affection, Giorgio writes letters to and dreams of his lover, Clara, and their happiness in Milan. He does not hide his interactions with Fosca, blaming them on his inferior status to Fosca's cousin-in-charge, his pity for her weak, ill state, and the way her feminine presence reminds him of Clara.[32] Despite all of Giorgio's attempts to avoid Fosca, including going out on maneuvers with his men and requesting leave, Fosca persists in pursuing him. She writes him a letter, covertly speaks to him and meets him, and successfully implores him to write letters to her while away.[33] But then, when she takes a turn for the worse, her doctor encourages Giorgio to visit her bedside: "You rejected her love ... and now this refusal has increased the gravity of her disease. This woman is letting herself die because of you."[34]

The doctor's statement shows that Fosca's obsession with loving Giorgio is, in fact, an action of survival. By extending her affection to another person, Fosca had been reversing her illness. But because Giorgio rejected her extended affection, her act of survival, Fosca chooses to hasten the progress of her diseased state. Unlike Lucy, who remained in her in/sanity and in-between-ness, Fosca plays dangerously with the descent into insanity and self-destruction. Giorgio reluctantly visits Fosca on her sickbed and again writes her a letter, at her insistence. Then, when Fosca confronts him, he leaves her without remorse, and Fosca's illness begins soon after.

Even after learning this, Giorgio continues fighting Fosca's attentions, calling her selfish and smothering, and eventually arguing loudly with her in the rain.[35] This experience causes them both to fall ill, and afterwards, Fosca calmly explains her all-consuming love for Giorgio as something she can't control. This honest confrontation marks a turning point for Giorgio. He leaves Fosca's all-consuming passion for Clara's now-seemingly superficial passion, and quickly returns to the military camp. The opening theme repeats as Giorgio sings, "I thought I knew what love was." This effectively reverses his original line to Clara, "I never knew what love was," from the opening scene.[36] By the end, Giorgio sees in Fosca's obsession a type of all-consuming, unselfish, unconditional love that he and Clara never came close to having. Giorgio realizes he still has much to learn about the differences between the passion of love and the passion of happiness.

For Fosca, Giorgio's love gives her the freedom to die in peace. Her last spoken words to Giorgio are, "To die loved is to have lived."[37] And in her last letter to him, she affirms that his love made her pain disappear.

In effect then, Giorgio's love healed her from her past trauma; his presence and his returning of her affections ended her liminal state of in/sanity. Fosca's comparatively happy ending shows the possibilities for Lucy in *Sweeney Todd*. If given a chance at repeating past actions with positive endings, these traumatized women have a chance. Even though Fosca dies just as Lucy, Fosca dies in a state of peace and contentment. Lucy, on the other hand, dies without receiving closure from her trauma. Only in death, with a peaceful face, does her husband recognize her and realize the ways in which Mrs. Lovett blinded him with her lies. Lucy does not feel love again and thus, according to Sondheim, does not have a chance at recuperating from her trauma. Fosca, on the other hand, has the ability to relentlessly pursue her love for Giorgio, and is rewarded with a blissful ending.

Thus, with these two women, Sondheim reveals the necessity of sympathetic supporters to healing the victims of traumatic events. Lucy and Fosca each posit two different scenarios: one to a violent death and one to a peaceful death. In the "great black pit" of London, Lucy's attempted suicide does not garner any sympathy or motivate any assistance from those around her. So she enters a liminal state where she wavers between sanity and insanity, and her lucid moments are overlooked due to her apparent instability. In the remote provincial military encampment, however, Fosca's attempted suicide and moments of lucid honesty motivates sympathy from Giorgio and redeems them both in the end.

Miss Saigon: Kim's Constant War

In *Miss Saigon*, Alain Boublil and Claude-Michel Schönberg adapted the story of *Madame Butterfly* to address the plight of Amerasian children, or *bui-doi*, from the Vietnam War. By highlighting Kim's struggle during and after the war, they reveal the effects of PTSD on simultaneously inspiring and crushing dreams. This balancing act again emphasizes the incomplete existence of a character with PTSD. Kim copes with two traumas within the play: the initial one of watching her village and parents burn before her eyes and then the Fall of Saigon that separates her from her lover, Chris, a United States Marine. Within Kim's struggle for escape and control, Boublil and Schönberg illustrate a PTSD-influenced trajectory to self-destruction that ends up liberating Kim from her constant war for peace.

Kim arrives in the "Onstage/Dreamland" sequence, a young woman of seventeen from the village, fresh to Saigon's streets and the club atmosphere of prostitution. She imagines a better future than as a bar girl, dreaming of the man who will allow her to escape that life.[38] In this way, early on, Kim reveals her dreams of safety and peace, away from violence.[39] This contrasts with her past trauma, a tale she reluctantly tells to Chris the next morning about her forced marriage, her family's death, and the destruction of her village.[40] Kim emphasizes her desire to recover from her past, not to belabor it or pretend many other young Vietnamese women have not suffered the same story. This confirms why she dreams of a man who will "keep us safe all day" from anyone who might "blow the dream away." Indeed, Kim illustrates her determined avoidance by resolving, "I would rather die," than face a similar trauma again.

After hearing this, Chris's feelings for Kim overtake his lingering cynicism: Kim leaves the club and they live together. Thuy, Kim's cousin and former betrothed, interrupts their happy sojourn with anger, violence, threats against Chris, and promises of a communist victory. Kim prevents Thuy from shooting, daring him to shoot her instead of Chris. So Thuy leaves, swearing her parents will curse her.[41] Kim's behavior in this scene confirms her earlier resolution: she would rather be killed than be dragged back to a violent past. In Kim's understanding, a return to Thuy would end her future dreams by throwing her back into the violent world of the past. For Kim, Chris represents the safe future of which she dreams, whereas Thuy represents the violent past from which she still runs.

After this violent encounter, Chris promises to take Kim to the United States with him "on the other side of the Earth" to "a place where life still has worth,"[42] and where they can escape the turmoil of Vietnam. They "dance like it's the last night of the world," and in fact, it is: the Fall of Saigon will happen the following day. After this song, the play fast forwards three years, showing Kim living in postwar Vietnam and Chris married to another woman. Thuy finds Kim again, telling her she must be his bride as their parents promised. Kim refuses, and Thuy calls in his men to beat her. Kim finally reveals the reason she can still believe in Chris's return: she gave birth to their son, Tam. "[T]his is my son, he has kept me alive."[43]

Then, after Thuy threatens to kill Tam, Kim shoots him with Chris's gun.[44] This further illustrates Kim's resolve to separate herself from her past by any means possible. Though now burdened by a second major trauma and still living in Vietnam, Kim shows resilience and even resorts to violence in order to attain a future for her son and herself. Tam now embodies the future, and Kim will do anything to protect him and the future he represents. With the help of her former employer at the bar, the Engineer, Kim and her son flee to Bangkok and she sings to her son that she would die for him if that would give her son a better chance at life.[45] This transformation marks Kim as a devoted mother above anything else, showing her son as both her lifeline for survival and her motivation for continuing to dream of a future with Chris.

Midway through Act 2, Kim learns from John, Chris's best friend, that Chris has arrived in Bangkok. Her dreams finally seem to be coming true, and her liminal state seems to be coming to an end. But, on the verge of achieving the final closure to her violent past, Thuy's ghost rises up and haunts her, reminding her that Chris abandoned her before. Kim flashes back to her second trauma, the Fall of Saigon, Chris leaving her to prepare their departure, and her unsuccessful attempts to gain access to the United States embassy.[46] This sequence begins as a nightmare and then unfolds in full up to the final helicopter rescue from the embassy. The flashback reveals the incomplete nature of Kim's recovery and that she does not yet have closure or a sense of normalcy.[47] After waking from the nightmare, Kim consoles herself by dreaming of their love being reborn when she finally sees Chris again. But, instead of finding Chris and a reborn love at his hotel, Kim finds Ellen, Chris's new wife.

As she sees her dreams evaporate, Kim's liminal state descends into desperation.[48] Realizing that her dream of living with Chris as his wife will not materialize, Kim tries to convince Ellen to take Tam back to the United States. Kim is willing to live without her own dream so that her son will "not live his life in the streets like a rat."[49] This scene reveals Kim's continued attempts to control her own life and provide her own ending to the trauma. Ellen adamantly refuses this option, as well. Denied both dreams, Kim's anger boils over. Then she demands that Chris tell her that his son has no future in person at her apartment.

With this, Kim sets in motion her final attempt at achieving a peaceful and hopeful future. She does not accept Ellen's refusal or denial, once more showing her struggle and persistence to achieve her dreams of a peaceful life. Even in the face of seeming failure, Kim perseveres, determined to bring about her desired future for her son. Driven simultaneously by her past nightmares and future dreams, Kim seeks to end the cycle of trauma that has so far defined both their lives. Back home, Kim sings about how she is now the one in control of the ending.[50] When Chris finally arrives, Kim shoots herself with his gun, forcing Chris and Ellen to take Tam with them back to the United States.

All along, then, Kim tries to flee from past trauma and redefine her life as normal, calm, and peaceful. Yet, she never fully deals with her traumas, dreaming instead of the future where no trauma will occur. When Chris arrives, she puts all these dreams on him and their love. By displacing her damage into future dreams, Kim creates a false sense of normalcy for herself that exists as a type of movie in her mind. In her liminal state, she can hope for a future that will resolve her suffering. Once Tam enters the picture, her dream movie plays out as Chris "teaching him to fly paper dragons in the sky."[51] Additionally, Tam embodies the future in his person, showing to Kim day after day that her time with Chris was not imagined and so a future is possible. Repeatedly, however, persons and memories from her violent past upset her dreams, reminding her of her origins, further trapping her in violence, and delaying or destroying any sense of security for her and Tam. As each obstacle presents itself and extends her feeling of liminality, Kim responds with increasing intensity: she offers herself to Thuy's gun, then kills Thuy, and eventually kills herself.

Thus, with each disturbance of her dream, Kim grows more and more desperate to escape the traumas that seem to envelop her. As Chris's best friend astutely observes, "You didn't see what was in that girl's head,"[52] recognizing Kim's formidable determination to provide a peaceful future for Tam, if not for herself. In the end, as with Lucy and Fosca, Kim hastens her own destruction. Her final act of suicide doubles as an act of self-sacrifice for her son, Tam, and also liberates all the main characters. She frees Chris from feeling obligated to her, Ellen from feeling jealous of Kim's connection to Chris, herself from a life of pain and violence, and Tam from a life on the streets as a physical reminder of the Vietnam War. Kim believes this act enables her to watch over her son from above, as well, freeing her from the potential guilt of abandoning her child. Above all, her final act of suicide brings an end to her liminal state, granting her peace and closure just as it granted these same things to Lucy and Fosca.

The Who's Tommy: *A Child Responds to Trauma*

In *The Who's Tommy*, a violent act also brings about the young protagonist's struggle, and this musical strongly emphasizes the physical effects brought on by PTSD.[53] It follows Tommy's journey as he attempts to deal with witnessing his father's murder of another man. Throughout the musical, Tommy has various selves who manifest themselves in flesh and in mirrors. These mirrors, Tommy's introspective numbers, and physical incapacitation all emphasize the dissociative symptoms of PTSD and the healing power of integrating past and present into one person's story.[54]

Captain Walker, Tommy's father, goes MIA in World War II, and his mother finds another lover. Captain Walker returns when Tommy is four years old, sees his wife with another man, and shoots the man dead before his wife and son. After this act, the adults turn to Tommy and insist that he heard nothing, saw nothing and will not say anything about it.[55] They repeat this mantra several times, not knowing it will soon manifest within Tommy's person: Tommy will not hear, see, or speak from that moment forward. The Walkers try several remedies to cure Tommy, all to no avail.

Upon Tommy's lapse into deafness, muteness, and blindness, the narrator Tommy appears onstage. Through the narrator, the audience learns of Tommy's feelings. The adult Tommy also communicates with the young Tommy, first the four-year-old then the ten-year-old. He sings of the Amazing Journey of sickness and delirium on which Tommy is about to embark.[56] In this haze of delirium, Tommy passes from doctor to doctor, among family members, and then surprisingly reveals his prowess at playing pinball. This gives him instant stardom, and his family continues trying cure after cure. His father, desperate to try anything, even sets up Tommy with a prostitute, but then cannot go through with it.[57] Throughout, Tommy encounters himself in the mirror, and the narrator reveals Tommy's inner monologue through song.

Eventually, his mother grows tired of Tommy always staring in the mirror but not interacting with anyone or anything besides a pinball machine. She smashes the mirror, and Tommy regains his sight, hearing, and speaking abilities.[58] This moment represents the breaking down of Tommy's dissociative barrier inside of himself, but he still has not fully dealt with his family's role in his past and his present life. As the cured pinball wizard, Tommy ascends to even greater celebrity status. When he tries to insist that he aspires to be a normal, average person, and regular folks should not aspire to attain his kind of celebrity, Tommy's fans desert him. At this moment, the mirror appears again with his younger selves inside of it. But instead of regressing back to his dissociative state, Tommy turns to his family and embraces them. This moment shows that Tommy has completed his healing process.

Thus, Tommy's journey ends only when he can complete two steps: breaking out of his dissociative behavior and reconciling his past with his present. Only when he fully accepts that his family and his past trauma will always remain as part of him and his story can Tommy finalize the healing process and bring closure to the event. In addition, his two younger selves disappear from their separated state, simultaneously moving into Tommy's past and into Tommy's narrative of self. This illustrates Tommy integrating them into his personal narrative, instead of trying to live the impossible paradox of separate selves within one person's body. In this way, the ending of Tommy's journey through PTSD and liminality ends with both Tommy and his family integrated into singular units, instead of physically and emotionally fractured.

Conclusion

In sum, these musicals reveal the challenges of living with PTSD without any effective means of resolving the liminal state created by that trauma. For Pippin, Fosca, and Kim, the PTSD escalated as their attempts at finding normalcy or closure continued failing. While Pippin's efforts ended with ordinary happiness, Fosca's and Kim's work ended in peaceful deaths that liberated the women from their constant struggle. For Lucy, her lengthy time suffering from PTSD highlighted her insanity above her sanity. This marginalized her lucid observations and influence over the musical's characters, allowing Sweeney to continue his path of vengeance. Finally, for Tommy, his lengthy time in the grips of PTSD sharply challenged his ability to grow and mature from childhood to adulthood. His only liberation lay in recognizing the connectedness already present within himself, which enabled him to move forward into a sense of normalcy.

Thus, these musicals do not gloss over the trials associated with recovering from a traumatic event such as rape, murder, war, or violence. In their own ways, each reveal multiple challenges to recovery, including the ghosts or voices goading a character into unproductive behaviors, the unbalanced state brought on by suicide attempts, the debilitating nature of long-term PTSD, the changing circumstances of life, and the fractured psyche that strengthens dissociative actions within a young victim. These musicals demonstrate that, at any point, a character suffering from PTSD can easily relapse or descend into deeply destructive behaviors and emphasize the need for rehabilitative therapy with family support when possible.

NOTES

1. For contrast, the recent Pulitzer prize–and Tony award–winning musical, *Next to Normal*, deals with bipolar depression more directly. Ben Brantley, "Fragmented Psyches, Uncomfortable Emotions: Sing Out!" nytimes.com, April 16, 2009, accessed December 23, 2010, http://theater.nytimes.com/2009/04/16/theater/reviews/16norm.html.

2. The dates in parentheses represent the years of each musical's world premiere, whether on the West End or Broadway.

3. *The Diagnostic and Statistical Manual of Mental Disorders Fourth Edition Text Revision* (Washington, DC: American Psychiatric Association, 2000).

4. Michael B. First, "309.81 Posttraumatic Stress Disorder," in *Diagnostic and Statistical Manual of Mental Disorders Fourth Edition* (Washington, DC: American Psychiatric Association, 2000), accessed Dec 23, 2010, http://online.statref.com/document.aspx?fxid=37&docid=230.

5. See also Matthew J. Friedman, Patricia A. Resick, and Terence M. Keane, "PTSD: Twenty-Five Years of Progress and Challenges," in *Handbook of PTSD: Science and Practice*, eds. Matthew J. Friedman, Terence M. Keane, and Patricia A. Resick (New York: Guilford Press, 2007), 4–6.

6. Stephen Schwartz and Robert O. Hirson, *Pippin: A Musical Comedy* (New York: Drama Book Specialists, 1975), 5. Stephen Schwartz, *Pippin (1972 Original Broadway Cast Recording)*, recorded in 1972 (New York: Universal Classics Group, 2000), compact disc. For all musicals, I consulted the most complete record of music and book available. For those for which a complete, published book and lyrics exist, I will cite the musical CD only in the first note pertaining to that particular musical.

7. Schwartz and Hirson, 6–7.

8. Ibid., 14.

9. Ibid., 20–21.

10. Ibid., 26.

11. Ibid., 30–35.

12. Cross-reference the definition of PTSD in the DSM-IV, which includes: "Traumatic events that are experienced directly include, but are not limited to, military combat" and "Witnessed events include, but are not limited to, observing the serious injury or unnatural death of another person due to violent assault, accident, war, or disaster or unexpectedly witnessing a dead body or body parts." First, "309.81."

13. Schwartz and Hilson, 42–46.

14. Ibid., 53–55.

15. Ibid., 75–76.

16. Ibid., 76.

17. For the comorbidity of depression and PTSD, see Leo Sher, "Suicide in War Veterans: The Role of Comorbidity of PTSD and Depression," in *Expert Review of Neurotherapeutics*, Vol. 9, No. 7 (2009), 921–923.

18. Schwartz and Hirson, 74.

19. Ibid., 81–83.

20. For a narrative correlation to the Players' role in *Pippin*, see Ron Capps' personal account of his PTSD struggle in "Back from the Brink: War, Suicide, and PTSD," in *Health Affairs* (2009): 1407–1410, doi: 10.1377/HLTHAFF.2009.0827.

21. Cross-reference the DSM-IV: "Traumatic events that are experienced directly include, but are not limited to ... violent personal assault (sexual assault, physical attack, robbery, mugging)." As far as symptoms and behaviors, "the disturbance must cause clinically significant distress or impairment in social, occupational, or other important areas of functioning." First, "309.81."

22. Stephen Sondheim and Hugh Wheeler, *Sweeney Todd: The Demon Barber of Fleet Street* (New York: Dodd, Mead, 1979), 6–7. Stephen Sondheim, *Sweeney Todd [Original Broadway Cast]*, recorded March 12 and 13, 1979 (New York: RCA, 1990), 2 compact discs. Lucy's behavior falls roughly into the described "numbing of general responsiveness" and "persistent symptoms of increased arousal" from First, "309.81," in DSM-IV. Her actions also fall into the previously noted "distress or impairment in social, occupational, or other important areas of functioning." Since Lucy has the added factor of arsenic poisoning, she has the additional complication of damage from that experience.

23. Sondheim and Wheeler, *Sweeney Todd*, 17–19.

24. Ibid., 6–7.

25. Ibid., 27–28.

26. Ibid., 112, 117, 127, 129, 130.

27. Ibid., 173–176.

28. Stephen Sondheim and James Lapine, *Passion: A Musical* (New York: Theatre Communications Group, 1994), 10–14. Stephen Sondheim, *Passion—A New Musical—Original Broadway Cast Recording*, recorded May 29, 1994 (New York: Universal Music, 2002), compact disc. Fosca's avoidance of men and personal interactions reflects a "response to the event must involve intense fear, helplessness, or horror," "persistent avoidance of stimuli associated with the trauma and numbing of general responsiveness," as well as "persistent symptoms of increased arousal." See First, "309.81," in DSM-IV.

29. Sondheim and Lapine, *Passion*, 17, 18.

30. Ibid., 23, 26.

31. Ibid., 34–36.

32. Ibid., 27, 31, 37.

33. Ibid., 39, 40.

34. Ibid., 54.

35. Ibid., 89–92.

36. Ibid., 8, 117. See also Giorgio's final letter to Clara, on 116, in which he says that love isn't convenient and can't be scheduled. He asks, "What's love unless it's unconditional?"

37. Ibid., 123.

38. Claude-Michel Schönberg, Alain Boublil and Richard Maltby, Jr., "The Movie in My Mind," from *Miss Saigon—1995 Complete Symphonic Recording*, recorded 1995 (London: Exallshow, 1995), 2 compact discs. This two-compact disc recording contains complete dialogue and lyrics that are missing from some of the earlier cast recordings. If necessary in later notes, I will note significant lyric differences between this recording and the original London recording.

39. Cross-reference earlier notes on avoidance behaviors in those suffering from PTSD.

40. Schönberg, Boublil, Maltby, Jr., "This Money's Yours," from *Miss Saigon*.

41. Ibid., "Thuy's Arrival."

42. Ibid., "The Last Night of the World."

43. Ibid., "Back in Town."

44. Before shooting, Kim repeatedly insists that Thuy will not harm Tam and that Tam is what she lives for and is her "only joy." Schönberg, Boublil, Maltby, Jr., "Thuy's Death/You Will Not Touch Him," from *Miss Saigon*.
Schönberg, Boublil, Maltby, Jr., "I'd Give My Life for You," from *Miss Saigon*.

45. Schönberg, Boublil, Maltby, Jr., "I'd Give My Life for You," from *Miss Saigon*.

46. Ibid., "Kim's Nightmare." See also Edward Behr and Mark Steyn, *The Story of Miss Saigon* (New York: Arcade Publishing, 1991), 104.

47. Kim's nightmare stands as the clearest example of a key PTSD symptom, that of reexperiencing the trauma. Since Pippin does not recall the war or violence in a flashback manner, and both Lucy's and Fosca's tragedies are narrated by external characters, they also do not directly fall into the reexperiencing symptom. "The traumatic event can be reexperienced in various ways. Commonly the person has recurrent and intrusive recollections of the event ... or recurrent distressing dreams during which the event can be replayed or otherwise represented." First, "309.81," in DSM-IV.

48. Schönberg, Boublil, Maltby, Jr., "Room 317," from *Miss Saigon*.

49. Ibid.

50. Schönberg, Boublil, Maltby, Jr., "Finale," from *Miss Saigon*.

51. Ibid., "The Confrontation."

52. Ibid., "The Confrontation." See also, "Please."

53. In the book published about the musical, Pete Townshend and Chad Sylvain emphasize how Tommy's symptoms are similar to autism. I differ, finding the musical more closely reflects PTSD than autism. Pete Townshend, *The Who's Tommy* (New York: Pantheon Books, 1993), 32, 46. Pete Townshend, *The Who's Tommy (Original Cast Recording)*, recorded in 1992 (New York: RCA Victor Broadway, 1993), 2 compact discs.

54. "In rare instances, the person experiences dissociative states that last from a few seconds to several hours, or even days, during which components of the event are relived and the person behaves as though experiencing the event at that moment." Also: "Diminished responsiveness to the external world, referred to as "psychic numbing" or 'emotional anesthesia,' usually begins soon after the traumatic event. The individual may complain of having markedly diminished interest or participation in previously enjoyed activities ..., of feeling detached or estranged from other people ..., or of having markedly reduced ability to feel emotions (especially those associated with intimacy, tenderness, and sexuality)." First, "309.81," in DSM-IV. See also John A. Fairbank, Frank W. Putnam, and William W. Harris, "The Prevalence and Impact of Child Traumatic Stress," in *Handbook of PTSD*, 229–251.

55. Townshend, *Tommy* (Pantheon Books), 32.
56. Ibid., 50.
57. Ibid., 75–77.
58. Ibid., 110.

BIBLIOGRAPHY

Behr, Edward, and Mark Steyn. *The Story of Miss Saigon*. New York: Arcade Publishing, 1991.
Brantley, Ben. "Fragmented Psyches, Uncomfortable Emotions: Sing Out!" nytimes.com, April 16, 2009. Accessed December 23, 2010, http://theater.nytimes.com/2009/04/16/theater/reviews/16norm.html.
Caps, Ron. "Back from the Brink: War, Suicide, and PTSD." In *Health Affairs* Vol. 29, No. 7 (2009): 1407–1410.
Fairbank, John A., Frank W. Putnam, and William W. Harris. "The Prevalence and Impact of Child Traumatic Stress." In *Handbook of PTSD: Science and Practice*, edited by Matthew J. Friedman, Terence M. Keane, and Patricia A. Resick, 229–251. New York: Guilford Press, 2007.
First, Michael B. *Diagnostic and Statistical Manual of Mental Disorders Fourth Edition*. Washington, DC: American Psychiatric Association, 2000. Accessed December 23, 2010. http://online.statref.com/document.aspx?fxid=37&docid=230.
Friedman, Matthew J., Patricia A. Resick, and Terence M. Keane. "PTSD: Twenty-Five Years of Progress and Challenges." In *Handbook of PTSD: Science and Practice*, edited by Matthew J. Friedman, Terence M. Keane, and Patricia A. Resick, 3–18. New York: Guilford Press, 2007.
Schönberg , Claude-Michel, Alain Boublil, and Richard Maltby, Jr. *Miss Saigon: 1995 Complete Symphonic Recording*. Recorded 1995. London: Exallshow, 1995. 2 compact discs.
Schwartz, Stephen, *Pippin (1972 Original Broadway Cast Recording)*. Recorded in 1972. New York: Universal Classics Group, 2000. Compact disc.
Schwartz, Stephen, and Robert O. Hirson. *Pippin: A Musical Comedy*. New York: Drama Book Specialists, 1975.
Sher, Leo. "Suicide in War Veterans: The Role of Comorbidity of PTSD and Depression." *Expert Review of Neurotherapeutics* Vol. 9, No. 7 (2009): 921–923.
Sondheim, Stephen. *Passion—A New Musical—Original Broadway Cast Recording*. Recorded May 29, 1994. New York: Universal Music, 2002. Compact disc.
Sondheim, Stephen. *Sweeney Todd [Original Broadway Cast]*. Recorded March 12 and 13, 1979. New York: RCA, 1990. 2 compact discs.
Sondheim, Stephen, and Hugh Wheeler. *Sweeney Todd: The Demon Barber of Fleet Street*. New York: Dodd, Mead, 1979.
Sondheim, Stephen, and James Lapine. *Passion: A Musical*. New York: Theatre Communications Group, 1994.
Townshend, Pete. *The Who's Tommy*. New York: Pantheon Books, 1993.
Townshend, Pete. *The Who's Tommy (Original Cast Recording)*. Recorded in 1992. New York: RCA Victor Broadway, 1993. 2 compact discs.

9

Bad Girls

From Eve to Britney

WANDA LITTLE FENIMORE

> Words have power. They have the power to hurt or soothe, to honor
> or insult, to inform or misinform. Words reflect and shape prevailing
> attitudes, attitudes that in turn shape social behavior. And words —
> disparaging and disrespectful labels in particular — inflict emotional
> pain to those to whom they are applied.[1]
> — Otto F. Wahl, *Media Madness: Public Images of Mental Illness*

In 2005, the National Institute of Mental Health reported that twenty-
six percent of adults in the United States have some type of serious mental
disorder.[2] Yet those with mental illness are one of the few remaining groups
who are subject to thoughtless labeling and ridicule; it is acceptable to parody
the mentally ill.[3] In their study of print media in New Zealand, Coverdale et
al. determined that "print media portrayals [of the mentally ill] are negative,
exaggerated, and do not reflect the reality of most people with mental illness.[4]
Other studies, in the United States and abroad, support these findings.[5] On
the whole, the media represent persons with mental illness as different, vulnerable, unpredictable, violent, and childlike. Richard Dyer states, "How we
are seen determines in part how we are treated; how we treat others is based
on how we see them; such seeing comes from representations."[6] Therefore,
media portrayals, both fictional and non-fictional, of marginalized groups
significantly influence public perceptions and, consequently, behavior towards
members of the groups.

   In this chapter, my purpose is to examine how the news production
process and gender biases impact the news media's reports of three female
celebrities: Britney Spears, Lindsay Lohan, and the late Amy Winehouse.[7]
Each woman has a reputation for sexuality and a history of substance abuse,

mental illness, and legal problems. The news media depict them as "bad girls," relying upon naturalized assumptions of the definition of a "bad girl." The taken-for-granted suppositions of a "bad girl" are rooted in the story of Biblical Eve, and are propounded further because journalists rely upon a commonly-held repertoire of cultural symbols. Instead of delving deeper into potential underlying causes of these women's behavior, the media construct them as the Other, or socially deviant. As a result, the bad girl persona, as developed by the media, perpetuates the stigma of mental illness and substance abuse. By further entrenching the shame and embarrassment associated with mental illness, the news media are not serving the public interest and in fact are doing a disservice to those people suffering with legitimate mental health issues.

Method

For my study, I will be employing a two-pronged approach that incorporates elements of political economy and critical discourse analysis. I will be examining various news articles, or discourses, about Spears, Lohan, and Winehouse, but am also suggesting that specific word choices and language in the articles are the by-product of the news media's overriding concern with the financial bottom line. Using two methods is necessary because my analysis is not one-dimensional; instead, it involves an assessment of how production values and profit motive (political economy) influence language and word choice (critical discourse analysis).

According to Robert McChesney, political economy is multi-faceted.[8] First, a political economy analysis examines how media and content reinforce, challenge, or influence existing class and social relations. Second, political economy explores how media ownership, support mechanisms (e.g., advertising), and government policies influence media behavior and content.[9] More specifically, political economy involves studying how advertising and commercial values "implicitly and explicitly determine or influence the nature of media content."[10] Also, political economy favors the value of extending democracy to all aspects of social life[11] and is driven by its "explicit commitment to participatory democracy."[12] The idea of a participatory democracy is significant especially as it relates to marginalized groups, because democracy "works best when there is minimal social inequality and when there is a general sense that any individual's well-being is closely related to the welfare of the community."[13] Participatory democracy depends upon a multitude of voices being heard. Unfortunately, negative and inaccurate portrayals of certain groups in the media mean their voices are left unheard.

Critical discourse analysis (CDA) is also concerned with social inequality.

It is not a specific method or theory, per se, but instead, an approach that is problem-oriented, focusing on relations of power and dominance. John Flowerdew states that CDA is a specific agenda for bringing about social change, or at least supporting struggle against inequality.[14] Critical discourse analysis focuses on how social relations, identity, knowledge, and power are constructed through written and spoken texts, and how these texts may, or may not, legitimize control and relations of inequality.

Allan Luke explains that discourses, or texts, construct representations of the world, social identities, and social relationships and that these same discourses constitute our ways of knowing, valuing, and experiencing the world.[15] Knowledge is generated and circulates through discourses. Dominance may be enacted and reproduced by subtle, routine, everyday forms of text and talk that appear quite natural and acceptable. One of the goals of critical discourse analysis is to reveal how these naturalized texts operate to maintain existing power relations and the oppression of certain groups.

Objects of Analysis

The news articles were selected from three electronic databases: Lexis-Nexis, Academic Search Complete, and Access World News. I used the individual woman's name (Britney Spears, Amy Winehouse, or Lindsay Lohan) as the search term, and specified articles of more than 500 words. The sources include *USA Today*, *People Magazine*, *New York Times*, *Rolling Stone Magazine*, *Guardian Unlimited* (England), and *Los Angeles Times* as well as additional mainstream news organizations. I gathered approximately twenty articles about Spears written at different points between 2004 and 2008; approximately twenty articles about Winehouse written between 2007 and 2009; and approximately twenty articles about Lohan written between 2008 and 2010.

News Media in the United States

Media in the United States are privately owned and operate within a capitalist economic structure. In other words, the government does not directly fund or subsidize them. As a result, the media depend on advertising for revenue. With this structure of advertiser-supported media, revenue is dependent upon ratings. What this means is that a news organization must increase its readership in order to sell enough advertising at a high enough rate to ensure it is profitable or as Gamson et al. explain, "Media organizations use news and other programming as a commodity to attract an audience which they can then sell to advertisers."[16] Most Americans would agree that advertiser-supported media is better than the alternative: news media that are owned, funded, or censored by the government. However, it places a burden on media, and in their attempt to garner ratings and advertising sales, news media resort to yellow or tabloid journalism. According to Croteau and Hoynes, yellow or tabloid journalism is a more sensational version of the news, full of inflammatory headlines and garish pictures, with stories that focus on sex and scandal.[17] Tabloid journalism is not emblematic of the twenty-first century; it's been around as long as there have been journalists and newspapers. But today, with technology offering immediate, no-holds barred access, and intense competition among news organizations, sensationalism has reached new heights. Or is it lows?

I would argue that the overarching search for profit results in news stories that are less substantive, more scandal-ridden, and more sensationalized. The production values inherent in profit-seeking result in news stories that are brief, trivialized, and depoliticized with news organizations placed between a rock and a hard place, an irresolvable dilemma, "Do they [news media] attempt to battle the tide, provide hard-hitting and powerful political journalism even if it costs more and may not have a great deal of immediate market demand, in the hope of generating a strong market for news down the road?"[18] Faced with the prospect of losing readers and advertising dollars, very few news organizations will battle the tide. Consequently, the bottom line triumphs over social and journalistic responsibility.

Just like any other business, news media try to keep expenses low and to increase sales to maximize profit. One way to keep expenses low is to write stories using a syntactical, or episodic, structure. Also known as the inverted pyramid, this structure emphasizes the most important aspects of a story first, allowing an editor to delete information from the end without losing the essence of the story.[19] This format is popular among newspaper editors because it offers flexibility when determining how much space to devote to a story and it also allows a busy reader to get the gist of the story just by reading the headline and first few paragraphs. Gamson et al. describe the episodic format as an event-oriented report that depicts concrete instances.[20] Also, as Murdock and Golding explain, this format concentrates on "superficial eruptions and the dramatic, on form rather than content [...]"[21] While technically accurate, this type of story is often misleading, because without any additional explanation or analysis, it often reinforces existing ideas and stereotypes.[22] However, because it is less costly to produce and takes less effort on the part of the reader, it is the dominant structure in the news.

An alternative to the episodic format is the thematic structure; however, it is most commonly found in non-news, or features, sections, because it is more time-consuming and costly. The thematic format is longer, more detailed, more complex, and more expensive to produce. Seiff explains, "These structures pull together events, sources, and propositions that flow together with logical reasoning to form a hypothesis or state a causal relationship."[23]Utilizing a thematic structure involves describing conditions, general outcomes, with supporting statistical evidence.[24] When considering mental illness, a story written in the thematic format would offer more than mere behavioral manifestations of the disorder, instead including an interview with a mental health service provider, discussion about the temporary nature of most disorders, or positive accounts of recovery.

Because the news media are profit-seeking businesses, their product, the news, is a commodity. News must be entertainment, because as a commodity, it must survive in the marketplace by attracting the largest audience that is attractive to advertisers,[25] often resorting to the titillating, sensational, and dramatic.[26] One way to entertain is to forgo "hard news" and instead focus on celebrities, especially their personal lives. These types of stories are popular, profitable, and easier to cover than political or other substantive reporting.[27] In other words, viewing pleasures (and sales) subordinate other concerns.[28]

To summarize, the news media resort to celebrity lifestyle reporting because it is less expensive and attracts the audiences needed to sell to advertisers. Stuart argues "[...] media coverage may be negative as a result of broader industry pressures that foster particular angles in storylines, such as the need to sensationalise in order to gain a competitive edge, a lack of time to do otherwise, lack of access to mental health experts to present opposing views and other industry constraints."[29] Using the less costly and less detailed episodic format to write about celebrities with mental health or substance abuse issues diminishes the opportunity for accurate, empathetic or positive reporting that could potentially increase the public's understanding of mental illness. Instead, sensational and dramatic headlines catch the attention of readers, increasing sales and potential profit.

Consensus: We-ness and Other-ness

The news media serve an important function in society by offering an integrated picture of reality. This reality is constructed so that it presents the most broadly held common social values and assumptions in order to establish common ground between the news organization and the audience.[30] Hall et al. identify this process as the consensual nature of society whereby journalists and readers "share a common stock of cultural knowledge with our fellow men; we have access to the same 'maps of meanings.'"[31] The news takes the unexplained, the unexpected, the problematic, and structures it as comprehensible.

"News becomes a means of handling change, a comforting reaffirmation of the existing social order."[32] This process depends upon the journalists and readers sharing knowledge, interpretative resources, and collective symbols. Therefore, as Hall et al. state, "An event only 'makes sense' if it can be located within a range of known social and cultural identifications."[33] Journalists must write stories that readers can comprehend, because if readers can't understand the story, they'll quit buying.

According to Murdock and Golding, consensus is affirmed by the news media when a "uniform moral community is reinforced, laying claim to what is generally accepted as right and proper, as well as what is generally known."[34] The assumption is that we all have the same fundamental interests, values, and concerns in common as well as an equal share of power in society.[35] This consensus constructs "we-ness, a common community between medium and audience, to encapsulate the widest possible audience."[36] Hall et al. state that this consensual view represents society as culturally united, without class divisions, conflict, or controversy. It is a view that is depoliticized but appeals to the most lucrative market, the middle and upper classes. Golding and Elliott offer that "[...] it is also the world view of particular social groups, and especially social classes."[37]

This consensual world view situates journalists and readers as a collective "We" with shared knowledge about what is socially acceptable, as well as what is morally good and right. This process reaffirms the existing social order whereby members of the "We" group belong, and those who do not belong are constructed as the Other. The Other consists of marginalized groups such as homosexuals, African-Americans, Muslims, and those with mental illness. Negative depictions of these marginalized groups in the media establish and solidify the boundaries between We and Them, or the Other. Through repeated exposure to these unflattering and one-dimensional representations, readers unquestionably accept these differences as natural. Also, by not resisting these boundaries, readers confirm their membership within "We," reassuring themselves of their rightness and goodness.

The Original Bad Girl: Biblical Eve

Mary Daly writes, "Society as we know it has a perverse need to create 'the other' as object of condemnation so those that condemn can judge themselves to be good. [...] Eve was such a production."[38] Eve, as the original woman, is held responsible for the Fall of Man — not Adam, not Satan disguised as the serpent, not God, but Eve, and Eve alone. The Bible paints a picture of women as the cause of sinful behavior among men, being the causal and active agents in bringing about the transgressions of men.[39] This view of Eve as the sinner who causes problems for men and for all of humankind pervades contemporary society.[40] As the original woman, Eve symbolizes all women, signifying the essence of female existence.[41] The essence of female existence is "all that is base, lustful, untrustworthy, wily, beguiling, deceitful, seducing, and *evil* in the universe [...]"[42]

This construction of Eve as evil, a temptress, and weak presents an interesting paradox — she is both powerful and powerless. Harris writes, "Eve is weak enough to succumb to evil and temptation, but she also has that 'feminine' strength and power capable of making a man succumb to her suggestions and desires."[43] Her power lies in her sexuality, which she uses to tempt Adam and bring about the Fall of Man. Female power, in this sense, is most often viewed as manipulative, disruptive, illegitimate, or unimportant.[44] Because she is unable to resist Satan, she is powerless, implying that women are morally weak. Lawless argues that Eve resides in all females, signifying sin, evil and "all that men cannot control."[45]

Eve, as the Other, represents bad women. However, as Daly points out, the existence of good women requires the existence of bad women.[46] Good women possess traditional feminine characteristics: passivity, submissiveness, powerlessness, and chastity. Good women also reflect Biblical notions of the proper role for women as man's helpmate, being inferior and subservient to men. When a woman exhibits behavior that is not good, she is likened to Eve. This association between Eve and evil is a naturalistic assumption, a cultural construct that defies explanation or inquiry because "that's the way things are."

Contemporary Bad Girls: Lindsay Lohan, Amy Winehouse, and Britney Spears

Lohan, Winehouse, and Spears are not what most newspaper readers would classify as good women. Instead, as they are or have been depicted in the media, they are more suited for the role of bad women, or bad girls, because they exhibit the behaviors associated with Eve, seemingly powerful and powerless at the same time. Their power is located in their sexuality, talent, fame, and wealth while their lack of power is most often reflected in their inability to resist temptation, i.e., drugs and alcohol, impulsive behavior, and lack of judgment. Women are generally seen as one of two archetypes: a virgin or the wicked, wanton woman.[47] With involuntary and voluntary hospitalizations and stays in rehabilitation centers, the women appear as if they are suffering from mental illness and substance abuse. However, the news stories about them incorporate harmful slang, stereotypes, and accounts without offering the context necessary to fully understand, or identify with, the women's behavior.

In 2004, *Rolling Stone* described the preteen Lindsay Lohan as "a charming screen presence in kid-friendly fare," but as an adult of eighteen, she was described as "what's technically known as a 'bad girl.'"[48] According to the article, Lohan is a bad girl because she'd already dated a rock star, frequented nightclubs in Los Angeles and Manhattan, and occasionally danced on tables — behaviors that journalists and readers categorize as socially unacceptable for good women.

From "charming presence" or "bad girl," journalists more recently use "train wreck" or "car wreck" to describe Lohan.[49] A train or car wreck is a mangled jumble resulting from thousands of pounds of steel careening out of control. Applying the labels of train or car wreck to a person focuses on behaviors, not underlying causes. It is demeaning, yet writers can use these terms because their readers understand the connotation. Unfortunately, Lohan was not the only woman described as a train wreck. The phrase was used on more than one occasion to describe Spears[50] and Winehouse.[51] Rush, et al. irresponsibly wrote "[...] several APA [American Psychoanalytic Association] members implored the media to stop speculating on the train wreck's [Spears's] supposed mental illness."[52] First, I'm confident that the APA did not use the words "train wreck" when speaking of Spears. Second, the journalists irreversibly linked the connotations associated with train wreck to mental illness, with the implication being that those suffering from mental illness are out of control and a jumbled mess. Using the phrases "train wreck" or "car wreck" when writing about these women confirms Stuart's assertion, "Stories are written in such a way that they require the reader to employ negative cultural stereotypes and common-sense understandings of what it means to be mentally ill, to interpret the story material and co-create the message."[53]

Common-sense understandings were abundant in story headlines with "Falling Apart,"[54] "Lindsay Lohan's Road to Ruin,"[55] "Britney Interrupted,"[55] "Britney in Crisis,"[57] "Britney Breaks into Pieces,"[58] "Yes, Amy's a tortured, mangled soul ...,"[59] "Amy's Sobering Transformation,"[60] "Amy Sent to Rehab — Help for Star after Crack Shame,"[61] and "In Real Time, Amy Winehouse's Deeper Descent."[62] News editors and journalists write headlines to grab readers' attention. These examples are inflammatory, sensational, and titillating — successful in drawing readers to articles. Generic terms for mental illness are abbreviated references that are utilized for limited space and headlines.[63] Instead of expanding or qualifying the brief snippet headlines, the articles merely provide more stereotypical language and imagery in regards to mental illness and substance abuse.

Prior to her death, in 2011 the following words or phrases were used in news articles about Amy Winehouse: chaotic personal life and being troubled[64];

trying to address her demons[65]; poster child for codependency and domestic abuse[66]; deluded[67]; exhibiting anti-social behavior[68]; junkie[69]; out of control[70]; troubled chanteuse[71]; shamed[72]; bumbling, unfocused[73]; self-sabotage[74]; and human crack pipe.[75]

The same type of language was used when writing about Britney Spears: troubled pop diva[76]; Spears saga[77]; downward spiral[78]; bizarre behavior[79]; breakdown diva, fragile persona, weird behavior[80]; out of control[81]; Britney Spears soap opera[82]; wacky chanteuse[83]; Unfitney[84]; fogged mental state[85]; deeply troubled, woman in crisis[86]; and outlandish behavior.[87]

Derogatory language was also used in the articles about Lindsay Lohan, with phrases like: wake of her latest meltdown, rehab veteran[88]; deeply troubled, out of control, self-destructive, erratic[89]; looking undone[90]; tainted image, tendencies towards self-destruction[91]; something of an idiot, watch her go down in flames[92]; thrice-rehabbed starlet[93]; serial rehabber[94]; indulged in more bad behavior than an entire rugby league team[95]; and defiant.[96]

This type of language is dramatic, but more importantly, it does not require any effort for readers to decipher because it employs existing negative imagery of the mentally ill. These women are portrayed as behaving in socially unacceptable ways that most certainly indicate mental instability. "Virtually all slang terms for mental illness have undertones of disapproval or negative judgment of some sort."[97] These slang terms are the residual of past unflattering conceptions of mental illness predating the nineteenth century: bizarre, deviant, dangerous, and unable to function in society like normal people. Attaching this type of language to these women's behavior constructs them as bad girls and consequently, links so-called bad girl behavior with mental illness.

All of the women are portrayed in the media as needing control by patriarchal institutions: Winehouse and Spears by their fathers, and Lohan by the legal system. These depictions correspond with Wahl's assertion that the media most often represent people with mental illness as needing forceful control.[98] Control of Lohan comes in the form of the court restrictions that are "meant to keep her on a short leash."[99] These restrictions include probation, community service, alcohol education classes, travel limitations, drug-testing, and an alcohol-monitoring bracelet.[100] She can't behave, or control herself, so the courts must do it for her.

Spears's father was appointed temporary conservator of her estate.[101] Mr. Spears then sought to have her manager, Howard Grossman, fired because he purportedly provided Ms. Spears with a car in violation of the court's order. Mr. Spears also requested a restraining order preventing Sam Lufti from having any contact with her.[102] Lufti reportedly drugged Spears and took "control of her life, home and finances."[103] According to *The Times*, "A court creates a conservatorship when it concludes a person no longer can care for themselves or their personal and financial affairs."[104] *People Magazine* quoted a court-appointed attorney as saying that Spears "does not understand the nature of these proceedings" and "lacks the capacity" to hire representation.[105] The articles paint a picture of Britney unable to defend herself against Lufti's machinations and having to be rescued by her father. While these reports are technically accurate, they offer minimal information about the legal requirements for a conservatorship, instead framing it as dramatically as possible. Other articles reporting on the same topic quoted Lynne Spears as saying that Britney was drugged, confused, and showing "the understanding of a very young girl,"[106] furthering the notion that the mentally ill are child-like, being incapable of independence or unable to take care of themselves.[107]

The lyrics from Winehouse's top-selling single, "Rehab," that described how her father tried to make her go into rehab despite her resistance were often quoted as a segue to interviews with Winehouse's father, Mitch Winehouse.[108] Mr. Winehouse's repeated statements to the press that he wanted his daughter forcibly locked up in a mental hospital for her own good and having her sectioned was the only way to keep her from killing herself with drugs unfortunately foreshadowed her death.[109] Amy's mother is quoted as saying, "the troubled singer needs to be rescued"[110] and that "Amy is just like a teenager who is out of control."[111] The Associated Press reports, "Concerned family members regularly beg Winehouse to seek help [...]"[112] While implying Winehouse is a danger to herself may seem an accurate representation especially since she died from alcohol toxicity, these statements construnct her as uncontrollable. The news media relied upon sensational instead of the substantial, furthering the commonly-held misconception that the mentally ill, particularly women, are unpredictable, unable to anticipate consequences or to account for one's behavior.[114] The cumulative effect is the view that sufferers are erratic, frightening unreliable, untrustworthy, and unable to cope or control their lives, therefore becoming subject to the will of others.[115]

The other implication is that Winehouse and Spears are powerless in the same sense as Eve; she is unable to resist temptation even if it means severe consequences. As with Spears, the news articles failed to elaborate on the legal requirements for a conservatorship, instead focusing on the age-old image of the mentally ill being unfit for society and having to be forcibly locked up. Reporting that Ms. Winehouse's family feared for her safety and Mr. Spears was appointed conservator over Ms. Spears's estate may make for good drama, but they are incomplete stories because they lack the details or context necessary to resist the stereotypical image of the mentally ill as being unable to care for themselves.

The image of the mentally ill needing to be forcibly restrained was asserted numerous times in the articles about Britney Spears. When reporting on Spears's hospitalizations, she was described as "being carted away in a daze by paramedics" and "taken from her home yet again by ambulance"[116]; "paramedics, flanked by police escort ... took Spears from her home to the psychiatric hospital before dawn"[117]; "a wild-eye Spears, 26, being carried out of her Studio City home on a gurney, her bare feet strapped down"[118]; "she was whisked to a hospital's psychiatric ward"[119]; and "police-escorted gurney."[120] Spears's first hospitalization was after she refused to relinquish her son after a court-ordered visit. "Paramedics then restrained Spears and delivered her to Cedars-Sinai Medical Center, where she was forcibly committed."[121] *People Magazine* then quoted a source as saying that at the hospital, "Spears was causing a ruckus ... like a caged prisoner."[122]

Spears's second hospitalization, at UCLA in January 2008, was extended for two weeks after the initial 72-hour evaluation because California law "allows patients to be kept for medical treatment if they are found to be disabled or a danger to themselves or others."[123] While this particular article cited the California law, it did not provide the criteria necessary to determine if a person was a danger to themselves, leaving readers to infer that Spears was most likely suicidal. *People Magazine* quoted a former UCLA student as saying, "The place is locked up tight ... you had to be escorted by one of the big guys with a set of keys. It was claustrophobic,"[124] echoing the public's worst images of psychiatric hospitals. Instead of being positive about Spears receiving psychiatric care or even framing her situation as being worthy of empathy or understanding, journalists depicted her being forcibly restrained and committed to a dudgeon-like facility. Such language and images reinforce the nightmarish visions the public has of psychiatric facilities and persons with mental health issues.

Another dominant media representation is that of the mentally ill as recognizably different by virtue of bizarre behavior and appearance.[125] This type of portrayal was most evident in stories about Amy Winehouse. She was described as frail-looking[126]; bruised and bloody[127]; wan and disheveled[128]; wild-eyed and whirling[129]; screeching[130]; and intoxicated.[131] Spears was also described as wild-eyed[132]; agitated[133]; confused[134]; along with manic and unstable.[135] These descriptors conjure an image of the stereotypical incoherent madwoman who is out of touch with reality and most definitely different from the rest of society. Choosing to use these adjectives to describe Winehouse and Spears results in the mentally ill being portrayed as a special, distinct, and flawed group who are different than the rest of us — a manifestation of we-ness and other-ness.

Conclusion: Why Do Images in the Media Matter?

The news media present information about events which occur outside the direct experience of the majority of society. Therefore, the media represent the primary, and often only, source of information about social and political processes.[136] As Wahl points out, "Americans themselves identify the mass media as the source from which they get most of their knowledge of mental illness."[137] Without direct, personal contact with a person with a mental illness, a reader's only exposure or knowledge about mental illness is through the media. When the media consistently offer derogatory and dehumanizing images of mental illness, the public has no other frame of reference. As Gamson et al. argue these negative images appear as transparent depictions of reality and are routinely taken for granted.[138]

Inaccurate media images lead to misconceptions and stigma, contributing to the confusion and misunderstanding about mental illness. Hinshaw defines stigma as the "global devaluation of certain individuals on the basis of some characteristics they possess, related to membership in a group that is disfavored, devalued, or disgraced by the general society."[139] Stigma involves harsh moral judgment that is directly related to the notion of the Other. Baker and MacPherson write, "It [stigma] plays a significant role in keeping people with diagnosed mental health problems at the very margins of society — perpetuating the 'them and us' culture."[140]

Once stigmatized, people are likely to be discriminated against and excluded from many forms of social exchange including employment, housing, financing, relationships, health services, and parenting. In a survey conducted by Mind in 1996, consisting of 778 people who had experienced mental health problems, forty-five percent thought that discrimination had increased in the last five years.[141] Sixty percent cited repeated negative media stories as allowing the stigma associated with mental illness to continue.[142] Popular media representations of the mentally ill as different and unworthy lessens our desire for contact and contributes to social rejection.[143]

Coverdale et al. write that media depictions could be more positive if individuals with mental illness could be directly quoted or present their own stories.[144] Hinshaw argues that realistic portrayals of mental illness should include the real-life, everyday pain and struggle of sufferers, as well as representations that promote interest, empathy, and compassion.[145] Mind, a mental health charity located in the United Kingdom, suggests that well-researched documentaries on mental health issues may improve attitudes, especially when people with direct experience of mental distress are involved in production and featured in the documentary.[146] Positive stories can help explode negative stereotypes of the mentally ill and, at the same time, putting a human face on mental illness can make it easier for people to empathize and identify.[147]

My assertion is not that these news articles are false, but instead, they inaccurately represent mental illness and its behavioral manifestations. With the news media relying on episodic reporting structures and being restrained by production values, news stories perpetuate negativity and stigma about mental illness. Wahl states, "The mass media are the storytellers of today, and, as such, they function as the primary socializing agent, ensuring that all members of our society are given the information and taught the lessons that form the shared basis of our culture."[148] Resorting to stereotypes ensures that news stories are comprehensible to readers, but repeatedly using these shortcuts ensures that stereotypes are not resisted. Without resistance and awareness, readers will continue to shun those with mental illness, resulting in continued stigma and shame.

NOTES

1. Otto F. Wahl, *Media Madness: Public Images of Mental Illness* (New Brunswick, NJ: Rutgers University Press, 1995), 14.

2. National Institute for Mental Health, "NIMH — Statistics — Prevalence of Serious Mental Illness Among U.S. Adults by Age, Sex, and Race," National Institute for Mental Health, accessed December 18, 2010, http://www.nimh.nih.gov/statistics/SMI_AASR.shtml.

3. Greg Philo, Greg McLaughlin, and Lesley Henderson, "Media Content," in *Media and Mental Distress*, ed. Glasgow University Media Group et al. (London: Longman, 1996), 49.

4. John Coverdale, Raymond Nairn, and Donna Claasen, "Depictions of Mental Illness in Print Media: A Prospective National Sample," *Australian and New Zealand Journal of Psychiatry* 26, no. 5 (2002): 697.

5. Wahl, *Media Madness*; Glasgow University Media Group and Greg Philo, *Media and Mental Distress* (London: Longman, 1996); Stephen P. Hinshaw, *The Mark of Shame: Stigma of Mental Illness and an Agenda for Change* (Oxford; New York: Oxford University Press, 2007); Elaine M. Seiff, "Media Frames of Mental Illness: The Potential Impact of Negative Frames," *Journal of Mental Health* 12, no. 3 (2003): 259; Heather Stuart, "Media Portrayal of Mental Illness and Its Treatments: What Effect Does It Have on People with Mental Illness?" *CNS Drugs* 20, no. 2 (2006): 99; Sue Baker and Julie MacPherson, *Counting the Cost: Mental Health in the Media* (London: MIND Publications, 2000).

6. Richard Dyer, *The Matter of Images: Essays on Representation* (London: Routledge, 1993), 1.

7. Amy Winehouse died on July 23, 2011. According to the London Times, the pathologist report determined cause of death as alcohol toxicity ("After Cleaning up Her Act, Winehouse Drank Herself to Death in Final Binge," October 27, 2011).

8. Robert W. McChesney, "The Political Economy of Global Communication," in *Capitalism and the Information Age: The Political Economy of the Global Communication Revolution*, ed. Robert W. McChesney et al. (New York: Monthly Review Press, 1998), 1.

9. Ibid.

10. Ibid., 6.

11. Vincent Mosco, *The Political Economy of Communication*, 2nd ed. (London: Sage, 2009), 4.

12. McChesney, "The Political Economy of Global Communication," 8.

13. Ibid.

14. John Flowerdew, "Critical Discourse Analysis and the Strategies of Resistance," in *Advances in Discourse Studies*, ed. V. K. Bhatia et al. (London: Taylor & Francis Routledge, 2008), 195.

15. Allan Luke, "Introduction: Theory and Practice in Critical Discourse Analysis," accessed March 17, 2010, http:gseis.ucla.edu/faculty/kellner/ed270/Luke/SAHA6.html.

16. William A. Gamson et al., "Media Images and the Social Construction of Reality," *Annual Review of Sociology* 18, no. 1 (1992): 377.

17. David Croteau and William Joynes, *The Business of Media: Corporate Media and the Public Interest*, 2nd ed. (Thousand Oaks, CA: Pine Forge Press, 2006), 52.

18. Robert W. McChesney, *The Political Economy of Media: Enduring Issues, Emerging Dilemmas* (New York: Monthly Review Press, 2008), 54.

19. Seiff, "Media Frames."

20. Gamson et al., "Media Images."

21. Graham Murdock and Peter Golding, "For a Political Economy of Mass Communications," *Socialist Register* 10 (1973), 228, accessed Dec. 10, 2010, http://socialistregister.com/index.php/srv/articles/view/5355.

22. Seiff, "Media Frames"; Robert A. Freidman, "Media and Madness: For Better and Worse, the News Media and Entertainment Industry Shape Public Opinion about Mental Illness," *The America Prospect* 19, no. 7 (July-Aug 2008): A2.

23. Seiff, "Media Frames," 264.

24. Gamson et al., "Media Images."

25. Murdock and Golding, "For a Political Economy."

26. Peter Golding and Philip Elliott, "News Values and News Production," in *Media Studies: A Reader*, 3rd ed., eds. Sue Thornham et al. (New York: New York University Press, 2009), 635.

27. McChesney, *The Political Economy of Media.*

28. Lesley Henderson, "Selling Suffering: Mental Illness and Media Values," in *Media and Mental Distress*, ed. Glasgow University Media Group and Greg Philo (London; New York: Longman, 1996), 18.

29. Stuart, "Media Portrayal," 104.

30. Golding and Elliott, "News Values."

31. Stuart Hall et al., "The Social Production of News," in *Media Studies: A Reader*, 3rd ed., eds. Sue Thornham et al. (New York: New York University Press, 2009), 649.

32. Murdock and Golding, "For a Political Economy," 227.

33. Hall et al., "The Social Production of News," 649.

34. Murdock and Golding, "For a Political Economy," 230.

35. Hall et al., "The Social Production of News."

36. Murdock and Golding, "For a Political Economy," 229.

37. Golding and Elliott, "News Values," 644.

38. Mary Daly, *Beyond God the Father: Toward a Philosophy of Women's Liberation* (Boston: Beacon Press, 1973), 60.

39. Kevin Harris, *Sex, Ideology, and Religion: Representation of Women in the Bible* (Totowa, NJ: Barnes & Noble, 1984), 94.

40. Elaine J. Lawless, "Woman as Abject: 'Resisting Cultural and Religious Myths that Condone Violence against Women,'" *Western Folklore* 62, no. 4 (2003): 237.

41. Carol L. Myers, *Discovering Eve: Ancient Israelite Women in Context* (New York; Oxford: Oxford University Press, 1988), 3.

42. Lawless, "Woman as Abject," 242.

43. Harris, *Sex, Ideology, and Religion*, 84.

44. Meyers, *Discovering Eve,* 42.

45. Lawless, "Woman as Abject," 242.

46. Daly, *Beyond God the Father,* 61.

47. Candace Hammond, "Is Celebrity News Gender-Biased?," *Cape Cod Times* (Hyannis, MA), March 31, 2008, accessed March 4, 2011, http://www.capecodonline.com/apps/pbcs.dll/article?AID=20080331/LIFE/80331032&CID=sitesearch.

48. Mark Binelli, "Confessions of a Teenage Drama Queen," *Rolling Stone*, August 19, 2004, 60.

49. Kenneth Hart, "'Mean Girl' Goes Too Far 7/11," *The Daily Independent*, July 11, 2010, accessed March 4, 2011, http://dailyindependent.com/columns/x73995246/KEN NETH-HART-Mean-Girl-goes-too-far-7–11; Slotek, "It's All About Me; Lindsay Lohan must be the only one who thinks she needs to focus more on herself," *The Toronto Sun*, April 9, 2009; D'Souza, 58,"The Lo Down," *Sunday Times* (London, England), June 1, 2008, 10.

50. Acuna, "Declaring a Britney-Free Zone: The Bee Says 'Moo!'" *The Sacramento Bee* (CA), Feb. 17, 2009; Rush et al., "Brit's No-Show Goes On," *New York Daily News*, Jan. 24, 2008, 20.

51. Bryant, "One Night with Amy," *The Mirror* (London), July 15, 2008, 18; Moody, "Grammy Triumph Fades as Winehouse Plight Deepens," *Associated Press Archive*, June 26, 2008, accessed December 8, 2010,via Access World News database, SQN: D91HVDMG0; Pareles, "In Real Time, Amy Winehouse's Deeper Descent," *New York Times*, January 24, 2008, E1(L).

52. Rush et al., "Brit's No-Show," 20.

53. Stuart, "Media Portrayal of Mental Illness," 101.

54. Karen S. Schneider et al., "Falling Apart," *People*, August 6, 2007, 56.

55. Michelle Tauber et al., "Lindsay Lohan's Road to Ruin," *People*, October 11, 2010, 52.

56. Karen S. Schneider and Jill Smolowe, "Britney Interrupted," *People*, February 18, 2008, 58.

57. Michelle Tauber and Michelle Tan, "Britney in Crisis," *People*, January 21, 2008, 62.

58. P. Corser, "Britney Breaks into Pieces," *Community Care*, January 17, 2008, 17.

59. Adrian Thrills, "Yes, Amy's a Tortured, Mangled Soul, That's Why She's So Great," *Daily Mail* (London), February 15, 2008, 52.

60. Edna Gundersen, "Amy's Sobering Transformation," *USA Today*, January 29, 2008.

61. Gordon Smart and Pete Samson, "Amy Sent to Rehab — Help for Star after Crack Shame," *The Sun* (London), January 25, 2008, 12.

62. Pareles, "In Real Time."

63. Wahl, *Media Madness*, 43.

64. "Embassy Tells Winehouse No," *The Daily Review*, February 8, 2008, accessed December 8, 2010 via Access World News database, SQN: 8205507.

65. Thrills, "Yes, Amy's a Tortured Soul"; Gundersen, "Amy's Sobering Transformation."

66. Bob Vines, "As Cool as a Celebrity in Rehab — Fresh from the Vine," *Northern Wyoming Daily News*, February 16, 2008, 004.

67. "Amy Must Be Less of a Lioness," *The Sunday Independent* (Ireland), February 17, 2008, accessed March 4, 2011, http://www.independent.ie/health/case-studies/amy-must-be-less-of-a-lioness-129123.html.

68. Ibid.

69. Taylor, "Lock Up My Amy," *The News of the World* (England), April 27, 2008; Smart and Samson, "Amy Sent to Rehab," 12.

70. Taylor, "Lock Up"; Moreton, "For God's Sake, Amy, It's Time to Get a Grip," *The Independent on Sunday* (London), April 27, 2008, 42.

71. Gundersen, "Amy's Sobering Transformation."

72. Smart and Samson, "Amy Sent to Rehab."

73. Moody, "Grammy Triumph."

74. Ibid.

75. "Skank Wars!" *Rolling Stone*, no. 1067, 75.

76. Acuna, "Declaring a Britney-Free Zone."

77. Ibid.

78. Linda Deutsch, "Restraining Order Accuses Manager of Taking over Britney

Spears' Life," *Rutland Herald*, February 6, 2008, 04; "Spears to Remain in Hospital 2 Weeks," *The Times*, February 4, 2008, A02.

79. Ibid.

80. Solvej Schou, "Celebrities Love Giving Advice for Britney Spears," *Charleston Daily Mail*, February 5, 2008, P2D.

81. Blade Staff, "Spears' Stay in Hospital Extended," *The Blade*, February 5, 2008, D3; Schneider and Smolowe, "Britney Interrupted," 58.

82. Jeremy Herron, "Spears' Sage Spreads Wealth — Many Benefit Economically from Her Public Antics," *Ventura County Star*, January 29, 2008, accessed October 29, 2010, via Access World News database, SQN:179543.

83. Maria Puente, "Celebrity Accents: It's All Very Tongue-in-Chic," *USA Today*, January 29, 2008, 3D.

84. Rush et al. "Brit's No Show."

85. Schneider and Smolowe, "Britney Interrupted."

86. Tauber and Tan, "Britney in Crisis."

87. Corser, "Britney Breaks."

88. Schneider et al., "Falling Apart."

89. Tauber et al., "Lindsay Lohan's Road to Ruin."

90. Virginia Heffernan, "Party and Punishment," *The New York Times Magazine*, October 24, 2010, 18(L).

91. Gina Bellafante, "Lohan Assumes the Pose: Monroe's Final Sitting," *The New York Times*, February 21, 2008, E3(L).

92. Hart, "'Mean Girl.'"

93. Rush et al., "Look Who's Posing as Marilyn Monroe," *New York Daily News*, February 19, 2008, 18.

94. Joshua Gillian, "Lilo Sues E-Trade for $100 Million," *St. Petersburg Times*, March 10, 2010, 2B.

95. Andrew Taylor, "Notes on a Scandal or Two," *The Sun Herald* (Sydney, Australia), March 23, 2008, 10.

96. Richard Winton and Andrew Blankstein, "Lohan is Expected to be Released from County Jail," *Los Angeles Times*, September 25, 2010, AA1.

97. Wahl, *Media Madness*, 22.

98. Ibid, 10.

99. Tauber et al., "Lindsay Lohan's Road to Ruin."

100. Sandy Cohen, "Judge Issues Warrant for Lindsay Lohan's Arrest," *The Lompoc Record* (CA), May 20, 2010, accessed October 27, 2010, via Access World News database SQN: 547564ed93e8daad7f81f44a64ae0bee2ea5db7.

101. Raquel Maria Dillon, "Court Documents Show Britney Spears' Father Sought to Fire Her Manager for Sending Her a Car," *Alvarado Post* (TX), February 12, 2008, accessed October 29, 2010, via Access World News database, record w/2008–02–12/arti cles/2008/02/08/business/business/doc47b1f87be087087418.txt.

102. Ibid.

103. Deutsch, "Restraining Order."

104. "Spears to Remain."

105. Schneider and Smolowe, "Britney Interrupted."

106. Ibid.

107. Seiff, "Media Frames."

108. Vines, "As Cool"; Moreton, "For God's Sake"; Gundersen, "Amy's Sobering."

109. P. Taylor, "Lock Up"; Smart and Samson, "Amy Sent."

110. Tirdad Derakhshani, "Sideshow: With Britney, It's Either/Or," *The Philadelphia Inquirer*, June 18, 2009, E02.

111. Moreton, "For God's Sake."

112. Raphael G. Satter, "Amy Winehouse Visa Denied But She Will Perform by Satellite at the Grammy Awards," *Associated Press Archive*, February 8, 2008, accessed December 8, 2010, via Access World News database, SQN: D8ULROD01.

113. P. Taylor, "Lock Up."

114. Coverdale et al., "Depictions of Mental Illness."

115. Ibid.

116. Schou, "Celebrities Love."

117. "Spears to Remain."

118. Tauber and Tan, "Britney in Crisis."

119. Deutsch, "Restraining Order."

120. Herron, "Spears' Saga."

121. Tauber and Tan, "Britney in Crisis."

122. Ibid.

123. Blade Staff, "Spears' Stay."

124. Schneider and Smolowe, "Britney Interrupted."

125. Wahl, *Media Madness*, 37.

126. P. Taylor, "Lock Up."

127. Gundersen, "Amy's Sobering Transformation."

128. Moody, "Grammy Triumph"; Bryant, "One Night"; Pareles, "In Real Time."

129. Bryant, "One Night"; Pareles, "In Real Time."

130. Bryant, "One Night."

131. Pareles, "In Real Time."

132. Tauber and Tan, "Britney in Crisis"; Croser, "Britney Breaks."

133. Deutsch, "Restraining Order."

134. Schneider and Smolowe, "Britney Interrupted."

135. Tauber and Tan, "Britney in Crisis."

136. Hall et al., "The Social Production of News."

137. Wahl, *Media Madness*, 3.

138. Gamson et al., "Media Images."

139. Hinshaw, *The Mark of Shame*, 23.

140. Baker and MacPherson, *Counting the Cost*, 2.

141. Jim Read and Sue Baker, *Not Just Sticks and Stones: A Survey of Stigma, Taboos, and Discrimination Experienced by People with Mental health Problems* (London: MIND Publications, 1996), 13.

142. Ibid.

143. Wahl, *Media Madness, 95.*

144. Coverdale et al., "Depictions of Mental Illness," 698.

145. Hinshaw, *The Mark of Shame*, 210.

146. "Public Attitudes to Mental Distress," accessed December 18, 2010, http://www.mind.org.uk/help/research_and_policy/public_attitudes_to_mental_distress.

147. For possible alternatives and positive representations in the media of the mentally ill, please see Stephen P. Hinshaw, *The Mark of Shame: Stigma of Mental Illness and an Agenda for Change* (Oxford [UK]: Oxford University Press, 2007); Otto F. Wahl, *Media Madness: Public Images of Mental Illness* (New Brunswick, NJ: Rutgers University Press, 1995); and Mind Publications (United Kingdom) www. Mind.org.uk.

148. Wahl, *Media Madness*, 121.

Bibliography

Baker, Sue, and Julie MacPherson. *Counting the Cost: Mental Health in the Media*. London: MIND Publications, 2000.

Coverdale, John, Raymond Nairn, and Donna Claasen. "Depictions of Mental Illness in Print Media: A Prospective National Sample." *Australian & New Zealand Journal of Psychiatry* 26, no. 5: 697–700.

Croteau, David, and William Hoynes. *The Business of Media: Corporate Media and the Public Interest.* 2nd ed. Thousand Oaks, CA: Pine Forge Press, 2006.

Daly, Mary. *Beyond God the Father: Toward a Philosophy of Women's Liberation.* Boston: Beacon Press, 1973.

Dyer, Richard. *The Matter of Images: Essays on Representation.* London: Routledge, 1993.

Flowerdew, John. "Critical Discourse Analysis and the Strategies of Resistance." In *Advances in Discourse Studies,* edited by V. K. Bhatia, John Flowerdew and Rodney H. Jones, 195–210. London: Taylor & Francis Routledge, 2008.

Freidman, Robert A. "Media and Madness: For Better and Worse, the News Media and Entertainment Industry Shape Public Opinion about Mental Illness." *The America Prospect* 19, no. 7 (July–Aug 2008).

Gamson, William A., David Croteau, William Hoynes, and Theodore Sasson. "Media Images and the Social Construction of Reality." *Annual Review of Sociology* 18, no. 1 (1992): 373–393.

Glasgow University Media Group and Greg Philo. *Media and Mental Distress.* London: Longman, 1996.

Golding, Peter, and Philip Elliott. "News Values and News Production." In *Media Studies: A Reader,* 3rd ed., edited by Sue Thornham, Caroline Bassett and Paul Marris. New York: New York University Press, 2009.

Hall, Stuart, Chas Critcher, Tony Jefferson, John Clarke, and Brian Roberts. "The Social Production of News." In *Media Studies: A Reader,* 3rd ed., edited by Sue Thornham, Caroline Bassett and Paul Marris. New York: New York University Press, 2009.

Harris, Kevin. *Sex, Ideology, and Religion: The Representation of Women in the Bible.* Totowa, NJ: Barnes & Noble, 1984.

Henderson, Lesley. "Selling Suffering: Mental Illness and Media Values." In *Media and Mental Distress,* edited by Glasgow University Media Group and Greg Philo. London; New York: Longman, 1996.

Hinshaw, Stephen P. *The Mark of Shame: Stigma of Mental Illness and an Agenda for Change.* Oxford: Oxford University Press, 2007.

Lawless, Elaine J. "Woman as Abject: 'Resisting Cultural and Religious Myths that Condone Violence Against Women.'" *Western Folklore* 62, no. 4 (2003): 237–269.

Luke, Allan. "Introduction: Theory and Practice in Critical Discourse Analysis." Accessed March 17, 2010, http://gseis.ucla.edu/faculty/kellner/ed270/Luke/SAHA6.html.

McChesney, Robert W. "The Political Economy of Global Communication." In *Capitalism and the Information Age: The Political Economy of the Global Communication Revolution,* edited by Robert W. McChesney, Ellen M. Wood and John Bellamy Foster. New York: Monthly Review Press, 1998.

_____. *The Political Economy of Media: Emerging Issues, Emerging Dilemmas.* New York: Monthly Review Press, 2008.

Myers, Carol L. *Discovering Eve: Ancient Israelite Women in Context.* Oxford: Oxford University Press, 1988.

Mosco, Vincent. *The Political Economy of Communication.* 2nd ed. London: Sage, 2009.

Murdock, Graham, and Peter Golding. "For a Political Economy of Mass Communications." *Socialist Register* 10 (1973). Accessed December 10, 2010, http:socialistregister.com/index/php/srv/article/view/5355.

National Institute for Mental Health. "NIMH — Statistics — Prevalence of Serious Mental Illness among U.S. Adults by Age, Sex, and Race." Accessed December 18, 2010. http://www.nimh.nih.gov/statistics/SMI_AASR.shtml.

Philo, Greg, Greg McLaughlin, and Lesley Henderson. "Media Content." In *Media and*

Mental Distress, edited by Glasgow University Media Group and Greg Philo. New York: Longman, 1996.

Read, Jim, and Sue Baker. *Not Just Sticks and Stones: A Survey of the Stigma, Taboos, and Discrimination Experienced by People with Mental Health Problems.* London: MIND Publications, 1996.

Seiff, Elaine M. "Media Frames of Mental Illness: The Potential Impact of Negative Frames." *Journal of Mental Health* 12, no. 3 (2003): 259.

Stuart, Heather. "Media Portrayal of Mental Illness and Its Treatments: What Effect Does It Have on People with Mental Illness?" *CNS Drugs* 20, no. 2 (2006): 99–106.

Wahl, Otto F. *Media Madness: Public Images of Mental Illness.* New Brunswick, NJ: Rutgers University Press, 1995.

10

Evolving Stages

Representations of Mental Illness in Contemporary American Theater

SARAH J. RUDOLPH

Throughout time, philosophers, physicians and artists have entertained a multitude of theories about mental illness. While theater has always found great fascination in probing madness, increasingly scientific understanding of mental illness has transformed the shape of this fascination. Where insanity once haunted tragic figures and the antics of crazed characters enlivened comedy, many plays on the modern American stage consider mental illness as complex condition. Along with evolving theories about the nature of disease, impressions of mental health professionals and treatment vary widely in these works. In some, treatment facilities offer refuge; in others, they lurk menacingly offstage or become extensions of an oppressive status quo. Struggling characters worry about heredity, resort to alcohol or drug abuse, and cope with perplexing questions about prescription drug treatment and other therapies. The relationship between patients and mental health professionals, at times, resembles that between child and parent and, at others, seem more akin to that of prisoner and jailer. The plays themselves range from the melodramatic to the bleakly despairing, from stark realism to expressionism to the Broadway musical, and offer representations of mental illness often running parallel to shifting attitudes in the wider culture.

The Melodramatic Stage: Charming Misfits

Melodrama is the first distinctly American form of drama. While not always featuring a villain who ties a helpless ingénue to the railroad tracks and a hero arriving to free her as the train barrels towards them; melodrama does rely upon rigid distinction between the heroic and the villainous. This simple formula well serves melodrama in its attempts to depict mental illness. In the place of the heroine on the tracks, we have the delicate eccentric on the verge of being crushed by cold conformists. Jon Patrick's painfully senti- mental 1950 play *The Curious Savage* exemplifies such attempt. Patrick assem- bles a cast of loveable misfits protected in a "home." Their primary caregiver, Miss Wilhelmina, tends to them with a kind of maternal devotion (and even- tually is revealed to be married to Jeffrey, one of the residents, and determined to remain by his side while he heals). The male psychiatrist, Dr. Emmett, visits the day room infrequently but proves a calm and caring father figure forced to comply with professional protocol. The title character of the play is a good-natured elderly woman, Ethel Savage, whose impatient and greedy adult children deem her "insane" as a means to take control of her substantial estate. As the sole representatives of the world beyond the cozy day room, these offspring stand in stark opposition to essentially "good" residents of the home. Even Mrs. Paddy, the grumbling pretender to artistic greatness, by play's end, proves loving.

Tom Griffin's 1987 play *The Boys Next Door* also finds inspiration in melodrama and the idealization of those deemed "different." The central char- acters consist of four men coping with various forms of mental disability and Jack, their young social worker, living together in a group home — a 1980s version of the Cloisters. Only one the four residents of the home, Barry Klem- per, is identified as having a severe mental illness (in one of Jack's narrative passages, he explains that Barry is schizophrenic). Barry's delusion takes the rather innocuous form of believing he is a golf pro and, throughout much of the play, he frequently boasts about the gifts of boxed chocolate he receives from his father, even though he cannot eat chocolate. When his father visits, he complains loudly about the difficulty he has had finding the place, makes ugly racist remarks about Barry's roommate, and bullies him for not speaking and calling him a "little sonovabitch."[1] The verbal attacks progress to physical violence: Barry cowers curled up into a fetal position, Jack intervenes, and Griffin. has fully established the link between a father's brutality and a son's mental illness. In addition to their clear definitions of good and evil, *The Boys Next Door* and *The Curious Savage* both use fantasy sequences to reveal the inner beauty of their principle characters. In *The Boys Next Door*, Norman, a friendly innocent with cognitive impairment, invites Sheila, a female version of himself, to his home. After some bumbling exchanges, the two begin to dance: "from their first shuffling awkward step, Norman and Sheila are trans- formed. The lights intensify. The music builds. They glide effortlessly across the floor.[2]

Later in the play, Lucien, a character with the mental capacity of a five-year-old, testifies before a Senate subcommittee on Health and Human Services. At first humiliated by his inability to form thoughts, a change overcomes him, and "he is no longer retarded Lucien, but rather a confident and articulate man."[3] In *The Curious Savage*, all the occupants of Patrick's day room end the play in the guise of the idealized selves of their dreams: in the place of the "crude canvas" that has been visible on Mrs. Paddy's easel throughout the play is "a finished seascape of great beauty;" Florence, unable to reconcile herself to the loss of a young child and carrying a ragged doll as if it were a living child, now holds the hand of little boy; and Fairy, clumsy, bespectacled ingénue, reclaims the stage as a graceful beauty.[4] While neither *The Curious Savage* nor *The Boys Next Door* figure prominently in the canon of American drama, their popularity after their Broadway openings attests to the ongoing attraction of a view of the mentally ill as charming harmless misfits and of a care system in which they are protected and content.

A variation on the theme of charming misfit is provided by Joseph Kesselring's much better known *Arsenic and Old Lace*, which opened on Broadway in 1941 and was later made into a film directed by Frank Capra and starring Cary Grant. Not melodrama, but rather full-throated comedy, the play makes subtle overtures to the hereditary nature of "difference." Mortimer Brewster, the play's protagonist, is burdened with two dotty but charming aunts gleefully poisoning elderly men, one brother who fancies himself as Teddy Roosevelt and another who is a serial killer. Given what this might bode for his future, he hesitates to marry and reproduce. Late in the play, he discovers that he is not related to the family through blood and is overcome with relief. Without overstating the play's significance as a depiction of mental illness, even a slight reference to genetics seems to anticipate ideas that become prevalent much later in the century.

The Damning Stage: Brutal Care

Eugene O'Neill, Tennessee Williams, and Arthur Miller gave shape to a movement bringing true stature to the American theater. Many of their most esteemed works feature characters grappling with mental illness; however, psychiatric intervention, medication, therapy and other treatments remain largely confined to ambiguous references. Perhaps the last moments of Tennessee Williams's *A Streetcar Named Desire* exemplify what seems common impulse in their drama. Flanked by psychiatric workers who have come to take her to the institution to which she has been committed, Blanche utters, "I have always depended on the kindness of strangers."[5] As Blanche and her new caretakers move across the stage, no other characters intervene; in fact, most of the men continue their card game. Within the dramaturgy of the play, Blanche does not simply leave her sister's home, but is forever banished from relevance. Similar dynamics shape Arthur Miller's *Death of a Salesman*. The play provides only two options for Willy Loman: suicide or ongoing pain marked by disabling delusion, alienation, recrimination and self-hatred. In *Long Day's Journey into Night* and other plays, Eugene O'Neill orchestrates dark family pathologies to fester while his characters self-medicate with alcohol and drugs; asylums and doctors lurk offstage, signifying terminal points in the plotline.

Ken Kesey's *One Flew Over the Cuckoo's Nest*—originally written as a novel but adapted for both stage and screen—represents a major turning point in the characterization of mental illness on the American stage. Kesey and many following his lead place asylums and doctors center stage. Far from challenging conceptions of the institution as a point of no return, *One Flew Over the Cuckoo's Nest* characterizes mental health treatment practices as brutal enough to devastate even the heartiest of spirits. For a beat generation inspired by R.D. Laing and Michel Foucault, the zealous free-spirited R.P. MacMurphy offered a new kind of hero just as Nurse Ratched embodied all the repression and sadism of the status quo. Dale Wasserman's stage version of *One Flew Over the Cuckoo's Nest* takes place in the day room of the acute ward of a state hospital. Emphasizing details such as "plastic-covered" furniture and "formidable steel grilles" covering the windows, Wasserman's set description conveys a wholly sterile environment that under "full lighting has the charm of a refrigerator interior."[6] Through the windows can be seen "a green and treed world"[7] The unfolding action consistently reinforces the divide between the cold artifice of the institution and the natural world beyond it. Chief Bromden (the character who narrates the Kesey novel) begins the play. Monologues in which the Chief speaks to his late father, "Papa," evoke purer times just as the frequent interplay between images of nature and machinery reveres the earth. In his first monologue, the Chief describes how hospital workers routinely "tip the whole world on its side" and when it is ripped open, those who fall to the bottom "bleed only rust."[8] This monologue establishes that the horrors of institutionalization have driven the Chief to feign the inability to speak or hear.

Before McMurphy enters, all the patients comply numbly with the cruel order exacted by Nurse Ratched. The vigor he brings to the room gradually inspires all the patients to reclaim their voices; the Chief's liberation from silence is only the most literal expression of that achievement. The play's main characters are the "Acute" patients whom Wasserman renders as a charmingly sympathetic group whom McMurphy rescues from timidity and joylessness. Indeed, while the "Chronic" patients—characters occupying their own area of the stage and present but not highly consequential — appear truly afflicted; the "Acutes" seem fragile and mistreated, not genuinely ill. When Nurse Ratched reads aloud McMurphy's commitment file, the story that emerges is one about lively individualism and utter disregard for propriety, not psychological disease.

> **Nurse Ratched**. (*Reading*.): McMurphy, Randle Patrick. Committed by the State for diagnosis and possible treatment. Thirty-five years old. Never married. Distinguished Service Cross for leading an escape from a Communist prison camp. A dishonorable discharge afterwards for insubordination. Followed by a history of street brawls, barroom fights and a series of arrests for drunkenness, assault and battery, disturbing the peace, *repeated* gambling, one arrest for rape.[9]

The reference to McMurphy's valor as a soldier safeguards against temptations to dismiss him as an ineffectual rebel, while information about the discharge and his interactions with the criminal justice system defines him as a man not to be bound by even the most entrenched power systems. That he meets his match ultimately in the hospital — not simply in the form of Nurse Ratched, whom he rattles but does not break, but in proscribed treatment in the form of frontal lobotomy — effectively casts the mental hospital as a ruthless oppressor. The cavalier treatment of sexual assault conforms to the play's larger uses of gender to articulate a specific vision of heroism. McMurphy's machismo attitudes and reckless sexuality help generate his defiant energy. Eager to accommodate McMurphy and sexually available, Candy becomes allied with all that is sympathetic in the play just as Nurse Ratched, who frequently exerts control over the male patients by ridiculing or repressing their sexuality, represents a stifling, unnatural power structure. These two conflicting visions of womanhood clash in the play's crisis scene. Nurse Ratched discovers Billy, the most delicate and boyish of the characters, in a sexual encounter with Candy. The relentless way she humiliates and shames Billy provokes McMurphy to assault her. His attack includes, significantly, ripping open her uniform to expose her breasts.[10] She regains her power by having McMurphy subject to a frontal lobotomy — the ultimate destruction of his spirit and a kind of psychic castration.

The frontal lobotomy (a very controversial and, by the time of the play's writing, a very rarely used psychiatric measure) is only the most extreme of those methods availed of people like Nurse Ratched. Throughout the play, electroshock treatment emerges as a barbaric form of discipline, and in one passage, Harding — who, as the most astute and well educated of the characters, occasionally assumes the voice of reason — likens medication to ammunition. The entire psychiatric system emerges as a mechanism for suppressing the passionate, sensitive, and abused.

Marta Caminero-Santangelo's *The Madwoman Can't Speak or Why Insanity is Not Subversive* adds considerable perspective to the sensibilities refined in *One Flew Over the Cuckoo's Nest* and similar and, in particular, the odd mix of blatant sexism and general condemnation of societal oppression in *One Flew Over the Cuckoo's Nest.* She writes, "The antipsychiatry movement failed to consider women explicitly, despite the obvious significance for women of a theory that defined madness in terms of deviation from social expectations."[11] According to Caminero-Santangelo, when feminists began to describe the mental health system as complicit in the oppression of women, they too simply relied upon broad generalization, regarding all designations of mental illness in women as part of larger efforts to silence voices at odds with patriarchy.[12] While the plays under discussion in this essay do not deal directly with women's oppression, Caminero-Santangelo's critique of feminist theory does reflect on ideas crucial to understanding developments in the representation of mental illness. She challenges the basic essentialism inherent in the antipsychiatry movement and the attending valorization of madness. Despite its reliance on broad assumptions, *One Flew Over the Cuckoo's Nest* did serve to expose the real abuse taking place in the name of treatment. However, making an icon of every individual who has been given a diagnosis of mental illness ultimately diminishes important individual realities. Representations of psychiatric systems — just as theories about mental illness and feminist critiques of literature — gain nuance as they evolve.

The Analytic Stage: The Puzzle of Mental Illness

Opening ten years after Wasserman's play, Peter Schaeffer's *Equus* provides a more mediated study of mental health treatment.[13] Not only does Schaeffer offer in Dysart a highly reflective and ethically minded child psychiatrist, his rendering of the frail and enigmatic Alan makes clear the presence of genuine illness. Like the earlier play, *Equus* uses monologues delivered by a character alone on stage to advance the emotional logic of his play. Where Chief Bromden addresses his "Papa," Dysart speaks his mind aloud to the audience. In stunning contrast to the ruthless conviction of Nurse Ratched, Dr. Dysart persistently questions the function and methods of his profession. The language he uses evokes metaphors similar to those that unify Wasserman's play. Medical intervention into the human psyche is characterized as the devastation of an organic — and thereby more authentic — state. Early in the play, speaking to the audience, Dysart describes his work as "being in the adjustment business."[14] Schaeffer uses Hester Solomon, a magistrate working with the psychiatric system, to counter Dysart's self-deprecating analysis of his efforts. The obvious affection the two characters have for one another helps dignify her point of view as does the genuine concern she has for Alan and the other children committed to the hospital. In contrast to Dysart's tendencies to equivocate and over-analyze, Hester manages to arrive deftly at decisions. She reasons that Alan is in pain and that Dysart has the ability to alleviate that pain.

Dysart shares with the audience dreams in which he ritualistically removes the entrails from children, and, as the play's central image, horses appear as holy figures that humans restrain with bit and bridle. The play's abundant reference to Greek and Christian iconography adds mythic dimension to the central metaphors of the play while the sexual form taken by Alan's reverence for the horses and Dysart's frequent references to his sexless marriage stress Schaeffer's indebtedness to Freudian thought. The rendering of Alan's parents, Dora and Frank, further contribute to this psychoanalytic bent. Alan's problems seem clearly rooted in the tension between Dora's fervent religious beliefs and Frank's cold intellectualism.

At first, Alan seems to have most in common with the "Chronics" depicted in *One Flew Over the Cuckoo's Nest*. Rather than meaningful interaction with Dysart, he repeats advertising slogans. As the play progresses, his determined resistance to Dysart suggests some kinship with McMurphy and evidence of his unhappy life — particularly the suggestion of an overbearing and sexually repressed mother — recalls something of Wasserman's characterization of the delicate Billy. The highly elaborate structure of Alan's pathology gives some complexity to Schaeffer's characterization of mental illness, just as the pains the play takes to articulate Dysart's misgivings about his profession offer a more flattering portrait of psychiatric systems. One on level, the play's characterization of treatment offers stark contrast to the savage use of electro-shock and lobotomy depicted in *One Flew Over the Cuckoo's Nest*. Dysart uses a placebo that Alan believes is a "truth pill" and hypnosis, dramatized as a simple and noninvasive event, to compel Alan to disclose the trauma haunting him. On another level, however, the play's vision of psychiatric treatment has clear affinities with understandings advanced by Kesey and Wasserman.

Once Dysart determines to "treat" Alan, the power and control he exercises are so immense that he effectively vanquishes the very identity of his young patient, in its place leaving but a "ghost" of the former person. As in the earlier play, psychiatric treatment is rendered as a means to squelch passion and produce citizens amenable to social control. Dysart reflects, "Passion, you see, can be destroyed by a doctor. It cannot be created."[15] He visualizes for the "cured" Alan an unremarkable life characterized by factory work and satisfaction with mundane pleasures such as that afforded by saving his modest pay and betting on horses, having entirely lost the sense of awe they once engendered in him. Working as an extension of the institution, Dr. Dysart admits he has squelched in Alan all that was expressive, fierce and unique, albeit taboo.

The link between profundity and madness made in *Equus* differs significantly from the pat idealization of those with mental health issues prevalent in many works and is given further investigation by David Auburn in *Proof*. Opening on Broadway in October of 2000, Auburn's play revolves around Robert and his adult daughter, Katherine, who share not only remarkable mathematical ability, but mental illness. These characters seem complex figures to neither idealize nor dismiss. Unlike the legions of earlier characters surrendering blindly or denying their own "madness," Robert and Katherine apply their extensive intellects to thinking about their conditions.

The critical acclaim that greeted *Proof* included both the Pulitzer Prize for Literature and Antoinette Perry Award for Best New Play in 2001 and interested theatre enthusiasts and mathematicians alike. Reviewing *Proof* for *Notices of the American Mathematical Society,* Dave Bayer reflects on the play's concern with the "sources, sanctuaries and emotional risks of intellectual passion in general" as well as Auburn's characterization of mathematical genius in particular with its "capacity for abstraction."[16] After reading this review, Ron Howard hired Bayer as a mathematics consultant for the film *A Beautiful Mind*. This film, Akiva Goldman's adaptation of Sylvia Nash's autobiography of brilliant mathematician John Nash, tells the story of a career interrupted by the psychosis of schizophrenia. Like Auburn's play, Howard's film proved an immense success, winning both the Golden Globe and Academy Awards for Best Picture in 2002. Together, the works indicate the existence of a public receptive relatively new thinking about mental illness. Despite the considerable differences between their scripts, Goldsman and Auburn sustain fascination with the figure of the mad genius without reducing the complex realities of mental illness to a glorified persecution.

While not based on actual events, Auburn's play captures the interplay between intensified thought, magnified feeling, mental illness, and extraordinary achievement highlighted by various studies, autobiographies and biographies including Nassar's work on Nash. In the process, *Proof* entertains the ambiguous line separating inspired work and obsession, seeks the point at which obsessions become delusions, and explores how, by assuming structures consistent with the individual's mind and experiences, hallucinations present themselves as wholly viable experiences looming larger than the reality beyond them. Also in keeping with transforming perceptions of mental illness as organic, *Proof* suggests that the manifestation of illness corresponds with the unique ways an individual intellect operates. Perhaps, hallucinations and delusions produced by mathematical minds became all the more compelling during a time when logic seemed to triumph over superstition in thinking about mental illness.

Auburn concentrates on the relationship between Robert, a University of Chicago mathematics professor whose mental problems seem to resemble either manic-depression or schizophrenia, and his daughter Katherine who has been taking care of him. He understands mental illness as a condition with predictable courses, symptoms, and meaningful organic structures rather than as product of either environmental factors or social oppression. By leaving more ambiguous the play's ending — in that we do not know precisely what course Katherine's mental health will take — Auburn also presents mental illness as an ongoing issue, not a plot event with clear beginning and ending points.

Proof opens with one of the play's best scenes, in which Katherine and Robert converse rather frankly about her fear for her mental health. Hoping to reassure her, Robert insists that the "simple fact that we can talk about this together is a good sign."[17] He goes on, "Crazy people don't sit around wondering if they're nuts," and explains that a "very good sign that you're crazy is an inability to ask the question, 'Am I crazy?'"[18] Even though Katherine points out that there is an obvious gap in his logic given his own earlier admission that he is "bughouse," Robert's remarks offer an amusing acknowledgement of the misconception that those with mental illness lack insight into their own conditions.

In what proves particularly effective theater, Auburn withholds until the end of Katherine and Robert's exchange the fact that the latter is actually dead. The resulting suggestion, that Katherine's grasp on reality is compromised, adds dimension to the concerns she has for her sanity. More significantly, this device applies a sense of internal logic and matter-of-fact quality to delusion. In this exchange Robert describes even Katherine's depression as "mathematical." In his review, Bayer sees in Auburn's characterization of Katherine a revelation of the "capacity for abstraction" that underlies both her mathematical gift and the strong connection she has to her father. He finds refreshing the play's treatment of such abstraction that "might have been more conventionally portrayed as social detachment." He finds laudable Auburn's approach in which the character's "continual recentering of discourse onto to its true subject is evocative of uncanny problem-solving ability."[19] Relating Katherine's interpersonal style to her mind's unique intellectual capabilities dignifies the larger connection between the mind's vulnerability to illness and its potential for extraordinary insight.

Through Robert, Auburn also reveals how illness can fully erode the capacities of even the most brilliant mind and, in so doing, captures the poignant interplay between the mind's most productive and most disabled states. In a flashback scene in the second act, Katherine returns home from college to find Robert, who has not been answering the phone, quite agitated. In a reference to his mind's mathematical capacity, he boasts, "(T)he machinery is working, Katherine, it's on full blast."[20] Inspired intellectual work may account for his seeming obliviousness to the cold weather — the scene takes place outdoors on the porch during a Chicago December — and his manic energy. However, when he shows Katherine the outline for a new proof he has written, the words on the paper make a sad mockery of the mind he once possessed. Katherine reads "slowly, and without inflection":

> "Let X equal the quantity of all quantities of X. Let X equal the cold. It is cold in December. The months of cold equal November through February. There are four months of cold and four of heat, leaving four months of indeterminate temperature. In February it snows. In March the lake is a lake of ice. In September the students come back and the bookstores are full. Let X equal the month of full bookstores." [21]

Robert's pathetic equation about months and weather seems to signal a point of no return.

The play's primary interest lies in watching Katherine grapple with the fear that just as she inherited her father's talents she may well have inherited the illness that deflated his genius. In the opening scene, Robert chastises her for "not keeping up with the medical literature. There are all kinds of factors. It's not simply something you inherit. Just because I went bughouse doesn't mean you will..."[22] While this is the only concrete reference to heredity, the extensive resemblance Auburn creates between Robert and Katherine raises questions about the extent to which people inherit identity: questions essential to the modern debate about the biological versus environmental roots of mental illness. Katherine eventually surrenders herself to never having the kind of "proof" about her mind or future that can she can have in relation to mathematical equations. Nonetheless, where characters like Williams's Blanch DuBois and Kesey's MacMurphy ultimately seem victims to forces beyond their control, Auburn's Katherine confronts the reality of her condition and seeks ways to survive. As is true with characterizations of all marginalized groups, moving beyond images of passivity and victimization represents a crucial step in dignifying those who have been oppressed.

The Musical Stage: Rethinking Form

Given the limited visibility of even the most critically acclaimed non-musical productions in the American theater, only a musical with widespread popular appeal could make widely visible the new sensibilities in portraying mental illness in the American theater. That musical came in the form of Tom Kitt and Brian Yorkey's *Next to Normal*, which opened on Broadway in April 2009. *Next to Normal* offers an in-depth study of the toll mental illness takes upon afflicted individuals as well as their family members, of the promises and disappointments of pharmaceutical, electroshock, hypnosis and talk therapy, and of the complicated interplay between experience, predisposition, repression and substance abuse in disease. Such dark material, a stark contrast with the dreamy love stories typically associated with musical theater, was not wholly unprecedented, but did break important new ground. Reviewing *Next to Normal* for *Time Out New York*, Adam Feldman describes it as "that rarest of Broadway species: a thoughtful, emotional musical for grown-ups" after acknowledging that "it is not easy to pull off a musical about psychotropic drugs and electroconvulsive therapy."[23]

Anthony Rapp, the actor who originated the role of Mark in Jonathon Larson's *Rent*, took part in the workshops that led to *Next to Normal*. In his foreword to the published text of the musical, he reflects upon the changing face of the American musical. While acknowledging the success he has enjoyed performing in mainstream musicals, he fully understands those who have "allegeric reactions to the cornball razzamatazz of the old-school shows."[24] Working on both musicals, he describes feeling "blessed to sing songs that expressed matters of life and death in a musical vocabulary."[25]

Rent's innovations take place mainly through form and tone and the later production advancing characterization and more sophisticated ideas. Based on Giacamo Puccini's *La Boheme*, Larson's update populates the stage with far more rebellious youth and transports the action from Paris's Latin Quarter to New York City. Most of the characters in *Rent* hail from middle- and upper middle-class homes and choose quite consciously to live in poverty. They clash with the "establishment" in the form of an old friend named Benny, who wants to develop property, and their bourgeoisie parents who become stereotypical footnotes in the plot; they struggle with drug addiction and fall victim to AIDS. Mimi, the alluring central female character in the musical, makes her living as an erotic dancer, has a passion for heroine and an AIDS diagnosis. Inspiring a heartbroken Roger to love again and returning miraculously from the brink of death, Mimi proves but a raucous variation on the "whore with heart of gold." *Rent* relies on other clichés of youthful idealism, but stages them imaginatively on a set more utilitarian than aesthetically pleasing. The musical became something of an overnight sensation, and Larson's untimely death the night prior to its Broadway opening enhanced the show's mystique. For many, *Rent* made theatre once again relevant to youth culture. In fact, in an interview shortly before his death, Larson himself described *Rent* as the *Hair* of his generation.[26] While its characters and storyline may not hold up over time, *Rent* did carry forward innovations initiated by *Hair* and musicals like Andrew Lloyd Weber's *Jesus Christ Superstar*, with edgy staging and vigorous rock scores.

Next to Normal benefitted from formal innovations in musical theater while enhancing character development and undertaking wholly original investigation of complex subject matter. While certainly not devoid of humor or spectacle, the main achievement of the musical lays in offering a multi-dimensional representation of serious mental illness. Weaving together a range of attitudes and beliefs about causation and treatment, by dignifying the pain not just of the ill person but that of her family members, and never suggesting the possibility of infallible, permanent solutions, *Next to Normal* engages meaningfully with earlier depictions of mental illness.

Next to Normal presents the protagonist's central delusion through a theatrical device similar to that Auburn employs in *Proof*. However, *Next to Normal* takes more time to reveal that Diana's son, Gabe, appears only to her; these scenes, however, are written to make him seem no different from the other characters. As a result, and again complementing the sensibilities articulated in *Proof*, the show portrays delusion as somewhat matter-of-fact, plausible, and fully ingrained into Diana's "normal" day-to-day world. Isolating Gabe through unique costuming or special effects or otherwise distancing him from the rest of the action might make for more sensational theater; however, in taking the approach they do, Kitt and Yorkey iterate the reality that mental illness frequently exists just beyond the surface of "normal." Their musical begins with a number sung by all four members of the family, indicating hectic lives and strained relations, but nothing apparently beyond the dysfunction experienced by many families. She calls her son "a little shit," her husband "boring" and her daughter a "freak."[27] The characters scramble to get ready for the day. Diana bustles about making sure everyone gets breakfasts and then begins to make sandwiches to pack for lunches. Only after this semblance of routine has been established does the façade of normal begin to erode. Diana's efficiency evolves into manic energy and she begins to deal loaves of sliced bread like cards covering the kitchen table and part of the floor.

Diana's long-suffering husband, Dan, copes with her illness through repeated insistence that life will improve; at this point in the plot, he places his faith in a psychiatrist — aptly named "Dr. Fine." Dan assures Diana: "Let's go see Doctor Fine. This is just a blip. Okay? Nothing to worry about. I'll wrap up the, um, sandwiches, and then we will go."[28] Such reassurances eventually sound hollow and even Dan must concede he has been struggling primarily to convince himself. Waiting outside while Diana sees Dr. Fine, Dan sings, "Who's crazy? The husband or the wife?"[29] Dan's fierce attachment to

Diana and his determination to remain supportive, which psychologists call co-dependency, erode his own emotional health. At play's end, Doctor Madden (notably portrayed by the same actor playing Dr. Fine earlier in the production) offers to find a psychologist for Dan, who replies, "Oh, no, I. Yes. I would. Thank you."[30] The basic shape of this response aligns with the musical's larger assessment of mental health treatment; in the end, an imperfect option trumps having no option.

Diana sees Dr. Fine, who offers her pills coming in all colors of the rainbow. When one regimen does not work, another is tried, with Fine admitting "eventually we will get it right."[31] These interactions enable a witty musical interlude set to the tune of "My Favorite Things," from *The Sound of Music*, with "Zoloft and Paxil and Buspar and Xanax" and a series of other drugs taking the place of "Girls in white dresses with blue satin sashes, snowflakes that stay on my nose and eyelashes" as the "favorite" things.[32] Fine's warnings about possible side effects and Diana's experience of them expose one of the downsides of pharmaceutical treatment. And when Dr. Fine determines that Diana is stable only when she tells him, "I don't feel like myself. I don't feel anything" clearly refers to other reservations about medication.[33] In one of the show's most striking musical numbers, "I Miss the Mountains," Diana mourns the loss of feeling brought on by medication. Numbing effects, diminished creativity, and the loss of individuality frequently propel arguments against the use of drug therapy and correspond with assertions that theories relying on the notion of "mental illness" functions only to denigrate individuals otherwise too passionate to conform to societal norms.

Next to Normal resists the impulse to define mental illness and the psychiatric profession with broad strokes, however, and acknowledges how psychotropic medication does prove effective. Bolstered by Gabe's insistence that going off her medication represents an act of bravery, Diana becomes manic. She finds these episodes liberating at first, and Dan is convinced that things are better than ever. Drifting further and further from reality, Diana throws a birthday celebration for Gabe. She displays a cake boasting eighteen candles and performs a solo rendition of "Happy Birthday." Dan and Natalie look on in horror. Making the spectacle particularly unbearable for Natalie is that Henry visits their home for the first time. Her hopes to keep Henry from knowing the whole story of her family collapse as she is forced to explain her mother's pathological denial of a child's death.

After the disastrous evening with Henry, Diana must admit the truth about going off her medication, and Dan locates a psychiatrist, Dr. Madden, who offers alternatives to drug therapy. Hypnosis leaves Diana with overwhelming sadness without resolving issues related to Gabe. Determined to make greater progress, Madden turns next to Electroconvulsive Therapy

(ECT) The prospect of ECT initially horrifies Dan. Scenes of Madden trying to convince Dan of the safety and effectiveness of the treatment are juxtaposed with scenes of Gabe urging a desperate Diana to join him "in a place" where "the pain goes away."[34] A parallel to the earlier scene about medication, an element seduction of underlies this exchange and Gabe again proves persuasive. Diana attempts to take her own life. This crisis convinces Dan to try ECT and when we see Diana again, she is on a gurney about to be rolled into a treatment room. Gabe materializes and again coaxes Diana to refuse treatment. Diana rediscovers her conviction in a song making allusions to *One Flew Over the Cuckoo's Nest*.[35] In other references to the larger context of her problem and to actual women who have succumbed to mental illness and suicide, she sings about not being Sylvia Plath or Frances Farmer.[36]

The Broadway production places Diana in between her husband and (late) son, suggesting a power struggle in a clear expression of oedipal tensions. For much of the time, Diana's gaze remains fixed on Gabe, but in the last moments of the act, she turns slowly towards Dan and gives her assent to ECT.

When the second act begins, a dummy lies on the gurney while Diana "watches" herself undergo shock therapy. Such staging gives physical expression to rather abstract philosophical thoughts about identity. Diana understands that on one level she remains the same woman she longs for in "I Miss the Mountains," however she also exists within the pain of her own dysfunction, fear, confusion and loss. After completing a series of ECT treatments, Diana has essentially no memory. She returns to Dan and Natalie something of a blank slate. Having been encouraged by Madden to use mementos to help free her memory, they sit with her at the table. In keeping with his determination to remain positive, Dan shares souvenirs from their wedding day and photos of a younger Natalie playing on the beach. The way he relishes the possibility of recreating Diana's emotional life poses perplexing existential questions. Should medical procedures truly enable an adult to bury memory of former experience, who does their patient really *become*? Without awareness of our own past and the way it has shaped us, can we have truly stable identity? Appalled by her father's plan, Natalie shares entirely different mementos, such as a newspaper story about an incident in which Diana created a public spectacle, photos capturing Diana's destruction of house and property (and even running over a family pet), and pieces of evidence documenting Diana's absence at key events in her daughter's childhood.

Natalie alternates verses with Diana in the Act Two opening number, "Wish I Were There." The two characters are separated from one another, with the staging of Diana's ECT experience on one level and Natalie's interactions on another. Natalie has begun abusing prescription drugs and gives an embarrassing performance playing wildly improvised piano music rather than the pieces she has prepared. The parallel scenes underscore the shared experience of a distancing from self: Diana alienated by the current running through her body and Natalie divided from herself by drug abuse. This staging also expresses Natalie's complex relationship to a mother she at once needs desperately and finds repellant. Understandably, Natalie fears suffering a fate similar to her mother's and there is even some suggestion that Diana's own mother may have been manic. (In consultation with her doctor, Diana explains that her mother too was "high-spirited, so much so that she was kicked out of the PTA").[37] In addition to raising the issue of genetics and chemical dependency, representation of Natalie's predicament provides other insights into mental illness. The lyrics in her first solo reveal plans to get a musical scholarship to attend Yale as means to escape her parents' home. The song also makes significant references to engage with the idea of "mad genius" and mental illness, contrasting Mozart's madness to the beauty of his compositions.[38]

When Henry enters the scene, early for his reservation of the same practice room, an interaction about opposing tastes in music and lifestyle helps throw into relief Natalie's disposition. References to Natalie in an earlier musical number have already characterized her as rigid and perfectionist. Her staunch defense of classical music against Henry's preoccupation with improvisational jazz and a generally prim tone reinforce this impression. As difficulties at home compound, she tries on a completely opposite demeanor. Her jump between two extremes — from an intolerance of even marijuana use to the abuse of potent chemicals, from a pianist dedicated to a narrow elitist definition of music to a the reckless improvisation at her recital — reflects impulses common in coping with mental illness. Indeed, drastic solutions to the puzzle presented by mental illness inform many of the trends discussed earlier in this chapter. What Natalie, and indeed all the characters come to accept, is the futility of searching for a formula to resolve the problem of living with mental illness.

Eventually, Diana's memory of the trauma of losing a child is freed. Realizing the need to sort out her difficulties alone, she moves out. Natalie finally trusts Henry's assurances that he can cope with the unpredictable course their relationship might take. She accepts that instincts may fluctuate, but need not be expressed in their totality: that identity is not stable but subject to constant, though often subtle, shifts in perspective. And, in one of the play's most gut-wrenching scenes, Gabe breaks down Dan's resistance to him. Forced to "see" and engage this son and all he represents, Dan allows himself to collapse into Gabe. And finally, as aforementioned, Dan agrees to seek help from a system that may be fallible, but is also capable of support. As the musical concludes, its entire cast of characters venture into unknown territory: For the first time in her illness, Diana lives alone; Henry and Natalie accept that they can neither predict nor control the course their relationship will take; and Dan is finally forced to focus on his own mental health instead of submerging himself in his wife's problems.

Conclusion

The discussion above reveals a range of ideas about mental illness articulated through different formal structures in the modern American theater. Equally vital to the evolution of these representations is the changing regard for theater in American culture.

Where the general public had some acquaintance with Eugene O'Neill, Tennessee Williams, and Arthur Miller when they were writing, theater has been become less visible alongside the rapidly growing appeal of film and television. Rising prices and a more rigid line dividing social classes reinforced this shift. As the twentieth century drew towards an end, the theater seemed relevant to an ever narrowing segment of the population. The scene began to shift once more as Broadway tours of popular musicals engaged audiences across the country, nudging theater back into mainstream American culture. In the course that the modern American theater has taken, *Next to Normal* was an important milestone. While not on an artistic level comparable to that achieved by Tennessee Williams, Arthur Miller, or Eugene O'Neill, and not arousing the same degree of passion as attended *One Flew over the Cuckoo's Nest*, the reception to Kitt and Yorkey's musical attests to shifting perspectives in the larger culture. A once taboo subject, mental illness has gradually emerged from the shadows of shame and mystery. More public discussion of mental illness and greater sophistication in thinking about its origins, the different forms it takes, and treatment options have created a unique audience. Thinking about mental illness as a complex and nuanced reality expands the possibilities for characterizing it on stage.

Early representations of mental illness in the modern American theater conformed to unity of form and content. While Patrick's *The Curious Savage* and Kesey's *One Flew over the Cuckoos Nest* offer markedly different ideas and vary immensely in tone, each one remains solidly within the convention it employs. Patrick stays true to the formula provided him by comedy just as completely as Kesey remains within the confines of serious realism. Despite working at opposing extremes, both playwrights depend on melodrama's rigid definitions of good and bad to resolve their discussions. Even though *One Flew over the Cuckoo's Nest* offers a far more complex and unforgiving rendering of mental health treatment, in final analysis, the play leaves as little room for ambiguity as the idealized portrait with which we are left in *The Curious Savage*. Their expression of the notion that those "sent away" are more misunderstood than ill differs only in terms of degree. The more revered drama of the mid-century, that written by O'Neill, Williams, and Miller, considers more deeply the suffering of imperfect characters; and, by capturing the sensation of dreams, Williams and Miller alike brought new dimensions to their images. To varying degrees, Shaffer's *Equus* and Auburn's *Proof* incorporate dream sequences and other conventions beyond strict theatrical realism. Additionally these plays leave their audiences with open-ended questions rather than rigid conclusions. Shaffer and Auburn recognize the complex issues and ideas surrounding mental illness. *Proof* also provides a mix of comic and serious moments which set it apart from earlier representations.

From the predictable to complex, from the melodramatic to the haunting, from reassuring sentiment to heated social commentary: evolving images of mental illness offered Kitt and Yorkey a rich legacy. The stage was set for serious consideration of a difficult reality through a form once largely associated with spectacle and optimism. The barriers that once separated various theatrical conventions, along with narrow concepts of the kind of material appropriate within the confines of these conventions, have gradually given way. Such development echoes the voices engaged in society's ongoing conversation about mental illness.

NOTES

1. Barry Griffin, *The Boys Next Door* (New York: Dramatists Play Service, 1983), 49–50.
2. Griffin, 34.
3. Griffin, 52.
4. John Patrick, *The Curious Savage* (New York: Dramatists Play Service, 1950), 76.
5. Tennessee Williams, *A Streetcar Named Desire* (New York: Signet, 1947), 142.
6. Dale Wasserman, *One Flew Over the Cuckoo's Nest* (New York: Samuel French, 1970), 9.
7. Wasserman, 7.
8. Wasserman, 9.
9. Wasserman, 25.
10. Wasserman, 93.
11. Marta Caminero-Santangelo, *The Madwoman Can't Speak: Why Madness Isn't Subversive* (Ithaca, NY: Cornell University Press, 1998), 8.
12. Caminero-Santangelo, 18.
13. While *Equus* debuted in 1973 at the Royal National Theatre in London, the play is included in a discussion of American theatre given the critical acclaim of its Broadway production. *Equus* received the Antoinette Perry Award for the Best Play of 1973.
14. Peter Shaffer, *Equus* (London: Samuel French, 1973), 4.
15. Shaffer, 69.

16. Dave Bayer, "Review of David Auburn's *Proof*," *Notices of the AMS* [American Mathematical Society], Volume 47, Number 4: 1082, http://www.ams.org/notices/200009/rev-bayer.

17. David Auburn, *Proof* (New York: Faber and Faber, 2001), 11.

18. Auburn, 12.

19. Bayer, 1083.

20. Auburn, 70.

21. Auburn, 73–74.

22. Auburn, 10.

23. Adam Feldman, "Review of *Next to Normal*," *Time Out: New York*, April 23, 2009, http://newyork.timeout.com/arts-culture/theater/35112/next-to-normal.

24. Anthony Rapp, "Foreword," *Next to Normal* by Tom Kitt and Brian Yorkey (New York: Theatre Communications Group, 2010), ix.

25. Rapp, xiii.

26. *New York Times* theatre critic Anthony Tommasini interviewed Jonathon Larson just hours before Larson's death. He writes about this interview and the reference to *Hair* in "The Seven Year Odyssey that Led to *Rent*," published on March 17, 1996, http://www.nytimes.com/1996/03/17/theater/theather-the-seven-year-odyssey-that-led-to-rent.html?ref=jonathanlarson.

27. Brian Kitt and Thomas Yorkey, *Next to Normal* (New York: Theatre Communications Group, 2010), 9.

28. Kitt and Yokey, 15.

29. Kitt and Yorkey, 17.

30. Kitt and Yorkey, 103.

31. Kitt and Yorkey, 18.

32. Kitt and Yorkey, 18.

33. Kitt and Yorkey, 18.

34. Kitt and Yorkey, 52.

35. Kitt and Yorkey, 6.

36. Kitt and Yorkey, 57.

37. Kitt and Yorkey, 39.

38. Kitt and Yorkey, 15.

BIBLIOGRAPHY

Auburn, David. *Proof.* New York: Faber and Faber, 2001.

Bayer, Dave. "Review of David Auburn's *Proof.*" *Notices of the AMS* [American Mathematical Society], Volume 47, Number 4: 1082–1084. Accessed October 22, 2010. http://www.ams.org/notices/200009/rev-bayer.pdfBayer, David.

Caminero-Santangelo, Marta. *The Madwoman Can't Speak or Why Madness Isn't Subversive.* Ithaca, NY: Cornell University Press, 1998.

Feldman, Adam. "Review of *Next to Normal. Time Out New York*, April 23, 2009. Accessed January 13, 2011. http://newyork.timeout.com/arts-culture/theater/35112/next-to-normal.

Griffin, Tom. *The Boys Next Door: A Play in Two Acts.* New York: Dramatists Play Service, 1988.

Kesey, Ken. *One Flew Over the Cuckoo's Nest.* New York: Signet, 1962.

Kesserling, Joseph. *Arsenic and Old Lace.* New York: Dramatists Play Service, 1969.

Kitt, Tom, and Brian Yorkey. *Next to Normal.* New York: Theatre Communications Group, 2010.

Miller, Arthur. *Death of a Salesman.* New York: Viking Press, 1949.

O'Neill, Eugene. *Long Day's Journey into Night.* New Haven: Yale University Press, 1955.
Patrick, John. *The Curious Savage.* New York: Dramatists Play Service, 1951.
Puccini, Giacomo. *La Boheme: In Full Script.* New York: Dover, 1987.
Rapp, Anthony. "Foreword." *Next to Normal,* xi-xiv. New York: Theatre Communications Group, 2010.
Shaffer, Peter. *Equus.* London: Samuel French, 1973.
Tommasini, Anthony. "The Seven Year Odyssey that Led to *Rent.*" *New York Times,* March 17, 1996. Accessed January 18, 2011. http://www.nytimes.com/1996/03/17/theater/theather-the-seven-year-odyssey-that-led-to-rent.html?ref=jonathanlarson.
Wasserman, Dale. *One Flew Over the Cuckoo's Nest.* New York: Samuel French, 1970.
Williams, Tennessee. *A Streetcar Named Desire.* New York: Signet, 1947.

11

New Media as a Powerful Ally in the Representation of Mental Illness

YouTube, Resistance and Change

KATIE ELLIS

YouTube.com is a user-generated video file-sharing platform where anyone with an Internet connection and digital video camera can upload their own video production. Ranging from the amateur to the professional, these user-generated videos allow a variety of representation not often seen in mainstream media. In May 2008 the Treatment Advocacy Centre of the United States blogged about a YouTube video that had been posted of an unmedicated woman with bipolar disorder confronting other passengers on an Atlanta train. The so-called "Solja girl" video went viral — not only had the woman become the face of mental illness for the other passengers on the train, but she reached a global audience. Other YouTube users posted mashups of the initial video to music and personal reflections on what they saw as unprovoked, antagonistic behaviour. With 847,638 views and 10,274 comments, conversations around the initial video reflected and reinforced stigma associated with mental illness. Some comments include:

> "Oh my God ... what a horrible person."
> "That was scary"
> "What a nutcase."
> "She needed to be popped in the mouth."
> "Someone forgot to take her meds.."
> "I'd hit her in the middle of the face with a baseball bat if i was just sitting there in the train going home or anything. i'm pretty sure i would have support"

"Yall can't see that this girl is mentally insane."
"Shes disturbeddd"
"If i had been on the train i would have —— — kicked her in the face."
"That chick needs to be medicated."
"THIZ FEMALE CRAZY"
"Somebody call the doctor. This girl is obviously not healthy in the head"
"Definitely psychotic"
"Schizophrenia is a terrible illness of the mind. She needs meds STAT! Or she needs to up her dosage."
"This girl is having a psychotic episode. Somebody should have called the doctors in white coats to take her to the nearest state mental hospital."
"...wow ... get this b —— a straight jacket..."
"nuuuuuuuuuuuuuuuttsssssssssss"[1]

While these comments represent a variety of opinion, they most clearly reflect the social stigma attached to people with mental health conditions and the association the general public has between mental illness and danger, criminal behaviour and unpredictability.[2] These kinds of labels create a cultural stigma around mental illness which may prevent people from seeking the treatment they require.[3]

These cultural stereotypes are usually initiated and reinforced through mainstream media while web-based video sharing sites are providing an opportunity for cultural change. The tendency to use slang or terminology which emphasizes disorders over people is a troubling aspect of media representation.[4] Although in this case, the stigmatizing conversation began on YouTube, the video-sharing platform also gave people close to the woman an opportunity to respond. A video post from her brother received 516,917 views and 3,558 comments and opened up a conversation around mental illness and the damaging effects of negative community attitudes.[5] Several others responded to both videos with videos of their own aimed at setting the record straight on mental illness. Following the brother's video, one woman even addressed her own initial video and encouraged others to think of the effects of their labelling and stigma — as she had. [6]

YouTube embraces the cultural phenomenon described by Bruns as produsage. Web 2.0 or the read-write web enables and encourages users to become producers — produsers. This in turn can lead to the challenging and updating of inequitable social tendencies.[7] Web 2.0 is characterized by networks that get stronger the more people are in and contributing to them. Web 2.0 applications are characterised by collaboration and contribution amongst disparate groups.[8] Popular zeitgeist suggests these platforms are accessible and supportive of collaboration and interaction. Blogs or "weblogs" were one of the first platforms allowed via Web 2.0 that resulted in critical attention, particularly within media and disability studies.[9] Unlike typical diaries or journals, blogs are characterized by community and encourage dialogue via the contribution of comments. Illness blogs are an important function of this new form of communication because they allow people experiencing illness to share their day-by-day, hour-by-hour feelings while gaining and sharing information and emotional support.[10] Social and medical constructions, topics frequently discussed in these spaces, hold relevance to the social model of disability (a critical framework I will discuss throughout this chapter).

As an extension of blogging, video-sharing sites such as YouTube provide an important opportunity to address social discrimination particularly in relation to stereotypes of mental illness. This chapter explores the way new media, and particularly YouTube, contributes to possibilities for resistance and change regarding media imagery of people with mental illness. YouTube provides an opportunity to address and revise the prejudice against people with mental illness and has been used by both people with mental illness for the purpose of autobiographical testimony and mental health advocates interested in "stigmabusting."[11]

I begin this chapter with a consideration of the ways mental illness is commonly represented in the mainstream media. Although classification of this kind is critiqued and problematized in the recent literature, there is still a powerful and pervasive idea about mental illness that structures the media agenda. Stereotypes associating mental illness with "violent criminals, helpless victims or laughable lunatics"[12] perpetuate stigma and can overturn positive perceptions of the ability of people experiencing these conditions to live safely in the community. Research shows that media constructions still negatively influence people's perceptions even when they have had positive personal interactions with people with mental illness.[13] As the social model of disability articulates, imagery and camera framing isolate and stigmatize this group as outside the norm.[14] While the social model is a useful tool to investigate these media tendencies, the discipline has been broadly criticized for neglecting to consider mental illness within its theorization. However, recent theorization in this area recognises that like people with disability, people with mental illness are discriminated against and their perspectives ignored.[15] As the chapter progresses, the significance of the conversations regarding mental illness taking place on YouTube and their potential contribution to the social model of disability will become clear.

Despite the deficiencies of the social model of disability with relation to a critical analysis of mental illness, some aspects of the theorization can be applied to mental illness in popular culture. The second section of the chapter will therefore move to consider the relevance of the disability cultural movement of the 1990s as activists, academics, and media producers began arguing that people with disability should be in charge of their own image because they had been subjugated by medicalized accounts for too long.[16] Often, the media frames stories around the expert opinions of medical professionals. As Goggin suggests in the context of empowering people with disability:

> It has been these experts to whom we have been asked, or directed, to listen about disability. Hence a key tenet about listening is the need to recognize the expertise of people with experience of disability in conversation, knowledge and research.[17]

Posts on YouTube by people with disability are addressing this medicalization by foregrounding the lived experience of disability, impairment and illness instead.[18] Likewise, people with mental illness upload, share, and view videos on YouTube to combat negative stereotypes perpetuated by mainstream media. This section will concentrate on a post by the Anti Stigma Project as it questions the stigmas attached to people with mental health conditions and reveals what it is like to live with mental illness.

These campaigns demonstrate the media as a potentially powerful ally in changing media representations which stigmatize and stereotype. Wahl argues that the frequency of stereotypical imagery and the lack of any alternative have a demonstrated impact on whether affected people will seek help.[19] While it is in these organisation's best interests to create a supportive environment, whereby affected people will feel comfortable to seek help, they do not necessarily address the issue of encouraging the stories made by people experiencing mental illness.

Personal narratives are of great significance to the cultural conversation taking place on YouTube. This is particularly so because the tendency to value the expert opinion of medical professionals has been shown to have a stifling effect on how individuals experience and retell the narrative of their own experience.[20] The third section of the paper considers the techniques adopted and narratives embraced in several video diaries made by a number of vloggers (video bloggers) with a variety of mental health conditions active on YouTube. Video enhances qualitative research by visually capturing lived experiences and emphasizing subjectivity.[21] This section will use autopathography as a theoretical framework to highlight the importance of allowing people experiencing mental illness to tell their own stories. YouTube uniquely enables these types of representations by putting distribution under the control of people actually experiencing the illness and associated social stigma. Further, YouTube's format allows the filmmaker to provide context and the audience to comment. Such a conversation invites the creation of community, which while not a replacement for traditional therapy, has potentially therapeutic and life-affirming benefits.[22] This feature of YouTube invites a consideration of production, text and reception as suggested by several theorists within disability media studies.[23] In this post-structural model, the filmmaker and the spectator have equal weighting, as ideology and context are acknowledged. I conclude with reflections towards this end.

Media Images

Research into mental illness and the media has traditionally focused on a sort of classification of images. While Wahl (2003) identifies the serial killer, psycho-rapist, child molester, homicidal maniac, loony artist, demented scientist, unstable roommate, rampaging escaped mental patient, insanely jealous lover, sociopathic murderer, and weird scientist, Stuart (2006) suggests media images emphasize associations with danger, criminal behaviour and unpredictability. Philo et al. (1994) trace stigmatization back to an emphasis by the media on violence where people experiencing mental illness are portrayed in three ways as "violent criminals, helpless victims or laughable lunatics."[24] However, with the more recent proliferation of participatory media, theorization has identified the need for a more comprehensive analysis, particularly into the potential for the media to act as a powerful ally in shifting prejudices about the experience of mental illness and who should talk about it.[25]

In the seminal book on media images of mental illness *Media Madness: Public Images of Mental Illness*, Otto Wahl argues that the media has a material effect on public opinion regarding mental illness. He posits that prejudice and negative stereotyping can be directly tied to the media.[26] His argument that filmic representation and news stories of deranged serial killers, homicidal maniacs, and escaped mental patients are internalized by the general public was backed up by a 1993 study of the impact of these types of images on audience beliefs.[27] In this study Philo et al. found that 40 percent of people surveyed associated mental illness with violence and gave media imagery as the origin of this belief. In a similar study conducted in 2009, this figure had increased to 44 percent.[28] The 2009 report argues that cinematic stereotypes of mental health conditions have not changed since the silent era and that these images and narratives have a lasting impact on cinema audiences who internalise these stereotypes as fact. For example, half of the almost 2000 people surveyed had seen a violent character with a mental health condition in a Hollywood film and 44 percent believed that people with mental illness will exhibit violent behaviour.[29] People with mental heath conditions themselves cite media as a common experience of stigma.[30]

Although mental illness could potentially affect one in every four people[31] and most of us have some experience with a person with mental illness, whether through personal experience or that of a family member or friend, the media tends to have the greatest effect on public perception of mental illness.[32] Images of mental illness in the media tend to be consistently unfavorable, with sufferers being described as different, dangerous or laughable. Negative images and ideas that emanate from these stereotypes, like inaccessible environments, disable people that live with certain illnesses and impairments.

Social Model of Disability

A theorization of representations of mental illness in the media can draw on frameworks established by the social model of disability. The social model looks to the ways society disables people through inaccessible environments and — extending to the media — prejudicial attitudes and negative stereotypes. This model is characterized by the simple separation of disability and impairment:

> Impairment is the material, bodily diversity, where people are born with, acquire, and develop particular kinds of bodies, conditions, and capacities. Disability is what happens to people with impairments in their encounters and dwelling in society and the world. It is socially created by particular relations, architectures and environments. People do not have disabilities, as they are believed to have diseases or illness. They are disabled through the way that they are treated in society.[33]

Building on the social model of disability, a number of academics and activists highlighted the significant role the media plays in disabling people that have impairments. As a disability cultural movement emerged around this concept, activists, academics, and media producers argued that people with disability should be in charge of their own image. An emphasis on establishing a counterculture of people with disability controlling the means of media production was seen as crucial in creating any sort of social change. Along with an active audience, images and narratives which did not reassure the able-bodied of their privileged position were seen as crucial.[34] Despite being long been portrayed negatively in both news and entertainment media, the portrayal of mental illness was largely left out of this discussion. People who are ill or who experience social disadvantage as a result of illness do not fit neatly into cultural and social theories, often being positioned as the real limitation from which to escape. For example, women, gay men, lesbians, and indigenous people have historically experienced a medical pathologization that has contributed to their social exclusion. Disability activists likewise refuse any association with illness, particularly within the social model which argues that most, if not all, of the problems experienced by people with disability can be solved via social manipulation. By rejecting an association with illness, impairment, and the effects of impairments, proponents of the social model believed their theoretical framework would be strengthened.[35] As such, the experience of people with mental illness was never a concern to the development or progression of the social model.[36]

Recent theorization in this area recognises that like people with disability, people with mental illness are not listened to. The fact that they were silenced by the social model is of particular concern and reveals a wider problem with this model. By focusing exclusively on disability as what society makes, the theoretical framework failed to fully deal with the material bodily differences experienced by many people with impairments, including those experiencing mental illness. As Goggin and Newell (2005) suggest:

> There is, of course, a physical and biological dimension to disability. For example, there can be significant practical issues to do with [...] dealing with the realities of mental illness [for example]. At the most profound level we dwell in our bodies. This means that it can be difficult to ascertain — whether for personal or political reasons, or a mix of both — the effects of the biological substrate of impairments as distinguished from the social shaping of disability.[37]

The reality that any experience of disability also includes an experience of impairment, illness or injury suggests any politicization must include subjectivity and embodiment. Therefore despite the tendency to silence people with mental illness as a way to strengthen the social model, media theorization around this model does have much to contribute. The representation of disability in the media is recognized as having an effect on the way disability is imagined in the wider community. In order to improve the social position of people with disability, media imagery must change. YouTube encourages an active audience that both use and produce the media agenda and as such has the greatest potential to change representation of people with disability, impairment and illness.

Nasa Begum (2000) urges mental health system survivors to reclaim the social model and use it as a way to address discrimination and prejudice as well as explain the experience of mental illness to society.[38] Mental health promoters have been called on to work with the media to ensure a more accurate portrayal of mental health.[39] Both people living with mental illness and organisations and individuals advocating on their behalf have turned to social media and Web 2.0 outlets such as YouTube to influence public perception and the media agenda.

Several organizations have used YouTube to challenge the stigma associated with mental illness. In a one-minute, thirty-second post from the Mental Health Association of Broward County in Florida, labels attributed to people with mental health conditions are considered.[40] In the *Mental Illness*

Stigma Project a woman asks people to come up with euphemisms for somebody with mental illness, and like the responses listed at the beginning of this chapter to the "Solja girl" video, a montage of disembodied lips repeat negative labels, including:

- Those people are crazy
- They're one of Gerry's kids
- *Those* people, you know, *those* people
- Space cadet
- Screws aren't too tight
- Aren't the sharpest tool in the shed
- Isn't rowing with both oars
- Crazy as a loon
- Bricks with no motar
- No light on
- Fruitcake
- Elevator doesn't quite reach the top floor

The effect of the shadowed lighting, fragmented lips and eerie music overlay is powerful. The short video opens with the statement that all of us know someone with a mental illness, and we may even be suffering from one ourselves, yet throughout the montage people with mental illness are excluded from the mainstream through the emphasis on words like "they're" and "those." This short video powerfully exposes the widespread social intolerance towards people with mental illness and reflects the way the public evaluates mental health issues. The video reshapes these labels as a form of social prejudice and cultural stigma when the narrator suggests the same exercise but for cancer instead. Following a brief silence a loud horn sounds and subtitles tell us that mental illness is "no laughing matter."

This short clip exposes stigma surrounding people with mental illness. These adverse attitudes, argues the Center for Disease Control and Prevention, communicate an uncaring and unsympathetic attitude towards people with these conditions, which in turn can prevent them from seeking help or even disclosing their condition to family and friends.[41] Reframing mainstream media is an important initiative, and Internet sites can reduce negative attitudes and stigma and encourage the seeking of help through information.[42] The *Mental Illness Stigma Project* ends with the suggestion to contact a local mental health practitioner if such help is required. Significantly, the video finishes with the words, "Working to challenge stigma and promote mental health is a goal for everyone!"

There are many other examples of anti-stigma campaigns on YouTube, including, for example, a number of 30-second videos that tap into the clip culture established by YouTube whereby audiences have limited concentration. Another campaign juxtaposes a man and a woman applying for the same job where the man discloses his mental illness and is rejected while the woman is celebrated for "overcoming" her diabetes.[43] A final anti-stigma initiative sees a young man advertise for a roommate or date using online platforms and highlights his declining responses once he discloses his mental illness.[44] This video reveals people's association between mental illness and violence as rejection emails emphasize the possibility that the man advertising for a roommate could become violent and hurt them in their sleep. While a significant move, these anti-stigma campaigns frame the narratives through the particular organization's agendas and do not necessarily foreground the lived experience of people that have mental illness. As a user-generated site, however, there are many other videos on YouTube that do center on individual's lived experiences of mental illness.

"Autopathography" Testimony

While traditional case histories stifle patients' own experiences of illness[45] and over time patients tire of having to retell their medical history to each health professional they encounter,[46] autopathography, or an autobiographical account centered on disease or disability, invites greater agency. Variously described as medical confessions, patient's tales, and plain tales from the ill,[47] I have previously emphasized their importance in a discussion of "illness narratives":

> Telling illness narratives is a valuable means of recovery when the body becomes what the individual never expected it would — damaged. Narrative is vital, as the ill person works out their changing identity, and position in the world of health, continuing when they are no longer ill, but remain marked by their experience.[48]

Autopathography possesses two distinct features —first, illness structures the narrative, and second, autopathography emphasises community.[49] According to Aronson (2000), autopathography is characterised by patients' writing their own narratives — usually out of a desire to help others, to come to terms with their own illness, for catharsis, or simply to make money. Aronson contends that stories usually contain fabrication or denial, but this is impossible to quantify. While the relevance of life writing to autopathography and psychotherapy is obvious, the emergence of new formats and ways to reflect self-identity available through Web 2.0 platforms is transforming the ways people use autopathography as a mode of self-expression and communication. Autopathography allows people the opportunity to reclaim the agency they lost when they became subjects or patients, with Web 2.0 allowing immediate publication and community:

> Blogs enable people an outlet and illness narrative blogs, which focus on the articulation of the experience of illness in order to understand it better and/ or provide support to others, have emerged as an important subgroup in the blogosphere. These online spaces hold significance for life writing as they allow sufferers (or recoverers) a way to recover a sense of agency while transforming the private into public.... Power imbalances and social constructions are de- and reconstructed within these narratives. Patients become the experts online in a massive power shift.[50]

Like Goggin and Newell's (2005) call to acknowledge subjectivity and the embodied experience of illness and disability, including for example mental illness, Couser describes autopathography as an exploration of embodied experiences and hence a sign of cultural health.[51] Autopathography embraces embodiment and rehabilitates the relevance of lived experienced within critical analysis by filtering the narrative through the author's illness.[52] Autopathography is characterized by an acknowledgement that we experience the world through our bodies and recognition that illness is more than an interruption to be overcome. Increasingly, autopathography also recognises that self-perception may be infected by cultural stereotypes and that health conditions are both culturally and physically constructed.[53]

A 2005 survey showed that 50 percent of bloggers blog for the purpose of self-therapy.[54] Therefore, it is reasonable to conclude that many video bloggers do so for psychosocial health gains.[55] The rapidly evolving online realm is having an impact on the lived experience of people experiencing illness, disease, disability, and, by extension, the way they perceive cultural stereotyping:

> Many authors currently examining the role of online spaces in the lives of sufferers of serious illness see online communication as providing a means for configuring experience as a meaningful and coherent story, and thus conferring, or we could say recovering, a sense of agency amidst a tumultuous and ongoing battle with serious illness.[56]

With the emergence and proliferation of the video-sharing site YouTube in 2005, blogging has progressed to include video blogs. Similar to blogs but using a video rather than written format, people can both watch and contribute in any way they choose. Community is emphasized through the comments section following each post. Video bloggers become broadcasters and find a space for their stories that are not generally listened to in the mainstream, allowing a reconfiguration of the experience of illness. Stream-of-consciousness writing is criticised by proponents of life writing in favour of more structure as a strategy for dealing with mental illness.[57] However, new media theorists suggest the stream-of-consciousness format can be therapeutic, especially when communities are established.[58]

In a post simply titled *Mental Illness*, prolific vlogger Reshmecka[59] engages in a stream-of-consciousness, self-described "rant" about people conflating her experiences of depression with their general everyday feelings of sadness. Having just had such an encounter in a chat room, she wants to get it off her chest. She concludes the video with a message to a recently diagnosed friend, "James," telling him she knows the difficulty and identity crisis he is experiencing in having recently been diagnosed.[60]

The video blogs in YouTube operate within a social network, and others subscribe to and comment on each other's video posts. The audience is active in exactly the way Hevey envisioned in 1997 regarding the utopian counter-culture movement that recorded the process of cultural change by identifying the socially disabling and bodily experiences of disability and impairment without projecting an overcoming-all-odds narrative.[61] This social network relieves tension and provides a supportive 24/7 environment.[62] Like the initial video diary, this representative comment in response is both supportive and an eloquent deconstruction of cultural stigma:

> Thanks for your honesty & bravery. I'm open bout my mental illness & attempt to educate people tho receiving ridicule as well. if I can help anyone my vulnerability is worth it no matter how much hurt. People suffer to varying degrees & mental health is still so stereotyped, shunned, denied. I've gone thru a lot & struggled 20+ yrs.-still get so frustrated by peoples ignorance. I'll always battle this disease daily, but must remember not alone & as lovable as any, even those "functional" peps![63]

Unlike traditional forms of life writing or illness narratives, the aupathography allowed through the use of video technology and sharing invites a variety of styles and interactions. Stream-of-consciousness is not just words; montages and lyrical documentary styles of narrative are often used, such as the video *My story* posted by someone claiming to want help, not attention. The film consists of montage, titles, still images, and a lyrical soundtrack and fits into the poetic mode of documentary identified by Nichols. Although not traditionally political, the poetic focus on subjectivity around a topic normally silenced by expert opinion is revolutionary. According to Nichols (2001), the poetic style of documentary emphasizes subjective interpretation to

> [open] up the possibility of alternative forms of knowledge to the straightforward transfer of information, the prosecution of a particular argument or point of view, or the presentation of reasoned propositions about problems that need a solution. This mode stresses mood, tone, and affect much more than displays of knowledge or acts of persuasion.[64]

This style of filmmaking rejects rhetoric and foregrounds audience interpretation. Many of the "commenters" seem to gain solace from this video, with conversations emerging around depression, grief, cutting, and the juxtaposition of a beautiful song with gruesome images in the video itself.

Unlike traditional media, the audience is not presented with a point of view or given a solution to a social problem; rather, they are encouraged through the mood, tone, and affect to start a conversation and support each other. While the filmmakers' voice is emphasized in this mode, reality is presented as "a series of fragments, subjective impressions, incoherent acts, and loose associations" in a way that allows the audience to ponder social reality. For example in *My story*, the filmmaker juxtaposes cliché greeting card poetics such as *take me as I am* with images of cuts. Poetic engagements and reconfiguring such as this allow the audience to see the experience of mental illness anew.[65]

Grassroots communities of people with disability, usually clustered around the experience of different impairments, have emerged on YouTube. The communities seek to offer support to members and often question the expert opinions of the favoured media narrative. YouTube, as a Web 2.0 platform, features characteristics typical of the read-write web; in particular, people comment following each other's video posting, and cultural conversations emerge to sustain the communities. This is an especially important feature in light of calls by disability media theorists to use digital media for social change by emphasizing the points of view of both the filmmaker and audience alongside the text itself:

> In this post-structural model the filmmaker and the spectator have equal weighting, as ideology and context are acknowledged. While wanting to effect social change is an important starting point for the filmmaker, audience reception is crucial to the acceptance of this change. An *active* audience engaged in politics accepts social responsibility.... YouTube certainly has an active audience with the potential to enact lasting change.[66]

This interactive space of an active audience of *produsers* creates a whole new relationship between the media and individuals, individuals having a material effect on the perception of community and our relationship to society. This image can be updated, developed, challenged and co-created.[67] Perhaps this produsage will result in the questioning of the long-standing stigma that surrounds mental illness. Despite the stigma reflected in the broader cultural mode of disability and media, the produsage enabled via Web 2.0 platforms such as YouTube offers a different type of image through a different type of media. The conversations that take place amongst the communities of producer users are revolutionizing disability representation because consideration of context, text and reception are possible.

Conclusion

YouTube is a good forum for resistance and change for several reasons, including, firstly, the anti-stigma public service announcements which dispel damaging stereotypes presented in more mainstream media but do not fully embrace personal narratives. Secondly, video blogs that invite autobiographical testimonials lead to group discussions of mental health. They also provide medical professionals and the general public greater insight and empathy.[68] Communities of people experiencing mental health conditions represent the counterculture movement that Hevey envisioned in the late 1990s, as they record the process of change, present counter-images from their own lives and points of view, and do not play into the culturally prescribed dominant media imagery. This is possible because on YouTube the users are the producers who are also the distributers. YouTube and the produsage taking place on it are important to disability studies because of the emphasis on embodiment and subjectivity as well as the conversations initiated around them.

In *Disability and New Media*, Ellis and Kent recognise the importance of new media technologies to people with disability and in turn the importance of these technologies in advancing any politicization of disability. They cite YouTube as a particularly important tool in revising negative stereotypes and stigma perpetuated by mainstream media:

> In the 1990s, activists, academics, and media producers of the disability cultural movement argued that people with disability should be in charge of their image and, further, those images must make the able-bodied audience feel uncomfortable in order for social change to occur.... Web 2.0 participatory media, such as Google's YouTube, realizes this vision, and allows people with disability a new voice — a way to tell their stories and force the non-disabled world to take responsibility for the disableism that devalues the perspectives of people with disability in film and media. Systemic ableism is perpetuated by traditional media which promotes individualized representations of disability to absolve society of responsibility for creating inaccessible environments.... Mainstream media frequently represent disability in a way that reassures able-bodied people of their normality.... Digital video has long been used to subvert this and offer more complex realities of disability. Web 2.0 now provides an effective platform for the dissemination of these grass-roots videos.[69]

I began this chapter with a description of a YouTube video that prompted a conversation that embraced the slang that Wahl warns is so damaging. Yet the format of YouTube allowed others with personal experience and greater understanding and empathy the opportunity to respond and work towards encouraging greater understanding for people who are mentally ill. While the media has been instrumental in encouraging negative stereotypes, more recent platforms can act as a powerful ally. YouTube is used by both mental health advocates and communities of people who have mental illness for the purpose of decreasing stigma and documenting autobiographical accounts to benefit self and others. Communities of active audiences have emerged, and their perspectives must be considered within a social model of disability.

NOTES

1. Treatment Advocacy Centre United States, "Personal Encounters with Untreated Mental Illness, Stigma & YouTube," *Treatment Advocacy Centre,* May 20, 2008, accessed December 16, 2010, http://psychlaws.blogspot.com/2008/05/personal-encounters-with-untreated.html.

2. Heather Stuart, "Media Portrayals of Mental Illness and Its Treatments: What Effect Does It Have on People with Mental Illness," *CNS Drugs* 20, no. 2 (2006): 99.

3. Peter Wollheim, "The Erratic Front: Youtube and Representations of Mental Illness," *Entrepreneur,* Sept-Oct 2007, accessed December 1, 2010, http://www.entrepreneur.com/tradejournals/article/170456711_2.html.

4. Otto Wahl, *Media Madness, Public Images of Mental Illness* (New Brunswick, NJ: Rutgers University Press, 2006), 21.

5. shadiya7, "Re: Brother of Crazy Girl On Train," *YouTube,* May 13, 2008, accessed December 12, 2010, http://www.youtube.com/watch?v=khgfXRgDQSI.

6. Ibid.

7. Axel Bruns and Joanne Jacobs, *Use of Blogs* (New York: Peter Lang, 2006), 7.

8. Patricia McGee and Veronica Diaz, "Wikis and Podcasts and Blogs! Oh, My! What Is a Faculty Member Supposed to Do?" *Educause Review* (2007), 28.

9. See Katie Ellis and Mike Kent, *Disability and New Media* (New York: Routledge, 2011), 44–62; Beth Haller, *Representing Disability in an Ableist World: Essays on Mass Media* (Louisville, KY: Avocado Press, 2010), 1–24.

10. Michael Keren, *Blogosphere: The New Political Arena* (Lanham, MD: Lexington Books, 2006), 119.

11. Wollheim, "The Erratic Front."

12. Greg Philo et al., "The Impact of the Mass Media on Public Images of Mental Illness: Media Content and Audience Belief," *Health Education Journal* 53 (1994): 279.

13. Ibid.

14. See Katie Ellis, *Disabling Diversity: The Social Construction of Disability in 1990s Australian National Cinema* (Saarbrücken: VDM-Verlag, 2008); Martin Norden, *The Cinema of Isolation: A History of Physical Disability in the Movies* (New Brunswick, NJ: Rutgers University Press, 1994), 35.

15. See Gerard Goggin, "Disability and the Ethics of Listening," *Continuum* 23, no. 4 (2009b): 489–502; Ellis, *Disabling Diversity.*

16. David Hevey, "Controlling Interests," in *Framed: Interrogating Disability in the Media,* eds. Ann Pointon and Chris Davies, 209–13 (London: British Film Institute, 1997).

17. Goggin, "Disability and the Ethics of Listening," 495.

18. Katie Ellis, "A Purposeful Rebuilding: YouTube, Representation, Accessibility and the Socio-Political Space of Disability," *Telecommunications Journal of Australia* 60, no. 2 (2010), 21.1–21.2.

19. Wahl, *Media Madness,* 102.

20. Jeffrey K Aronson, "Autopathography: The Patient's Tale," *BMJ* 321, no. 23–30 (2000): 1599.

21. Martin Downing, "Why Video? How Technology Advances Method," *The Qualitative Report* 13, no. 2 (2008): 173.

22. Leon Tan, "Psychotherapy 2.0: MySpace Blogging as Self-Therapy," *American Journal of Psychology* 62, no. 2 (2008): 159.

23. See Ellis, *Disabling Diversity*; Tom Shakespeare, "Art and Lies? Representations

of Disability on Film," in *Disability Discourse*, eds. Mairian Corker and Sally French, 164–72 (Buckingham: Open University Press, 1999); Liz Ferrier, "Vulnerable Bodies: Creative Disabilities in Contemporary Australian Film," in *Australian Cinema in the 1990s*, ed. Ian Craven, 57–78 (London: Frank Cass, 2001).

    24. Philo et al., "Impact of the Mass Media," 279.

    25. Stuart, "Media Portrayals"; Wollheim, "The Erratic Front."

    26. Wahl, *Media Madness,* 137.

    27. Philo et al., "Impact of the Mass Media," 271.

    28. William Little, "Mental Health Stereotypes in the Movies Crueller Than Ever, New Report Claims," *Time to Change,* August 17, 2009, accessed December 1, 2010, http://www.time-to-change.org.uk/news/mental-health-stereotypes-movies-crueler-ever-new-report-claims.

    29. Ibid.

    30. Wahl, *Media Madness,* ix.

    31. "One in Four Affected," *NHS Choices,* December 12, 2009, accessed December 12, 2010, http://www.nhs.uk/Livewell/mentalhealth/Pages/Mentalhealthoverview.aspx.

    32. Philo et al., "Impact of the Mass Media."

    33. Goggin, "Ethics of Listening," 492.

    34. Hevey, "Controlling Interests."

    35. Ellis and Kent, *Disability and New Media,* 92.

    36. Peter Beresford, "Madness, Distress, Research and a Social Model," *Disability Studies Archive University of Leeds,* 2004, accessed December 14, 2010, http://www.leeds.ac.uk/disability-studies/archiveuk/Barnes/implementing%20the%20social%20model%20-%20chapter%2013.pdf.

    37. Gerard Goggin and Christopher Newell, *Disability in Australia: Exposing a Social Apartheid* (Sydney: University of New South Wales Press, 2005), 53.

    38. Nasum Begum, "Reclaiming the Social Model of Disability," Greater London Action on Disability (glad) Report, 2000, accessed December 16, 2010, http://www.leeds.ac.uk/disability-studies/archiveuk/GLAD/Social%20Model%200f%20Disability%20Conference%20Report.pdf.

    39. Rachel Harris, "Media Representation of People with Mental Health Problems," *Nursing Time.net,* August 24, 2004, accessed November 15, 2010, http://www.nursingtimes.net/nursing-practice-clinical-research/media-representation-of-people-with-mental-health-problems/204177.article.

    40. cliffordbeers, "Mental Illness Stigma Project," *YouTube* February 26, 2007, accessed December 1, 2010, http://www.youtube.com/watch?v=C0BFzvjkDcc&feature=related.

    41. "Attitudes Towards Mental Illness 35 States, District of Columbia, and Puerto Rico, 2007," *JAMA* 304, no. 2 (2010).

    42. Ibid.

    43. jwj40504, "Mental Illness Stigma Commercial," *YouTube,* December 29, 2008, accessed November 29, 2010, http://www.youtube.com/watch?v=Dw_I-G1smoo.

    44. ttcnow2008, "Don't Get Me Wrong," *YouTube,* September 14 , 2010 accessed December 1, 2010, http://www.youtube.com/watch?v=CUzHK97wdWw.

    45. Aronson, "Autopathography: The Patient's Tale," 1599.

    46. Philip Neilsen and Fiona Murphy, "The Potential Role of Life-Writing Therapy in Facilitating 'Recovery' for Those with Mental Illness," *Media-Culture* 11, no. 6 (2008).

    47. Jeffrey Aronson, "Autopathography: The Patient's Tale," 1599.

    48. Katie Ellis, "A Quest Through Chaos: My Narrative of Illness and Recovery," *Gender Forum: An Internet Journal for Gender Studies* vol. 26, issue 2 (2009), accessed December 10, 2010, http://www.genderforum.org/issues/literature-and-medicine-ii/a-quest-through-chaos/http://www.genderforum.org/issues/literature-and-medicine-ii/a-quest-through-chaos/.

49. Stephen Moran, "Autopathography and Depression: Describing the 'Despair Beyond Despair,'" *J Med Hummanit* 27 (2006): 79.

50. Ellis, "A Quest Through Chaos," accessed December 10, 2010, http://www.genderforum.org/issues/literature-and-medicine-ii/a-quest-through-chaos/.

51. Thomas Couser, "AutoPathography: Women, Illness and Life Writing *Women and Autobiography* (Washington: Scholarly Resources Inc., 1999), 164.

52. Stephen Moran, "Autopathography and Depression: Describing the 'Despair Beyond Despair,'" *J Med Humanit* 27, no. 2 (2006): 79–91.

53. Thomas Couser, "AutoPathography: Women, Illness and Life Writing."

54. Business Wire, "AOL Survey Says: People Blog as Therapy," September 16, 2005, accessed January 1, 2011, http://www.thefreelibrary.com/AOL+Survey+Says%3A+People+Blog+as+Therapy.-a0136251614.

55. Leon Tan, "Psychotherapy 2.0."

56. Anthony McCosker, "Blogging Illness: Recovering in Public," *M/C Journal* Vol. 11, No. 6 (2008), accessed December 12, 2010, http://journal.media-culture.org.au/index.php/mcjournal/article/viewArticle/104.

57. Neilsen and Murphy, "Potential Role of Life-Writing Therapy."

58. Tan, "Psychotherapy 2.0"; Ellis, "A Purposeful Rebuilding."

59. This profile shows an uploaded video total of 292,284.

60. Reshmecka, "Mental Illness," *YouTube,* November 15, 2006, accessed December 10, 2010, http://www.youtube.com/watch?v=fNZfPNMffzA.

61. Hevey, "Controlling Interests."

62. Tan, "Psychotherapy 2.0."

63. Alora666, cited on Reshmecka, "Mental Illness."

64. Bill Nichols, *Introduction to Documentary* (Bloomington: Indiana University Press, 2001), 103.

65. 03267324, "My Story," *YouTube,* July 7, 2007, accessed December 1, 2010, http://www.youtube.com/watch?v=Ee03HqOseM8&feature=related.

66. Ellis, "Purposeful Rebuilding."

67. Bruns and Jacobs, *Use of Blogs,* 6–7.

68. Wollheim, "Erratic Front."

69. Ellis and Kent, *Disability & New Media,* 69.

BIBLIOGRAPHY

03267324. "My Story." YouTube. Accessed December 1, 2010. http://www.youtube.com/watch?v=Ee03HqOseM8&feature=related.

Aronson, Jeffrey K. "Autopathography: The Patient's Tale." *BMJ* 321, no. 23–30 (2000): 1599–602.

"Attitudes Towards Mental Illness 35 States, District of Columbia, and Puerto Rico, 2007." *JAMA* 304, no. 2 (2010): 149–52.

Begum, Nasum. "Reclaiming the Social Model of Disability." Greater London Action on Disability (GLAD) Report. Accessed December 16, 2010. http://www.leeds.ac.uk/disability-studies/archiveuk/GLAD/Social%20Model%20of%20Disability%20Conference%20Report.pdf.

Beresford, Peter. "Madness, Distress, Research and a Social Model." Disability Studies Archive University of Leeds. Accessed December 14, 2010. http://www.leeds.ac.uk/disability-studies/archiveuk/Barnes/implementing%20the%20social%20model%20-%20chapter%2013.pdf.

Bruns, Axel, and Joanne Jacobs. *Use of Blogs.* New York: Peter Lang, 2006.

Business Wire. "AOL Survey Says: People Blog as Therapy." The Free Library. Accessed

January 1, 2010. http://www.thefreelibrary.com/AOL+Survey+Says%3A+People+Blog +as+Therapy.-a0136251614.

cliffordbeers. "Mental Illness Stigma Project." YouTube. Accessed December 1, 2010. http://www.youtube.com/watch?v=C0BFzvjkDcc&feature=related.

Couser, Thomas. "Autopathography: Women, Illness and Life Writing." In *Women and Autobiography*, eds. Martine Watson Brownley and Allison B. Kimmich, 167–176. Washington: Scholarly Resources Inc., 1999.

Downing, Martin. "Why Video? How Technology Advances Method." *The Qualitative Report* 13, no. 2 (2008): 173–77.

Ellis, Katie. *Disabling Diversity: The Social Construction of Disability in 1990s Australian National Cinema.* Saarbrücken: VDM-Verlag, 2008.

_____. "A Purposeful Rebuilding: YouTube, Representation, Accessibility and the Socio-Political Space of Disability." *Telecommunications Journal of Australia* 60, no. 2 (2010): 21.1–21.12.

_____. "A Quest through Chaos: My Narrative of Illness and Recovery." *Gender Forum: An Internet Journal for Gender Studies* 26, no. 2 (2009). Accessed December 10, 2010. http://www.genderforum.org/issues/literature-and-medicine-ii/a-quest-through-choase/.

Ellis, Katie, and Mike Kent. *Disability and New Media, Routledge Studies in New Media and Cyberculture.* New York: Routledge, 2011.

Ferrier, Liz. "Vulnerable Bodies: Creative Disabilities in Contemporary Australian Film." In *Australian Cinema in the 1990s*, ed. Ian Craven, 57–78. London: Frank Cass, 2001.

Goggin, Gerard. "Disability and the Ethics of Listening." *Continuum* 23, no. 4 (2009b): 489–502.

Goggin, Gerard, and Christopher Newell. *Disability in Australia: Exposing a Social Apartheid.* Sydney: University of New South Wales, 2005.

Haller, Beth. *Representing Disability in an Ableist World: Essays on Mass Media.* Louisville, KY: Avocado Press, 2010.

Harris, Rachel. "Media Representation of People with Mental Health Problems." Nursing Time.net. Accessed December 10, 2010. http://www.nursingtimes.net/nursing-prac tice-clinical-research/media-representation-of-people-with-mental-health-prob lems/204177.article.

Hevey, David. "Controlling Interests." In *Framed: Interrogating Disability in the Media*, eds. Ann Pointon and Chris Davies, 209–13. London: British Film Institute, 1997.

jwj40504. "Mental Illness Stigma Commercial." YouTube. Accessed November 29, 2010. http://www.youtube.com/watch?v=Dw_I-G1smoo.

Keren, Michael. *Blogosphere: The New Political Arena.* Lanham, MD: Lexington Books, 2006.

Little, William. "Mental Health Stereotypes in the Movies Crueler Than Ever, New Report Claims." Time to Change. Accessed November 29, 2010. http://www.time-to-change. org.uk/news/mental-health-stereotypes-movies-crueler-ever-new-report-claims.

McCosker, Anthony. "Blogging Illness: Recovering in Public." *M/C Journal* 11 no. 6 'recover' (2008). Accessed December 10, 2010. http://journal.media-culture.org.au/index. php/mcjournal/article/viewArticle/104.

McGee, Patricia, and Veronica Diaz. "Wikis and Podcasts and Blogs! Oh, My! What Is a Faculty Member Supposed to Do?" *Educause Review* Vol. 43 no 5 (2007): 28–40.

Moran, Stephen. "Autopathography and Depression: Describing the 'Despair Beyond Despair.'" *J Med Hummanit*, no. 27 (2006): 79–91.

Neilsen, Philip Max, and Fiona Murphy. "The Potential Role of Life-Writing Therapy in Facilitating 'Recovery' for Those with Mental Illness." *Media-Culture* 11, no. 6 'recover' (2008). Accessed December 10, 2010. http://journal.media-culture.org.au/index.php/ mcjournal/article/viewArticle/110.

Nichols, Bill. *Introduction to Documentary*. Bloomington: Indiana University Press, 2001.

Norden, Martin. *The Cinema of Isolation : A History of Physical Disability in the Movies*. New Brunswick, NJ: Rutgers University Press, 1994.

"One in Four Affected." NHS Choices. Accessed December 1, 2010. http://www.nhs.uk/ Livewell/mentalhealth/Pages/Mentalhealthoverview.aspx.

Philo, Greg. "Changing Media Representations of Mental Health." *Psychiatry and the Media* 21 (1997): 171–72.

Philo, Greg, Jenny Secker, Steve Platt, Lesley Hendersen, Greg McLaughlin, and Jenny Burnside. "The Impact of the Mass Media on Public Images of Mental Illness: Media Content and Audience Belief." *Health Education Journal* 53 (1994): 271–81.

Reshmecka. "Mental Illness." *YouTube*. Accessed December 10, 2010. http://www.youtube. com/watch?v=fNZfPNMffzA.

shadiya7. "Re: Brother of Crazy Girl On Train." YouTube. Accessed December 10, 2010. http://www.youtube.com/watch?v=khgfXRgDQSI.

Shakespeare, Tom. "Art and Lies? Representations of Disability on Film." In *Disability Discourse*, eds. Mairian Corker and Sally French, 164–72. Buckingham: Open University Press, 1999.

Stuart, Heather. "Media Portrayals of Mental Illness and Its Treatments: What Effect Does It Have on People with Mental Illness." *CNS Drugs* 20, no. 2 (2006): 99–106.

Tan, Leon. "Psychotherapy 2.0: Myspace Blogging as Self-Therapy." *American Journal of Psychology* 62, no. 2 (2008): 143–63.

Treatment Advocacy Centre United States. "Personal Encounters with Untreated Mental Illness, Stigma & YouTube." Accessed December 16, 2010. http://psychlaws.blogspot.com /2008/05/personal-encounters-with-untreated.html.

ttcnow2008. "Don't Get Me Wrong." YouTube. http://www.youtube.com/watch?v=CUz HK97wdWw.

Wahl, Otto. *Media Madness: Public Images of Mental Illness*. 2d ed. New Brunswick, NJ: Rutgers University Press, 2003.

Wollheim, Peter. "The Erratic Front: YouTube and Representations of Mental Illness." *Entrepreneur*. Accessed December 1, 2010. http://www.entrepreneur.com/tradejournals/ article/170456711_2.html.

12

On the Wings of Icarus

Exploring the Flawed Superhero

LAWRENCE C. RUBIN

Why We Need Superheroes

In their *Myth of the American Superhero,* John Lawrence and Robert Jewett suggested that contemporary superhero tales are no less than modern-day mythological epics, which have had profound and important effects on American (and world) culture. Their position was antidotal to the lament of psychologist Rollo May, who, in *The Cry for Myth,* proclaimed that contemporary societies have lost their direction because their mythologies and, by association, their histories have been marginalized

Lawrence and Jewett believed that it was the superhero story, or "American monomyth," with its historical epicenter in the American Revolution and later in the conquest of the Wild West, that seemed to revitalize our society's eroded historical and moral foundation. Their "myth" of the American superhero, which centered on the selfless hero's redemptive mission to restore a threatened community to its formerly paradisiacal state, while illusory, was important in consolidating the mythos of the American spirit. Just as their mythological precursors did, superhero tales provide a stage upon which deeply human passion plays are (re)enacted and, most importantly and once again, offer us heroes to inspire, guide, and teach. For Gerard Jones, these tales of mighty men and women "distill the passions of children and outsiders to such pure glowing symbols that they can be passed from generation to generation without dimming [and are thus able to] find their way to some hidden yearning."[1] And just as America symbolizes strength, stability, and power in a chaotic and dangerous world, these uniquely American characters, according to Loeb and Morris, "believe in themselves and in their cause, and they go all out to achieve their goals ... by showing us how even very powerful people have to fight to struggle to stick to what is right in order to prevail."[2]

By providing an organic link to stories of mythological heroes and deeds, superhero stories anchor us firmly in the past while orienting us toward the future. Whether it is Batman crusading against the demons of Gotham, The Fantastic Four sacrificing themselves to save the planet from deadly cosmic radiation, or the Watchmen once again bringing order to a misguided society, these stories are signifiers of hope and perseverance actualized. As such, according to William Marston, creator of Wonder Woman, superhero stories "satisfy the universal longing to be stronger than all opposing obstacles and the equally universal desire to see good overcome evil, to see wrongs righted, underdogs nip at the parts of their oppressors, and withal, to experience vicariously the supreme gratification of the deus ex machina who accomplishes these monthly miracles of right triumphing over not-so-mighty might."[3]

At the core of these stories is the hero, the conflicted and, more often than not, reluctant do-gooder who must simultaneously fend off inner demons and "real-life" ne'er-do-wells who forever test their conviction and vision for a better world. They are gods, and we worship them with the same conviction our ancestors offered up. We ask much of them — out of both hope and desperation for solutions and answers. We expect no less from them but greatness, and in the process, we strip them of their humanity — as Lucy Hughes-Hallet suggests, so that we may project both our inadequacies and fantasies upon them.[4] They are colorful and powerful, yet irredeemably flawed blank slates who stand in and stand up for us. In this way, according to Ira Talpin, these heroes "enable us to externalize the inner contradictions of our lives ... are also a safety valve for our collective frustrations"[5] and as such help us to reconcile the inescapable discordance between the promises and disappointments inherent in contemporary society.

Emergence of the "Real" Superhero

Early superhero tales, often referred to as those of the "golden age," drew heavily from the realm of fantasy and mythology. Superman came from another planet, Wonder Woman was an Amazonian princess, Aquaman inhabited the lost continent of Atlantis, and Thor descended from the Norse gods. These golden-age heroes were, according to Mordecai Richler, "invulnerable, all-conquering champions for children providing revenge against what seemed a gratuitously cruel adult world."[6] In the spirit of their literary predecessors, who braved the western frontier and traveled to the far reaches of outer space, these early superheroes were self-reliant and rugged individualists who rarely, if ever, doubted themselves, answered to no one, and often rose above the law and prevailing legal and political authority in order to get the job done. They were, as Jamie Hughes observed, black and white figures with a very simplistic goal: protecting the world from evil. In order to embrace such adventures, the reader had to engage willingly in "primary process thinking," a primitive form of cognition characteristic of fantasy, dreams and the unconscious. The reader had little to do other than sit back, suspend reality, and enjoy the bold adventures.

Just as the primary process thinking of childhood must give way to the more mature reality-based "secondary process thinking" of adulthood, which relies upon logic, reason and reality, the fantastic figures of the golden age had to evolve in order to meet the demands of a maturing genre and its readership. Jamie Hughes noted, "With each passing year, superheroes [became] more involved in 'real world' scenarios that mirrored current political and social problems."[7] Superheroes became more complex and multi-layered characters that, in spite of their inescapable disconnect from society, lived and functioned within it. For comic historian Peter Coogan, events and places from the real world became incorporated to the point where superhero characters took on more complex characteristics and personal self-reflection became important.

The self-doubting and deeply flawed superheroes of the so-called "Silver Age" began their ascent to the pantheon once reserved for their physically and psychologically flawless predecessors. Simply, superheroes became more human and their motives more grounded in the reality of day-to-day struggles. As opposed to the perennial good guys of Superman and Captain America, the "brooding psychopath of Batman, Rorschach and the other Minutemen," according to Jamie Huges, "chose to do it for more mundane reasons — money, power, fame or to promote their own ideology."[8] It is likely no coincidence that the political and ideological upheaval of the 1960s contributed to the emergence of this new breed of angst-ridden superheroes who suffered and struggled to make sense of a world that was in chaos and on the brink of self-destruction. The X-Men were a prime example of a living metaphor for racial inequality and persecution, and as Salvatore Mondello posited, "the conflicts within and between the X-men stressed cooperation among individuals and minorities rather than conflict, moderation in politics rather than extremism, and the right of each American to social recognition and economic opportunity."[9]

According to Richard Reynolds, "in place of the mythologized perfect being embodying strength, intelligence, wisdom, compassion, loyalty and courage, we [began to] read of fragmented virtues and signs, operating in isolation, but drawing such significance as they can from their common origin and shared cultural roots."[10] As a result of this demythification, the growing concern over the detrimental effects of comic book violence on youth, the implementation of restrictions on comic book content, and the growing sophistication of the average comic book reader, the plots and character of the superhero became more grounded in reality.

Reflecting on Marvel Comics' early focus on real-world issues, Stan Lee, in an interview with Roy Thomas, suggested that "one thing that made our work different from anyone else's is the fact that we tried to make our characters as real and believable as possible. Even though they were in fantasy stories, our formula was 'what if somebody like this existed in the real world and what would his or her life be like?' In a similar vein, Bradford Wright noted that people continue to face a confusing, lonely and sometimes frightening world that so often seems to spin out of control ... in this culture [of pain and isolation], comic books do have a place and they will continue to endure so long as they bring out the superhero in us all."[11] In their *Superheroes and Philosophy: Truth, Justice and the Socratic Way,* Tom and Matt Morris explain that "the best superhero comics [raise] questions regarding ethics, personal and social responsibility, justice, crime and punishment, the mind and human emotions, personal identity, the soul, the notion of destiny, the meaning of our lives."[12]

It is within this "real world" of human experience that the stories of flawed superheroes have gained and maintained their appeal. Elektra's quest for dominance over childhood trauma, Ironman's need for atonement, the twisted vigilantism of Rorschach from the Alan Moore and Dave Gibbons's *Watchmen,* and the inner torment of Norman Osborne, aka the Green Goblin, are but a few examples. While their stories of both power and powerlessness may indeed kindle our own deep-seated (or repressed) and childlike primary process longings and fantasies for power, dominance and revenge, it is our resonance with their very human limitations and fallibilities that is so engaging. Stories of invincible and unassailable (super)heroes are far less interesting and far more predictable than those of their tormented, complex and flawed counterparts. Quoting fictional superhero Billy Button, aka Captain Mantra, Paul Gravett notes, in *Superheroes: Nothing Will Ever be the Same Again,* "It's not a comic book world anymore.... Our time has passed. Problems don't come in neat little boxes anymore, with 'The End' scrawled in the corner. There is no end. Only new versions of reality. People don't talk in balloons anymore. They curse. They shout obscenities. The world is no place for children or heroes which may be the same thing."[13] Mental illness has entered the superhero world.

Marks of Greatness, Scars of Pain

With this emergence of the comic-book superheroes into the real world, it becomes critical to view them as real people who just happen to be "super"

in one way or another. This hybridization compels us to consider that along
with their gifts and (super)abilities come very real and very human frailties.
Superheroes are intriguing characters; they can fly, travel through time, move
mountains, change shape, alter the weather and cheat death. Movie fans as
well as readers of superhero comics know of the now-famous axiom offered
to young Peter Parker, aka Spider-Man, by his uncle Ben: "With great power,
there must also come great responsibility." But can anyone truly appreciate
the kind of responsibility these caped crusaders have to shoulder on a daily
basis? Their tasks range from the more mundane re-routing of a speeding
train in order to save a school bus, to changing history in order to save entire
civilizations. In the course of a day, they must shield us from bullets, radiation,
and vile and unimaginable creatures as well as from the evil machinations of
megalomaniacal ne'r-do-wells.

Superheroes are rarely understood by those whom they serve, are often
vilified, ostracized and persecuted. In this vein, Colonel Ross stalks Bruce
Banner, *Daily Bugle* Editor J. Jonah Jameson constantly persecutes Spider-
Man, and the X-Men are forever on Senator Kelly's most-wanted mutants
list. Their secret identities are constantly threatened, their powers are the
target for villainous plots, they must constantly live a shadowy double life by
lying about their alter-identities, and their loved ones are always in peril.

While powerful and heroic, these superheroes are nevertheless tormented,
alienated and angst-ridden. Themes of human frailty permeate their tales.
For example, after being lured to Gotham City's infamous Arkham Asylum
for the Criminally Insane by the Joker in Grant Morrison and Dave McKean's
Arkham Asylum: A Serious House on Serious Earth, Batman is forced to confront, yet again, his own dark demons. In a perverse game of cat and mouse
that culminates in a dramatic denouement, the Joker says, "Just don't forget—if it ever gets too tough—there's always a place for you here."[14] Similarly,
wealthy industrialist Tony Stark, aka The Invincible Ironman, battles alcohol
and a weakened heart and is thus far more vulnerable than most of his com-
patriots. In David Michilinie's *Demon in a Bottle*, we find him staring at his
haggard reflection lamenting, 'Iron Man, ol' buddy, I thought I knew you.
But, I don't. I don't know you at all." [15] And then there is Ben Grimm, aka
The Thing, who in a particularly poignant issue of *Fantastic Four* by Karl
Kesel called *Remembrance of Things Past,* travels back to Brooklyn to confront
the anti–Semitism that plagued him as a child and the renunciation of his
faith as an adult. Along similar lines, in Greg Pak's *World War Hulk,* The
Incredible Hulk suffers from a painful betrayal by his so-called friends that
launches him on an unparalleled mission of revenge. In *Welcome to Tranquility*,
by Gail Simone and Neil Googe, a retirement community for superheroes
contains the likes of Bad Dog, Pink Bunny, Colonel Gragg, Judge Fury, and

Astral Man, who battle primarily with obscurity and a profound feeling of unimportance. In a powerful issue of Judd Winick's *Green Arrow* entitled *HIV Positive,* the hero's sidekick, Speedy, must contend with her recent HIV diagnosis. When friends innocently and naively query into the origin of her affliction, she erupts with, "Meth. I was living on the street ... we all shot speed ... staying awake is a pretty high priority ... keeps the number of rapes down to a minimum."[16] In Scott Lobdell's *The Walking Wounded,* Jean-Paul Baubier, aka Northstar of the Canadian crime fighting organization Alpha Flight, was the first comic book superhero to smash his way out of the closet, revealing his homosexuality, and in so doing, paved the way for contemporaries including Rainmaker, Apollo, and Midnighter.

And finally, there are the unique circumstances of Frank Castle, aka The Punisher, a former U.S. Marine who, along with his beloved wife and children, were attacked in New York's Central Park after witnessing a gangland shooting. While only Castle survived the onslaught, he was forever changed — into a revenge-seeking vigilante who stops at nothing to exact vengeance against the mob and other criminals. According to psychologist Andrew Getzfield, his black-and white mentality, irresponsibility in the management of his own affairs, absolute disregard for others, lack of remorse for the death and destruction he causes, and willingness to use lethal force, including torture, suggests that he has been forever damaged by the circumstances of his life and the means he uses to correct them.

The question remains: "Shouldn't superheroes, who are endowed with such extraordinary gifts, be spared the ravages of being human?" What is it about superherodom that accentuates, rather than mitigates, vulnerability? Simply, to be "super" is to face unrelenting enemies wishing only to upset the status quo. To constantly protect a secret identity is to be forever denied the peace that comes with stability and consistency; to be reified is to worry always about acceptance and the "fall from grace," and constantly to have to make choices is to live in fear of making the wrong ones. Further, to live above or outside the law is, as Jamie Hughes suggests, to be ostracized and persecuted by "figures of authority [who] deem the superheroes they depend upon to be menaces,"[17] and to have experienced traumatic origins including betrayal and parental abandonment means, as Richard Reynolds points out, to "reach maturity without ever having a relationship with his [or her] parents."[18] Further compromising their efforts to reach "maturity" are inescapable childhood conflicts that cartoon writer and armchair psychoanalyst R.C. Harvey accurately addresses. He suggests that "in their customary endeavors, then, superheroes are tainted by two characteristics normally associated in the subconscious with forbidden behavior: they are excessively aggressive and they challenge [traditional] authority."[19] Clearly, then, the glow of superheroism is forever tarnished by the loneliness, fragmentation, fallibility, and self-doubt that marks the existential legacy of humankind.

Superheroes Enter the World of Psychiatry

If, as Ira Talpin opines, "[super] heroes are a welcome symbolic relief from the reluctance to confront our own inadequacies,"[20] is there a price they, and we by association, must pay for what he also refers to as our abrogation of collective responsibility? Surely, as noted above, superheroes are not immune from the slings and arrows of human (and superhuman) misfortune. They rage, lament, despair, worry and rejoice just like the rest of us. But what value inheres in casting these gods and demigods in such a fragile mold?

Perhaps, as projections of our own unrelenting need to conquer death and to overcome our mortal bonds, they vicariously pay the price for our hubris. In our effort to transcend mortality, we fly too close to the sun, cast off responsibility for the journey to them, and in turn, they take the heat for us. Ironically, since they cannot physically die, we must create a ways for them to suffer with the burden from which we have freed ourselves. In a sense, we make them crazy! Mental illness is the price they pay for our sins. As Ira Talpin suggests, "Outwardly, we gain satisfaction in the knowledge that others are solving major crises for us, so inwardly we can continue our search for that mental sanctuary. While it is paradoxical that the mental anguish of our superheroes is really our own, it is the temporary externalization of our suffering in the form of their mental illness that provides us with the mental reprieve that Talpin alludes to. This is not dissimilar to the Platonic notion of catharsis that comes from witnessing someone's tragedy, even if it is being performed on stage.

The trope of the wounded warrior dates to antiquity, but it is only in the genre of the comic-book superhero—which coincides with the height of the Psychoanalytic movement in America—that we witness an attempt to psychologically scrutinize these characters. For practicing psychiatrist Sharon Packer, "wounded warrior stories offer much more than temporary solace through fantasy escape."[21] While Lauretta Bender and Reginald Lourie, also practicing psychiatrists, albeit decades ago, recognized the importance of psychological relevance of superheroes when they compared them with heroes of folklore and mythology, it has been Packer who has brought psychiatry to bear in understanding our superheroes and ourselves. She adds, "If superheroes were not fiction, and if they were not so much fun and if they were not so funny, they could [readily] be substituted for psychiatric case studies."[22]

While superhero stories may indeed be entertaining, and are occasionally punctuated by humor, they are very often, as Packer suggests, psychiatric case histories. Paranoia, for example, is defined by the American Psychiatric Association's *Diagnostic and Statistical Manual of Mental Disorders-fourth Edition-Text Revision [DSM-IV-TR]* as a "pervasive distrust and suspiciousness of others such that their motives are interpreted as malevolent, beginning by early adulthood and present in a variety of contexts."[23] It is further characterized by suspicion without sufficient basis, preoccupation with doubts about others' loyalty, reluctance to confide in people for fear of betrayal and reading hidden meaning into others' behaviors. While superheroes must on the one hand rely upon hypervigilance, suspicion, and mistrust in order to ward off the potential threats that their nemeses constantly pose, that very same paranoia isolates and alienates them. As Packer suggests, "Among the persecuted, only the paranoid survive."[24] Batman relies upon fear and anxiety in order to dominate his foes, but also lives a life of tortured isolation, cloistered away in his underground lair, forever scanning the outside world for signs and warnings of danger.

While paranoia actually helps the superhero to remain on guard for threats, and as such is a job asset (in spite of its deleterious effects), narcissism is not quite as helpful a psychological symptom and in fact often undermines the superhero's best efforts. According to the DSM-IV-TR, narcissism, when taken to the extreme, results in a condition known as narcissistic personality disorder. It is defined as "a pervasive pattern of grandiosity (in fantasy or behavior), need for admiration, and lack of empathy, beginning by early adulthood and present in a variety of contexts."[25] It is further characterized by an exaggerated sense of self-importance, a preoccupation with fantasies of unlimited power and success, a sense of entitlement and need for excessive admiration, arrogance, and difficulty empathizing with the thoughts and feelings of other people. Granted, many of these characteristics may indeed be warranted by the various caped crusaders; however, such a narrow and self-focused worldview further deepens the divide between the superhero and the everyday mortals that she is charged with protecting. Early tales of Spider-Man were very much stories of unbridled narcissism and its often painful effects on the young Peter Parker. While grandstanding and showing off are also the signature of the Fantastic Four's Flame, envy and jealousy prove every bit as incendiary to him and his team as do his flames.

Another interesting form of psychopathology that afflicts a portion of the superhero universe is "body dysmorphic disorder," which is defined by the DSM-IV-TR as a "preoccupation with an imagined defect in appearance ... if a slight physical anomaly is present, the person's concern is markedly excessive."[26] While The Thing is certainly preoccupied with his grotesque appearance, which often sends bystanders running in fear, his perennial difficulty adjusting to the permanence of his disfigurations results in great inner pain, anger, and a profound sense of disconnection. Other superheroes, who rely upon their muscular prowess to inspire fear and vanquish their enemies, are very likely a shadowy reflection, accorder to Packer, of society's preoccupation with muscle mass — an "unofficial subcategory of body dysmorphic disorder."[27]

Intermittent Explosive Disorder is yet another form of psychopathology that undermines the efficacy of several more prominent superheroes, including Wolverine and the Incredible Hulk. The DSM-IV-TR defines this disorder as "the occurrence of discrete episodes of failure to resist aggressive impulses that result in serious assaultive acts or destruction of property."[28] In a sense, superhero stories would not be as entertaining or compelling if their protagonists could not explode into righteous or otherwise morally justified rage against one of the many villains that threaten or accost them. We rely on heroes to do heroic things, but the price in destruction of property, loss of life, and the generalized chaos that follows these destructive rampages call into question the sanity of the superhero.

And finally, what would a discussion about mental illness and superheroes be without reference to Post Traumatic Stress Disorder (PTSD), which is characterized in the DSM-IV-TR by "recurrent and intrusive distressing recollections of the [traumatizing] event, including images, thoughts, or perceptions, recurrent distressing dreams of the event, acting or feeling as if the traumatic event were recurring, and intense psychological distress at exposure to internal or external cues that symbolize or resemble an aspect of the traumatic event."[29] Most notably among traumatized superheroes are Bruce Wayne and Elektra, who lost their parents to brutal murders during childhood; Superman, who was orphaned when his home planet of Krypton exploded; Frank Castle, aka The Punisher, who lost his wife and child to violence; Daredevil, who lost his vision to an untimely accident; and Bruce Banner, who lost his humanity through genetic experiments by his father and then to gamma radiation.

Clearly then, the backstories of many superheroes are filled with myriad psychological tragedies and would satisfy the diagnostic criteria on any psychologist's or psychiatrist's symptom checklist. The suffering of these wounded warriors are testament to the pain not only of being alive, but of bearing the image of man. Yet, as we shall see, they are also stories of hope and resiliency in the face of seemingly insurmountable odds.

Stories of Recovery, Stories of Hope

Tony Stark, or Ironman as his legions of hero worshippers prefer to call him, embodies hope. A wealthy and deeply narcissistic military industrialist who built his fortune through death and destruction, Stark suffers from both heart damage and alcoholism. Nevertheless, he uses his scientific prowess to build a device that corrects his heart problem and ultimately attains sobriety. In a tour de force of art imitating life, the actor chosen to portray the tormented superhero was Robert Downey, Jr., also notorious for his narcissism and substance abuse. And just like his fictional counterpart, Downey eventually attains sobriety and reclaims his place among the Hollywood glitterati. Both characters embody resilience and hope, both of which are the flip side to the pathos and psychopatholgy that characterizes so many superheroes.

While comic book fans and moviegoers are drawn to the violence, destruction, displays of absolute power, and vanquishing of evil in superhero stories, it is also arguable that the redemptive stories of the protagonists are every bit as compelling. If superheroes are, on the one hand, poster children for the pernicious effects of childhood (and adulthood) trauma, the stories of conquest over their "inner demons" are every bit as appealing as that of their tragedies.

In their discussion of the "myth" of the American superhero, John Lawrence and Robert Jewett note that "the monomythic superhero is distinguished by disguised origins, a redemptive task and extraordinary powers."[30] The notion of redemptive task is key to appreciating the relationship between the superhero's suffering and his/her ultimate triumph over personal demons. For while the superhero uses her powers to redeem society by purging it of evil, she also redeems herself through ongoing self-sacrifice and renunciation of true membership in that society.

Superman is a prime example of redemption, reconciliation and healing. Jettisoned to Earth by loving parents, adopted by a kind farming couple, and ultimately embraced by society, he is nevertheless an orphan who bears the scars of early abandonment. In order to maintain his secret identity so that he may enjoy a semblance of a normal he must adopt the identity of the meek and mild-mannered Clark Kent, who by psychiatric reckoning has a severe case of Social Anxiety Disorder. However, his own kindness, selfless dedication to the cause of vanquishing evil, and renunciation of human temptations reveal him as a survivor. Similarly, Wolverine, the poster child for the angry, disaffected, and disillusioned "superhero" loners, finds solace, connection, and meaning through his dedication to the cause and members of the X-Men. With a steel-like skeleton and ability to heal instantly from physical assault, he slowly learns to reach out, trust, and rely on his fellow cast-offs. Matt Murdock, aka Daredevil, who grew up in the Hell's Kitchen section of New York as the son of a down-on-his-luck prizefighter, is similarly no stranger to adversity — and triumph. After losing his father to the mob and then his sight, he dedicates himself to fighting crime as an attorney by day and vigilante crime fighter by night.

These stories of salvation, redemption and resilience undergird the super-hero universe, and while one need only scratch the surface of any superhero story to find tales of despair and grief, the stories of hope lie close by. Batgirl rebuilds herself after a spinal cord injury and sexual assault, Batman becomes a force for good even after losing his parents to the dark forces, Professor Xavier transcends incapacitation by developing his genetic predisposition for telekinesis, Dr. Strange travels to Tibet to hone his mystical skills after an automobile accident deprives him of his surgical prowess, and even the twisted and perverse Rorschach of the Watchmen, who endured extensive childhood abuse, is able to step up for good.

In 2007, Margaret Haglund and her clinical team, writing in *Current Psychiatry,* offered six protective factors against Post Traumatic Stress Disorder (PTSD). They included an active coping style, physical exercise, a positive outlook, a moral compass, social support and cognitive flexibility. [31] Each of the superheroes noted above, and those in the larger pantheon who have tri-umphed over demons, particularly inner ones, implement each of these factors in the course of their everyday lives. They are by definition solvers of problems whose moral compasses usually point due north, and who more often than not have a small yet supportive social network. Physical exercise, of course, goes with the territory. Packer refers to superheroes' triumph over personal adversity as "Post Traumatic Strength Disorder." Although Post Traumatic Strength Syndrome is a better name because of its non-pathological focus, it nicely captures the essence of strength, hope, and resilience that is also very much a part of the mythos of the American superhero

Conclusion

Superheroes are first and foremost figures of great strength and moral resolve. As Lawrence and Jewett note, "the superhero's aim is unerring, his fists irresistible, and his [her] body capable of suffering fatal injury ... his motivation is a selfless zeal for justice..." [32] Superheroes have historically been black and white figures whose straight-on approach to matters of both state and the heart nicely side step the vagaries, ambiguities and paradoxes of every-day life. This was especially true for early incarnations who single-handedly fought Nazis, crime lords and commies.

As the genre matured, so too did the themes and characters of superhero tales. Feet of clay replaced the sturdy boot, unswerving moral resolve gave way to inner turmoil and self-doubt, and idealistic loners banded together out of the basic need for affiliation. As superheroes took on more Earthbound and reality-based nemeses such as infectious disease, terrorism, racism and poverty, the divide separating these gallant shepherds from us humble and mortal sheep lessened. Their traditional retreat upon the mission's completion gave way to the need to live among us and to be more like us.

Superheroes have dared to be more human — perhaps their greatest act of hubris. For in donning the fragile wings of humanity in hopes of experiencing, as Joseph Campbell referred to it, the rapture of being alive, they have at the same time exposed themselves to the searing heat of human suffering. The price they have paid has been no less than debilitating mental illness, every bit as torturous as a shard of Kryptonite or (in the case of Green Lantern) the color yellow. While superheroes have historically fended off attacks from the most vile, vicious and violent of creatures, they have had far less success in staving off the ravages of depression, anxiety, and psychosis-demons that have eaten at them from the inside.

However, and true to superhero form, our valiant crusaders continue to fight back to overcome the demons of childhood abuse, parental loss, societal rejection and personal betrayal. Some by reaching out for help and support, others through the sheer power of will. Superheroes continue to fight ... even as they plummet to earth.

NOTES

1. Gerard Jones, *Men of Tomorrow: Geeks, Gangsters and the Birth of the Comic Book* (New York: Basic Books, 2004), 340.

2. Joseph Loeb and Tom Morris, "Heroes and superheroes," in *Superheroes and Philosophy: Truth, Justice and the Socratic Way,* eds. Tom Morris and Matt Morris (Chicago: Open Court Books, 2005), 17.

3. William Moulton Marston, "Why 100,000,000 Americans Read Comics," *American Scholar* 13 (1944): 39.

4. Lucie Hughes-Hallett, *Heroes: Saviors, Traitors and Supermen* (London: Fourth Estate, 2004), 2.

5. Ira Taplin, "Why We Need Heroes to Be Heroic," *Journal of Popular Culture* 22 (1988): 142.

6. Mordecai Richler, "The Great Comic Book Heroes," in *The Cool Web: Pattern of Children's Reading,* eds. Margaret Meek, Aidan Warlow and Griselda Barton (London: Bodley Head, 1977), 300.

7. Jamie Hughes, "Who Watches the Watchmen? Ideology and 'Real World' Superheroes, *Journal of Popular Culture* 39, no. 4 (2006): 547.

8. Hughes, 548.

9. Salvatore Mondello, "Spider-Man: Superhero in the Liberal Tradition," *Journal of Popular Culture* 10 (1976): 238.

10. Richard Reynolds, *Super Heroes: A Modern Mythology* (Jackson: Mississippi University Press, 1992), 123.

11. Bradford Wright, *Comic Book Nation: The Transformation of Youth Culture in America* (Baltimore: Johns Hopkins University Press, 2001), 284.

12. Wright, *Comic Book Nation,* 17.

13. Paul Gravett, "Superheroes: Nothing Will Ever Be the Same Again," accessed November 10, 2010, http://www.paulgravett.com/index.php/articles/article/superheroes/.

14. Grant Morrison and Dave McKean, *Arkham Asylum: A Serious House on Serious Earth* (New York: DC Comics, 2004), n.p.

15. David Michelinie and Bob Layton (w), John Romita and Carmine Infantino (p), and Bob Layton (i), "Demon in a Bottle," *The Invincible Iron Man* (April 2008), Marvel Comics, n.p.

16. Judd Winick (w), Phil Hester (p), and Ande Parks (i), "H.I.V. Positive," *Green Arrow* #44 (January 2005), DC Comics, 2.

17. Hughes, 547.

18. Reynolds, 16.

19. R. C. Harvey, "Superheroes on the Couch," *Comics Journal* 104 (1986), 80.

20. Taplin, 139.

21. Sharon Packer, *Superheroes and Superegos: Analyzing the Minds Behind the Masks* (Santa Barbara, CA: Praeger, 2010), 238.

22. Ibid, 230.

23. American Psychiatric Association (APA), *The Diagnostic and Statistical Manual of Mental Disorders IV-TR* (Washington, DC: APA Press, 2000), 697.

24. Packer, 225.

25. American Psychiatric Association, 717.

26. American Psychiatric Association, 510.

27. Packer, 231.

28. American Psychiatric Association, 667.

29. American Psychiatric Association, 467.

30. John Shelton Lawrence and Robert Jewett, *The Myth of the American Super Hero* (Cambridge, England: Wm. B. Erdmans Publishing, 2002), 47.

31. Margaret Haglund et al., "6 Keys to Resilience for PTSD and Everyday Stress," *Current Psychiatry* 6 (2007), 23.

32. Lawrence and Jewett, 47.

BIBLIOGRAPHY

American Psychiatric Association (APA). *The Diagnostic and Statistical Manual of Mental Disorders IV-TR.* Washington, DC: APA Press, 2000.

Bender, Lauretta, and Reginald Lourie. "The Effects of Comic Books on the Ideology of Children." *The American Journal of Orthopsychiatry* 11, no. 3 (1941): 540–550.

Coogan, Peter. *Superhero: The Secret Origin of a Genre.* Austin, TX: Monkey Brain Books, 2006.

Getzfeld, Andrew. "What Would Freud Say: Psychopathology and the Punisher." In *The Psychology of Superheroes: An Unauthorized Exploration,* ed. Robin Rosenberg, 163–174. Dallas, TX: Benbella Books, 2008.

Gravett, Paul. "Superheroes: Nothing Will Ever Be the Same Again." Paul Gravett. September 30, 2007. http://www.paulgravett.com/index.php/articles/article/superheroes/

Haglund, Margaret, Nicole Cooper, Steven Southwick, and Dennis Charney. "6 Keys to Resilience for PTSD and Everyday Stress." *Current Psychiatry* 6, no. 4 (2007): 23–30.

Harvey, R.C. "Superheroes on the Couch." *Comics Journal* 104 (1986): 78–82.

Hughes, Jamie. "Who Watches the Watchmen? Ideology and 'Real World' Superheroes." *Journal of Popular Culture* 39, no. 4 (2006): 546–557.

Hughes-Hallett, Lucy. *Heroes: Saviors, Traitors and Supermen.* London: Fourth Estate, 2004.

Jones, Gerard. *Men of Tomorrow: Geeks, Gangsters and the Birth of the Comic Book.* New York: Basic Books, 2004.

Kesel, Karl (w), Stuart Immonen (p), and Scott Koblish (i). "Remembrance of Things Past." *Fantastic Four* #56 (Aug. 2002), Marvel Comics.

Lawrence, John Shelton, and Robert Jewett. *The Myth of the American Super Hero* Cambridge, England: Wm. B. Erdmans, 2002.

Lobdell, Scott (w), Mark Pacella (p), and Dan Panosian (i). "The Walking Wounded." *Alpha Flight* #106 (March 1992), Marvel Comics.

Loeb, Joseph, and Tom Morris. "Heroes and Superheroes." In *Superheroes and Philosophy: Truth, Justice and the Socratic Way,* eds. Tom Morris and Matt Morris, 11–20. Chicago: Open Court Books, 2005.

Marston, William Moulton. "Why 100,000,000 Americans Read Comics." *American Scholar* 13 (1944): 35–44.

May, Rollo. *The Cry for Myth.* New York: Delta, 1991.

Michelinie, David, and Bob Layton (w), John Romita and Carmine Infantino (p), and Bob Layton (i). "Demon in a Bottle." *The Invincible Iron Man* (April 2008), Marvel Comics.

Mondello, Salvatore. "Spider-Man: Superhero in the Liberal Tradition." *Journal of Popular Culture* 10, no. 1 (1976): 232–238.

Moore, Alan, and Dave Gibbons. *Watchmen.* New York: DC Comics, 1986.

Morris, Matt, and Tom Morris. *Superheroes and Philosophy: Truth, Justice, and the Socratic Way.* Chicago: Open Court, 2005.

Morrison, Grant, and Dave McKean. *Arkham Asylum: A Serious House on Serious Earth.* New York: DC Comics, 2004.

Packer, Sharon. *Superheroes and Superegos: Analyzing the Minds Behind the Masks.* Santa Barbara, CA: Praeger, 2010.

Pak, Greg (w), John Romita, Jr. (p), and Klaus Janson (i). "World War Hulk." *The Incredible Hulk* (August 2007), Marvel Comics.

Reynolds, Richard. *Super Heroes: A Modern Mythology.* Jackson: Mississippi University Press, 1992.

Richler, Mordecai. "The Great Comic Book Heroes." In *The Cool Web: Pattern of Children's Reading,* eds. Margaret Meek, Aidan Warlow, and Griselda Barton, 299–308. London: Bodley Head, 1977.

Simone, Gail, and Neil Googe. *Welcome to Tranquility.* La Jolla, CA: Wildstorm Productions, 2008.

Taplin, Ira. "Why We Need Heroes to be Heroic." *Journal of Popular Culture* 22, no. 2 (1988): 133–142.

Thomas, Roy. "Stan the Man & Roy the Boy: A Conversation between Stan Lee and Roy Thomas." *TwoMorrows Magazine,* January 29, 2009. http://twomorrows.com/comicbookartist/articles/02stanroy.html.

Winick, Judd (w), Phil Hester (p), and Ande Parks (i). "H.I.V. Positive." *Green Arrow* #44 (January 2005), DC Comics.

Wright, Bradford. *Comic Book Nation: the Transformation of Youth Culture in America.* Baltimore, MD: Johns Hopkins University Press, 2001.

Mental Illness and Popular Culture Abroad

13

The Aesthetics of Mad Spaces

Policing the Public Image of Graffiti and Mental Illness in Canada

KIMBERLEY WHITE

This chapter introduces a way of thinking about mental illness *as* popular culture.[1] While popular culture is often criticized and even dismissed as a sensationalized rendering of reality, heavily influenced by mass media and dumbed-down for mass consumption, it is also a contentious and highly politicized site of subordination and resistance, one through which history is mediated and hegemonic order is maintained. To examine mental illness *as* popular culture is to consider how, as modern disease concept, mental illness has come to permeate our popular consciousness to the extent that its manifestations can be seen in and as cultural practice. I use the term "mental illness" as a contextually specific construct of modern science and consider its meanings in popular culture to be different from that of "madness," a broader, more socially and historically inclusive reference.[2] Therefore while the rise of mental illness represents an important event in the longer history of madness, it is essential that it not become ideologically dislodged from that history. Powerful symbolic images and metonymical representations of madness (as a disease, a state of chaos or disorder, and an economic threat) continue to inform and define the dominant closed interpretation of mental illness that is made popular today.[3] We can also see various interesting manifestations of madness/mental illness in other cultural spaces that have been imbued with popular disease ideology. Two especially vivid Canadian illustrations of the processes through which popular ideas about illness and disease become cultural practices can be found in the socio-legal regulation of graffiti and "graffiti crime" and in the establishment of anti-stigma campaigns designed to dispel representations of "mental illness" as dangerous.

218

Over the past decade, anti-graffiti and community safety programs in Canada have unflinchingly defined graffiti as pathologic and criminogenic. The appearance of graffiti is quickly diagnosed by police and city officials as a symptom of "spatial disorder" and a sign that other, more catastrophic, social conditions may develop. However, this is hardly a new or unique framework through which to interpret and manage the urban madness that graffiti has come to represent. The graffiti-as-crime/disease message is a classic public relations strategy that has been widely used in North American cities for more than 40 years, with little variation, and has given rise to a regime of crime-control responses premised on a cultivated fear of chaos and commonsense historical knowledge regarding the nature and dangers of "illness." It is therefore essential for anti-graffiti propaganda[4] to maintain the conceptual links between graffiti, disease, and danger in order to *appear* legitimate.

Anti-graffiti campaigns in Canada, like any other public interest/awareness campaigns, make considerable use of social marketing and consensus-building technologies that rely on the narrative conventions of retrospection, repetition and self-quotation. A typical campaign strategy is to develop a sharply focused message stating the social costs of "graffiti crime," deliver it over and over through various media outlets, use the same (often unreferenced) quantitative research, and offer reassurance that through community support, a shared vision of a healthy city, and adequate funding, a solution can be found and transformation can begin. This is similar to the approach currently used in public interest/awareness campaigns targeting stigma associated with mental illness: develop a sharply focused message stating the social costs of "mental illness," deliver it over and over through various media outlets, use the same (often unreferenced) quantitative research, and offer reassurance that through community support, a shared vision of a healthy nation, and adequate funding, a solution can be found and transformation can begin.

In *Part One*, "Policing Graffiti and Spatial Disorder," I explore the policing of graffiti and "spatial disorder" (sometimes termed "urban disorder") through an analysis of the nature, conceptual significance, and cultural imperatives of anti-graffiti campaigns in Canada. I am particularly interested in the recent turn toward urban "beautification" programs as a less explicit, but perhaps more powerful, regulatory regime through which graffiti and "graffiti crime" is morally and aesthetically policed.[5] Rather than the crude crime-control framework of most anti-graffiti campaigns, beautification campaigns have the expressed goal of *visual transformation*— transforming not only *what* we see, but also *how* we see. I then shift in *Part Two*, "Policing 'Mental Illness': A Disease Like Any Other" to explore some of the conceptual resemblances between anti-graffiti/beautification campaigns and the practice of anti-stigma campaigns in Canada. Here I am particularly interested in examining the structure and social significance of the "Opening Minds" campaign, launched in 2009 by the Mental Health Commission of Canada (MHCC), which was designed to eliminate stigma and "transform the lives of those living with mental illness."[6] By definition, a *transformation* requires a dramatic change in the form, appearance or character of some thing or some idea — that which can be seen. This is very different from the concept of social *reform*, which would require deeper changes in social, political and economic institutions and practices in order to improve structural conditions.

At first glance, it appears that anti-graffiti campaigns depicting "graffiti crime" as a dangerous form of urban madness are at odds with concurrent anti-stigma campaigns intended to correct popular misperceptions of "mental illness" as dangerous and something to fear.[7] However, in considering public interest/awareness campaigns themselves as cultural practices — designed to transform that which is deemed undesirable and unhealthy — we can detect some interesting conceptual, as well as practical, resemblances. Here I propose that urban beautification/anti-graffiti campaigns and mental illness anti-stigma campaigns occupy similar cultural spaces (mad spaces) and serve similar socio-political functions. Further, I argue that the "Opening Minds" anti-stigma campaign, and similar campaigns aimed at transforming the way we see "mental illness," are, in essence, beautification projects.

Policing Graffiti and Spatial Disorder

> Who writes? For whom is the writing being done? In what circum-
> stances? These it seems to me are questions whose answers provide us
> with the ingredients making for a politics of interpretations.[8]

Considerable work has been done on the criminalization of graffiti and the various crime-control measures now used to detect and prevent "graffiti crime." The political dominance of associations between graffiti and spatial/urban disorder can be credited in large part to the popularity of the "broken windows" theory of criminal behaviour applied most ambitiously to the perceived graffiti crisis in New York City during the 1990s.[9] A recent Canadian example of the broken windows approach to graffiti can be seen in the City of Toronto and is summarized in a magazine article titled "Graffiti vandalism linked to urban decay." In the article, Sgt. Heinz Kuck, the lead coordinator of the Toronto Police Services Graffiti Eradication Program, enlists the broken window model to explain how certain neighborhoods in Toronto have been "visually immobilized" by graffiti and *appear* to the public to be unsafe and unprotected. If left untreated, the afflicted neighborhood and communities within will eventually degenerate into spaces of crime and disorder.[10]

In order to move beyond the broken window theory, and instead to analyze "graffiti crime" and anti-graffiti campaigns as cultural manifestations of the linkages forged between madness, disorder, danger, and disease, I turn to the work of critical interdisciplinary scholars interested in understanding graffiti more as a cultural practice than a criminal act.[11]

Works by Alison Young and Tim Cresswell suggest that graffiti in various contexts came to acquire a criminal and distasteful status in part through a series of pejorative and provocative metonymical associations with waste, decay, criminality, disease, obscenity, and irrationality. As Young argues, "Graffiti is rarely considered *as itself* (whatever that would mean), but rather always by reference to and through some other — usually quite distanced — phenomenon."[12] Young also suggests that the metonymical associations that define the way we *see* graffiti expose a politics of aesthetic order,[13] which in turn dictates only certain responses to graffiti to be socially appropriate:

> Despite the contemporary saturation of the urban visual field with corporate or official signage to an extent that far exceeds anything graffiti writers could hope to accomplish, graffiti is still commonly represented as a polluting flood of dirty signifiers. As is to be expected with the discourse of dirt and waste, these media representations animate a common cultural imperative to remove the polluting substance or fluid. When skin is scarred, we long for its healing; when a surface is dirtied, we work to clean it…. Such is the impact imperative underlying the representation of graffiti as waste: it establishes the need for its removal as an unquestioned precondition of its existence.[14]

Given the cultural imperatives associated with commonsense interpretations, or what Jacques Ranciére calls a dominant "distribution of the sensible," it is important to pay attention to the processes through which common sensibilities are structured and maintained. In examining *how* things are made sense of, we also learn who is entitled to participate in community life, who has the ability (or inability) to control what is "common," and generally who is permitted (or not) to be seen and heard in a given socio-political and historical context.[15]

In a 2006 article titled "City Space: A Semiotic and Visual Exploration of Graffiti and Public Space in Vancouver," Craig Noble reveals how some graffiti writers share a distinctly counter-hegemonic idea about social order, political power, and the ownership of public space in a city that vigilantly polices its self-image as safe, clean, and beautiful.[16] Nobel argues that one reason why graffiti is routinely represented as dangerous is that it brings to light those who are typically rendered invisible. It exposes a human presence and expression on the street that is "free from institutionalized markers of taste, appropriateness and permission."[17] Unlike *legitimate* forms of public expression and propaganda, such as censored and paid-for public messaging or commercial advertising that tends to exclude marginalized members of society, graffiti, as a cultural practice, is not so obviously about production and consumption.[18] Graffiti, like madness, is decidedly and uncomfortably free, unpredictable, anti-democratic, and difficult to control. In translating the chaos of graffiti into "graffiti crime," it immediately appears to be more contained — authorized as a definable, and thus manageable, social problem. Similarly, in translating the complex conditions of madness into "mental illness," or a problem of "mental health," it is immediately brought in line with a predetermined set of associated characteristics and solutions.

In representing graffiti as a vile and dirty by-product, a symptom of a more subversive underlying social disorder, there is also a tendency for anti-graffiti organizers (and some behavioral social scientists) to extend assumptions about the anti-social nature of graffiti writing to the body and mind of the graffiti writer, often depicted as a deviant and disturbed individual.[19] In constructing a politics of difference between the deviant (dirty and unhealthy) individuals who *do* graffiti crime and those (clean and healthy) citizens who are *victims* of graffiti crime, attention is pulled away from the social and political conditions that often inspire graffiti writing and the pre-existing social anxieties that so easily allow for graffiti to be framed in terms of pathology. Historically, we know that other bodies perceived as socially deviant were/are pathologized and marked by ascriptions of dirt and disease (gay men, addicts, the homeless, and criminals for instance).[20] It follows that as "diseased" bodies come to occupy certain spaces and places, these too become marked (stigmatized) as sites of disease and disorder. The marked bodies of graffiti writers are often elusive, unfixed, and difficult to control; therefore it is the *evidence* of their transgression — the writing — that becomes the target of criminalization, transformation, and treatment.

Some graffiti writers and their supporters have attempted to bring graffiti into popular consciousness as a legitimate art form and to have the practice of graffiti seen as more than mindless scrawling on walls. At the same time, many consider it important to also maintain the subversive character and resistant politics that underwrite the history and cultural practice of graffiti. As Cresswell argues:

> Much of the meaning of graffiti lies in its subversion of the authority of urban spaces. This is also the source of its criminality. Graffiti is not a crime that actually harms anyone.... The criminality of graffiti, unlike most crimes, lies in its being seen, it its transgression of official appearances.[21]

Also, the dispute over the significance of graffiti in urban space and culture (as with most disputes over space, place, culture, or ideology) is confined to a cultural context that does not easily allow for more than one legitimate "system of thought"[22] pertaining to the same social phenomenon, particularly if they are incongruous thoughts. In other words, it seems graffiti can't be seen as beautiful, coherent, and productive at the same time it is seen as vulgar, disorderly, and useless.[23]

In what appears to be an attempt to clean up the image of graffiti, the City of Toronto recently initiated a series of urban "beautification" projects that would "elevate" graffiti from a sign of transgression to a sign of unity and community safety.[24] A common mandate of public interest/awareness campaigns is to refashion that which is considered dysfunctional, ugly, or unhealthy into something productive, beautiful, and healthy. This was made explicit in 2005, when the City of Toronto awarded Style in Progress, a not-for-profit organization that promotes urban art, music, dance, and fashion, a "Clean and Beautiful City" award and a grant to commission 10 graffiti artists to paint "art murals" on Bell Canada's "defaced" telephone utility boxes located around the city. Not only would this beautification campaign transform the outward appearance of the city, organizers claimed it would also engage inner-city street culture by offering a *legal* space and opportunity for some "well-known graffiti artists" to be seen in a more positive light and earn public acceptance.[25] In doing so, the campaign would also allow public official to demonstrate that lost, rebellious graffiti criminals could, with intervention, be rehabilitated into disciplined and productive members of the community. The introduction of *legal* spaces for graffiti artists to work suggests a progressive move, but in effect, beautification projects primarily serve as a means for city officials to reclaim and maintain control over public spaces. Through beautification, the marks of graffiti are "painted out" and replaced with aesthetically neutralized "art murals," the form and content of which is strictly policed. Therefore, the legality of a space is only a matter of perception, defined through processes of official aesthetic judgment and according to its transformability.

The "art mural designers," as selected graffiti artists came to be called, were permitted to choose the Bell Canada utility box they wished to paint but were certainly not free to produce images of their own choosing. Bell management and Toronto city councillors first had to approve each designer's submission as well as did the owner of the property on which the Bell utility box resided. Each "design" submitted for consideration was also expected to convey a popular image that reflected the desired commercial character of a particular neighbourhood. In the Toronto neighbourhood known as "Little Italy" for instance, the selected design depicted someone enjoying a slice of pizza. I simply fail to see how beautification programs work to legitimize graffiti as art, or graffiti writers as artists — perhaps because bringing graffiti into a positive light is not the primary social function of such programs. By design, beautification programs are structured and implemented to perform judgments of sentiment and taste.[26] In deciding which characteristics constitute an acceptable "art mural," certain other images retain their "graffiti" status and thus continue to be seen as suitable subjects for criminalization and stigmatization.

In November 2010, Torontonians elected a new socially conservative mayor, Rob Ford. While Mr. Ford has been in office for only a short time, he has already made it a priority to "crack down on the street scrawl," proclaiming in a recent newspaper interview that in six months' time "there will not be graffiti" on the streets of Toronto.[27] City staff members have been reassigned from other "enforcement areas" to focus on graffiti abatement. There is also support for a new "murals program" (a revitalization of the 2005 beautification campaign) designed to "divert would-be taggers' energies into constructive projects." [sic] The crime-control aspect of this newest murals program is more explicit, promoted as "a legal alternative for graffiti artists, [one which] promotes artistic expression and dissuades graffiti vandals."[28] However, there is little evidence to suggest graffiti writers are dissuaded by paint-outs, art murals, or any other anti-graffiti tactic.[29] At least some graffiti writers in Toronto seem unaffected by the threat of having their images "erased" and are well aware of the aesthetic politics at work. One artist interviewed insists she is not a "vandal" but an "artist" and explains that street art will continue to be seen as vandalism only "[a]s long as society does not provide a safe space for artists to work a large space that is not dictated by a money-driven agenda."[30] The idea of "safe spaces," as specified by graffiti artists, is quite different from the idea of "legal spaces" as specified by city officials. They are, in mental health terms, akin to different qualities of care.

When graffiti is removed from public view — washed away, painted over, or reinterpreted as an art mural — it is politically displaced from its historical and cultural location as "graffiti." Through processes of beautificaiton, graffiti is rendered ugly, disruptive, ahistorical, and inaudible, and by extension graffiti writers, too, cease to be seen and heard on their own terms. Cresswell is astute in his observation that the incompatibility of certain interpretations (graffiti as both disruptive and productive) is not natural, but culturally realized. Things or ideas are only "*said* to be incompatible by someone whose interests lie in preserving a particular set of meanings." [31] To take this analysis further, I return to Ranciére's argument that politics lies in interrupting the distribution of the sensible. The policing of graffiti as a disorder of space, and graffiti writers as dangerous individuals, has been premised on the mistaken generalization that "we are all equal," when in fact, the policing of graffiti necessitates the political subjectification (or "subjectivization" as Ranciére would put it) of both graffiti and graffiti writers as having no part in the established social order.[32] They are only brought *into* order through the politics of subjectification, which at once makes them into a legitimate target of dispute, treatment and transformation.

The City of Toronto's beautification campaign is subtler, but arguably more powerful, than the classic anti-graffiti crime-control campaign organized by the Toronto Police Services. Rather than propagating an explicit anti-graffiti message, beautification campaigns reflect more of an anti-stigma approach, trying to break down the barriers between graffiti writers and the broader community. However, much more can be seen going on here, and it brings us back to Young's analysis of the "impact imperative" that underlies the representation of graffiti as waste — it must either be removed or treated.[33] In the context of the "Clean and Beautiful City" program, anti-social "graffiti vandals" are transformed into productive "art mural designers." In this light, beautification programs can be seen as also performing a sort of therapeutic function, much like treatment programs. Or perhaps administering a beautification program is more analogous to administering anti-psychotic medication — an attempt to sedate graffiti and present it to the public in a safer and more palatable form.

As a cultural site imbued with disease ideology, the moral and aesthetic policing of graffiti and "spatial disorder" can be understood as a manifestation of the same symbolic images and metonymical representations of madness that inform and define popularized interpretations of "mental illness." As I move on to *Part Two*, I propose to demonstrate how, in policing the image of "mental illness" as a disease, anti-stigma campaigns with mandates of transformation must both summon and disavow the historical and political subjectification of madness and the mad. Similar to selective processes through which beautification/anti-graffiti campaigns render some images public art and others a public threat, anti-stigma campaigns work to bring some representations (and representatives) of mental illness into public view, while others are deemed unsuitable for public displays of treatment or transformation. In this way, anti-stigma campaigns might also be conceptualized as beautification projects.

Policing "Mental Illness" — A Disease Just Like Any Other

If one considers the ideas of disease — all disease, including mental illness — as realities, but as realities mirrored in and conceptualized through the pressures of social forces and psychological models, then the question becomes much more complex and indeed, much more interesting.[34]

Early in the establishment of the Mental Health Commission of Canada (MHCC)[35] there emerged a general consensus from the Board of Directors to employ the trope of "disease" in order to promote the idea that individuals and families are not to blame for mental illness — that mental illness is a disease just like any other.[36] The expressed hope in naming mental illness a disease, like diabetes or heart disease, was that it would help lift associated feelings of shame and reassure Canadians that the experience of mental illness (directly or indirectly) is relatively common. But this attempt to *naturalize* mental illness rests somewhat uncomfortably alongside the commission's larger public relations initiative, which has been to bring national attention to Canada's looming "mental health crisis."

In the months leading up to the launch of the "Opening Minds" anti-stigma campaign, the public was primed with warnings delivered through mass media that "mental health" has reached a point of "crisis" in Canada.[37] The official mandate of the MHCC anti-stigma initiative is, like most other anti-stigma campaigns, to dispel popular myths about the nature and danger of mental illness and to educate the public on what mental illness *really is.* The MHCC has strictly adopted the language of "mental illness" and considers other terms such as "madness" to be derogatory and loaded with negative connotations. However, in employing targeted social marketing strategies to peak public concern and gain political buy-in for the anti-stigma project, the commission's official messages on "mental illness," as a disease, calls forth the very histories and representations of madness they claim they wish to dispel.[38] Perhaps more disconcerting is the fact that there does not seem to be any awareness or appreciation of this irony.

MHCC officials claim that while mental illness *is* a disease, at the core we are all the same and thus should not think in terms of "us" and "them."[39] On that premise, the central theme of the "Opening Minds" campaign is to bring "mental illness out of the shadows" and calls for those living with mental illness to come "into the light" in order to make themselves seen and heard in every aspect of social life.[40] Similar to the goals of anti-graffiti/beautification programs to transform graffiti into something that appears normal and recognizable to an anxious public, the assumption behind the be-seen-and-heard strategy in the "Opening Minds" campaign is that increased exposure will help to demystify mental illness in the eyes of the (healthy) public and help normalize the experience for those living with mental illness. However, as Gilman points out: "The banality of real mental illness comes into conflict with our need to have the mad be identifiable, different from ourselves," and thus "madness must express itself in a way that is inherently different."[41] It is therefore significant that the call is for those living with "mental illness" to come out of the shadows, and not the "mad." Those who do not reflect the desired, enlightened vision of mental illness are likely to remain in the shadows, where they will retain their status as mad and dangerous.

In June 2008, in the midst of the economic downturn, *The Globe and Mail*, one of Canada's national newspapers, published the first in a series of Special Reports titled, "Breakdown: Canada's Mental Health Crisis."[42] The introduction to the series assuredly outlined the parameters and severity of Canada's mental health problem:

> *FACE IT. FUND IT. FIX IT. At least 1 in 5 Canadians will experience some form of mental illness in their lifetimes. "There's nobody in our country,"* renowned psychiatrist David Goldbloom says, "who can stand up and say, 'Not my family — not my aunts or uncles or cousins or grandparents, children, siblings, spouse or self.'" Yet unlike any other group of diseases, mental illness today remains surrounded by shame and silence, concealing the almost unequalled devastation it wreaks on Canadian families, workplaces and health-care and justice systems. Through the next week, The Globe and Mail will tell those stories and seek solutions.[43]

The seven-day "Breakdown" series included full-page articles on a range of mental health issues including: the cost of mental illness to the workforce and corporate revenue; practical strategies to "solve" the crisis; the virtues of "deep brain stimulation" (electric shock therapy); and the pressures that the mentally ill put on Canada's bulging criminal justice system. The series wrapped up with an essay written by Michael Kirby, Chair of the MHCC, titled "Fighting the Stigma."[44] Here the public is informed of the many ways in which stigma prevents those suffering with mental illness from seeking the appropriate professional treatment they need in order to recover into fully functioning, productive citizens.

Authors of the "Breakdown" series do not make reference to past and present state policies and practices that give credence to many of the most stigmatizing representations of madness and mental illness to endure in popular culture.[45] For instance, we know that historically the mad often occupied the same physical and ideological spaces as criminals and that these proximities have over time produced and maintained strong associations between crime, madness, disease, and danger.[46] Today still, it is typically these individuals (the mad *and* criminal) who are represented as the most disordered, dangerous and unrecoverable, and thus make unsuitable candidates for anti-stigma programs.

To illustrate this delineation, I refer to a different news report titled "To Heal and Protect." The full-spread article was intended to expose the inability of Canadian Correctional Services to manage and treat the "staggering" number of "mentally damaged" individuals currently "flooding" the criminal justice system and "clogging" jail cells.[47] However, the three-page special feature also exposed the ease with which we are able to recall and deploy historically informed alignments between crime, madness, disease, and danger. In outlining the inevitable social costs that come with failing to properly manage the "sick and demented" through appropriate risk assessment and medication, the report describes the situation in Canadian prisons as a "revolving door to disaster" and recounts the increased severity of one man's mental state as a "slowly creeping calamity." The article is punctuated with fearful messages about a decaying system out of control and the inability of mental health experts to effectively detect dangerous individuals before "disaster" strikes.

Concern regarding the effects of stigma seem not so prominent in this context, as one medical expert explained: "The vast majority will not be violent. But who will be?... If you don't want to stigmatize everyone, you should know who is at higher risk."[48] Here mentally ill inmates are likened to animals on a "range" wandering around "like a herd of deer, they appear docile, yet leery; most are heavily medicated." In describing "some unusual inmates," the deputy superintendent of the Maplehurst correctional facility in Ontario said, "[i]t is like putting four-year-olds in custody. They cry all day for their mommies. Social workers give them colouring books and crayons." She went on to say that the "primary concern" at Maplehurst "is getting medication and the right treatment."[49]

In many ways, this story represents the other side of mental illness where the hopeless, nameless, faceless, and feared reside. The images marshaled in the "To Heal and Protect" article at first appear to conflict with the anti-stigma message the MHCC would officially like to convey. However, it is precisely this *other* story that helps define and give meaning to anti-stigma campaigns as transformation/beautification projects. We must be able to recall and retain images of *madness* in order to characterize and control the image of *mental illness*. The "Opening Minds" anti-stigma campaign is designed to ensure people living with mental illness are treated as full citizens with equal opportunities to participate in society and in everyday life. Those who will remain locked away and out of sight — the herds of damaged, deranged, and disorderly — will never have such an opportunity.

Several market research consultants employed by the MHCC recommended early on in developing the campaign that they focus on messages that will put a "human face on mental illness" in order to appeal to "public empathy," suggesting that the popular tendency is still to imagine and fear the mentally ill as something *other* than human. The human-face-strategy aims to promote sameness/universality, predictability, and rationality in order to eradicate stigma and change public perceptions, not through programs of social *reform* or a politics of rights, inclusion and diversity, but by transforming the appearance of mental illness to look more like *us* and less like the madness we fear. The commission's official website is now filled with face-to-face testimonials from selected spokespeople willing to tell stories of "shared experiences" and convey images of hope and recovery. Similar to the strategy seen in the anti-graffiti/beautification campaign, the strategy here is also to shine a light on a selection of recognizable and aesthetically pleasing images that convey health, productivity, and responsible citizenship.

Despite the unprecedented resources that have been poured into the "Opening Minds" campaign, the MHCC has encountered some challenges in making their messages heard. The work, and even existence, of the MHCC is not well known among the general Canadian public, and particularly among those whom the work of the MHCC is supposedly intended help. Chair Michael Kirby recently defended the fact that over the past three years there has been little reporting in Alberta (where the MHCC is based) about the commission in general and anti-stigma efforts in particular. According to Kirby, "[I]f people get the *right* help, there is hope. But you can't even get started if people aren't willing to talk about it. Once we take away the stigma, we can begin the work."[50] The very proposition that the necessary starting point is getting the mentally ill to talk about mental illness immediately screens out those who are unable or unwilling to talk, as well as denies the historical processes of social, political, and economic exclusion that silenced mad people in the first place.

The invitation for the mentally ill to speak up is also the central theme of Bell Canada's new "Let's Talk" anti-stigma campaign, officially launched on February 9, 2011, following several lead-up weeks of advertising and celebrity media spots.[51] While it may be coincidence, it is also noteworthy that Bell Canada has recently participated in both an anti-graffiti/beautification program and a mental illness anti-stigma campaign. Recycling statistical claims from the MHCC, as well as the Canadian Mental Health Association and the Canadian Medical Association, that stigma is "the primary reason two-thirds of people living with mental health problems don't seek help," the five-year $50-million Bell Mental Health Initiative calls for an "open" and "respectful" conversation about mental illness in Canada.

In a radio interview, the chair of the Bell Canada "Let's Talk" campaign, Mary Deacon, claimed that taking about the "disease" of mental illness will keep it "visible," and that has the "potential to be transformative." When asked by the host, Matt Galloway, "What will transformation look like?" Deacon responded that by openly talking about mental illness we ensure support for "research that seeks solutions." In encouraging research that seeks solutions, the goal of the "Let's Talk" campaign is to "paint a different picture of mental illness."[52] But this does not answer the previous question regarding what transformation, or a "different picture," would look like. One thing that the "Let's Talk" campaign is more likely to ensure is that those who resist or challenge the bio-medical label of mental illness, or may instead choose to identify as mad, will not generally be part of the conversation. In resisting narrow agendas of recovery and the absolute authority of psychiatric treatment, "mad" people and activists associated with the "mad" movement do not represent the desired political aesthetic of mental illness as a disease from which one aspires to recover and be restored as a productive member of society. The self-identified "mad" (as apposed to the diagnosed mentally ill) and those willing to talk about it on their own terms have been pushed aside as unreasonable, absurd, and dangerous, in a way that can't help but bring to mind the histories that contributed to the stigma which the MHCC believes has caused Canada's mental health crisis.

In May, 2010, the *National Post,* another of Canada's national newspapers, published an article titled: "Mad Pride: Movement to Depose Psychiatry Emerges from the Shadows." Here readers are warned of the counter-hegemonic Mad Pride movement's plan to "overthrow" psychiatry. In the report, the Mad Pride movement, an international grass-roots organization, is sharply dismissed by well-known Canadian medical historian Edward Shorter as a group inspired by the "hidden hand of Scientology," a cult-like "hobby" that also "opposes medical psychiatry even as it believes in aliens," suggesting that to reject psychiatry is a sure sign of madness itself.[53] The article refers to delegates (academic and non-academic) of an international conference titled "PsychOUT," held at the University of Toronto in the spring of 2010, as "fringe advocates," "self-absorbed crackpots" and "ideological zealots" who deserve no place (or voice) in a respected university. The risk of such movements, the reporter explains, is that they will "discourage people from seeking mental health care, and increase stigma and suicide." The message is that there is only one rational course of treatment for mental illness and that resistance to the institution of psychiatry is not only *crazy,* but also subversive and dangerous to society. The article triggered a number of heated responses and revealed, as with the dispute over graffiti, the challenges in reconciling, or making space for, different systems of thought. The dispute regarding mental illness also lays bare the strict policing of hegemonic order, a process that keeps at the periphery those perspectives and practices interpreted as social transgressions, or simply "at odds with the mainstream."[54]

In an article following the "Mad Pride" report, the MHCC is criticized for including on one of its advisory committees Professor Neree St-Amand, an outspoken critic of psychiatry. According to the author: "His presence there as a supporter of the anti-psychiatry movement — which generally sees mental illness as a bogus corporate invention, and medical psychiatry as a caricatured memory of One Flew Over the Cuckoo's Nest — has put a wedge between allies at the MHCC."[55] Professor St-Amand's participation on the Family and Caregiver Advisory Committee is explained by one MHCC Board member as evidence of the commission's "openness to diverse opinions." But later in the article, perhaps in an effort to put distance between St-Amand and the commission, an unnamed "spokeswoman" for the MHCC reassures readers that "[a]nti-psychiatry is not a widespread concern at the commission" and further that "Mr. St-Amand's views are his own." The MHCC must work continuously to maintain its legitimacy by appearing focused, decided and strategic, not open and flexible.[56] According to this report, to be seen as accepting of different or incompatible views is to be seen as "ignorant and dangerous."[57]

In 1983, Edward Said made the following observation regarding the imperative of reductionist interpretations:

> The universalizing habit by which a system of thought is believed to account for everything too quickly slides into a quasi-religious synthesis.... In fact, interpretation and its demands add up to a rough game, once we allow ourselves to step out of the shelter offered by specialized fields and by all-embracing mythologies. The trouble with visions, reductive answers and systems is that they homogenize evidence very easily. Criticism as such is crowded out and disallowed from the start, hence impossible.... Far from taking in a great deal, the universal system as a universal type of explanation either screens out everything it cannot directly absorb or it repetitively churns out the same sort of thing all the time."

In this chapter I have argued that anti-graffiti/beautification campaigns, such as the "Clean and Beautiful City" initiative in Toronto, effectively produce, maintain, and disseminate a universal vision of what is socially acceptable and manageable, and in doing so mandates the treatment, transformation, and criminalization of that which is not. Through similar processes of "beautification," the "Opening Minds" anti-stigma campaign also produces, maintains, and disseminates a universal vision of "mental illness," a disease that is socially acceptable and manageable, and in doing so mandates a regime of response imperatives. In socially, morally, and aesthetically policing the public images of graffiti and mental illness, we crowd out diversity, individuality and freedom of expression. Indeed for some, to be called mad is preferable to being called mentally ill. And perhaps for some it is preferable to be seen as politically subversive graffiti writers rather than politically neutralized mural designers.

Conclusion

In bringing together two seemingly unrelated social constructs of "mental illness" and "graffiti crime," I do not suggest that madness and graffiti are the same in terms of history, social relevance, and individual impact. However, I do suggest that in examining public interest/awareness campaigns designed to manage the *problem* of mental illness and the *problem* of graffiti crime, we gain insight into the variable ways in which manifestations of mental illness, as a disease concept, are structured, maintained, and performed, not *in*, but *as* popular culture. This analysis also demonstrates how an insistence on universality and the promotion of a reductive "system of thought" (as is necessary for any social marketing campaign), not only displaces or excludes other/different/new ways of seeing and being, but also interferes with the possibility of deep and meaningful social change.

In manifesting historical knowledge of illness and disease, public interest/awareness campaigns are designed to bracket and bring attention to the perilous consequences of an untreated social problem and legitimize politically engineered programs of transformation or "beautification." In order for such programs to *appear* legitimate, a line must be drawn between good and bad, healthy and diseased, order and chaos, light and dark. To delineate between graffiti and art murals is therefore an attempt to neutralize and control some aspects of graffiti by reinterpreting it as art. Likewise, madness appears less chaotic when it is reinterpreted as mental illness. While each of the social marketing campaigns explored in this chapter claim in one way or another to move us away from problematic histories of criminalization and stigmatization, it is necessary for these histories to remain intact and in full view in order to legitimize and give meaning to processes of transformation.

The increasingly popular practice of employing social marketing techniques to identify and manage social disorders has in some ways opened a new chapter in the social and legal regulation of disorderly people. But it is a chapter that must be read in context and as a product of a broader cultural trend in the West to identify and solve social problems caused by various forms of transgression — non-conformity, disobedience, indecorousness — through state-authorized "projects of change."[58] As Dawn Moore suggests in her analysis of the historical governance of drugs and drug users in Canada, even as contexts change with time, place, and political climate, the particulars of a transformation project can be refashioned to suit different and changing situations, all the while keeping the basic design intact.

NOTES

1. Popular culture is used here to capture the collective of accepted, mainstream ideologies, discourses, representations, images, memes and/or attitudes that permeate and influence social practices and everyday life. Where popular/common knowledge may be seen as informally organized and structured, and official/expert knowledge as more formally organized through institutional structures and practices (such as law, government or medicine), I do not consider "the popular" and "the official" mutually exclusive cultural terrains, rather they are one in the same.

2. I use "madness" in this chapter as a broader cultural reference and which includes various other terms that are more temporally and contextually specific such as lunacy, insanity, mental disorder, psychotic, mental disability and mental illness.

3. The implications of imposing a "closed space" on the interpretation of social events (through "techniques of analysis, disciplinary attitudes and commonly held views") is explored by Edward Said in "Opponents, Audiences, Constituencies and Community," in *The Anti-Aesthetic: Essays on Postmodern Culture,* ed. Hal Foster (Seattle: Bay Press, 1983), 142.

4. I use propaganda in a broad sense to include communications developed for the purposes of persuasion, manipulation and political warfare, but also communications developed to deliver seemingly neutral messages associated with public health, community participation and safety.

5. In general, I use Ranciére's notion of *policing* to stand for an "organizational system of coordinates that establishes a distribution of the sensible or a law that divides the community into groups, social positions and functions" and which "implicitly separates those who take part from those who are excluded." Jacques Rancière, *The Politics of Aesthetics* (London: Versa Press, 2004), 3.

6. MHCC, "Opening Minds," accessed January 5, 2010, http://www.mentalhealthcommission.ca/English/Pages/OpeningMinds.aspx. There was a very similar campaign launched in 2005, by the Centre for Addiction and Mental Health (CAMH) in Toronto, Ontario, called "Transforming Lives." The language of "transformation" is also central to MHCC discourse where key initiatives are focused on "transforming the mental health system" and "transforming the lives of those living with mental illness." The MHCC and CAMH anti-stigma campaigns are virtually indistinguishable in their visions of "mental illness," the characteristics and effect of stigma, and access to services as key to treatment and recovery.

7. For a couple of good analyses on popular representations of madness/mental illness see: Stephen Harper, "Media, Madness and Misrepresentation: Critical Reflections on Anti-Stigma Discourse," *European Journal of Communication* 20, no. 4 (2005): 460–483; and Simon Cross, "Visualizing Madness: Mental Illness and Public Representation," *Television & New Media* 5, n0.3 (2004): 197–216.

8. Edward Said, "Opponents, Audiences, Constituencies and Community," In *The Anti-Aesthetic: Essays on Postmodern Culture,* ed. Hal Foster (Seattle: Bay Press, 1983): 135.

9. See George L. Kelling and Catherine M. Coles, *Fixing Broken Windows: Restoring Order and Reducing Crime in Our Communities* (New York: Free Press, 1996); and Joe Austin, *Taking the Train: How Graffiti Art Became an Urban Crisis in New York City* (New York: Columbia University Press, 2001).

10. Heinz Kuck, "Graffiti Vandalism Linked to Urban Decay," *Blue Line Magazine,* April 2006: 45, accessed December 14, 2010, http://www.paintedproblems.com/files/Pages_from_2006.04.pdf .

11. For example: Joe Austin, *Taking the Train* (2001); Tim Cresswell, *In Place / Out of Place: Geography, Ideology and Transgression* (Minneapolis: University of Minnesota Press, 1996), chapter 3; Simon Morley, *Writing on the Wall: Word and Image in Modern Art* (Berkeley: University of California Press, 2003); Craig Noble, "City Space: A Semiotic and Visual Exploration of Graffiti and Public Space in Vancouver" (2006), accessed July 10, 2010, http://www.graffiti.org/faq/noble_semiotic_warfare2004.html; and Alison Young, *Judging the Image: Art, Value, Law* (London: Routledge, 2005), chapter 3 in particular.

12. Young, *Judging the Image,* 53.

13. For an elaborated analysis of the politics of aesthetic order, see John Berger, *Ways of Seeing* (New York: Viking Press, 1973); and Jacques Rancière, *The Politics of Aesthetics* (London: Versa Press, 2004).

14. Young, *Judging the Image,* 55.

15. Ranciére, *The Politics of Aesthetics,* 12–13.

16. Craig Noble, "City Space," 1.

17. Ibid., 9.

18. Ibid., 11.

19. For a good example see *Vandal Watch*, accessed December 10, 2010, http://www.vandalwatch.citysoup.ca/Graffiti/default.htm.

20. See Cresswell, *In Place / Out of Place*, 4–5, 67; Wilbert Gesler and Robin Kearns, *Culture, Place and Health* (Abington UK: Routledge, 2002), 97–98; David Horn, "Bodies of Evidence," in *The Criminal Body* (New York: Routledge, 2003): 1–27; Steven Maynard, "Through the Hole in the Lavatory Wall: Homosexual Subcultures, Police Surveillance, and the Dialectics of Discovery, Toronto, 1890–1930," *Journal of the History of Sexuality* 5, no. 2 (1994): 207–242; and Dawn Moore, *Criminal Artifacts: Governing Drugs and Users* (Vancouver: University of British Columbia Press, 2007).

21. Tim Cresswell, *In Place / Out of Place*, 58.

22. Said, "Opponents, Audiences, Constituencies and Community," 143.

23. The battle for legitimacy is a concern for anti-graffiti fighters as well. On the official website for the Toronto Graffiti Eradication Project is a link titled "Building Legitimacy" which provides several examples of local, provincial and federal politicians bestowing praise upon the Toronto Police for helping to improve the "quality of life" for the citizens of Toronto by (ironically) "not tolerating messages of violence and fear." Toronto Police Services, Graffiti Eradication Program, "Building Legitimacy," accessed December 10, 2010, http://www.torontopolice.on.ca/graffiti/legitimacy.php. See letters from former provincial minister, John Godfrey; former Prime Minister, Jean Chrétien; former Premier of Ontario, Mike Harris; and former Mayor of Toronto, Mel Lastman.

24. This is not unique to Toronto. Municipal programs that aim in part to contain "graffiti crime" through city "beautification" projects are increasingly popular in North America.

25. City of Toronto, June 14, 2006, accessed December 15, 2010, http://wx.toronto.ca/inter/it/newsrel.nsf/0/e56f8b49e2348da28525718d0063ab7c?OpenDocument.

26. Pierre Bourdieu, *Distinction: A Social Critique of the Judgement of Taste* (Cambridge: Harvard University Press, 1984).

27. Erin Hershberg, "Graffiti Is in the Eye of the Beholder," *The Globe and Mail*, January 29, 2011, M1 and M6.

28. Ibid., M6.

29. In a 2003 documentary, one Vancouver graffiti artist appeared confident that abatement programs will never stop graffiti, but rather suggested that as an adaptive form of resistance, graffiti writers will turn their focus to mastering the art of tagging rather than developing full color pieces that require a good amount of safe space and uninterrupted time. From this graffiti writer's perspective, tagging is not considered mindless scrawling or a lesser form of graffiti art; it is practiced as a "stripped down," more spontaneous and "pure" form of graffiti that showcases an artist's unique and well-developed "hand style." *City Space*, directed by Craig Noble (Vancouver: Pixel One, 2003), DVD.

30. Hershberg, "Graffiti," M6.

31. Cresswell, *In Place / Out of Place*, 57–59.

32. Ranciére, *The Politics of Aesthetics*, 3 and 92.

33. Young, *Judging the Image*, 55.

34. Gilman, *Disease and Representation*, 9.

35. The creation of a permanent Mental Health Commission of Canada (MHCC) was first proposed in November 2005, and officially mandated and incorporated in March 2007. The official MHCC website is under a steady state of reconstruction and much of the information on the original terms of reference and early initiatives has been "updated" or edited out. Mental Health Commission of Canada, accessed Jan 20, 2011, http://www.mentalhealthcommission.ca/English/Pages/TheMHCC.aspx.

36. The diseases the MHCC most often align with mental illness are diabetes and heart disease, not other historically stigmatized diseases such as leprosy, cancer or AIDS. Occasionally breast cancer is mentioned as a comparator, but it is the success of the Pink

Ribbon campaign to bring awareness to breast cancer that is aligned with the Opening Minds campaign, not breast cancer the disease.

37. The use of the term "crisis" is particularly significant here if we consider that a crisis in health typically marks a turning point of a disease when an important change takes place, indicating either recover or death.

38. I have argued elsewhere that the corporate organization of the MHCC has forced a particular set of administrative structures that in every way has directed the production of knowledge within that organization. Kimberley White, "Out of the Shadows and Into the Spotlight: The Politics of (In)visibility and the Implementation of the Mental Health Commission of Canada," in *Configuring Madness: Representation, Context & Meaning,* ed. Kimberley White (Oxford: Inter-Disciplinary Press, 2009), 225–249.

39. Mental Health Commission of Canada, "Toward Recovery & Well-being: A Framework for a Mental Health Strategy for Canada," November 2009, 13.

40. The metaphors of shadow and light play an important role in MHCC messages. For example, the banner on the MHCC website home page reads "out of the shadows forever" which is taken from a Senate report in 2006 titled "Out of the Shadows at Last: Transforming Mental Health, Mental Illness and Addiction Services in Canada." Also, in 2009, the MHCC organized a national conference titled "Into the Light: Transforming Mental Health in Canada" as a forum to discuss the "framework" for the national mental health strategy. MHCC, "Into the Light," accessed December 10, 2010, http://www.men talhealthcommission.ca/English/Pages/IntotheLight.aspx.

41. Gilman, "Disease and Representation," 13 and 14.

42. While the Breakdown series was not explicitly presented to *Globe and Mail* readers (demographically identified as upper-middle class, educated and right-leaning) as an advertisement for the MHCC, neither can it be said to be an independent news report. The idea for the special report was originally conceived by the commission's then director of communications as a strategic initiative to shine a spotlight on pre-selected issues to be addressed by the MHCC. An open forum (including an official Facebook group) for the ongoing *The Globe and Mail* Special Report can be accessed through the MHCC website under "resources," accessed December 5, 2010, http://v1.theglobeandmail.com/breakdown/.

43. "Breakdown: Canada's Mental Health Crisis," *The Globe and Mail,* June 21, 2008, 1. Dr. David Goldbloom is also member of the MHCC Board of Directors and a senior administrator at the Centre for Addiction and Mental Health in Toronto. This is not mentioned in the news coverage.

44. Ibid., F1.

45. One rare, and brief, reference to historical processes — the only I have seen in official MHCC publications — states: "For far too long, people who have been given a diagnosis of mental illness have been seen as fundamentally different. There was a time — not that long ago, even in Canada — when they were sent away and locked up, never to be seen again." This quote seems quite out of touch with institutional reality in Canada, where people are still locked up, some to never be seen again. MHCC, "Toward Recovery and Well-being," 13.

46. Micheal Foucault, *Madness and Civilization: A History of Insanity in the Age of Reason* (New York: Random House, 1965); Robert Menzies, *Survival of the Sanest: Order and Disorder in a Pre-Trial Psychiatric Clinic* (Toronto: University of Toronto Press, 1989); and "The Making of Criminal Insanity in British Columbia: Granby Farrant and the Provincial Mental Home, Colquitz, 1919–1933," in *Essays in the History of Criminal Law Volume 6,* eds. H. Foster and J. McLaren (Toronto: University of Toronto Press, 1999), 274–313.

47. Kirk Makin, "To Heal and Protect," *The Globe and Mail,* January 22, 2011, F6–7.

48. Ibid., F7.

49. Ibid., F6.

50. Valerie Fortney, "Former Senator Michael Kirby Saluted for Mental Health

Work," *Calgary Herald*, August 13, 2010, accessed December 10, 2010, http://spon.ca/for mer-senator-michael-kirby-saluted-for-mental-health-work/2010/08/14/.

51. Bell Canada, "Let's Talk," accessed February 13, 2010, http://letstalk.bell.ca/ ?EXT=CORP_OFF_URL_letstalk_en.

52. Matt Galloway, "Let's Talk Day," *Metro Morning*, CBC Radio, February 9, 2011. Interview with Mary Deacon, chair of the Bell Mental Health Initiative. accessed Feb 11, 2011, http://www.cbc.ca/metromorning/episodes/2011/02/09/lets-talk-day/.

53. Joseph Brean, "Mad Pride: Movement to Depose Psychiatry Emerges from the Shadows," *National Post*, May 7, 2010, accessed January 25, 2011, http://www.national post.com/Mental+block+Opposers+Pride+protest+anti+psychiatrist/399658l/story.html.

54. Joseph Brean, "Mental Block: Opposers of Mad Pride Protest Anti-Psychiatry," *National Post*, Saturday, December 18, 2010.

55. Ibid.

56. In studying the organization and governance of the MHCC, I have observed many instances where the Board has delivered a narrow or simplified message to the public, not because they all agree, but because they recognize that in social marketing it is important to present an agenda of consensus.

57. Joseph Brean, "*Mental Block*," 2010.

58. Dawn Moore, *Criminal Artifacts: Governing Drugs and Drug Users* (Vancouver: University of British Columbia Press, 2007): 24.

BIBLIOGRAPHY

Austin, Joe. *Taking the Train: How Graffiti Art Became an Urban Crisis in New York City.* New York: Columbia University Press, 2001.

Bell Canada. "Let's Talk." Accessed February 13, 2011, http://letstalk.bell.ca/?EXT=CORP_OFF_URL_letstalk_en.

Berger, John. *Ways of Seeing.* New York: Viking Press, 1973.

Bourdieu, Pierre. *Distinction: A Social Critique of the Judgment of Taste.* Cambridge: Harvard University Press, 1984.

Cresswell, Tim. *In Place / Out of Place: Geography, Ideology and Transgression.* Minneapolis: University of Minnesota Press, 1996.

Cross, Simon. "Visualizing Madness: Mental Illness and Public Representation." *Television & New Media* 5, no. 3 (2004): 197–216.

Fortney, Valerie. "Former Senator Michael Kirby Saluted for Mental Health Work." *Calgary Herald*, August 13, 2010. Accessed December 10, 2010, http://spon.ca/former-sena tor-michael-kirby-saluted-for-mental-health-work/2010/08/14/.

Foucault, Michel. *Madness and Civilization: A History of Insanity in the Age of Reason.* New York: Random House, 1965.

Galloway, Matt. "Let's Talk Day." *Metro Morning*. CBC Radio, February 9, 2011, accessed Feb 11, 2011, http://www.cbc.ca/metromorning/episodes/2011/02/09/lets-talk-day/.

Gelser, Wilbert, and Robin Kearns. *Culture, Place and Health.* Abington, UK: Routledge, 2002.

Gilman, Sander L. *Difference and Pathology: Stereotypes of Sexuality, Race and Madness.* Ithaca, NY: Cornell University Press, 1985.

_____. *Disease and Representation: Images of Illness from Madness to Aids.* Ithaca, NY: Cornell University Press, 1988.

_____. *Illness and Health: Images of Difference.* London: Reaktion Books, 1995.

The Globe and Mail. Special Report. "Breakdown: Canada's Mental Health Crisis." June 21, 2008, A1, F1–14.

Harper, Stephen. "Media, Madness and Misrepresentation: Critical Reflections on Anti-Stigma Discourse." *European Journal of Communication* 20, no. 4 (2005): 460–483.

Hershberg, Erin. "Graffiti is in the Eye of the Beholder." *The Globe and Mail*, January 29, 2011, M1 and M6.

Horn, David. *The Criminal Body*. New York: Routledge, 2003.

Kelling, George L, and Catherine M. Coles. *Fixing Broken Windows: Restoring Order and Reducing Crime in Our Communities*. New York: Free Press, 1996.

Kirby, Michael. "Speaking Notes: The Honourable Michael Kirby, Chair, Mental Health Commission of Canada," *Calgary Chamber of Commerce*, Calgary, May 4, 2009, accessed May, 30, 2009, http://www.mentalhealthcommission.ca/English/Pages/keyDocuments.aspx.

Kuck, Heinz. "Graffiti Vandalism Linked to Urban Decay." *Blue Line Magazine*, April 2006, 45.

Makin, Kirk. "To Heal and Protect." *The Globe and Mail*, January 22, 2011, F7.

Martin, N., and V. Johnston. *A Time for Action: Tackling Stigma and Discrimination*, accessed June 15, 2009, http://www.mentalhealthcommission.ca/English/Pages/AntiStigmaCampaign.aspx.

Maynard, Steven. "Through the Hole in the Lavatory Wall: Homosexual Subcultures, Police Surveillance, and the Dialectics of Discovery, Toronto, 1890–1930." *Journal of the History of Sexuality* 5, no. 2 (1994): 207–242.

Mental Health Commission of Canada, accessed Jan 20, 2011, http://www.mentalhealthcommission.ca/English/Pages/TheMHCC.aspx.

Menzies, Robert. "The Making of Criminal Insanity in British Columbia: Granby Farrant and the Provincial Mental Home, Colquitz, 1919–1933." In *Essays in the History of Criminal Law Volume 6*, eds. H. Foster and J. McLaren, 274–313. Toronto: University of Toronto Press, 1999.

_____. *Survival of the Sanest: Order and Disorder in a Pre-Trial Psychiatric Clinic*. Toronto: University of Toronto Press, 1989.

Moore, Dawn. *Criminal Artefacts: Governing Drugs and Users*. Vancouver: University of British Columbia Press, 2007.

Morley, Simon. *Writing on the Wall: Word and Image in Modern Art*. Berkeley: University of California Press, 2003.

Noble, Craig. *City Space*. Directed by Craig Noble. Vancouver: Pixel One, 2003. DVD.

_____. "City Space: A Semiotic and Visual Exploration of Graffiti and Public Space in Vancouver," 2006, accessed July 10, 2010, http://www.graffiti.org/faq/noble_semiotic_warfare2004.html.

Phillips, Susan. *Wallbangin': Graffiti and Gangs in L.A.* Chicago: University of Chicago Press, 1999.

Rancière, Jacques. *The Politics of Aesthetics*. London: Versa Press, 2004.

Said, Edward W. "Opponents, Audiences, Constituencies and Community." In *The Anti-Aesthetic: Essays on Postmodern Culture*, ed. Hal Foster, 135–159. Seattle: Bay Press, 1983.

Sontag, Susan. *Illness as Metaphor and AIDS and Its Metaphors*. New York: Picador, 1977.

Toronto Police Services. *Graffiti Eradication Program*, accessed on December 14, 2010, http://www.torontopolice.on.ca/graffiti/.

_____. "Building Legitimacy." Accessed December 10, 2010, http://www.torontopolice.on.ca/graffiti/legitimacy.php.

Vandal Watch. Accessed December 10, 2010, http://www.vandalwatch.citysoup.ca/Graffiti/default.htm.

White, Kimberley. "Out of the Shadows and Into the Spotlight: The Politics of (In)visibility and the Implementation of the Mental Health Commission of Canada." In *Configuring Madness: Representation, Context & Meaning*, ed. Kimberley White, 225–249. Oxford: Inter-Disciplinary Press, 2009.

Young, Alison. *Judging the Image: Art, Value, Law*. London: Routledge, 2005.

14

Beyond Beyond Reason

Images of People with Mental Disabilities in Australian Film Since the 1970s

PHILIPPA MARTYR

Shine (1996), the Australian film loosely based on the life of pianist David Helfgott (who lives with a mental illness), won Australian actor Geoffrey Rush an Oscar for Best Actor in 1997. In his acceptance speech, Rush thanked Helfgott for his inspirational life: "And to those people who say it's a circus, then with your celebration of life you show me that the circus is a place of daring and risk-taking and working without a safety net and giving us your personal poetry."[1] But how much "daring and risk-taking and working without a safety net" has there been in Australian film's depiction of people living with mental illness? And what are we talking about — "movie madness," which is a very flexible and accommodating eccentricity, or genuine mental illness in all its complexity and difficulty? In this chapter, I will be examining Australian film since the 1970s and how it has presented characters or situations involving mental illness or psychiatric disability.

Far from breaking out and trying new and more accessible approaches, Australian film since the 1970s has been plagued by the stereotypes of "dramatic" therapies, "exciting" behaviors, and "tragic but inevitable" suicides. Nonetheless, there are some promising signs of change also, but these are coming not from within but from concerted pressure applied outside the industry. I will also be focusing on "fictional" film, rather than documentary, which means I will have to exclude works like Brian McKenzie's *On the Waves of the Adriatic* (1991). This is not to say that the documentary format lacks validity; rather, my principal focus is films in which mental illness is used as a dramatic and creative element in its own right: when Australian writers and directors have shown us — intentionally or not — what they think it is like to live with a mental illness.

Mental Illness in Australian Film Since the 1970s

The history of madness in Australia has been dominated by what Australian disability theorist Robert Cettl calls "a prolonged period of government imposition of medical model theories and the subsequent creation of disability as a social crisis as much as an individual impairment."[2] The institution has been the dominant form of mental health care provision in Australia, and almost all its mental institutions in the last 150 years have been government-owned and operated. Appropriately enough, the first Australian film to subvert this, in which social destruction through nuclear war forces a group of survivors out of a psychiatric hospital and into a dangerous and uncertain future, was independent filmmaker Giorgio Miangamele's *Beyond Reason* (1970; not to be confused with the 1977 film with Telly Savalas). This symbolic "deinstitutionalization" — a breakdown of social and medical government — is a good point from which to begin a discussion of how Australian filmmakers have approached the question of mental illness.

Following the repeal of Australia's notoriously strict film censorship laws in the early 1970s, the industry has produced some internationally acclaimed critical and commercial successes. These include *Strictly Ballroom* (1992), *The Piano* (1993), *Muriel's Wedding* (1994), and recently *Animal Kingdom* (2010), which won the dramatic jury prize for world cinema at the 2010 Sundance Film Festival and at the time of writing had opened strongly in the United States. Yet despite a huge increase in the number of independent Australian filmmakers and productions in the last three decades, the Australian film industry has also been criticised for making too many "depressing" films. Australia has a small population (around 23 million), and without that critical mass — as Karl Quinn noted — there is always the temptation to be over-serious, in order to be taken seriously.[3]

In 2005, the Australian Government's Department of Health and Ageing commissioned two literature reviews to explore the portrayal of suicide and mental illness in film and drama. The second of these two studies, by Pirkis et al., entitled *A Review of the Literature Regarding Film and Television Drama Portrayals of Mental Illness (2005)*, scoped international as well as local productions and found broadly negative portrayals of people with mental illness: violent, aggressive, simpletons, failures, (female) seductresses, and self-obsessives.[4] However, Pirkis et al. also found that mental health professionals were portrayed with equal malevolence: manipulative, deceitful, power-mad, exploitative, or excessively rationalistic. Importantly, the review also found a very limited presentation of mental health treatments, with an over-emphasis on "dramatic" therapies such as ECT and psychotherapy, and less focus on the more common but visually less exciting use of medication. A follow-up literature review in 2010 by Pirkis and Blood found that international research largely supported an association between film/television portrayal of suicide and suicide attempts and completions.[5]

There have been positive responses to these claims, but these have not come from within the film industry: instead, the responses have come from clinicians and government. Australian critics such as Rosen, et al.,[6] Tam,[7] Quadrio,[8] Wilson et al.,[9] and Macfarlane[10]— all from clinical backgrounds — have begun to unpack the more unhelpful images of mental illness in mainstream film. The Australian government has taken the issue seriously enough to fund the *Response Ability* and *Mindframe* projects, which provide pre-packaged response materials to support a more accurate and positive presentation of mental health issues in the public forum. Consumer groups like SANE Australia (which has a "StigmaWatch" project) have also campaigned for change in the news media.

Pirkis et al. determined that the "entertainment media may exert a more powerful influence than the news media,"[11] and yet in Australia, it seems to have become the last bastion of stereotype. Why is this? Entertainment media are expected to make profits from people who pay to consume their product; news media is consumed with a different set of expectations. Successful film is expected to entertain: to trigger certain emotional responses that are comfortable and familiar enough to reassure, and yet different enough to generate creative friction. Rosen and Walter have also queried the "rules of the game" that seem to operate in Australian film treatment of mental illness, even allowing for what they identify as the constraints within which filmmakers operate: the battle between education and entertainment; artistic integrity; the pressures of narrative pace; and the need to accommodate multiple stakeholders.[12]

"Going Full Retard": Confronting Some Existing Prejudices

The Australian mainstream film industry's development has been largely dominated by American tropes and techniques. If anyone had any doubts about what the mainstream film industry thought of disability, the recent satire *Tropic Thunder* (2008) put them to rest. There is a scene where Kirk Lazarus (Robert Downey, Jr.) lectures action movie star Tugg Speedman (Ben Stiller) on Speedman's recent career-wrecking flop called *Simple Jack*, in which he plays a severely disabled man. Lazarus explains: "You went full retard, man. Never go full retard." Even though mental illness has been understood and used as a dramatic trope for centuries, this thus-far-and-no-farther attitude has still broadly influenced the depiction of people with mental illnesses in contemporary film.

Cettl describes the subversive potential of mental illness, because it represents a sometimes-violent rejection of normal thinking rather than a disempowered state of physical dependence and weakness,[13] and Shakespeare certainly appreciated the dramatic value of a "mad" character who can speak the truth where others cannot. But who has really tried it on screen? It is unthinkable to write about mental illness in film without mentioning the treasured shibboleth *One Flew Over the Cuckoo's Nest* (1975). Yet Jack Nicholson as McMurphy is portraying someone who is not really mentally unwell: McMurphy feigns madness in order to escape hard labour in prison, and the audience's knowledge of this is integral to the viewing experience.

Even today, mainstream American film still seems to be prone to sliding into the extremes of ultra-violence or mawkish sentimentality and unable to turn a more nuanced presentation of disabling mental illness into a commercial success. *The Soloist* (2009) is an example of a well-intentioned film that somehow got lost in translation: it proved to be neither a critical nor a commercial success due to a perceived lack of narrative focus. Film reviewer Roger Ebert came to the point in his review: " 'Explaining madness is the most limiting and generally least convincing thing a movie can do,' Pauline Kael once wrote. *The Soloist* doesn't even seem sure how to depict it.... [T]he musician here seems more of a loose cannon, unpredictable in random ways. Yes, mental illness can be like that, but can successful drama?"[14]

The recent U.S. film *Adam* (2009) is another case in point. This mainstream attempt to present life with Asperger's Syndrome was reasonably balanced, but was also sanitised and didactic. Adam (Hugh Dancy) was given good looks, a degree of financial security, a best friend who helped to make the world safe for him, and considerable insight into his own disability. By contrast, the Australian mainstream film *Malcolm* (1986) anticipated *Adam* by more than two decades and managed to leave its Aspergerish main character ignored but triumphant. Malcolm's experience of stigma, disability, and social isolation turn out to be his greatest assets, especially in the comic life of crime to which he turns, and the film was an unusual commercial, critical, and cult success, winning eight AFI (Australian Film Industry) awards.

These mainstream American films illuminate some of the limitations within which the Australian film industry has also operated when confronted with mental illness. Rosen and Walter have called these the "rules of the game," which include: never spoil a good story with the facts; lend credibility by linking an actual person to a fictional plot; and — most painfully — stereotype at will.[15] How much these "rules" have persisted can be seen when we examine how Australian film has presented people with mental illnesses.

What Constitutes a "Psychiatric Theme" in a Film?

I mentioned earlier the idea of "movie madness"—a convenient and only minimally disabling condition with occasionally dramatic symptoms. There is an abundance of films with characters who are unpleasant, sociopathic, blood-thirsty and very violent, but are they mentally ill—*really* mentally ill, and not just conveniently "deranged" for the purposes of supporting a paper-thin plot?

"Madness" has many levels of meaning in film; for example, the "mad" character who is a very marked (and occasionally rugged) individual, living many miles from citified and *ipso facto* desensitized folk. Examples can be found throughout the offbeat Australian science-fiction comedy *As Time Goes By* (1988) and more recently the film *Charlie and Boots* (2009), which took its protagonists through an outback densely populated with "characters" of varying degrees of eccentricity. This can devolve into the *Steppenwolf* or rogue male who now lives on the fringes of acceptable patterns of behaviour: an example is the recently re-released *Wake in Fright* (1971, 2009), where a man stranded in the Australian outback falls among a group of menacing characters. These men may be mad, but the real issue is that they are very dangerous and violent. (One of Australia's most famous movies, *Mad Max* (1979), is not about "madness" at all).

I have chosen to focus on films which have more coherent psychiatric themes and have organised these thematically into four groups: developmental disability, the "mad genius," institutionalization, and social dysfunction. With several films in each group, it is also possible to trace changes taking place over time since the 1970s. Pirkis et al. found that mental health literacy has improved when viewers can identify with the person on screen and the issues are not over-simplified,[16] so a number of litmus tests can be applied to these films: how their directors have approached the casting and interpretation of key characters with a mental illness; how these films approached treatment issues; and whether the consumer-characters are presented as complex people with redeeming features, or oversimplified into merely negative and disruptive elements in the storyline.

Developmental Disability: Tim (1979); Struck by Lightning (1990)

It seems rare to find a positive presentation of a character with a devel-opmental disability in any film, Australian or otherwise. However, there have been some attempts by Australian filmmakers to incorporate the concept of developmental disability into mainstream film. Colleen McCullough's novel *Tim*,[17] which was published in 1971 and filmed in 1979, is an example of how mental health themes can be trumped by the more potent offering of transgressive love.

Tim is played by a handsome young Mel Gibson, who shows few signs of disability: a decision which Cettl indicates was deliberately made by director Michael Pate, because the audience would laugh if Tim's character were shown with a greater degree of intellectual disability.[18] Kirk Lazarus's comments about "going full retard" ring very true here. Tim works as a builder's labourer and is the butt of practical jokes and unkindness from his workmates. He is out of his depth when the mature, beautiful and kind Mary (Piper Laurie) takes him under her wing as an odd-job man. Like McCullough's other novel *An Indecent Obsession*,[19] filmed in 1981, this film appears to be less about psychiatric disability and more about transgressive love, this time across a substantial age barrier.

A more satisfying film is Jerzy Domaradzki's *Struck By Lightning* (1990; released in the US as *Saltmarsh*). Ollie (Australian actor Garry Macdonald, himself the veteran of a very public nervous breakdown in the early 1990s) runs Saltmarsh, a halfway house for young people with developmental disabilities. Ollie is a complex character; he is a committed social worker, but he is also a self-pitying alcoholic who calls his clients "retards." Into this underfunded and failing environment comes Pat, a sports teacher whose brother is also, according to him, a "retard."

Pat — sometimes helped and sometimes resisted by the conflicted Ollie — manages to get the center's clients involved in soccer and helps them to develop skills like teamwork. The film culminates in a soccer match with predictable results, but the overall impact of *Struck by Lightning* is uplifting without being too sentimental. It slips into stereotyping at times, but this is done at the expense of perceived "do gooders" and ineffectual charity managers rather than the clients. *Struck by Lightning* represents an enormous leap forward from *Tim*, but disabilities advocates would likely argue that there is still a long way to go before people with developmental disabilities can appear as mainstream characters in any commercially successful Australian film.

Institutionalization: Beyond Reason (1970), 27A (1974), Così (March 1996), Lilian's Story (May 1996)

Historically most people with serious mental illness in Australia were institutionalized, often for many years, but unfortunately the mental hospital is also a B-movie icon, which makes it difficult to express creatively a person's lived experience of institutionalization without falling into cliché. I have chosen four Australian films which have explored this issue, all in different ways and with different degrees of success.

Cettl argues that the few Australian filmic references to either mental or physical disability before 1970 presented people with disabilities as "overcoming" them with the help of a largely benign medical establishment.[20] The apocalyptic *Beyond Reason* cut directly across this and, despite poor distribution, proved to be influential.[21] After a nuclear war, the surviving staff and patients of a psychiatric hospital re-create the institution in an underground shelter and attempt to continue to maintain medication-based behavioral discipline. However, as the drugs begin to run out, the patients begin to question medical authority, engage in forbidden sexual relationships, and eventually kill the psychiatrist in charge as the survivors' world disintegrates: what Cettl describes as "the disabled anti-hero's confirmation of victorious self-determination through the anarchic destruction of the disabling authority."[22] It would be nice to think that this was true, but in reality *Beyond Reason* appears to be struggling to escape the aura of the B-movie, while playing on collective fears of un-medicated "escaped lunatics" and sexual maniacs.

27A also cuts directly across the established genre, but was produced as a deliberate polemic to expose the limitations of the state-run mental health system in Queensland in the 1970s—the title refers to a clause in the state's mental health legislation that allowed indefinite detention. In this film Billy Donald, a middle-aged derelict and alcoholic (played by Robert McDarra, in real life also an alcoholic), joins Alcoholics Anonymous. This leads to a psychiatric evaluation, after which he is committed to a hospital indefinitely. The film was based on a true story and was released at a time when Queensland psychiatric facilities were undergoing increasing public scrutiny: a campaign driven by Robert Somerville, who fought his detention and questioned the validity of the law. The direction is deliberately documentary-style and impressionistic, and although it won two AFI awards, *27A* was not a mainstream commercial success.

In 1996 Australian film lived dangerously: three films were released with strong themes involving people living with mental illness, two of which became outstanding commercial successes: *Così*, directed by Mark Joffe and released in March 1996, *Lilian's Story* directed by Jerzy Domaradzki and released in May 1996, and *Shine*, directed by Scott Hicks and released in August 1996. Coincidentally, two of these films feature Toni Colette, who recently won an Emmy for her portrayal of the dissociative Tara in the 2009 television series *The United States of Tara*.

In *Così*, an immature university student (Ben Mendelsohn) is offered a job with a government-funded program to undertake the "rehabilitation" of a group institutionalized people. He decides he will help the patients to put on a play, only to find that his intention is utterly subverted by their decision to perform a full-costume, full-length production of Mozart's *Così Fan Tutte* (mimed to vinyl records). The patients in their performance mock the "charitable" performers who have so often come to entertain: they mime with delighted enthusiasm, dressed in dazzling and bizarre costumes of their own making, simply for their own satisfaction. *Così*, as such, is unashamedly mythopoeic: fantasy and imagination are happier places, and madness is a far more enjoyable country to live in than modern-day Australia.

Così does provide a critical commentary on institutionalization; nonetheless, Rosen et al. have commented adversely on *Così*, noting that the film's writer, Louis Nowra (who wrote the play upon which the film was based) had to rewrite the original 1971 script to make it correspond with the changed realities of the mental health system.[23] Yet the hospital's decrepit wards, chilly performance hall, and institutionalized staff still have plenty of real-life parallels in Australian mental health care today. Nowra's difficult personal history, theatrical background, and lived experience of head injury, combined with his undeniable gift for writing and imaginative communication, all help to make *Così* a complex and interesting film.

Lilian's Story (May 1996) also examines the impact of mental illness and how one individual can process and cope with years of institutionalization. It was neither a commercial nor critical success, with some reviewers comparing it unfavorably to Kate Grenville's novel on which it was based. Real-life celebrated Sydney vagrant Bea Miles was the original model for Lilian, whose character is released from a mental hospital after forty years of institutionalization. Unable to return to the home where she had been sexually abused by her father, she takes to living on the streets, reciting poetry and trying to gather together the fragments of her existence.

Clea Jones has pointed out that one of the problems with *Lilian's Story* is that it is questionable to what degree it is actually "Lilian's story."[24] The film relies on the extraordinary external behaviours displayed by Lilian throughout her life (in youth played by Toni Collette, and in old age by superb Australian character actor the late Ruth Cracknell), rather than sharing with the audience what it is like to "be Lilian." Lilian quotes Shakespeare throughout the film, but Ruth Cracknell is well-known in Australia as a theatre performer, and so the film sometimes tips over into a vehicle for her talents, rather than involving us in a "real" character called Lilian, whose life is supposed to be of interest to us. Colette's performance is perhaps more affecting, especially when the young Lilian experiences rape and responds by engaging in self-mutilation. Yet even with this, it is difficult to become involved with Lilian, and instead too much of the film becomes a vehicle for two very talented actors.

The "Mad Genius": Shine (1996)

The Australian pianist David Helfgott's career is inseparable from his mental illness. Institutionalized repeatedly for schizoaffective disorder and yet still performing publicly, Helfgott's story is a real-life example of the "mad genius" trope, and was as such a prize for any filmmaker. The movie *Shine*, a fictionalized version of his life, is uncompromising in its portrayal of Helfgott's repeated nervous breakdowns and triumphant piano performances.

So do we at last have a film that presents a person with a serious and disabling mental illness who is also high-functioning? This film raises more questions than it answers. Certainly the portrayal of Mozart in *Amadeus* (1984) has something in common with this: the idea that a high degree of artistic ability must go hand in hand with a certain degree of mental instability, but there are other issues which problematize *Shine*'s depiction of Helfgott. The accuracy of the film has been questioned, notably by his sister Margaret in her book *Out of Tune*.[25] Helfgott's real-life live performances and recordings are not "acclaimed" at all; in fact, critics have been less than impressed with his work, even allowing for his obvious psychiatric disability. (Helfgott almost never receives a negative review in Australia, but overseas reviewers such as Tomasini,[26] Dutton[27] and Smith[28] have been more pointed about his live performances and recordings.) The Helfgott of the film is actually a fictional character: a highly successful musical genius whose mental illness was either brought about or severely aggravated by a domineering Mozart-like father. This is fits the *Amadeus* mould of the "mad genius," but leaves the real Helfgott high and dry.

Ruth Hessey has cited director Scott Hicks's (somewhat *faux-naïf*) description of *Shine* as a movie about "an unlikely hero who nonetheless achieves the one thing we all desire: he finds his own place in the world, and someone with whom to share life, love, and music."[29] Perhaps Simon Wessely's summary is more accurate: "Films that combine genius, the Holocaust, dysfunctional families, romantic music, nail-biting competitions, mental illness, and a happy ending are bound to succeed."[30] Helfgott's genuinely complex life story has been transformed into a much more "commonplace story" of brilliant achievement in the teeth of great suffering. It is inspirational, but it is also fictional.

Hicks has consistently defended his use of creative license in *Shine*, and Jan Sardi, its screenwriter, said, "When you are dealing with someone's life, you tread that fine line between events that are known to have happened, and your own creative license. And of course the film must be entertaining. It must begin and end within 100 minutes and take the audience on an emotional rollercoaster ride."[31] Pirkis et al. noted that the film has sharply polarized critical and psychiatric opinion,[32] and Rosen and Walter have also commented adversely on *Shine*'s tendency to reinforce negative stereotypes. *Shine* was an opportunity to show some real complexity in the life of a person with a mental illness, someone whose psychiatric disability may actually have damaged his musical gifts and ability to perform, but it is questionable how much in the long run it has helped advance Australian society's thinking about "ordinary, everyday" people with mental illnesses.

Social Dysfunction: *Sweetie* (1989), *Angel Baby* (1995), *Animal Kingdom* (2010), *The Waiting City* (2010)

Sweetie (1989), director Jane Campion's first feature film, comes perilously close to the horror movie genre. Again, it was not a commercial success, and both Australian and overseas critics found aspects of it bewildering (notably Roger Ebert, who had to see it twice before he could make any sense of it).[33] Kay, a woman struggling with deep-seated neuroses apparently connected with incest, forms a relationship with Louis and moves in with him, but one night they return home to find that someone has broken into their home. Kay claims that the intruder is a "friend" of hers, but in reality it is her loathed sister Dawn, known in the family as "Sweetie." Sweetie is a monstrous creation; allegedly suffering from some delusional illness and requiring medication, she is a domineering, attention-seeking arch-controller who manipulates the entire family. The emotional turmoil generated within one small family is both a cause of mental illness and aggravated by it, as the increasingly unbalanced Sweetie exploits her own family's inability to cope with her. *Sweetie* is a bitterly astringent commentary on family dysfunction, but a less positive portrayal of a person living with delusion cannot be imagined.

Angel Baby (1995) is a bleak tragedy which nonetheless won seven AFI awards in the year it was released and also collected awards from the Gijón International Film Festival, Rotterdam International Film Festival, and the Valenciennes International Festival of Action and Adventure Films. More pointedly, the film won the (Australian) Human Rights and Equal Opportunity Commission Feature Film Award in 1995. Yet it was also not a commercial success, and it is easy to see why. The story involves Harry, who lives with schizophrenia and who is managing to achieve a level of social functioning while using his medication. He meets Kate, also schizophrenic and medicated, but who is still experiencing delusions. Harry and Kate move in together, but then Kate becomes pregnant, so the couple decide to stop taking their medication. Both become psychotic and Kate is hospitalized, but Harry manages to help her escape. They end up living in a construction site, from where Kate has to be rushed to hospital to deliver the baby, and the film ends with Harry's (implied) suicide shortly after the birth.

To its credit, *Angel Baby* grapples with the spiral of poverty and welfare dependence in which so many people with a mental illness in Australia, living in the "community" and shuttling between social isolation and relapses, are trapped. However, it is hard to avoid the implication that people with schizophrenia can never find true, lasting, or stable love in a relationship, and that if they decide to have a family, this will end in disaster. This quasi-eugenic attitude has been challenged by the recent development of specialist antenatal clinics for women and couples with serious mental illness who are expecting children, and who simply need more consistent support through this process than is normally available to people on low incomes in Australia.

The film was the first directorial effort by Michael Rymer, who prepared by spending four months attending an informal day care centre for people with mental illnesses. In an interview with Andrew Urban, Rymer claimed that the film does not come close to presenting the awfulness of daily life with schizophrenia: "It's a cleaned up version ... what they have to go through is messy, ugly and half the challenge [of making the film] is to make it watchable. But the script is not about crazy people.... If I'd set out to make a film about schizophrenics, it would have been more about the symptoms than about the people."[34]

This quote is telling: it shows that Rymer still subscribes internally to the idea that a film about "schizophrenics" would have to focus on symptoms, on the "performance" of the illness, rather than the person involved. Rymer's film is about people with schizophrenia who also have considerable psychiatric disability — they are low-functioning, and this has clearly been influenced by his experience of a limited group of clients. The idea that there may be people living with schizophrenia in the community who are reasonably high-functioning has yet to be explored in Australian film.

I am including two powerful and very recent Australian films, *Animal Kingdom* and *The Waiting City* (both 2010). *Animal Kingdom* is the story of a small-time gangland family in inner-city Melbourne, presided over by Janine, a serenely detached, cheerful and utterly ruthless matriarch. Her eldest son, "Pope," is mentally ill, but is also a heroin user and murderer. He is slow-moving, slow-speaking, very withdrawn and every bit as detached from reality as his adoring mother, who at one point suggests — not very seriously — that he should "start taking his pills again." While this may seem a step backward in associating a mentally unwell person with violence and offending, it actually represents a genuine attempt to present mental illness as a consequence of socioeconomic disadvantage: the mental illness — which is never named — is presented here not as the source of his violence, but rather as a product of his life of social deprivation.

The Waiting City, which I have reviewed elsewhere,[35] is different again.

Ben, a former musician who has had drug problems and too much success too young, is married to Fiona, a high-powered lawyer. Ben has been hospitalized in the past for depression, and is still on antidepressants, and the film captures this lived experience well: his lack of interest in sex, his inability to concentrate, and tendency to bewilderment. As the story progresses and Ben begins to recover, this process gradually reverses: he is more alert, more affectionate, and more in control. The couple travel to India to adopt a baby girl, but nothing goes as planned, and the two are unexpectedly caught up in a transcendental process of redemption and healing.

Both *Animal Kingdom* and *The Waiting City* offer more accurate and accessible depictions of a character living with depression in a serious film — where the illness is not caricatured or turned into a horror-movie performance, but where it remains simply a part of the character's life, real and unavoidable. Significantly, both characters are presented as using medication, rather than ECT or psychoanalysis: the absence of medication in film presentations of mental illness has been noted by Pirkis et al.,[36] so its incorporation here represents a real step forward.

Conclusion: Waiting for Gilliam? A Possible Future for Mental Illness in Australian Film

So how do these films measure up? Directors do not on the whole appear to have distinguished themselves in their casting and interpretation of key characters with a mental illness. Michael Pate chose to make *Tim* an unintelligent but handsome young man, because he believed audiences would laugh if he portrayed Tim as living with serious intellectual disability; Michael Rymer also admitted that what he presented in *Angel Baby* was a sanitized version of what he believed life with schizophrenia to be really like. Similarly, treatment issues have been generally handled negatively: "running out of drugs" in *Beyond Reason*, archaic brutality in *Lilian's Story* and *Shine*. Director Scott Hicks has been strongly criticised for *Shine*, but both he and screenwriter Jan Sardi have maintained that it was a valid artistic interpretation, and also that they were constrained by the "rules of the game" (as defined by Rosen and Walter).

But the most striking failure has been in the presentation of mental health consumers themselves: for the most part, they have not been allowed to appear as complex people with redeeming features, nor as people with whom an ordinary audience could identify. Rosen and Walter have cited Simon Champ's comments as inaugural Chair of the Australian Mental Health Consumer Network: "There is plenty enough drama available if you care to accurately tune in to the subjective experience of an individual or family who has survived mental illness."[37] Yet characters like the eponymous *Sweetie* (repellent and dangerous) and Harry and Kate in *Angel Baby* (suicidal failures) do little to lift the burden of stigma, and in the case of *Shine*, David Helfgott's real-life character has been distorted beyond recognition, leaving its contribution to real change questionable at best. What is even more interesting is that the use of mental illness as a critical creative device in Australian film has almost never been accompanied by commercial success. The standout exceptions to this have been *Shine* and *Così*, both of which managed to combine music and madness in digestible form. Australian film would thus appear to be at a critical turning point: one where the public is perhaps beginning to tire of conventional portrayals of "madness" in film, but has as yet been unchallenged by any real alternatives.

Perhaps the problem is that many Australian filmmakers do not appear to know very much about mental illness and institutionalization, apart from what they have absorbed from American and British film, and perhaps a rare or nominal visit to some institution or community group for "artistic development" purposes. Film from the "outside"—stories written at second hand by people who have not made much effort to engage with individuals affected by a mental illness, and produced and directed by equally disengaged people—will never capture the lived experience of mental illness.

Australia's smaller population and lack of critical mass are also factors beyond the film industry's control. However, related to this—and perhaps caused by it—is Australian film's tendency to live and move within an affluent urban enclave. Theater critic Michael Connor has described the artistic *nomenklatura* whose exasperation with "middle Australians" (who refuse to pay to watch fashionably self-hating or depressing Australian film and theater) is often rancorous.[38] Filmmakers thus run the risk of becoming disengaged from the very communities where there are families with Down Syndrome children, families living as carers for their schizophrenic son or daughter, or families with a member who has Alzheimer's disease.

It is worth noting that the drive for change in the presentation of people with mental illness has come from outside the Australian film industry, in other areas of the media. This presents a new danger: that the drive for change outside the industry will be interpreted as the imposition of "political correctness," a new form of hegemony which the truly "independent" filmmaker must resist and subvert. It would be a pity if the campaign for more accuracy and fairness towards consumers was seen as an unjustifiable intrusion into the comfortable world of Australian "movie madness." Rosen and Walter have argued that creativity and innovation can flourish while respecting social responsibility, asking for a more level playing field, "but also one with less mud to kick up and sling around."[39]

So what are we waiting for? The films of American director Terry Gilliam are some of the best examples of an original and highly artistic engagement with characters diagnosed with mental illness, notably *The Fisher King* and *12 Monkeys*. It is a great help that Gilliam has led an unusual life and has used his intelligence and filmmaker's eye to process this experience and provide both catharsis and communication to his audiences. Gilliam is not patronising, but is able to give his characters a freedom and depth: in Gilliam's film, mental illness is often an opening into a richer world of perception, part gift and part curse. Australian film, perhaps, is waiting for a Gilliam: for an Australian filmmaker who can draw upon a personal and lived experience of mental illness to show the world a truly original vision of this experience.

It could be argued that a really talented filmmaker does not need to experience mental illness to portray it. I do not agree. A really talented *actor* does not need to have experienced mental illness in order to portray it, because that is, after all, what acting is. But a director or producer may be a different kettle of fish: they are responsible for the overall look of a film, for the interpretation of the script and the way in which the film communicates with its audience. It is here that a more intimate or lived experience of mental illness would be very useful, especially if combined with real talent and breadth of vision as a director.

People with lived experience of mental illnesses can produce scripts and should be encouraged to do so, especially if they have the talent for film-writing. An opportunity surely must exist for a filmmaker to consider an autobiographical work like the recent *Strange Places: A Memoir of Mental Illness* by Will Elliot.[40] But until a director or producer can really engage with a script — and not alter it beyond recognition into what they consider to be a marketable presentation of mental illness — Australian film will continue to be self-limiting in its depiction of mental illness from an individual perspective, falling into well-worn stereotypes that will eventually no longer interest the audience, and at the same time fail to advocate for those who need to see real change.

NOTES

1. Geoffrey Rush, "Acceptance Speech," *1996 Academy Awards,* March 24, 1997, accessed July 20, 2010, http://aaspeechesdb.oscars.org/.

2. Robert Cettl, *Always an Other? Representations of Disability in Australian Film* (Canberra: National Film and Sound Archive, 2010): 7.

3. Karl Quinn, "Last Chance to See," *The Age,* November 29, 2009, accessed August 19, 2010, http://www.theage.com.au/news/entertainment/film/last-chance-to-see/2009/11/28/1258824863094.html.

4. Jane Pirkis, Warwick Blood, Catherine Francis, and Kerry McCallum, *A Review of the Literature Regarding Film and Television Drama Portrayals of Mental Illness* (Canberra: Australian Government Department of Health and Aged Care, 2005), accessed November 1, 2010, http://www.mindframe-media.info/client_images/372828.pdf.

5. Jane Pirkis and Warwick Blood, *Suicide and the Entertainment Media: A Critical Review* (Canberra: Mindframe/Commonwealth of Australia, 2010), accessed November 1, 2010, http://www.mindframe-media.info/client_images/900016.pdf.

6. Alan Rosen, Garry Walter, Tom Politis, and Michael Shortland, "From Shunned to Shining: Doctors, Madness and Psychiatry in Australian and New Zealand Cinema," *Medical Journal of Australia* 167 (1997): 640–644; Alan Rosen and Garry Walter, "Way Out of Tune: Lessons from *Shine* and Its Exposé," *Australian and New Zealand Journal of Psychiatry* 34, no. 2 (2000): 237–244.

7. Philip Tam, "Psychiatry and the Cinema," *Australasian Psychiatry* 10, no. 2 (2002): 178.

8. Carolyn Quadrio, "Current Cinematic Portrayals of the Female Psychiatrist," *Australian Feminist Studies* 11, no. 23 (1996): 115–128.

9. Claire Wilson, Raymond Nairn, John Coverdale, John, and Aroha Panapa, "Mental Illness Depictions in Prime-Time Drama: Identifying the Discursive Resources," *Australian and New Zealand Journal of Psychiatry* 33, no. 2 (1999): 232–239; Claire Wilson, Raymond Nairn, John Coverdale, and Aroha Panapa, "Constructing Mental Illness as Dangerous: A Pilot Study," *Australian and New Zealand Journal of Psychiatry* 33, no. 2 (1999): 240–247.

10. Stephen Macfarlane, "*Antwone Fisher*: How Dangerous is 'Dr Wonderful'?" *Australasian Psychiatry* 12, no. 2 (2004): 176–178.

11. Pirkis et al., 3.

12. Rosen and Walter, 238–242.

13. Cettl, 5.

14. Roger Ebert, "*The Soloist*," *Roger Ebert:* April 22, 2009, accessed August 19, 2010, http://rogerebert.suntimes.com/apps/pbcs.dll/article?AID=/20090422/REVIEWS/904229989.

15. Rosen and Walter, 238–239.

16. Pirkis et al., 3.

17. Colleen McCullough, *Tim* (Sydney: Angus and Robertson, 1975).

18. Cettl, 131.

19. Colleen McCullough, *An Indecent Obsession* (Sydney: Harper and Row, 1981).

20. Cettl, 34.

21. Cettl, 64.

22. Cettl, 65.

23. Rosen et al., 642.

24. Clea Jones, *Lilian's Story* (Perth: Murdoch University, 2004), accessed August 26, 2010, http://wwwmcc.murdoch.edu.au/ReadingRoom/film/dbase/2004/lilian.htm.

25. Margaret Helfgott and Tom Gross, *Out of Tune: David Helfgott and the Myth of 'Shine'* (New York: Warner Books, 1998).

26. Anthony Tomasini, "For Audience at a Recital, the Shine Is Undiminished," *New York Times,* March 6, 1997, accessed August 30, 2010, http://www.nytimes.com/1997/03/06/arts/for-audience-at-a-recital-the-shine-is-undiminished.html?n.

27. Denis Dutton, "Please Shoot the Piano Player! The David Helfgott Debate," *Philosophy and Literature* 21, no. 2, (1997): 332–391.

28. Steve Smith, "Less Famous Now, a Pianist Returns," *New York Times,* April 9, 2008, accessed August 30, 2010, http://www.nytimes.com/2008/04/09/arts/music/09helf.html.

29. Ruth Hessey, "Production Background," In *Shine: the Screenplay,* ed. Jan Sardi (London: Bloomsbury, 1997): 154.

30. Simon Wessely, "Mental Illness as Metaphor, Yet Again," *British Medical Journal* 314, no. 7074 (1997): 153.

31. Cited in Hessey, 144.

32. Pirkis et al., 9.

33. Roger Ebert, *"Sweetie," Roger Ebert,* March 23, 1990, accessed September 15, 2010, http://rogerebert.suntimes.com/apps/pbcs.dll/article?AID=/19900323/REVIEWS/3230307/1023.
34. Andrew Urban, "Making of: *Angel Baby* (1995)," *Urban Cinefile,* accessed August 12, 2010, http://www.urbancinefile.com.au/home/view.asp?Article_ID=1186.
35. Philippa Martyr, "Juno-esque in Saffron (review of *The Waiting City*)," *Quadrant* 54, no. 9 (2010): 112–114.
36. Pirkis et al., 12.
37. Rosen and Walter, 239.
38. Michael Connor, "Theatre Is Dead, Not," *Quadrant* 54, no. 9 (2010): 106–108.
39. Rosen and Walter, 243.
40. Will Elliott, *Strange Places: A Memoir of Mental Illness* (Pymble, NSW: ABC Books, 2009).

BIBLIOGRAPHY

Adam. Directed by Max Mayer. 2010. Los Angeles: 20th Century–Fox, 2010. DVD.
Amadeus. Directed by Milos Forman. 1984. Burbank, CA: Warner Home Video, 2002. DVD.
Angel Baby. Directed by Michael Rymer. 1995. Los Angeles: Republic Pictures, 1998. VHS.
Animal Kingdom. Directed by David Michôd. 2010. New York: Sony Pictures Classics, 2011. DVD.
As Time Goes By. Directed by Barry Peak. 1988. Sydney: Australian Film Commission (AFC) & Monroe Stahr Productions, 1988. Film.
Beyond Reason. Directed by Giorgio Mangiamele. 1970. Melbourne: Giorgio Mangiamele, 1970. Film.
Cettl, Robert. *Always an Other? Representations of Disability in Australian Film.* Canberra: National Film and Sound Archive, Canberra, Act, 2010.
Charlie and Boots. Directed by Dean Murphy. 2009. Hollywood: Paramount, 2010. DVD.
Connor, Michael. "Theatre Is Dead, Not." *Quadrant* 54, no. 9 (2010): 106–108.
Così. Directed by Mark Joffe. 1996. New York: Miramax Films, 2003. DVD.
Dutton, Denis. "Please Shoot the Piano Player! The David Helfgott Debate." *Philosophy and Literature* 21, no. 2 (1997): 332–391.
Ebert, Roger. *"The Soloist." Roger Ebert,* April 22, 2009. Accessed August 19, 2010. http://rogerebert.suntimes.com/apps/pbcs.dll/article?AID=/20090422/REVIEWS/904229989.
Ebert, Roger. *"Sweetie." Roger Ebert,* March 23, 1990. Accessed September 15, 2010. http://rogerebert.suntimes.com/apps/pbcs.dll/article?AID=/19900323/REVIEWS/3230307/1023.
Elliott, Will. *Strange Places: A Memoir of Mental Illness.* Pymble, NSW: ABC Books, 2009.
The Fisher King. Directed by Terry Gilliam. 1991. Hollywood: Image Entertainment, 2010. DVD.
Helfgott, Margaret, and Tom Gross. *Out of Tune: David Helfgott and the Myth of* Shine. New York: Warner Books, 1998.
Hessey, Ruth. "Production Background." In *Shine: the Screenplay,* ed. Jan Sardi, 144–160. London: Bloomsbury, 1997.
An Indecent Obsession. Directed by Lex Marinos. 1985. Melbourne: Umbrella Entertainment, 2006. DVD.
Jones, Clea. *Lilian's Story.* Perth: Murdoch University, 2004. Accessed August 26, 2010. http://wwwmcc.murdoch.edu.au/ReadingRoom/film/dbase/2004/lilian.htm
Lilian's Story. Directed by Jerzy Domaradski. 1996. Los Angeles: Vanguard Cinema, 2000. DVD.

Macfarlane, Stephen. "*Antwone Fisher*: How Dangerous Is 'Dr Wonderful'?" *Australasian Psychiatry* 12, no. 2 (2004): 176–178.

Mad Max. Directed by George Miller. 1979. Los Angeles: MGM, 2002. DVD.

Malcolm. Directed by Nadia Tess. 1986. USA: Televista, 2007. DVD.

Martyr, Philippa. "Juno-esque in Saffron (review of *The Waiting City*)." *Quadrant* 54, no. 9 (2010): 112–114.

McCullough, Colleen. *Tim*. Sydney: Angus and Robertson, 1975.

McCullough, Colleen. *An Indecent Obsession*. Sydney: Harper and Row, 1981.

Muriel's Wedding. Directed by P J Hogan. 1994. New York: Miramax Films, 1999. DVD.

On the Waves of the Adriatic. Directed by Brian McKenzie. 1991. Australia: Standard Films, 1991. Film.

One Flew Over the Cuckoo's Nest. Directed by Milos Forman. 1975. Burbank: Warner Home Video, 1997. DVD.

The Piano. Directed by Jane Campion. 1993. Santa Monica, CA: Lions Gate, 1998. DVD.

Pirkis, Jane, and Warwick Blood. *Suicide and the Entertainment Media: A Critical Review*. Canberra: Mindframe/Commonwealth of Australia, 2010. Accessed November 1, 2010.

Pirkis, Jane, Warwick Blood, Catherine Francis, and Kerry McCallum. *A Review of the Literature Regarding Film and Television Drama Portrayals of Mental Illness*. Canberra: Australian Government Department of Health and Aged Care, 2005. Accessed November 1, 2010. http://www.mindframe-media.info/client_images/372828.pdf. http://www.mindframe-media.info/client_images/900016.pdf.

Quadrio, Carolyn. "Current Cinematic Portrayals of the Female Psychiatrist." *Australian Feminist Studies* 11, no. 23 (1996): 115–128.

Quinn, Karl. "Last Chance to See." *The Age,* November 29, 2009. Accessed August 19, 2010. http://www.theage.com.au/news/entertainment/film/last-chance-to-see/2009/11/28/1258824863094.html.

Rosen, Alan, and Garry Walter. "Way Out of Tune: Lessons from *Shine* and Its Exposé." *Australian and New Zealand Journal of Psychiatry* 34, no. 2 (2000): 237–244.

Rosen, Alan, Garry Walter, Tom Politis, and Michael Shortland. "From Shunned to Shining: Doctors, Madness and Psychiatry in Australian and New Zealand Cinema." *Medical Journal of Australia* 167 (1997): 640–644.

Rush, Geoffrey. "Acceptance Speech." *1996 Academy Awards*. March 24, 1997. Accessed August 19, 2010. http://aaspeechesdb.oscars.org/.

Shine. Directed by Scott Hicks. 1997. New York: New Line Home Video, 2004. DVD.

Smith, Steve. "Less Famous Now, a Pianist Returns." *New York Times*. April 9, 2010. Accessed August 15, 2010. http://www.nytimes.com/2008/04/09/arts/music/09helf.html.

The Soloist. Directed by Joe Wright. 2009. Universal City, CA: Dreamworks Video, 2009. DVD.

Strictly Ballroom. Directed by Baz Luhrmann. 1992. New York: Miramax Films, 2010. DVD.

Struck by Lightning. Directed by Jerzy Domaradski. 1990. Sydney: Capricorn Pictures, 1990. Film.

Sweetie. Directed by Jane Campion. 1989. New York: Criterion, 2006. DVD.

Tam, Philip. "Psychiatry and the Cinema." *Australasian Psychiatry* 10, no. 2 (2002): 178.

Tim. Directed by Michael Pate. 1979. Toronto: Peace Arch Home Entertainment, 2009. DVD.

Tomasini, Anthony. "For Audience at a Recital, the Shine Is Undiminished." *New York Times*, March 6, 1997. Accessed August 19, 2010. http://www.nytimes.com/1997/03/06/arts/for-audience-at-a-recital-the-shine-is-undiminished.html?n.

Tropic Thunder. Directed by Ben Stiller. 2008, Universal City, CA: Dreamworks Video, 2008. DVD.

12 Monkeys. Directed by Terry Gilliam. 1995. Los Angeles: Universal Studios, 2005. DVD.

Urban, Andrew. "Making of: *Angel Baby* (1995)." *Urban Cinefile.* http://www.urbancinefile. com.au/home/view.asp?Article_ID=1186.

The Waiting City. Directed by Claire McCarthy. 2010. Croydon, Victoria, Australia: Roadshow, 2010. DVD.

Wake in Fright. Directed by Ted Kotcheff. 1971. Melbourne: Umbrella Entertainment, 2010. DVD.

Wessely, Simon. "Mental Illness as Metaphor, Yet Again." *British Medical Journal* 314, no. 7074 (1997): 153.

Wilson, Claire, Raymond Nairn, John Coverdale, and Aroha Panapa. "Mental Illness Depictions in Prime-Time Drama: Identifying the Discursive Resources." *Australian and New Zealand Journal of Psychiatry* 33, no. 2 (1999): 232–239.

Wilson, Claire, Raymond Nairn, John Coverdale, and Aroha Panapa. "Constructing Mental Illness as Dangerous: A Pilot Study." *Australian and New Zealand Journal of Psychiatry* 33, no. 2 (1999): 240–247.

15

Representing "Tradition," Confusing "Modernity"

Love and Mental Illness in Yoruba (Nigerian) Video Films

SAHEED ADERINTO

Prominent scholars, notably Jonathan Hayes, Onookome Okome, and Foluke Ogunleye, have carried out critical study of Nigerian societies through home video rendition of post-colonial identity; political critiques and challenges of nation building; witchcraft and fetishism; crime and violence; power, agency and self-fashioning. However, they have largely under-researched the representation of mental illness and love in the highly influential medium of popular culture.[1] As a result, and drawing evidence from a spectrum of scholarly work on mental illness and popular culture, I set out to uncover the multitudinous interpretations given to the intersection of love and mental illness among the Yoruba, one of the numerous ethno-cultural cleavages in Nigeria.[2] These genres of data complement the representation of mental illness in Nigerian video films called Nollywood — the second largest home video industry in the world, and the most influential and representative of mainstream Nigerian popular culture.[3]

A theme that threads through this chapter is the resilience and adaptation of traditional ideas about epidemiology of mental illness and the reconfiguration of masculinity and femininity in post-colonial Yoruba society. While recognizing the significance of exotic ideas and knowledge in human development, the Yoruba, like most African peoples, are able to creatively and selectively deploy indigenous and foreign ideas in interpreting and solving some of the challenges and realities of everyday life. I argue that the video films, more than any other forms of artistic production, effectively (though inadvertently) capture the contradiction accentuated by the desire and struggle to reconcile tradition with modernity.[4] For critical analysis, I select two films, namely *Ayo Ni Mo Fe* (I Want Joy) and *Iyawo Were* (Madman's Wife) from among several others because they best illuminate the intersection between mental illness and love on the one hand, and on the other, what Hayes appropriately termed "contradictory modernity" arising from the inability of video production to fully capture tradition and/or modernity in its fullest extent.[5]

A brief discussion of the Yoruba and their culture will serve this chapter well and help lay the context of several conjectures that we are about to engage. The Yoruba are the second most populous ethnic groups in Nigeria, with an estimated population of 30 to 40 million. Although their original home is the southwestern parts of Nigeria, they have considerable cultural and physical diasporic presence all over Africa and beyond. Their presence in the Atlantic World before the 20th century is largely attributable to the infamous trans–Atlantic slave trade which the people actively participated in during the seventeenth and eighteenth centuries.[6] The survival of Yoruba custom permeates the cultural landscape of modern Haiti, Cuba, and Brazil where Yoruba gods and goddesses were syncretized into Catholicism and other extra–African religious faith. Religious syncretism contributed imponderably in helping Yoruba culture to stand the test of time in the highly repressive slave culture of the Western hemisphere.[7] Representative religions such as *Candomble*, now widely practiced in the Caribbean, South and North America, is of Yoruba root.[8] Voluntary migration of Yoruba people to the Western hemisphere and Europe took place in the 20th century, reaching its peak in the 1980s, when African countries began to witness enormous economic crisis that forced their citizens to seek better livelihood in these developed parts of the world.[9] This new diaspora of Africans are principally responsible for globalizing contemporary Yoruba ideas in the 20th and 21st centuries.

The Yoruba, like most other African ethnicities, came under European colonial rule from the 19th century. Colonialism created significant social and economic change as European-styled education, culture, and values were introduced to supplant indigenous ones. As devastating the eroding force of colonial culture is, pre-colonial norms and ideas, philosophy and cosmology, survived into the 21st century. In fact, 21st-century Yoruba society showcases a tripartite identity of the traditional/pre-colonial, the modern/colonial, and the hybrid — a combination of both the modern and the traditional. Although scholars have recognized the complexity of establishing rigid binaries of the "modernity" and "tradition" on imperial sites, in the case of the Yoruba this categories is relevant for understanding the social structure and transformative process since the late 19th century. For our purpose in this chapter, we shall be dealing with the traditional and modern culture, along with contradictions or identity crises that emerge due to the inability to reconcile the difference between these compelling forces of social change.

Mental Illness in Yoruba Films and Culture

Scholars have established the significance of popular culture in understanding African experience across time, space, and place. In his seminal work *The Popular Yoruba Traveling Theatre of Nigeria*, Biodun Jeyifo establishes the traveling theater as an important aspect of artistic and cultural creation, and should be called "popular" not "folks" as they are usually designated, because the troupes played to the public, not a privileged few or members of the aristocracy.[10] Indeed, the traveling theater plays represent and embody the viewpoint of the masses and their engagement with the realities of social existence. Jeyifo and Karin Barber's highly influential scholarship charts multiple discursive terrains as they effectively capture Yoruba history, culture, and society using plays and oral recitation as entry points.[11]

Recently, scholars, especially Hayes, Ogunleye, and Okome, among others, have begun to show that in order to fully come to terms with the varied definitions of cultural codes in post-colonial Africa, the challenges of nation-building, and the making of a "new" Nigerian identity, attention should be given to emerging forms of popular culture like the home video production known as Nollywood, which emerged in the early 1990s from the relic of the celluloid and traveling theater culture of the 1970s and 1980s.[12] Nollywood currently releases an estimated 1000 new films each year and is a major employer of labor, especially in the eastern and southwestern regions of the country.[13] With budgets as low as 800,000 naira (about 5,000 dollars) and films shot sometimes within a fortnight, the home video industry feeds a growing Nigerian and international market, creating the opportunity for ambitious Nigerians to showcase their artistic talents.[14] The diasporic presence of Nigerians in Europe and North America is responsible for globalizing the films outside the African littoral,[15] while the poor quality of a good number of them in terms of editing, technology, and directing reflect (in part) the technological backwardness of the country and lack of governmental or institutionalized support.

Although Nollywood movies touch on nearly all areas of the Nigerian society, the aspects of evil and witchcraft feature prominently because an average Yoruba, and Nigerian in general, recognizes the existence of spiritual and metaphysical power.[16] If success is interpreted as the product of hard work and triumph over the militating forces of the spiritual enemies, failure is viewed as the inability to manipulate and suppress the evil powers (*aje, aye, oso*).[17] The causation of sickness, including mental illness, is mainly coded spiritually, not scientifically. In addition, mental illness is perceived as a state of metaphysical existence controlled by the "spirit of madness" (*aunjonu were*).[18] For the Yoruba, evil or bad conduct is the main causation of mental illness; a witch or "evil doer" could run mad after losing a spiritual battle with a superior/good power.[19] Yet, Yoruba cosmology, which the Nollywood films interpret, also recognizes that a promising individual could be inflicted with the spirit of madness by "wicked" people operating under the cover of nightly and unfathomable power.[20] Hence, a mentally ill person, both in the films and in real life, is represented and perceived either as a witch or victim of witchcraft.[21] Even when people develop mental illness due to observable and verifiable causes such as drug abuse and sudden change in lifestyle (as we shall shortly see), the Yoruba would still render a metaphysical explanation because of the notion that "nothing happens without a reason" (*bio ba ni 'di obinrin kii ke Kumolu*).

Native psychiatrists are usually highly revered traditional elites who derive their professional credentials and legitimacy from the ability to manipulate or deploy unseen forces and herbs in healing.[22] Although the native doctor/psychiatrist is primarily responsible for caring for the mentally ill, therapy is facilitated by the serene and friendly environment of rural communities where most of the asylums are located. Indeed, the Yoruba village as a therapeutic community helps the mentally ill to recover through everyday practice of oral recitation, music, and dance. Native psychiatry practice is guided by a number of complex customary laws. For instance, they are not expected to charge money for healing a mentally sick individual, but could receive gifts, which in theory and reality are not considered as a medical bill. In sum, the survival of pre-colonial cultural ideas about mental illness and therapy into the 21st century is attributable to the accessibility of native medical practitioners and the cardinal position that religion and spirituality occupy in the Yoruba people's worldview. In addition, the inability of biomedicine introduced through colonialism to adequately cater to the medical well-being of the people and the crisis of underdevelopment which engulfed the African states inhibit accessibility to the so-called superior Western alternatives.

Ayo Ni Mo Fe: Deceit, Heartbreak, and Mental Illness

Dedicated to Tai Solarin, a revered social crusader and "all those dedicated to the cause of the mentally ill" and directed by Tunde Kelani, whose name is almost synonymous with the best culturally grounded Yoruba movies,

Ayo Ni Mo Fe renders the crisis of legitimacy between Western and African ideas about marriage, love, the epidemiology of mental illness, and the perception of the mentally ill from two different but closely overlapping angles.[23] First, it explicates the gendered character of modern Yoruba society and the reconfiguration of traditional gender roles, a product of colonial implantation. The realignment of gender as a historical and social construction represents a paradox: on the one hand, it empowered men and women, and on the other it introduces new forms of tension which saw women losing the power and status accorded to them in traditional societies. Second, *Ayo Ni Mo Fe* reproduces a complex but widely accepted knowledge of the mentally ill's power (through spiritual means) to remedy barrenness. It is not unusual in big and small Yoruba towns to see mentally ill nursing or pregnant women, roving the streets with their infant children or toddlers. The public knowledge is that they are impregnated by men who were advised by native doctors to have sex with the mentally ill in order to help their wife/wives to conceive and have children. The popular saying *Olorun ni wo omo were* (it is God that nurses the child of the mentally ill) is rooted in the identity of the mentally ill woman and the accompanying miseries of her survival. Although the community, not the government, tends to give alms to mentally ill women, the fact that they are able to nurse their children (mostly without any help) constitutes what the Yoruba calls miracle (*iyanu*). In Yoruba daily life, reference (through proverbs and sayings as seen above) is regularly made to the personality of a mentally ill, the power of motherhood and mothering, and possibilities in the face of difficult situation.

The main characters of *Ayo Ni Mo Fe* are Bola Obot (as Jumoke) and Yomi Ogunmola (as Ayo), college-educated lovers who plan to get married. Other important characters include Lere Paimo (as Chief Adeleke), a rich, uneducated Muslim polygamist who seeks Jumoke's hand in marriage, and Karem Adepoju (as Chief Tomobi), another rich polygamist whose family is confronting a protracted problem of barrenness. The movie starts with a vivid description of romance between Ayo and Jumoke, and Adeleke's relentless persuasiveness to add the latter to his harem of wives. Although Chief Adeleke is not contravening any known Yoruba norm by wanting to marry Jumoke, the spinster found excuse in her status as an educated single who would prefer to start a new family with a young and educated man (Ayo). While Chief Adeleke is influenced by traditional Yoruba culture that endorses polygamy, Jumoke's stance found solace in the "new" or "modern" culture of an influential (but small) class of educated Yoruba that embraces the British-styled monogamous type of marriage.

When Jumoke discovers that the cheating Ayo impregnates Adunni, the teenage daughter of Police Commissioner Dabiri, and subsequently marries her secretly, she develops mental illness and is admitted into the local asylum run by a fake native psychiatrist, who gives a spiritual explanation for her illness. When the native doctor tries to rape her, she runs away, becomes homeless and roves the town, while her family searches for her. It is during this period that her path crosses with Chief Tomobi, who, as previously mentioned, could not get his wives pregnant. After numerous consultations with the oracles, Chief Tomobi finally receives the oracular revelation that he was cursed by a man his mother humiliated while attempting to have sex with a mentally ill woman; and would have to impregnate a mentally ill woman in order to neutralize this dangerous curse (*egun*). He finds the homeless Jumoke and impregnates her.

Eventually, Adeleke, who has become an important element in the struggle to save Jumoke, finds and takes her to a Western-styled psychiatric hospital. While the fake native psychiatrist diagnoses Jumoke's illness as spiritually induced, the psychiatrist trained in Western medicine reviews her life story and rightly concludes that her sickness is caused by the heartbreak occasioned by Ayo's wedding to another woman. The Western remedy proves effective, as Jumoke recovers from her illness and marries Adeleke, who stood by her during the period of tribulation. Her professional life takes a positive stride as she becomes the head of Adeleke's business empire. But her happiness is short-lived: she relapses when a jealous co-wife tries to kill her infant child and later recovers for the second time.

Ayo's marriage to Adunni is marred with total chaos, in part because they were forced to marry by Adunni's parents, who feared the public stigma associated with her being a single mother. Ayo's decision to "be a man" by making Adunni cook and perform house chores she is not accustomed to because she is *ajebota* (stereotype name for children of well-to-do or educated families) landed him in trouble. Adunni's parents drove Ayo out of the apartment they gave the couple as a wedding gift; he loses his jobs and becomes homeless when he can no longer cope with the new reality of life. He soon adapts well in his new life, becoming the "captain" of homeless thugs (known as area boys). Events take a good turn when Adunni's father, Police Commissioner Dabiri, is killed by armed thieves and Adunni decides to reunite with her estranged husband. This phase in Ayo and Adunni's life sees them traveling to the U.S. to pursue a doctorate and masters degree respectively.

Ayo Ni Mo Fe firmly establishes the Yoruba idea of binary complementarity as regards the order or circle of occurrences — i.e., good and bad; success and failure; happiness and sadness; living and dying. In Yoruba cosmology, individuals are expected to witness crisis at some point in their lives, but must see the light at the end of the long tunnel. While a basic sense of human judgment and Western scientific psychiatry would blame Ayo for causing Jumoke's mental illness, the Yoruba, in addition to apportioning blame, would plainly interpret the entire situation as "the work of destiny" (*kadara or ayanmo*). So, when Ayo shows up at Jumoke's magnificent office to apologize for all his wrongs, he blames destiny for directing the course of his life. The Yoruba believe that destiny, as the most important component of human existence, cannot be altered or modified. It was permanently engrained by God (*Olorun* or *Olodumare*) during the process of creation. To modify or change destiny, an individual would have to revisit the process of his or her creation — a task that is impossible. Love as well as success in marriage, family, and career is predominantly interpreted as destiny. Although Ayo and Jumoke's destiny took them through the agony of mental illness and homelessness, the end was good: Jumoke runs a big firm and enjoys her marriage; Ayo and Adunni reconcile and head to the U.S. for graduate education. In the end, Jumoke and Ayo both agree that they are not destined to be husband and wife and that they would not have achieved enormous professional and material success if they had married.

Ayo Ni Mo Fe offers some counter-narratives to established ideas about the superiority of African over Western psychiatry. The Yoruba promote native remedies over Western-styled psychiatry because they believe mental illness to be a spiritual problem that is best be treated by native psychiatrists who are trained to deploy metaphysical power in fighting the "dangerous spirit" that causes mental illness. *Ayo Ni Mo Fe* not only establishes the efficacy of the Western-styled psychiatric hospital over the native asylum, but paints the latter as fake, violent, and retrogressive. In another vein, it reinforces the public idea that sex with mentally ill women could help solve the problem of barrenness, as seen in the case of Adeleke, whose wives later become pregnant.

Iyawo Were: Becoming a Victim of Love

Iyawo Were is a story of both love and hate coexisting in an atmosphere of competition for financial success and social mobility. The main character of the movie is Toyin Afolayan (as Busayo), who is dating Segun, a college student reputed for cheating on his lovers and dumping them. After seeing Segun publicly breaking up with and humiliating two of his ex-girlfriends, Busayo feels highly insecure and envisions that Segun would soon break up with her. Busayo expresses her concern to her sister, who encourages her to consult a native doctor for love medicine/charm (*ogun ife*). Of the numerous types of love charms presented by the native doctor, Busayo picks the most potent one, "mad love" (*ife were*), which would permanently seal Segun's affection for her. But like most, if not all Yoruba medicine, the love charm comes with a condition: Busayo must not leave Segun for another man, or else he (Segun) would develop mental illness. Faced with this possibility, Busayo decides never to leave the relationship.

However, life takes a new turn when Busayo's ex-boyfriend, based in the U.S., returns home, not only with "tons of dollars," but with a marriage proposal. Busayo becomes confused, contacts her sister and begins to deliberate about deserting Segun. She defies the native doctor's warning that Segun will become mad if she leaves the relationship and elopes with her U.S. based lover. Segun, after learning of Busayo's departure to the U.S., develops mental illness, roves the streets, causing public disorder. When the mentally ill Segun harasses a female resident, the angry community attacks and kills him. Convinced that his son's mental illness, which eventually led to his death, was spiritually induced, Segun's mother goes to his graveside, curses his murderers and commands his spirit to avenge. This part of the film effectively portrays the Yoruba tradition of "making the spirit to fight" (*oku riro*), which entails commanding the ghost of the murdered to avenge by killing the murderer. The practice of seeking metaphysical redress or intervention in solving crime remains relevant in 21st-century Nigeria, which is characterized by poor policing, underdevelopment of forensic science, and corruption of the criminal justice system. In addition, Yoruba custom, as correctly rendered in the film, differentiates between spiritual death (like mental illness or state of dysfunctionality) and physical death (real death). In its larger and more complex application, death metaphorically represents a state of existence or situation that contravenes established values. Hence, Segun was dead spiritually (*iku aye*) before being put to death physically (*iku orun*). And his real murderer is Busayo, who caused his spiritual death, not the community that attacks and kills him physically.

More than twenty years after his demise, Segun's ghost begins to torment Busayo's apparently successful and happy family, causing her first child to be brutally murdered on her wedding day. Shortly afterwards, Busayo's second child suddenly develops mental illness on his 25th birthday and dies in circumstances similar to Segun's. The third child, while looking after their depressed mother in the hospital, begins to exhibit symptoms of mental illness and is immediately hospitalized. Busayo's family's search for the causes of their troubles takes them through several metaphysical terrains — the only means of explaining multiple crises of mental illness and death during important ceremonies like weddings and birthdays. In Yoruba cosmology, death during significant ceremonies such as a wedding or birthday is interpreted as the handiwork of witches or evil apparitional forces, which need to be appeased in order to put a halt to incessant misfortune. After several consultations with the native doctors who have the power to uncover the past and decode unseen narratives, Busayo is taken back to the days of her youth and reminded that the ghost of Segun which she disappointed is responsible for her misfortune.

Iyawo Were unveils a number of interesting ideas about love and loving and the causation of mental illness. In the first instance, it effectively narrates Yoruba belief that love or affection can be initiated and induced with the help of supernatural powers. Although Busayo is a "modern" lady influenced by Western culture, she sought a traditional solution to a problem that threatened her source of happiness by consulting a native doctor for love charm. Contemporary Yoruba still believe in the efficacy of charms in securing and sustaining love and relationship — especially in cases where one of the partners appears insecure.[24] In another movie, titled *Bolajoko* (*Sit with Wealth*), Omobola (female) who would later become mentally ill, is charmed in order for her to marry the U.S.-based Adekele. The rhetoric of securing financial mobility by marrying a U.S.- or Europe-based Nigerian features prominently in Nollywood's narrative about the place of Western societies as sites of "wealth" and "splendor." The Yoruba perceive themselves both as a member of a global system and their immediate ethnic and geographic enclave.

Iyawo Were also highlights the preeminent belief in *esan* (retribution) for "wickedness" or "evil" behavior. Busayo as an "evil" person reaps the fruit of her wickedness when misfortune befalls her family; likewise Chief Tomobi in *Ayo Ni Mo Fe*, whose wives suffer barrenness because his mother humiliated a man who wants to have sex with a mentally ill individual. Overall, the constant practice of depicting retribution in Nollywood films represent one of the goals of Yoruba movie artistes to use films to pass along the message of good conduct or behavior (*iwapele*) in a society under the siege of violence, greed, institutionalized corruption, and obsession with power.[25]

Conclusion

Although the major focus of this chapter is the representation of mental illness and love in several Yoruba video films, it is obvious that we have engaged a number of complex and broader issues about Yoruba culture and society. Indeed, it is not accidental that our discussion borders such themes as tradition, spirituality, and cosmology, because the Yoruba, like most Africans, mainly interpret mental illness as a spiritual problem. The systemic nature of Yoruba society means that one aspect of an individual's existence is capable of influencing the other and initiating a vicious process. This explains why Chief Tomobi encounters barrenness when his mother publicly humiliated someone who wanted to have sex with a mad woman, and why Segun developed mental illness when his girlfriend eloped with another man. Perceptions and attitudes toward the mentally ill unveil an important perspective for viewing the interrelatedness of violence and mental illness. Chief Tomobi committed sexual violence and rape because the oracle asked him to have sex with a mentally ill woman, and Segun is put to death by a hostile community. In both cases, spirituality influenced the attitude of people toward the causation of mental illness. The mentally ill in popular video films as well as in the real world unveil and reveal anti-social sentiments and are either brutalized or killed. The poor state of institutionalized medical facilities and social services, illiteracy, and poverty all combine to put the faith of the mentally ill in the hands of the public who would either feed and clothe them, or assault them. As interpreters of Yoruba popular culture, Nollywood movies continue to depict the contradiction associated with the new forces of modernity and globalism. They present the clash of ideas about metaphysical and scientific interpretation of epidemiology of mental illness and the interrelatedness of love and emotions.

NOTES

1. Jonathan Haynes, "Political Critique in Nigerian Video Films," *African Affairs* 105, no. 421 (2006): 511–533; John C. McCall, "Madness, Money, and Movies: Watching a Nigerian Popular Video with the Guidance of a Native Doctor," *Africa Today* 49, no. 3 (Autumn 2002): 79–94; Foluke Ogunleye, ed., *Africa through the Eye of the Video Camera* (Manzini, Swaziland: Academic Publishers, 2008); Foluke Ogunleye, ed., *African Video Film Today* (Manzini, Swaziland: Academic Publishers, 2003); Onookome Okome, "Nollywood and Its Critics: The Anxiety of the Local," in *Viewing African Cinema: FESPACO Art Films and the Nollywood Video Revolution,* eds. Mahir Saul and Ralph A. Austen (Athens: Ohio University Press, 2010), 26–39; Onookome Okome ed., *Special Issue on Nollywood — Africa at the Movies: West African Video Film Postcolonial Text,* March 1, 2007; Jenkeri Zakari Okwori, "A Dramatized Society: Representing Rituals of Human Sacrifice as Efficacious Action in Nigerian Home Video Movies," *Journal of African Cultural Studies* 16, n0.1 (2003): 7–23; John C. McCall, "Juju and Justice at the Movies: Vigilantes in Nigerian Popular Videos," *African Studies Review* 47, no. 3 (2004): 51–67; Akin Adesokan, "Practicing 'Democracy' in Nigerian Films," *African Affairs* 108, no. 433 (2009): 599–619; Brian Larkin, "Indian Films and Nigerian Lovers: Media and the Creation of Parrallel Modernitys," *Africa* 67, no. 3 (1997): 406–440; Paul Ushang Ugor, "Youth Culture and the Struggle for Social Space: The Nigerian Video Films" (PhD diss., University of Alberta, 2009).

2. The Yoruba are one of the most researched ethnic groups in Nigeria and Africa as a whole. Their geographical location along the fringes of the West African coastal water coupled with the socio-cultural and economic development that followed the abolition of the transatlantic slave trade laid the foundation for the emergence of a class of highly educated Africans and their descendants who spearheaded literary, intellectual and academic writing about the Yoruba. For more on the academic and historical writing about the Yoruba and the major authors, see Toyin Falola and Saheed Aderinto, *Nigeria, Nationalism, and Writing History* (Rochester, NY: University of Rochester Press, 2010), chapters 8–10.

3. A recent book-length work on Nollywood is Mahir Saul and Ralph A. Austen, eds., *Viewing African Cinema: FESPACO Art Films and the Nollywood Video Revolution* (Athens: Ohio University Press, 2010).

4. Hayes takes on the subject of modernity and tradition in Yoruba film in his foundation work on Nigerian Video Films. See Jonathan Hayes, "Introduction," in *Nigerian Video Films,* ed. Jonathan Hayes (Athens: Ohio University Center for International Studies, 200), 13–16. A new book *How Colonialism Preempted Modernity in Africa* is unable to identify popular culture within the matrix of Western imperialism and identity formation. See Olufemi Taiwo, *How Colonialism Preempted Modernity in Africa* (Bloomington: Indiana University Press, 2010).

5. *Ayo Ni Mo Fe,* VCD, directed by Tunde Kelani, 1996 (Lagos, Nigeria: Mainframe Productions, 1996) and *Iyawo Were,* VCD, directed by Segun Ogungbe, 2008 (Lagos, Nigeria: Das Motion Picture, 2008). For more on contradictory modernity, see Hayes, "Introduction," in *Nigerian Video Films,* ed. Hayes, 32–34.

6. See the following works: Robin Law, *The Oyo Empire c. 1600–1836: A West African Imperialism in the Era of Atlantic Slave Trade* (Oxford: Clarendon Press, 1977); and Kristin Mann, *Slavery and the Birth of an African City: Lagos, 1760–1900* (Bloomington: Indiana University Press, 2007).

7. For more on Yoruba diaspora and culture, see James Lorand Matory, *Black Atlantic Religion: Tradition, Transnationalism, and Matriarchy in the Afro-Brazilian Candomble* (Princeton: Princeton University Press, 2005); Solimar Otero, *Afro-Cuban Diasporas in the Atlantic World* (Rochester, NY: University of Rochester Press, 2010); and Toyin Falola and Matt D. Childs, ed., *The Yoruba Diaspora in the Atlantic World* (Bloomington: Indiana University Press, 2004).

8. Nathaniel Samuel Murrell, *Afro-Caribbean Religions: An Introduction to Their Historical, Cultural, and Sacred Traditions* (Philadelphia: Temple University Press, 2010).

9. A good book on the new African Diaspora is Isidore Okpewho and Nkiru Nzegwu, eds., *The New African Diaspora* (Bloomington: University of Indiana Press, 2009).

10. Biodun Jeyofo, *The Yoruba Popular Traveling Theatre of Nigeria* (Lagos, Nigeria: Nigerian Magazine, 1984), Chapter 1.

11. Karin Barber, *The Generation of Plays: Yoruba Popular Life in Theater* (Bloomington: Indiana University Press, 2000).

12. A foundational work on the history of Nigerian Video film is Jonathan Hayes, ed., *Nigerian Video Films.* For an exhaustive literature review of Nigerian home video, see Jonathan Hayes, "Nigerian and Ghanaian Videos: A Literature Review," *Journal of African Cultural Studies* 22, n0.1 (2010): 105–120.

13. Duro Oni, *Lighting Beyond Illumination: Inaugural Lecture* (Lagos: University of Lagos, 2010), 39.

14. Pierre Barrot, *Nollywood: The Video Phenomenon in Nigeria* (Oxford: James Currey, 2008).

15. See Akin Adesokan, "Excess Luggage: Nigerian Films and the World of Immigrants," in *The New African Diaspora,* eds. Isadore Okpewho and Nkiru Nzegwu, 401–421.

16. Foluke Ogunleye, "'That We May Serve Him Without Fear': Nigerian Christian Video Film and Battle Against Cultism," *International Journal of Humanistic Studies,* no. 2 (2003): 16–27.

17. For multiple representation of the power of *Aje* both as evil and forces of blessing see Teresa Washington, *Our Mothers, Our Powers, Our Texts: Manifestation of Aje in Africana Literature* (Bloomington: Indiana University Press, 2005).

18. Academic research on mental illness among the Yoruba has taken a multidisciplinary approach and featured scholars from the humanities, social sciences and medicine. The following list is not exhaustive but shows the wide range of approaches adopted in studying mental illness: Ayodele Samuel Jegede, "The Notion of 'Were' in Yoruba Conception of Mental Illness," *Nordic Journal of African Studies* 14, no. 1 (2005): 117–126; A.O. Odejide et. al. "Traditional Healers and Mental Illness in the City of Ibadan," *Journal of*

Black Studies 9 no. 2 (1978): 195–205; O.A. Erinosho, "Belief-System and the Concept of Mental Illness among Medical Students in a Developing Country: A Nigerian Example," *Journal of Anthropological Research* 33, no. 2 (1977): 158–166; Raymond H. Prince, "The Problem of 'Spirit Possession' as Treatment for Psychiatric Disorder," *Ethos* 2, no. 4 (1974): 315–333; Jane M. Murphy, "Sociocultural Change and Psychiatric Disorder among Rural Yorubas of Nigeria," *Ethos* 1 no. 2 (1973): 239–262; Robert B. Edgerton, "A Traditional African Psychiatrist," *Southwestern Journal of Anthropology* 27 no. 3 (1971): 259–278; Edward L. Margaret, "Traditional Yoruba Healers in Nigeria," *Man* 65 (1965): 115–118; Supo Laosebikan, "Mental Health in Nigeria: The Promise of a Behavioural Approach in Treatment and Rehabilitation," *Journal of Black Studies* 4, no. 2 (1973): 221–228; Leigh Bienen, "The Determination of Criminal Insanity in Western Nigeria," *The Journal of Modern African Studies* 14 no. 2 (1976): 219–245.

19. *Baluwe*, directed by Afeez Abiodun, 2010 (Lagos, Nigeria: Time Pictures Nigeria Limited, 2010), VCD.

20. *Bolajoko*, directed by Abiodun Olanrewaju, 2008 (Lagos, Nigeria: High Level Digital Studio, 2008). VCD.

21. *Baluwe*.

22. The rendition of native doctor as *onisegun* and *adehunse* is not absolute because the nature and methods of practices vary widely. Some babalawos (Ifa priest) also heal through divination. For more on Yoruba medicine, see Olufunmilayo Adekson, *The Yoruba Traditional Healers of Nigeria* (New York: Routledge, 2004).

23. Email correspondence between the author and director Tunde Kelani, January 21, 2011. Solarin, the founder of the famous Mayflower School is reputed for his critique of government's ineptitude towards the delivery of social welfare and service. He would pick dead bodies of homeless people who were likely to be mentally ill and deposit them at the doorstep of appropriate government officers.

24. See *Bolajoko*.

25. For more on this see, B. Hallen, *The Good, the Bad, and the Beautiful: Discourse about Values in Yoruba Culture* (Bloomington: Indiana University Press, 2000).

BIBLIOGRAPHY

Adekson, Olufunmilayo. *The Yoruba Traditional Healers of Nigeria*. New York: Routledge, 2004.

Adesokan, Akin. "Excess Luggage: Nigerian Films and the World of Immigrants." In *The New African Diaspora*, eds. Isidore Okpewho and Nkiru Nzegwu, 401–421. Bloomington: University of Indiana Press, 2009.

_____. "Practicing 'Democracy' in Nigerian Films." *African Affairs* 108, no. 433 (2009): 599–619.

Barber, Karin. *The Generation of Plays: Yoruba Popular Life in Theater*. Bloomington: Indiana University Press, 2000.

Barrot, Pierre. *Nollywood: The Video Phenomenon in Nigeria*. Oxford: James Currey, 2008.

Bienen, Leigh. "The Determination of Criminal Insanity in Western Nigeria." *The Journal of Modern African Studies* 14, no. 2 (1976): 219–245.

Edgerton, Robert B. "A Traditional African Psychiatrist." *Southwestern Journal of Anthropology* 27, no. 3 (1971): 259–278.

Erinosho, O.A. "Belief-System and the Concept of Mental Illness among Medical Students in a Developing Country: A Nigerian Example." *Journal of Anthropological Research* 33, no. 2 (1977): 158–166.

Falola, Toyin, and Matt D. Childs, eds. *The Yoruba Diaspora in the Atlantic World*. Bloomington: Indiana University Press, 2004.

Hallen, B. *The Good, the Bad, and the Beautiful: Discourse about Values in Yoruba Culture.* Bloomington: Indiana University Press, 2000.

Haynes, Jonathan, "Nigerian and Ghanaian Videos: A Literature Review." *Journal of African Cultural Studies* 22, no. 1 (2010): 105–120.

_____, ed. *Nigerian Video Films.* Athens: Ohio University Research in International Studies, Africa Series No. 73, 2000.

_____. "Political Critique in Nigerian Video Films." *African Affairs* 105, no. 421 (2006): 511–533.

Jegede, Ayodele Samuel. "The Notion of 'Were' in Yoruba Conception of Mental Illness." *Nordic Journal of African Studies* 14, no. 1 (2005): 117–126.

Jeyofo, Biodun. *The Yoruba Popular Traveling Theatre of Nigeria.* Lagos, Nigeria: Nigerian Magazine, 1984.

Laosebikan, Supo. "Mental Health in Nigeria: The Promise of a Behavioural Approach in Treatment and Rehabilitation." *Journal of Black Studies* 4, no. 2 (1973): 221–228.

Larkin, Brian. "Indian Films and Nigerian Lovers: Media and the Creation of Parallel Modernitys." *Africa* 67, no. 3 (1997): 406–440.

Law, Robin. *The Oyo Empire c. 1600–1836: A West African Imperialism in the Era of Atlantic Slave Trade.* Oxford: Clarendon Press, 1977.

Mann, Kristin. *Slavery and the Birth of an African City: Lagos, 1760–1900.* Bloomington: Indiana University Press, 2007.

Margaret, Edward L. "Traditional Yoruba Healers in Nigeria." *Man* 65 (1965): 115–118.

Matory, James Lorand. *Black Atlantic Religion: Tradition, Transnationalism, and Matriarchy in the Afro-Brazilian Candomble.* Princeton: Princeton University Press, 2005.

McCall, John C. "Juju and Justice at the Movies: Vigilantes in Nigerian Popular Videos." *African Studies Review* 47, no. 3 (2004): 51–67.

_____. "Madness, Money, and Movies: Watching a Nigerian Popular Video with the Guidance of a Native Doctor." *Africa Today* 49, no. 3 (Autumn 2002): 79–94.

Murphy, Jane M. "Sociocultural Change and Psychiatric Disorder among Rural Yorubas of Nigeria." *Ethos* 1 no. 2 (1973): 239–262.

Murrell, Nathaniel Samuel. *Afro-Caribbean Religions: An Introduction to their Historical, Cultural and Sacred Traditions.* Philadelphia: Temple University Press, 2010.

Odejide, A.O., M.O. Olatuwura, Sanda O. Akinude, and A.O. Oyeneye, "Traditional Healers and Mental Illness in the City of Ibadan." *Journal of Black Studies* 9 no. 2 (1978): 195–205.

Ogunleye, Foluke. *Africa through the Eye of the Video Camera.* Manzini, Swaziland: Academic Publishers, 2008.

_____. *African Video Film Today.* Manzini, Swaziland: Academic Publishers, 2003.

Okome, Onookome. "Nollywood and Its Critics: The Anxiety of the Local." In *Viewing African Cinema: FESPACO Art Films and the Nollywood Video Revolution*, eds. Mahir Saul and Ralph A. Austen, 26–39. Athens: Ohio University Press, 2010.

_____, ed. *Special Issue on Nollywood—Africa at the Movies: West African Video Film Postcolonial Text* 3, no. 1 (2007).

Okpewho, Isidore, and Nkiru Nzegwu, eds. *The New African Diaspora.* Bloomington: University of Indiana Press, 2009.

Okwori, Jenkeri Zakari. "A Dramatized Society: Representing Rituals of Human Sacrifice as Efficacious Action in Nigerian Home Video Movies." *Journal of African Cultural Studies* 16, no. 1 (2003): 7–23.

Oni, Duro. *Lighting Beyond Illumination: Inaugural Lecture.* Lagos: University of Lagos, 2010.

Otero, Solimar. *Afro-Cuban Diasporas in the Atlantic World.* Rochester, NY: University of Rochester Press, 2010.

Oyebode, Femi. "Obituary: Thomas Adeoye Lambo." *The Psychiatrist* 28 (2004): 469.

Prince, Raymond H. "The Problem of 'Spirit Possession' as Treatment for Psychiatric Disorder." *Ethos* 2, no. 4 (1974): 315–333.

Sadowsky, Jonathan. *Imperial Bedlam: Institutions of Madness and Colonialism in Southwest Nigeria.* Berkeley: University of California Press, 1999.

Saul, Mahir, and Ralph A. Austen, eds. *Viewing African Cinema: FESPACO Art Films and the Nollywood Video Revolution.* Athens: Ohio University Press, 2010.

Taiwo, Olufemi. *How Colonialism Preempted Modernity in Africa.* Bloomington: Indiana University Press, 2010.

Ugor, Paul Ushang. "Youth Culture and the Struggle for Social Space: The Nigerian Video Films." PhD diss., University of Alberta, 2009.

FILMS AND DOCUMENTARIES

Ayo Ni Mo Fe. Directed by Tunde Kelani. 1996. Lagos, Nigeria: Mainframe Productions, 1996. DVD.

Baluwe. Directed by Afeez Abiodun. 2010. Lagos, Nigeria: Time Pictures Nigeria Limited, 2010. VCD.

Bolajoko. Directed by Abiodun Olanrewaju. 2008. High Level Digital Studio, 2008. VCD.

Iyawo Were. Directed by Segun Ogungbe. 2008. Das Motion Picture, 2008. VCD.

The Strength of Africa: A Dutch Documentary on the Nigerian Movie Industry (Nollywood). A Double Entertainment, 2000.

Welcome to Nollywood. Directed by Jamie Meltzer. 2009. Cayce Lindner, 2009. DVD.

16

Reframing Mental Health and Illness

Perspectives from the Scottish Mental Health Arts and Film Festival

LEE KNIFTON

Scotland is a small country of six million people with an international reputation for scenic landscapes, established cultural traditions, and a strong national identity. However, this masks a darker side. Inequality is ubiquitous. Regions of Scotland have life expectancies for men of less than sixty years and exhibit high levels of suicide, mental illness, and poor mental health. In response, the government developed a national program to improve mental health in 2001, entitled "Towards a Mentally Flourishing Scotland."[1] It adopted a population health approach and conceptualized mental health as a dual continuum acknowledging illness related to, but distinct from, positive mental health that everyone can experience.[2] Programs were developed to tackle the stigma associated with mental illness, while others promoted positive mental health for all. Although progress was made, a review in 2006 highlighted the need to engage with communities more effectively to achieve and embed change, a view supported by research showing that media reporting had not improved significantly[3] and that improvements in public attitudes were modest, particularly among low income and ethnic minority communities.[4]

Our response was to adopt a cultural approach to achieving social change through the development of a national mental health arts and film festival. Since 2007, it has supported over two hundred arts, public and community groups co-producing over six hundred film, music, theater, dance, comedy, and literary events to over forty thousand members of the public — each contextualized with debate and dialogue. The Scottish Mental Health Arts and Film Festival (the Festival) takes place across the country throughout October in settings ranging from small community centers in the Highlands and Islands to major iconic arts venues in the cities of Glasgow and the capital, Edinburgh.

The Festival has developed a collective model that sees hundreds of partners working at a national and community level. They include the government, the Royal College of Psychiatrists, the National Film Agency and most of Scotland's major arts organizations. It has a collaborative funding and management model; regional planning networks spanning numerous sectors of civil society; and co-curation of events involving artists, mental health service users, community activists, and health practitioners. The Festival's vision is to achieve positive social change towards mental health through arts and film by challenging perceptions of and stigma towards mental health issues; making connections between organizations that would not otherwise engage; developing audiences and reaching those who are often missed; encouraging participation in the creative process by those who have experienced mental health issues alongside the wider community; and creating a platform for great arts events.

The scope of the Festival work and partners creates debates about notions of mental health and the purpose of the arts. Accordingly, the nature of the Festival is viewed differently by partners. Some see it as a human rights initiative, others as a health campaign, others as an artistic platform. A paper providing more detailed consideration of these issues and processes, and the ethical challenges they raise, can be found in *The Journal of Ethics in Mental Health*.[5]

In this chapter, I narrow our focus to three areas. I begin by examining mental health, illness, and stigma and the case for a cultural approach. I then explore the process of creative organizing in the Festival, focusing upon the perspectives of professional artists and curators. Finally, I summarize the evidence of social and cultural impact and conclude by considering the implications for international initiatives in arts and mental health spheres.

Mental Health, Mental Illness, and the Persistence of Stigma

Representations of mental health and illness in the arts, film, and media shape our beliefs about human identity and wellbeing and about "the mentally ill." These perceptions filter into our everyday interactions with others to shape the cultural context within which we understand and respond to mental health and illness. Consistent negative representations are both subtle and overt and result in stigmatizing beliefs and perceptions.

Stigma

Current understandings of mental health stigma unite interactionist perspectives, which view stigma at an interpersonal level,[6] with structuralist perspectives that instead emphasize institutional discrimination and service user voices and experience.[7] Link and Phelan describe stigma as the co-occurrence of labeling, separation, stereotyping, discrimination, and status loss. They acknowledge that this is mediated by power differentials, which result in discrimination and inequality.[8] A range of negative stereotypes held about people with mental illness persist, including dangerousness, unpredictability, recovery pessimism, incapability, pitifulness, shame, and blame. This actual and anticipated discrimination can be as significant as the symptoms of mental illness. It inhibits recovery and self-esteem,[9] increases social exclusion,[10] and stifles life chances.[11] Stigma also inhibits help-seeking from those affected.[12] Unemployment rates in Europe are higher than for any other social group at over eighty percent despite people wanting to work,[13] and people remain stigmatized in the most fundamental aspects of life: in friendships, relationships, and love.[14]

Current Approaches to Addressing Stigma

Few countries have adopted a cultural approach to tackling stigma, using and influencing arts and film directly. Most higher-income countries have responded to calls from the World Health Organization to improve mental health and address stigma through a series of structural reforms, such as rights-based legislation in areas including employment, deinstitutionalization, and recovery-focused care to advance people's basic human rights.[15] Yet this has not resulted in the improvements in equality achieved by other groups, including race, gender, and sexuality, nor compared to other health issues such as HIV/AIDS. Indeed there is some evidence that stigma can worsen. As we moved to community care, public attitudes and deep-seated fears shifted from a fear of becoming mad to fear of those others who have a mental illness and who now reside close by.[16] We can observe this reflected in art and film, particularly horror movies in the last century.

There are two essential explanations for the entrenched persistence of stigma. The first concerns mental illness itself. Some theorists argue that prejudice is instinctive and inevitable.[17] Others argue that the "mind" is so fundamental to our sense of self that it creates taboos that stifle meaningful public discourse. This is reinforced by the fact that mental illness stigma is culturally embedded through generations.

There is an alternative explanation, though, which is that existing approaches to addressing mental health stigma are flawed or limited. Imagine for a moment that we were instead pursuing gender equality. What might the response be to a campaign developed by men (but including representatives from women's groups, as volunteers!) using posters and other educational materials with "key messages" such as "women are not dangerous," "women can contribute to the workforce," or even "women can and do recover!" There would, quite rightly, be a swathe of protest and righteous indignation. But it is emblematic of some current thinking. Anti-stigma campaigns are largely rooted in positivistic notions of self and society and are dominated by medical models, psychiatry, pharmaceutical companies, and social marketers. They broadly view the problem as ignorance of facts and see the challenge as providing the right information to the less well-informed public in the right way. This, it is argued, will reduce stigmatizing judgements and actions in everyday social interactions with people with mental health problems. However, the problem is that evidence suggests that increasing psychiatric knowledge alone is unlikely to solve the issue or engage with communities holding diverse cultural beliefs.[18]

This problem is compounded by under-resourcing — public education campaigns are drowned out by wider popular cultural representations, and what is known to work to reduce stigma — positive contact and empowerment — are not a common feature. People with longer-term mental illnesses are socially and economically disenfranchised through unemployment and social drift.[19] But they are also culturally disenfranchised. With some admirable exceptions, such as the "survivors" movement and survivors poets whom we encounter later in this chapter, social movements in mental health have not had the same impact as in other areas. The social and cultural response to the stigma of HIV/AIDS, the outrage led by those affected and supported by the gay community and others was incredible. Arts and media were central to this, but it was enabled by the fact that the movement had begun to change the master narrative to one in which homophobia was rightly becoming stigmatized. This was enabled by many group members being relatively economically and socially powerful and holding positions as key "opinion formers"[20] and role models in arts and film organizations.

The Case for an Artistic and Cultural Response

If we can agree that mental illnesses are *essentially contested* concepts and *socially constructed,* then the case for a cultural response to engaging and shaping public perceptions is compelling regardless of the weaknesses of current approaches.[21] The potential value of arts and film include:

The arts explore rather than inform, creating new possibilities, allowing us to create and challenge dominant discourses and beliefs.

All cultures use arts to convey complex ideas. The arts may reach and engage diverse cultural groups, where there is evidence stigma manifests itself in different ways.[22]

Arts explore the human condition. By considering everyone's mental health identities we can undermine the dehumanization and label of absolute difference necessary to perpetuate stigma.

Stigma is emotional rather than rational. Arts and film experiences can create emotional engagement and are often collective experiences that have the scope to promote affirming experiences and positive contact.

We tell stories to influence others. Stories and narratives engage us. Conveying mental health narratives through art and film can be particularly effective.[23]

Participation has the potential to empower mental health service users and promote recovery, and to consolidate a wider community of support.

What is attractive about engaging with arts and film is its authentic and cutting-edge nature, and the potential it provides to create partnerships with organizations that already engage effectively with the public through established infrastructures. None of this, however, would work without professional artists and organisations seeing value in the Festival.

Creative Organizing: Perspectives of Artists

Creative organizing in the Festival is challenging — practically, ethically, and conceptually. The Festival attempts to provide a platform for artists to explore, create, curate, and collaborate with mental health service users, practitioners, community organizers, and academics. They develop, produce, and contextualize over two hundred projects and events each year. Collaborations can range from a modest community event to a major national project, such as creating a new album of music and a large-scale concert involving international musicians and numerous agencies. This model creates many possibilities for artists but means compromising and negotiating. It raises interesting questions about what they try to achieve, and their motivations and identities. We explore these issues in this section through the reflections of eight participating artists.

We begin with two artists who created and performed new theater productions. Maite Delafin created and performed a physical theater piece at the Glasgow Centre for Contemporary Art, and she is followed by Leann O'Kasi, a stage director, who wrote and performed a run of her critically acclaimed play, *Dirty Paradise*, at Glasgow's Tron Theatre:

> For my project I collaborated with an actor, musician and sound designer. It resulted in *Imprints*, a physical theatre piece telling the story of how a couple's lives change as the symptoms of Alzheimer's disease start to show. Previously I worked mostly on abstract concepts. For *Imprints* it's been different. I had this obsession to work on memory for a while but didn't really know where to start ... my father was quite old and without obvious reasons I started to record some memories of my childhood with him. A few weeks later, quite unexpectedly, he passed away.... I was scared to forget him, lose the beautiful memories. So somehow I thought I would face that fear by doing a piece. My dad was in the last years forgetting a lot already and my grandmother has severe dementia, so the subject was somehow familiar already. Consequently I started to do research on the disease, reading studies, watching films, but mostly spending time with my grandmother and other people with Alzheimer's, trying to really understand that journey. Making work with a social value has been an important change in my career, being able to raise awareness, making people reflect and talk about it.... Despite showing a very difficult journey, *Imprints* is a love story.[24]

> I wanted to create a piece which challenged preconceptions of "voice hearers," including my own. I didn't want the piece to be "issue led," but rather driven by a real human story.... Having experienced mental ill-health in my teens and seeing it through loved ones, I had some experience, but when it came to auditory hallucinations, I didn't have a clue! *Dirty Paradise* was inspired from a short story by Gabriel Garcia Marquez ("I Only Came to Use the Phone"). It tells the story of Maria, a streetwise young woman who has suffered from auditory hallucinations from an early age and her battle to dissect and accept it. The story is a fantastical road trip through Maria's life, from her frustrating existence in the UK to her vibrant adventures in Brazil where she finds love, magic, and LSD, but one night by a weird twist of fate finds herself in an asylum. Paradoxically, as significant memories surface, she starts to gain some sense of serenity. I found the festival through a friend, and was supported to contact organisations and people with lived experience of poor mental health. I conducted interviews with voice hearers through one-to-one chats, telephone conversations, and preliminary workshops. I had begun writing specific scenes, but the more I spoke to people about their own experiences, the more the scenes would change, so it was certainly a very "organic" process. A work-in-progress showing of the piece was presented to those who I had consulted about the original idea ... it was terrifying for me as I realised the weight of the responsibility I had taken on.... One value of the festival was to reach an audience outside of the normal 'theatre going' sphere. I was astounded by the amount of audience members who turned up to the show via the festival's advertising campaign, which clearly resonated as mental health being something which effects everyone. We will all go through some rough patches, and for many this may result in something more severe, which we

may want to talk about, but others won't know how to. The fact that the festival celebrates mental health in all its guises helps people to get talking about it no matter what.[25]

Both reflections introduce important points. The Festival encourages new work, here developing nascent ideas, rather than just providing a platform for existing art. It stimulates the use of multiple connecting art forms, reflecting an approach taken by many curators from different genres, in many ways reflecting the complexity of mental health and illness itself. Significantly, participating in the Festival has shaped future artistic practice and direction. This may be due to creative reasons or to the development of new audiences through their work, which they also recognize. The personal connection of the artist to mental illness is clear as a source of motivation for both, and both productions offer hope in difficult times, the "love story" and the "serenity."

The next pairing of artists developed participatory events on behalf of their organizations. Connections are at the heart of the Festival's dance program, which Satya Dunning of Dance House describes; followed by Emma Hagen of Solar Bear Company, who leads the Festival's therapeutic theater activity:

> Dance House is driven by a belief in the transformative impact of dance. We programme with the Festival through support, collaborations and partnerships. This included Mad for Dance, a series of illuminating and inspiring films that sensitively demonstrated the restorative benefits that dance can bring to people with mental health issues. To contextualise this, featured dancers share their experiences with the audience. We supported the development of a new work about bipolar disorder by young choreographer Emma Park.... We recently focused upon the theme of childhood and organised with partners "Moving Memories," an afternoon of text, movement workshops, and film screenings of work such as *Dance Like Your Old Man* by Australian Gideon Obarzanek and *5 Memories* by Spanish Alejandra Marquez and Mexican Oriana Alcaine. They celebrate the spirit and experience of childhood and its relationship to mind and body.[26]

> Our belief is that creativity, spontaneity, self-expression, and playfulness are essential for emotional health. Our approach is closely aligned with the recovery model, supporting individuals who access mental health services to explore their own stories, focusing on their strengths and hopes as well as addressing the difficulties they face. At every stage of the process participants retain total control. Our drama workshops, rehearsals, and performances have had sell-out audiences every year and take place at the renowned Citizens Theatre. It plays a role in challenging stigma. There is always a real feeling of celebration, achievement and pride in participating in a major arts festival. Group members have described an increase in confidence, self-esteem and greater sense of self. Being part of the group provides a sense of purpose and connection with others. The festival showcases the wide-ranging creative approaches that can support individuals to express themselves and have their voices heard on a national level.[27]

Satya illustrates how making connections motivates Dance House's involvement in the Festival, in her case connections across art forms and between organizations. Also impressive is their ability to work with the complexity of the spectrum of mental health; from mental illness through to seamlessly connecting with the general public audience's mental health identities. Both artists share the hopefulness and positive approach to mental health of the earlier artists, and have been stimulated to develop new work and ideas. Emma works more intensively with people who have experienced enduring mental health problems using a strengths–based recovery model, stressing the importance of using mainstream venues to avoid stigma, an approach that shows the Festival's reach is more year-round.[28]

The ethos of recovery and hopefulness is central to the Festival's literary program, where new writers with experience of mental health illness write and perform alongside established, professional authors, a surprising number of whom are open in their work and performances about their own experiences of mental illness. This is captured in reflections from Larry Butler and Willy Maley, who lead this strand:

> My favourite quote is from the Pulitzer prize-winning poet William Carlos Williams: "That's the way writing often starts, a disaster or a catastrophe of some sort, as happened to me.... And I think that's the basis for my continued interest in writing, because by writing I rescue myself under all sorts of conditions, whatever it may be that has upset me, then I can write and it relieves the feeling of distress."
>
> In my late teens I was sectioned and spent several months on locked wards of a mental hospital in California — sometimes in solitary confinement. I witnessed both kindness and healing as well as injustice, prejudice, edging towards cruelty.... After training as an artist and relocating to the UK, I worked as a community artist. We launched Survivors Poetry Scotland with Janice Galloway doing us the honour, then Lapidus Scotland promoting creative words for health and wellbeing, which over the past four years has organised the literary strand of the Festival. We began with a collaboration with Project Ability's international exhibition ... inspired by the art we used storytelling and songwriting, short story, and poetry and published a CD and booklet. In 2008, we extended our artistic remit, organising a showcase event with more 20 mental health user groups from throughout Scotland presenting their creative writing, songs and stories launched by Glasgow's poet laureate, Liz Lochhead. In 2009, we facilitated workshops with Voices of Experience, whose work was shared alongside that of established writers. In 2010 our theme broadened further and Lapidus designed an integrated programme collaborating with the Centre for Contemporary Art, Glasgow University, and Women's Aid. I see the value of the Festival as keeping the flag flying promoting the therapeutic benefits of engaging with the arts. Our belief is that the best arts and health projects place equal emphasis on process and product. I think the Festival does just that. By

having so many partners throughout Scotland, year by year it has been building a network linking many diverse groups and blurring the divide between arts and health. By integrating established artists with aspiring artists with a history of mental illness, the festival begins to normalise creativity and reduce stigma.[29]

I came to mental health through literature, and have a strong belief in the healing power of words and in particular the therapeutic effects of storytelling. In the past, I've worked as writer-in-residence in HM Prison Barlinnie and a Drama Worker in Milton Unemployed Workers Centre. My interest in mental health goes back to teaching a course entitled "Madness and Literature" at the University of Glasgow in 1995, using the work of Michel Foucault, R.D. Laing, and David Cooper as a way of exploring issues of mental health in writing from Shakespeare to Virginia Woolf. In 2008, as part of the Festival, I gave a preshow talk for the Lyceum Theatre's production of *Macbeth*, in which I reflected on the play's treatment of questions arising from the aftershock of violence. Since then I have co-curated the literary strand of the Festival, bringing together writers, mental health practitioners, and service users in a series of lectures, readings, and workshops. In 2008, I brought together a group of writers under the heading "Mind Readers/Writers Mind," featuring readings and panel discussions with authors — emerging and established — including Alan Bissett, Karen Campbell, Tom Leonard, Alison Miller, Denise Mina, Rachel Seiffert, and Zoe Strachan. The one-day event was remarkable both for the range and richness of readings and for the active engagement of those who listened and intervened. Tom Leonard's standout performance, moving and profound, will remain in the memory for a long time. In 2009 I co-curated with Rachel Clive "The Trick Is to Keep Writing" with Alan Bissett, Denise Mina, Kei Miller, Zoe Strachan, and Louise Welsh. In 2010 I co-curated with Lapidus and Juana Adcock. The theme of "Growing Pains: Writing the Road to Adulthood" was addressed by writers with considerable experience of depicting the challenges and changes of childhood, including Janice and Bernard MacLaverty. I said at the beginning that I came to mental health through literature. I meant that to be as ambiguous as it sounds, because I both learned about mental health by reading, recovered too from traumas of my own. The process of healing is a slow one, and as the poet Edmund Spenser says of his writing, "'O what an endless work have I in hand!'"[30]

Both writers build upon the themes of earlier artists. Making connections is central to their motivation, between professional writers, students, and mental health service users. Both explore the historical portrayal of mental health and traditional interpretations of literature. Personal connections with mental illness motivate these artists and ensure a balance between process and performance, leading to a strong ethos of equality, survival, and rights. But in their reflections, the centrality of mental health and illness in life and art really emerges.

We complete our explorations of artist perceptions with two documentary filmmakers. Nick Higgins's film *Hidden Gifts* won the jury prize in 2008, and Richard Adams's 1972 film *Asylum* was screened on the anniversary of Laing's death in 2007 with a debate involving a large audience comprising the general public, service users, Laing's family, academics and psychiatrists:

> The Chilean filmmaker Patricio Guzman once said that a country without documentary films is like a family without a photo album. It is an attractive formulation that immediately communicates both the sense of intimacy that documentary films can achieve and the cultural importance of looking back at ourselves through film. In many ways the Scottish Mental Health Film and Arts Festival provides an opportunity to reflect upon some of the more difficult and challenging moments in the cultural history of Scotland. As a filmmaker, my own contribution to this ongoing reflection was the documentary film *Hidden Gifts*. It is a film that tells the true story of Angus MacPhee, the "quiet big man" from south Uist. Angus was a man who struggled with the brutality of the Second World War and soon after found himself committed to Craig Dunain mental asylum in Inverness, where he was to remain for some 50 years. What was exceptional about Angus was that whilst he withdrew from the world, refusing to speak to any hospital staff, he began to create extraordinary objects from grass. These included coats, trousers, hats, gloves, and shoes, all of which he wore at various times. In the early 1970s his work was discovered by the art therapist Joyce Laing. Thanks to Joyce, Angus's work became known to the outside world, and the emotional and intellectual provocation of his art became the basis for the film I made. Angus died before having the chance to speak about his work; instead we are left with an artistic legacy that questions the very relationship between creativity and mental health. It is a relationship that was little understood in the days that Angus was first treated, but the very specific nature of his creative response to his own predicament tells us much about our own culture and the limits of understanding with which we necessarily operate. To return to Guzman's original analogy, the Festival makes it possible for all the members of the family to gather round, watch and discuss the often painful but also inspirational moments that make up our shared cultural lives. It is this function that makes the Festival such an invaluable part of Scottish society.[31]

> The Festival became a moving way for me to re-enter the very special ambience of a milieu I had tasted 36 years earlier when shooting Peter Robinson's *Asylum* in R.D. Laing's Archway community in London. Before coming I met a young intern at a preeminent New York psychiatric hospital who said that essentially "Nothing has changed since Foucault!" So it occurred to me as I headed for Laing's birthplace on the anniversary of his 80th birthday that he has two legacies— both his marginalization by mainstream psychiatry, and the emergence of varied initiatives worldwide — like the Scottish Festival itself, that directly or indirectly reflect Laing's willingness to connect with the mentally ill as fellow human beings. The Festival bridges the gap in countless ways, from the generous gift of a huge electronic billboard overlooking the city's main square, to the Festival

staffers and volunteers who had invited me to join them for an office lunch the day I arrived ... as open in some cases about their mental health challenges as they were warm in their welcome. It reminded me of my first day at Archway. The six weeks there, and my ten days at the Festival, made one thing clear: that mental health and mental illness are not so easily segregated along the broad spectrum of human joy and suffering.[32]

Both filmmakers explore what mental illness means in a historical context and challenge us to reconsider our perspectives on what mental illness means and the existing assumptions that we hold. They challenge diagnostic labels and the assumptions about people who have them. They focus upon the common humanity we all share, drawing upon memory and experience. Nick, particularly, explores the links between madness and creativity. The documentaries challenge and provoke us, but again the consistent theme that emerges is one of hopefulness and possibilities for change through reflection.

Whilst motivations and creative processes are unique to each artist and highly complex, some themes emerge across the reflections that are important considerations for arts and health initiatives more widely. The artists frequently draw upon personal experience of mental health issues, or the experience of a loved one, to motivate and inform their involvement. A blend of artistic, social, and personal reasons are most often stated, and mental health as an issue consistently stimulates most artists to create new work and to make connections across artistic genres and with diverse social groups. The diversity of responses to the issues, often building upon existing ideas, suggests that imposing a set of artistic themes and approaches would be counterproductive and light-touch programming will encourage and capture the widest range of creative responses. The artists challenge dominant beliefs and power structures in subtle and overt ways; social justice and equality are common threads throughout their work, as is hopefulness, which is important when considering the potential impact upon participants and audience members and the media.

Social and Cultural Impact of the Festival

Academics from a range of universities including Strathclyde, St. Andrews and University College London have collaborated to evaluate the Festival. Their disciplinary backgrounds include public health, psychiatry, psychology, social sciences, arts and humanities, and management. Primarily university-based, they also include working practitioners and service-user researchers. The studies undertaken have engaged over two thousand people including the Festival collaborators and audiences. They have employed techniques including analyzing audience data, surveys, questionnaires, interviews, focus groups, service user-led research and participant observation. In gauging whether the Festival has contributed to wider social change, studies are framed based upon the Festival's core aims.

Mental Health Service Users

Studies of mental health service users who collaborate with our professional artists to produce events have involved "service user research." The emerging findings indicate that the primary motivation for taking part is about individuals promoting personal wellbeing, making friends, and, for some participants, taking the opportunity to tackle social stigma. For some service users, there is a clear recovery dimension, but this was not the case for most respondents. Rather, the Festival provided an opportunity to offset their negative mental illness label by reinforcing a positive identity as meaningful artist or arts organizer. It is this positive identity formation that results in a reduction in self-stigma and an increase in reported wellbeing.[33] While empowering and positive overall, service users stressed the importance of not expecting people to be "ambassadors" for the wider population of people who experience mental illness and reinforced the fact that sharing stories and narratives at the Festival events risks eliciting negative emotions and negative public reactions. Effective support systems should be maintained. The issues of fluid identities, personal motivation, and making social and artistic connections have parallels in the responses of professional artists (many of whom have also experienced mental illness and distress) and will form the basis of future studies with the Festival participants.

Audience Impact

Almost two thousand audience members have taken part in studies using a range of approaches, including pre-post validated attitudinal surveys, semi-structured questionnaires, and interviews. The findings are complex, and fuller detail can be found in a paper just published in *Acta*,[34] although the main themes are summarized here. Across studies, the dominant theme is that audiences leave events with more positive beliefs about stigma, acceptance, and recovery. Significant reductions in stigma were found for fear and danger constructs, but the most significant gains were about promoting the positive — that people living with mental illnesses can contribute, have relationships, make good employees. It appears that the particular contribution of the Festival is to promote positive perceptions rather then dampen down negative ones. However, arts and film events also have the potential to reinforce and polarize preexisting bias, which was the case in a Festival screening of a film entitled *The Devil and Daniel Johnston*.

Programmers, in deciding whether to portray people who are the subjects of art, in this case documentary, in moments where they are unpredictable and dangerous, and where there is poor prognosis, must balance social impact with artistic value and merit. The likely audiences and the context must be carefully considered. A less anticipated finding was the extent to which audience members generalize their learning and positive perceptions across to other social groups who experience social injustice. Two other aspects of audience impact are noteworthy, one related to "self." Audiences reported greater willingness to seek help, to support others, and to acknowledge that we are all vulnerable to poor mental health. People identified steps they would take to actively promote mental wellbeing in their lives; the further consistent and powerful theme was the "value of the arts," being recognized for their instrumental and intrinsic value.

Meaningful contributions from people with experience of mental illness as artists, subjects, or in panels had the most impact on respondents. It is also important to acknowledge the differential impact of different arts forms upon the audience experience of events. The term "arts" like the term "mental illness" is an umbrella for an incredibly diverse range of forms. There is no reason to assume that film will create a similar impact to music or, say, a visual art exhibition. However some trends and patterns are emerging. Film and theater appear to be very effective at creating clear and consistent messages and impressions about mental illness, especially in relation to stigma and recovery. Music events more often generate emotional responses about wellbeing, acceptance, and positive mental health. This area is subject to ongoing analysis.

Audience Reach

The Festival attracts a very wide spectrum of the public, but, encouragingly, this includes higher proportions than are present in the Scottish population of people from low-income households, black and minority ethnic communities, and those who have experienced mental illness.[35] This is as unexpected as it is important, as these are groups who have reported dual stigma, vulnerability to poor mental health, and low arts attendance generally.[36] This is attributed to a number of factors, but primarily to the co-production model where community organizers and mental health service user groups play a full part in developing, producing, and marketing events.

Cultural Impact

The impact of the Festival on those who create and attend it, a broad cross section of society, appears effective. But social change depends upon how the wider population responds to it, especially the media and the powerful opinion formers who mediate and shape social opinions. The effects will unfold over time, but the signs are promising both in the media and politically.

The media represent the Festival events and their messages to the wider public. An ongoing study of media content indicates that coverage is extensive across television, radio, and press and is positive in content, tone, and sophistication. Celebrities talking about mental health were important in the Festival's first year, and this retains some value, but this dependence has been reduced as events create stories that are newsworthy and authentic. The relationships have evolved to the point that we have developed formal partnerships and worked on events with major institutions including the BBC. For the Festival to endure and maintain the buy-in of arts partners, arts critics in the national press are important. Fortunately they have, to date, embraced the Festival. Among a number of plaudits, *The Herald* described it as "more inclusive than any other festival in the country,"[37] *The Scotsman* as "one of the best ideas to hit the Scottish cultural scene in years."[38] Journalists now frequently take part in post-event panels with artists, service users, practitioners, and government officials to genuinely enable debate. It is a cyclical effect that makes it easier for us to build positive relationships with the media.

Politically, the Festival has exceeded initial expectations. The government now provides some financial support, even in challenging economic times, through its national program. It has had practical influence; for example the 2009 jury prize-winning film *Irene* was used to inform consultations on the National Dementia Strategy. The Scottish government identified the Festival as an example of good practice at a recent American/European mental health exchange, and it was selected as an example of success by the European Commission social inclusion pact in 2010. Other countries are now developing their own festivals on this model.

Reflections

The Festival provides a valuable example of a creative and energetic community of practice.[39] The creative processes undertaken by both artists and activists are shaped by and shape their identities. Motivation is often driven by personal experience of mental distress and a desire to connect with others, but also by a need to understand the cultural and historical context of mental illness and create and develop new artistic work. Ethical issues must be considered on an ongoing basis, and there are lessons being learned as the Festival evolves.

Encouragingly, the emerging evidence suggests that artistic and social value need not be balanced but can be synergistic. However, the balance must be maintained. If artistic leadership is diminished, we risk losing artistic value and credibility and becoming an arts "campaign" with little authenticity; without the voices of experience of people who have experienced mental illness co-programming projects, arts and film events risk reinforcing public prejudice and becoming disempowering experiences.

The Festival's social impact is promising, empowering service users, reaching diverse communities with greatest need, exerting positive effects, and engaging the media and opinion formers. Artistically there is considerable audience development, artists value the opportunity to collaborate, and the results are receiving critical acclaim. The arts, film, and popular culture deserve a central rather then supporting role in creating mentally flourishing societies.

NOTES

1. Scottish Government Health Department, *Towards a Mentally Flourishing Scotland: Policy and Action Plan 2009–2011* (Edinburgh: Scottish Government, 2009), 3.

2. Corey L.M. Keyes, "Promoting and Protecting Mental Health as Flourishing: A Complementary Strategy for Improving National Mental Health," *American Psychologist* 62 (2007): 95–108.

3. Lee Knifton and Neil Quinn, "Media, Mental Health and Discrimination: A Frame of Reference for Understanding Reporting Trends," *International Journal of Mental Health Promotion* 10 (2008): 23–31.

4. Neil Quinn and Lee Knifton, "Addressing Stigma and Discrimination Through Community Conversation," in *Social Work and Global Health Inequalities: Policy and Practice Developments,* eds. Paul Bywaters, Eileen McLeod and Lyndsay Napier (Bristol: Policy Press, 2009).

5. Lee Knifton et al., "Ethical Issues in a National Mental Health Arts and Film Festival," *Journal of Ethics in Mental Health* 4, no. 2 (Nov. 2009), accessed December 15, 2010, www.jemh.ca/issues/v4/n2/JEMH-Vol.4No.2.November2009.htm.

6. Erving Goffman, *Stigma: Notes on Management of Spoiled Identity* (London: Penguin, 1990), 11–12.

7. Graham Scrambler, "Health Related Stigma," *Sociology of Health and Illness* 31 (2009): 441–55.

8. Bruce G. Link and Jo C. Phelan, "Conceptualising Stigma," *Annual Review of Sociology* 27 (2001): 363–85.

9. Eric R. Wright et al., "Deinstitutionalization, Social Rejection, and the Self-Esteem of Former Mental Patients," *Journal of Health Social Behaviour* 41 (2000): 68–90.

10. Bruce G. Link et al., "A Modified Labelling Theory Approach in the Area of Mental Disorders: An Empirical Assessment," *American Sociological Review* 54 (1989): 100–123.

11. Sarah Rosenfield, "Labelling Mental Illness: The Effects of Received Services and Perceived Stigma on Life Satisfaction," *American Journal of Sociology* 62 (1997): 660–672.

12. Georg Schomerus and Matthias C. Angermeyer, "Stigma and Its Impact on Help-Seeking for Mental Disorders: What Do We Know?" *Epidemiologica Psichiatria Sociale* 17 (2008): 31–37.

13. Bridget Williams et al., *Experiences and Expectations of Disabled People* (London: Office for Disability Issues, Department of Work and Pension, 2008), 15.

14. Graham Thornicroft et al., "Global Pattern of Experienced and Anticipated Discrimination against People with Schizophrenia," *The Lancet* 373 (2009): 408–415.

15. World Health Organization, *The World Health Report 2001— Mental Health: New Understanding, New Hope* (Geneva: WHO, 2001), 110.

16. Una Maclean, "Community Attitudes to Mental Illness in Edinburgh," *British Journal of Preventative and Social Medicine* 23 (1969): 45–52.

17. Rahman Haghighat, "A Unitary Theory of Stigmatisation: Pursuit of Self Interest and Routes to Destigmatisation," *British Journal of Psychiatry* 178 (2001): 207–215.

18. Alan Rosen, "What Developed Countries Can Learn from Developing Countries in Challenging Psychiatric Stigma," *Australasian Psychiatry* 11 (2003): 589–595; Lee Knifton et al., "Community Conversation: Addressing Mental Health Stigma with Ethnic Minority Communities," *Social Psychiatry and Psychiatric Epidemiology* 45 (2010): 497–504.

19. John W. Fox, "Social Class, Mental Illness and Social Mobility: The Social Selection-Drift Hypothesis for Serious Mental Illness," *Journal of Health and Social Behaviour* 31 (1990): 344–53.

20. Elihu Katz and Paul F. Lazarsfeld, *Personal Influence: The Part Played by People in the Flow of Mass Communication* (New Brunswick, NJ: Transaction Publishers, 2009), 33.

21. Walter B. Gallie, "Essentially Contested Concepts," in *Proceedings of the Aristotelian Society*," 56 (Blackwell Publishing on behalf of The Aristotelian Society, 1955–1956), accessed December 10, 2010, www.jstor.org/stable.4544562; Kenneth J. Gergen and Mary Gergen, *Social Construction: A Reader* (London: Sage, 2003), 15.

22. Wim Van Brakel, "Measuring Health-Related Stigma: A Literature Review," *Psychology, Health and Medicine* 11 (2006): 307–34.

23. Neil Quinn, Lee Knifton and Jane Donald, "The Role of Narratives in Addressing Stigma," In *21st Century Social Workers*, eds. Raymond Taylor, Malcolm Hill and Fergus McNeill (Birmingham: Venture Press, 2011).

24. Maite Delafin, Artistic Director, NUX Company, Scotland.

25. Leann O'Kasi, Artist in Residence, Tron Theatre, Glasgow.

26. Satya Dunning, Dance House, Scotland.

27. Emma Hagen, Solar Bear Theatre Productions, Scotland.

28. Scottish Recovery Network, *Raising Expectations and Sharing Ideas for Mental Health Recovery.* (Glasgow, 2009), 9.

29. Larry Butler, Convenor of Lapidus, creative words for health and wellbeing, Scotland.

30. Professor Willy Maley, English Literature, School of Critical Studies, University of Glasgow.

31. Dr. Nick Higgins, Graduate School of Literatures, Languages and Cultures, Edinburgh University.

32. Richard W. Adams, cameraman-editor of *Asylum*, New York.

33. Morgan Garret, "The Experience of Service Users in a Mental Health Arts Festival" (M.A. diss., University of Strathclyde, 2010).

34. Neil Quinn et al., "The Impact of a National Mental Health Arts and Film Festival on Stigma and Recovery," *Acta Psychiatrica Scandinavica* 123 (2011): 71–81.

35. Greig Inglis et al., *The Reach of a National Mental Health Arts and Film Festival* (Glasgow: Mental Health Foundation, 2011), 6.

36. Scottish Arts Council, *Travel and Tourism. Taking Part in Scotland* (Scottish Arts Council: Edinburgh, 2008), 29.

37. Neil Cooper, "Open Your Mind to the Power of the Arts," *Herald Scotland,* 27 September 2010, accessed March 4, 2010, www.heraldscotland.com/arts-ents/more-arts-entertainment-news/open-your-mind-to-the-power-of-the-arts-1.1057805.

38. Joyce McMillan, "Theatre Review," *The Scotsman*, October 9, 2010, accessed March 4, 2010, http://joycemcmillan.wordpress.com/2010/10/08/dirty-paradise/.

39. Ettiene Wenger, *Communities of Practice: Learning, Meaning and Identity* (New York: Cambridge University Press, 1998), 6.

BIBLIOGRAPHY

Cooper, Neil. "Open Your Mind to the Power of the Arts." *Herald Scotland,* September 27, 2010.

Fox, John W. "Social Class, Mental Illness and Social Mobility: The Social Selection-Drift Hypothesis for Serious Mental Illness."*Journal of Health and Social Behaviour* 31, 4 (1990): 344–53.

Gallie, Walter B. "Essentially Contested Concepts." *Proceedings of the Aristotelian Society* 56 (1956): 167–198.

Garret, Morgan. "The Experience of Service Users in a Mental Health Arts Festival." M.A.in Social Work. PhD diss., University of Strathclyde, 2010.

Gergen, Kenneth J., and Mary Gergen. *Social Construction: A Reader.* London: Sage, 2003.

Goffman, Erving. *Stigma: Notes on Management of Spoiled Identity.* Upper Saddle River, NJ: Prentice Hall, 1963.

Haghighat, Rahman. "A Unitary Theory of Stigmatisation: Pursuit of Self Interest and Routes to Destigmatisation." *British Journal of Psychiatry* 178, 3 (2001): 207–215.

Inglis, Grieg, Lee Knifton, Neil Quinn, Rona Dougal, and Peter Byrne. *The Reach of a National Mental Health Arts and Film Festival.* Glasgow: Mental Health Foundation, 2011.

Katz, Elihu, and Paul F. Lazarsfeld. *Personal Influence: The Part Played by People in the Flow of Mass Communication.* New York: Free Press, 1955.

Keyes, Corey L.M. "Promoting and Protecting Mental Health as Flourishing: A Complementary Strategy for Improving National Mental Health." *American Psychologist* 62 (2007): 95–108.

Knifton, Lee, Mhairi Gervais, Karen Newbigging, Nuzhat Mirza, Neil Quinn, Neil Wilson, and Evette Hunkins-Hutchison. "Community Conversation: Addressing Mental Health Stigma with Ethnic Minority Communities." *Social Psychiatry and Psychiatric Epidemiology* 45, 4 (2010): 497–504.

Knifton, Lee, and Neil Quinn. "Media, Mental Health and Discrimination: A Frame of Reference for Understanding Reporting Trends." *International Journal of Mental Health Promotion* 10, 1 (2008): 23–31.

Knifton, Lee, Neil Quinn, Greig Inglis, and Peter Byrne."Ethical Issues in a National Mental Health Arts and Film Festival."*Journal of Ethics in Mental Health* 4, no. 2 (2009): 1–5.

Link, Bruce G., Francis T. Cullen, Elmer Struening, Patrick E. Shrout, and Bruce P. Dohrenwend. "A Modified Labelling Theory Approach in the Area of Mental Disorders: An Empirical Assessment." *American Sociological Review* 54 (1989): 100–123.

Link, Bruce G., and Jo C. Phelan. "Conceptualising Stigma."*Annual Review of Sociology* 27 (2001): 363–85.

Maclean, Una. "Community Attitudes to Mental Illness in Edinburgh." *British Journal of Preventative and Social Medicine* 23, 1 (1969): 45–52.

McMillan, Joyce. "Theatre Review." *The Scotsman.* October 9, 2010.

Quinn, Neil, and Lee Knifton. "Addressing Stigma and Discrimination Through Community Conversation," in *Social Work and Global Health Inequalities: Policy and Practice Developments,* eds. P. Bywaters, E. McLeod, and L. Napier (Bristol: Policy Press, 2009).

Quinn, Neil, Amanda Shulman, Lee Knifton, and Peter Byrne. "The Impact of a National Mental Health Arts and Film Festival on Stigma and Recovery." *Acta Psychiatrica Scandinavica* 123, 1 (2011): 71–81.

Quinn, Neil, Lee Knifton, and Jane Donald. "The Role of Narratives in Addressing Stigma," in *21st Century Social Workers: A Resource for Early Professional Development,* eds. R. Taylor, M. Hill, and F. McNeill (Birmingham: Venture Press, 2011).

Rosen, Alan. "What Developed Countries Can Learn from Developing Countries in Challenging Psychiatric Stigma." *Australasian Psychiatry* 11 (2003): 589–595.

Rosenfield, Sarah. "Labelling Mental Illness: The Effects of Received Services and Perceived Stigma on Life Satisfaction." *American Journal of Sociology* 62, 4 (1997): 660–672.

Schomerus, Georg, and Matthias C. Angermeyer. "Stigma and Its Impact on Help-Seeking for Mental Disorders: What Do We Know?" *Epidemiologica Psichiatria Sociale* 17, 1 (2008): 31–37.

Scottish Arts Council. *Travel and Tourism. Taking Part in Scotland.* Scottish Arts Council: Edinburgh, 2008.

Scottish Government Health Department. *Towards a Mentally Flourishing Scotland: Policy and Action Plan 2009–2011.* Scottish Government: Edinburgh, 2009.

Scottish Recovery Network. *What is Recovery?* Glasgow, 2009.

Scrambler, Graham. "Health Related Stigma." *Sociology of Health and Illness* 31, 3 (2009): 441–55.

Thornicroft, Graham, Elaine Brohan, Diana Rose, Norman Sartorius, and the INDIGO study group. "Global Pattern of Experienced and Anticipated Discrimination against People with Schizophrenia." *The Lancet* 373 (2009): 408–415.

Van Brakel, Wim. "Measuring Health-Related Stigma: A Literature Review." *Psychology, Health and Medicine* 11, 3 (2006): 307–34.

Wenger, Ettiene. *Communities of Practice: Learning, Meaning and Identity.* New York: Cambridge University Press, 1998.

Williams, Bridget, Phil Copestake, John Eversley, and Bruce Stafford. *Experiences and Expectations of Disabled People.* London: Office for Disability Issues, Department of Work and Pension, 2008.

World Health Organization. *The World Health Report 2001— Mental Health: New Understanding, New Hope.* Geneva: WHO, 2001.

Wright, Eric R., William P. Gronfein, and Timothy J. Owens. "Deinstitutionalization, Social Rejection, and the Self-Esteem of Former Mental Patients." *Journal of Health Social Behaviour* 41, 1 (2000): 68–90.

Afterword

The credits dash across the screen; a television commercial rushes in to fill the uneasy silence; the players gather at center stage for their final bow; and as the train leaves the station, the last few images of colorful graffiti blur in the gathering distance. Fade to black! In turn, we click off our television, eject our Blu Ray disc, slowly make our way to the rear of the theater, or settle in for the long thought-filled ride that lies ahead.

We try to shake the disturbing images, thoughts, and sounds that have flooded our consciousness, but words linger as potent reminders. And these words, like the images that accompanied them, are not without power! Speech dysfluency, attention deficit hyperactivity disorder, post-traumatic stress disorder, post-partum depression, sociopathy, and psychosis — powerful words that can and do influence the very manner in which we look upon and attempt to make sense of others and "the other." And in response to these words, we try to ask all of the right, or perhaps necessary questions. "What separates mental health from mental illness?" "Is mental illness, like its putative counterpart, physical disease, real or perhaps mere social construction or sociopolitical artifact?" "If, indeed, we are co-constructors of the edifice of mental illness, what is our role and responsibility as consumers of the numerous popular venues through which it is depicted?"

That people struggle with these and countless other "psychiatric conditions and disorders" is not now, nor has it been, debated in this volume. What has and is being considered is the extent to which the popular stage, or perhaps more accurately, the various stages upon which all that is popular is displayed and enacted, is a suitable and valid vehicle for the construction of mental illness.

What are we to do with the haunting images of the sociopathic killer, the suffering military veteran, the deranged psychotic lesbian or pathetic stutterer? How easily and casually do we compartmentalize, and in so doing, separate ourselves from the stories of both real celebrities-gone-mad and the fictionalized depictions of the mentally suffering protagonist in a television series, movie, Broadway musical, social media website, or even favorite comic book? And are the popular and popularized stories of the mentally ill in foreign lands so far removed from our daily lives as to have no relevance? Or are these stories of human suffering universal?

These are questions that I hope have been raised through the thoughtful essays in this volume and that you will take with you as both consumers and co-creators of popular culture representations of the mentally healthy and the mentally ill. — L.C.R.

About the Contributors

Saheed **Aderinto** is assistant professor of African history at Western Carolina University. His areas of expertise include gender and sexuality, nationalism and historiography, peace and conflict, and the African Diaspora. In addition to numerous journal articles, book chapters, encyclopedia entries, and book reviews, Aderinto is the co-author of *Nigeria, Nationalism, and Writing History* (2010).

Katie **Ellis** is a lecturer in media and communications at Murdoch University in Australia and an adjunct research fellow at the Centre for Research in Entertainment, Arts, Technology, Education and Communications at Edith Cowan University. She is the author of *Disabling Diversity* (2008) and *Disability and New Media* (2011, with Mike Kent), as well as published articles. She is investigating the digital cultures of youth with disabilities and writing a book with Gerard Goggin on disability and the media.

Elizabeth S. **EnglandKennedy** is a research associate and senior ethnographer with the Pacific Institute for Research and Evaluation. She received her Ph.D. in cultural anthropology from the University of Arizona, where she specialized in ethnomedicine, medical anthropology, sociolinguistics, and hidden disability. Her dissertation was on learning disabilities and attention deficit disorders. Her research focuses on mental illnesses and co-occurring disorders.

Jeffrey K. **Johnson** is a World War II historian for the Joint POW/MIA Accounting Command in Honolulu, Hawaii. He is the author of *American Advertising in Poland: A Study of Cultural Interactions Since 1990* (McFarland, 2009). A recent journal article is "The Countryside Triumphant: Jefferson's Ideal of Rural Superiority in Modern Superhero Mythology" (*Journal of Popular Culture*, August 2010). He is writing a book about comic books as historical texts.

Lee **Knifton** is a director of the Scottish Mental Health Arts and Film Festival (mhfestival.com); associate head of the Mental Health Foundation in Scotland (a leading NGO undertaking research, policy, and communication projects), health improvement lead in the National Health Service; co-chair of the UK Public Health Association section on mental health; and visiting academic in applied social sciences at Strathclyde University, Glasgow. He has published widely on mental health, stigma, media, and the arts and is a member of the editorial board of the *Journal of Public Mental Health*.

Wanda **Little Fenimore** is a doctoral student in the School of Communication at Florida State University. She earned her bachelor's degree from Randolph-Macon Woman's College and master's degree from Hollins University. Her research interests include sport studies, critical theory, and gender studies.

Philippa **Martyr** works at the Centre for Clinical Research in Neuropsychiatry, a joint Health Department/University of Western Australia research unit based at Graylands Hospital, Western Australia, and has also taught at the University of Western Australia and the University of Tasmania. Her research focuses on the history of medicine, mental health history and research, historical epidemiology, women's history, history of religion, film criticism, new technologies in history writing, and institutional histories. Her book *Paradise of Quacks* (2002) set out to present an alternative history of Australian medicine.

Debra **Merskin** is an associate professor in communication studies at the School of Journalism and Communication at the University of Oregon. She has also published in the journals *Sex Roles, American Behavioral Scientist,* and *Mass Communication and Society* and in books such as *Mediated Women: Representations in Popular Culture; Sexual Rhetoric: Media Perspectives on Sexuality, Gender, and Identity*; and *Dressing in Feathers: The Construction of the Indian in American Popular Culture.* Her book *Media, Minorities, and Meaning: A Critical Introduction* (2010) addresses the social, psychological, and cultural context for stereotyping in American mass media.

Alena **Papayanis** is a Ph.D. candidate in history at the University of London, Birkbeck College. She received bachelor's and master's degrees in media, information, and technoculture from the University of Western Ontario. Her research interests have focused on the contemporary cultural history of war within the United States, in particular from the Vietnam War to the Persian Gulf War of 1990–91. Her dissertation examines how the Vietnam War was inflected in the Gulf War, specifically through constructions of the U.S. soldier figure, gender, and national identity.

Shawn M. **Phillips** is an associate professor of anthropology at Indiana State University in the Department of Earth and Environmental Systems. His ongoing research is into the extent to which any disease or disability can acquire a powerful enough presence in the popular culture to affect the identity and experience of those with such a condition. He continues to explore the dynamic of deviancy in prehistoric and historic archaeological populations as well as mainstream American popular culture.

Lawrence C. **Rubin** is a professor of counselor education at St. Thomas University in Miami, Florida, where he directs the Mental Health Counseling Program and is a psychologist, counselor and play therapist in private practice. His books include *Psychotropic Drugs and Popular Culture: Medicine, Mental Health and the Media* (McFarland, 2006; it won the 2006 Ray and Pat Browne Award for best anthology), *Food for Thought: Essays on Eating and Culture* (McFarland, 2008), *Popular Culture in Counseling, Psychotherapy and Play-based Intervention* (2008), and *Using Superheroes in Counseling and Play Therapy* (2007). He blogs for *Psychology Today* on popular culture and psychology.

Sarah J. **Rudolph** is a professor of communication and theatre arts and director of theatre at the University of Wisconsin–Marathon County. She holds a Ph.D. in theatre and drama from the University of Wisconsin–Madison. She is cofounder of Under the Rug Theatre, a collaborative effort between theatre enthusiasts, mental health consumers, and professionals. She lives in Wausau, Wisconsin.

Esther **Terry** is an M.A./Ph.D. student in theatre and performance studies at the University of Pittsburgh. *The Journal of African American Studies* recently published her article, "Rural as Racialized Plantation vs. Rural as Modern Reconnection: Blackness and Agency in Disney's *Song of the South* and *The Princess and the Frog*." In 2010, she traveled to Tanzania as a recipient of a Fulbright–Hays Group Project Abroad. Her research focuses on changing narratives in Richmond, Virginia, as evidenced by monument construction and placement; historiographical trends in blackface minstrelsy; and representations of Mau Mau onstage by African and African American playwrights.

Laura **Tropp** is an associate professor and chair of the Communication Arts Department at Marymount Manhattan College. She has published in the areas of the mediated representations of pregancy and motherhood, political communication, and the study of media culture. She teaches a course titled "Mediating Motherhood: Contemporary and Historical Images of Motherhood." She is writing a book, *A Womb with a View: Pregnancy in Changing Media Environments*.

Julian **Vigo** is an independent scholar, filmmaker, and artist whose latest book is *Performative Bodies, Hybrid Tongues: Race, Gender, Sex and Modernity in Latin America and the Maghreb* (2010). Recently she has been working on the theory and anthropology of biopower specific to development work of NGOs and the United Nations in Haiti and finishing up post-production work on a film about the public mourning of Michael Jackson, *To Neverland and Back*. She is also lecturing and studying the Vedas, the Sutras, and Asana in India.

Kimberley **White** is an associate professor of law and society at York University in Toronto, Canada. Her research focuses on cultural representations and manifestations of madness, mental illness and health; the corporatization of mental health/illness; politics of identity and difference; aesthetics, graffiti and "dangerous" art; and processes of exclusion.

Index